German Philosophy i Twentieth Century

The course of German philosophy in the twentieth century is one of the most exciting, diverse and controversial periods in the history of human thought. It is widely studied and its legacy is hotly contested.

In this outstanding introduction, Julian Young explains and assesses the two dominant traditions in modern German philosophy – critical theory and phenomenology – by examining the following key thinkers and topics:

- Max Weber's setting the agenda for modern German philosophy: the 'rationalization' and 'disenchantment' of modernity resulting in 'loss of freedom' and 'loss of meaning'
- Horkheimer and Adorno: rationalization and the 'culture industry'
- Habermas' defence of Enlightenment rationalization, the 'unfinished project of modernity'
- Marcuse: a Freud-based vision of a repression-free utopia
- Husserl: overcoming the 'crisis of humanity' through phenomenology
- Early Heidegger's existential phenomenology: 'authenticity' as loyalty to 'heritage'
- Gadamer and 'fusion of horizons'
- Arendt: the human condition
- Later Heidegger: the re-enchantment of reality.

German Philosophy in the Twentieth Century: Weber to Heidegger is essential reading for students of German philosophy, phenomenology, and critical theory, and will also be of interest to students in related fields such as literature, religious studies and political theory.

Julian Young is William R. Kenan Jr. Professor of Humanities and Professor of Philosophy at Wake Forest University, USA. He is the author of thirteen books including *Schopenhauer* (Routledge, 2005); *Friedrich Nietzsche: A Philosophical Biography*, which won the Association of American Publishers' 2010 PROSE award for philosophy; *The Philosophy of Tragedy: From Plato to Žižek* (2013); and *The Death of God and the Meaning of Life* (2nd edition 2014, Routledge).

German Philosophy in the Twentieth Century

Weber to Heidegger

Julian Young

Routledge
Taylor & Francis Group

LONDON AND NEW YORK

First published 2018
by Routledge
2 Park Square, Milton Park, Abingdon, Oxon OX14 4RN

and by Routledge
711 Third Avenue, New York, NY 10017

Routledge is an imprint of the Taylor & Francis Group, an informa business

British Library Cataloguing-in-Publication Data
A catalogue record for this book is available from the British Library

Library of Congress Cataloging-in-Publication Data
Names: Young, Julian, author.
Title: German philosophy in the twentieth century : Weber to Habermas / Julian Young.
Description: 1 [edition]. | New York : Routledge, 2018. | Includes bibliographical references and index.
Identifiers: LCCN 2017054002| ISBN 9781138220003 (hardback : alk. paper) | ISBN 9781138220010 (pbk. : alk. paper) | ISBN 9781315409818 (e-book)
Subjects: LCSH: Philosophy, German--20th century.
Classification: LCC B3181 .Y68 2018 | DDC 193--dc23
LC record available at https://lccn.loc.gov/2017054002

ISBN: 978-1-138-22000-3 (hbk)
ISBN: 978-1-138-22001-0 (pbk)
ISBN: 978-1-315-40981-8 (ebk)

Typeset in Times New Roman
by Taylor & Francis Books
Printed and bound by CPI Group (UK) Ltd, Croydon, CR0 4YY

For August

Contents

Acknowledgements

I am grateful to my colleagues in the Wake Forest Philosophy Department who 'workshopped' drafts of several of the following chapters, in particular to Ralph Kennedy, Charles Lewis and Win Chiat-Lee. I am grateful also to the members of the Wake Forest Social Sciences Research Seminar and to Michael Hughes, who provided useful comments on my first chapter. Jason Baldwin, Christine Swanton and the two anonymous Routledge referees saved me from various errors. Tony Bruce suggested the addition of the Afterword, which gives the book a better literary and intellectual shape.

Abbreviations

The bibliographical details of the works cited are to be found in the Bibliography. I have sometimes made minor alterations to the translations cited. Where I have made major alterations, I have included the German original.

Arendt

BPF	*Between Past and Future*
EIU	*Essays in Understanding*
HC	*The Human Condition*
IB	*Introduction to Walter Benjamin's* Illuminations
LM	*The Life of the Mind* (two volumes)
MDT	*Men in Dark Times*
OT	*The Origins of Totalitarianism*
Y-B	*Hannah Arendt: For Love of the World* (biography by Elizabeth Young-Bruehl)

Gadamer

HT	*The Hermeneutic Tradition* (eds. G. Ormison and J. Schrift)
PG	*The Philosophy of Hans-Georg Gadamer*
TM	*Truth and Method*

Habermas

TCA I	*The Theory of Communicative Action* (volume I)
TCA II	*The Theory of Communicative Action* (volume II)

Heidegger

BP	*The Basic Problems of Phenomenology*
BT	*Being and Time* (Numerals refer to the seventh German edition of *Sein und Zeit*, given in the margins of the Macquarrie and Robinson translation.)
DT	*Discourse on Thinking*

EHP	*Elucidations of Hölderlin's Poetry*
GA	*Gesamtausgabe*
I	*Hölderlin's Hymn 'The Ister'*
ID	*Identity and Difference*
IM	*An Introduction to Metaphysics*
N	*Nietzsche*
OWL	*On the Way to Language*
P	*Pathmarks*
PLT	*Poetry, Language, Thought*
QCT	*The Question Concerning Technology and Other Essays*
TB	*On Time and Being*
WCT	*What Is Called Thinking?*

Horkheimer and Adorno

DE	*Dialectics of Enlightenment*
ER	*The Eclipse of Reason*
SE	*Critical Theory: Selected Essays*

Husserl

CM	*Cartesian Mediations*
CS	*The Crisis of the European Sciences and Transcendental Phenomenology*
Ideas I	*Ideas Pertaining to a Pure Phenomenology and a Phenomenological Philosophy: General Introduction to a Pure Phenomenology*
Ideas II	*Ideas Pertaining to a Pure Phenomenology and a Phenomenological Philosophy: Studies in the Phenomenology of Constitution*
LI	*Logical Investigations* (two volumes)
PRS	*Philosophy as a Rigorous Science*

Marcuse

EC	*Eros and Civilization*
ODM	*One-Dimensional Man*

Weber

ES	*Economy and Society* (two volumes with continuously numbered pages)
FMW	*From Max Weber: Essays in Sociology*
PE	*The Protestant Ethic and the Spirit of Capitalism*

Introduction

This book is the first instalment of a two-part attempt at a critical engagement with the major figures of twentieth-century German philosophy. Among the philosophers who will appear in the second rather than the current instalment are: Walter Benjamin, Ernst Bloch, Georg Lukács, Max Scheler, Carl Schmidt, and Leo Strauss. This first instalment focusses on Horkheimer, Adorno, Marcuse, and Habermas, the leading exponents of Frankfurt-based 'critical theory', and on Husserl, Heidegger, Gadamer and Arendt, the leading exponents of Freiburg-based 'phenomenology'. Max Weber appears as a foundational influence on both traditions.

Ever since Plato, philosophers have wanted to concern themselves with eternal things: with universal, necessary, 'transcendental' truths, truths that have no greater relevance to one time or place than another. Traditionally, philosophers have found the realm of 'becoming' uninteresting. In the shape of Neo-Kantianism, the 'transcendental' conception of philosophy dominated the early twentieth-century German academy. But given the awfulness of twentieth-century German history – the loss of the First World War, the great inflation, Nazism, the Holocaust, the loss of the Second World War, a country occupied and divided – the need for a different conception of philosophy, a philosophy that could focus specifically on the modern condition, was enormous. Such a conception had already been proposed by Nietzsche, who, on several occasions, defines the philosopher as the 'doctor of culture',[1] a metaphor that requires the philosopher to attend to the 'diseases' specific to his or her own cultural environment.

All of the Frankfurt thinkers discussed in Part I of this book, Horkheimer and Adorno (Chapter 2), Habermas (Chapter 3), and Marcuse (Chapter 4), subscribe to the Nietzschean conception of the philosopher. Influenced by Marx, they start from the position that capitalist, Western modernity is in a 'diseased' condition and take it to be their task to contribute to the struggle to overcome the disease. With respect to the phenomenologists the situation is more complicated. Husserl (Chapter 5), the founder of phenomenology, though critical of Kant, began his career with the 'transcendental' conception of philosophy, with the assumption that his task was to identify and describe the 'a priori', 'transcendental' structure of consciousness. Yet as his thought progressed, he was forced by the exigencies of the times to become, more and more, a Nietzschean philosopher. The modern world, he observes in 1935, is in crisis, a crisis that is nothing less than a 'crisis of humanity' as such, and it is the task of phenomenology to map out a path to its resolution. Similarly Husserl's one-time student Heidegger: though he begins his 'path of thinking' subscribing to the 'transcendental' conception of philosophy (Chapter 6) he ends it by providing an analysis specific to the crisis of modernity, a crisis, he argues, that can only be resolved by a 'turning' to a (genuine) post-modernity (Chapter 9). Heidegger's own students, Gadamer (Chapter 7) and Arendt (Chapter 8), are similarly convinced that something in the modern world is fundamentally 'broken' and in desperate need of repair.

'Crisis', then, as it lies at the heart of modern German history, lies at the heart of modern German philosophy. And in spite of the personal, philosophical, and above all political animosities that marred relations between Frankfurt and Freiburg, that the modern world is in crisis is a point on which they agree. The thinker who, at the beginning of the twentieth century, provided the most significant articulation of the nature of the crisis was the sociologist Max Weber. Yet, as I argue in Chapter 1, Weber's real significance for twentieth-century philosophy is that of a transmitter rather than initiator. For in German thought, the conception of Western modernity as a 'crisis of humanity' reaches back to the end of the eighteenth century, to the critique of the Industrial Revolution initiated by Goethe and the German Romantics. Weber's primary significance for philosophy, I argue, is that he transmits this critique to the twentieth century.

What is the source and nature of the crisis that all of my nine (or ten) thinkers address? Why does modern culture need a 'doctor'? Surprisingly, there is a high degree of agreement between Freiburg and Frankfurt, not merely on the fact of crisis, but also on its cause. The source of the crisis, it is agreed, is what Weber calls 'rationalization' (Horkheimer and Adorno call it 'reification' and the later Heidegger, 'enframing'), the exercise of 'control through calculation': 'control' over natural and – more problematically – human phenomena by means of scientific 'calculation' and technology. According to Weber, the rationalization of modernity has spawned two, as Habermas calls them, 'pathologies': 'loss of freedom' and 'loss of meaning'. In their own ways, all of the thinkers discussed in this book recognise these pathologies and search for ways to overcome them.

Horkheimer and Adorno's word for 'rationalization' is 'enlightenment'. As this suggests, the sense that the crisis of modernity is a product of rationalization is the sense that it is the product of the Enlightenment, the movement Habermas identifies as the defining 'project of modernity'. In general, and with varying degrees of confidence, the critical theorists hold that enlightenment rationality is capable of healing the wounds it itself has created. The phenomenologists on the other hand, tend to hold that something anathematized by the Enlightenment – authority, tradition, religion, mystery, holiness, or all of these – needs to be recovered if the crisis is to be overcome. In this respect, the phenomenological tradition (with which the present author identifies) is a continuation of the critique of the Enlightenment initiated by the German Romantics.

Note

1   Nietzsche (2005), *The Antichrist* section 7, Nietzsche (1999b) 7 23 [15], Nietzsche (2003) section 52. Sometimes his phrase is 'physician of the soul'.

Part I

FRANKFURT

1   Weber

Rationalization, disenchantment and charisma

Max Weber (1864–1920) wore many hats. Principally he is remembered as a sociologist, as, indeed, one of the founders of sociology as an academic discipline. In business schools he is remembered as a founder of 'management science'. But he was also deeply engaged with nineteenth-century German philosophy, above all with Nietzsche. And he represents an appropriate starting point for this book in virtue of having, at the beginning of the twentieth century, articulated, with memorable force, the problems that would come to be the central concern of each of the philosophers to be discussed in the chapters that follow. The most accessible of the texts in which he does this is a lecture delivered towards the end of his life to students at Munich University on 7 November 1917, entitled 'Wissenschaft als Beruf' ('Science as a Vocation', or 'Science as a Calling').

On the surface, the lecture looks to be something like a commencement address, an address to the Munich students engaged, as they already were, in 'science': 'science (*Wissenschaft*)', that is, in the broad German sense in which any disciplined intellectual activity counts as 'science', the 'human sciences (*Geisteswissenschaften*)' such as *Literaturwissenschaft* just as much as the 'natural sciences (*Naturwissenschaften*)'. Unexpectedly, however, the lecture is far from a celebration of science as a 'vocation'. One reason for this, one can hypothesize, is the fact that the First World War, still in progress, had deployed the fruits of modern science to kill people on a hitherto unimaginable scale (38 million in total).[1] ('No one born after 1914', Bertrand Russell once remarked, 'is capable of happiness'.) Whatever the original intention that led to the delivery of the lecture, in the event, its central force is to place a serious question mark against the value of science, against, indeed the entire post-Enlightenment development of the West. Since Weber had devoted his entire life to science, this gives the lecture something of the character of a self-critique.

In the lecture, Weber identifies 'rationalization' (sometimes 'intellectualization'), which he defines as 'control [or "mastery"] *(beherrschen)*] through calculation', as the defining characteristic of Western modernity. Since the control in question is 'created by science and science-based technology' (FMW 139), the 'calculation' in question is scientific theory.

The two areas of rationalization are 'external objects' and 'man's activities' (FMW 150), nature and society. Weber has no concerns about the rationalization of nature. (Had he lived in the age of climate change one doubts that he would have exhibited such equanimity.) What concerns him is the rationalization of society, the application of the methodology of natural science to social phenomena. The rationalization of society is, says Weber, an historical phenomenon – unique to the West, he thinks – that has been slowly developing for thousands of years (FMW 138). What is distinctive of modernity, however, is that the process has become so rigorous and so all-encompassing as to generate – here I follow Habermas' presentation of Weber's discussion – two 'pathological' consequences: 'loss of freedom' and 'loss of meaning' (TCA I 244).

Bureaucratization

The rationalization of social phenomena consists in the extension of the 'scientific point of view' from nature to humanity (PE 36, FMW 139). Weber is never very specific as to his conception of scientific method, but since he says that the progress of natural science consists in the 'transformation of nature into a causal mechanism' (FMW 350), it can be assumed that he understands it in terms of the standard 'covering law' model: explanation and prediction of events consist in their subsumption under causal laws, their control in the manipulation of the antecedents of such laws. The rationalization of a social phenomenon thus consists in the development of 'technolog[ies] of control' (FMW 150) on the basis of the relevant causal (or at least statistical) laws. The principal manifestation of the rationalization of society is what Weber calls 'bureaucratization'.

Bureaucracies are social organizations that are designed to produce a given result as efficiently and reliably as possible. They are characterized by the division of labour into specific tasks within a hierarchy of command and control (Foucault speaks here of the 'military dream of society'), where the tasks to be performed at each level are defined by rigid (and hence often stupid and inhuman) rules and procedures (FMW 196). Weber's key insight is that bureaucracies are technological devices, kinds of machines. Bureaucratization, he sees, is 'mechaniz[ation]' (PE 124): the point of the rigidity and inflexibility of bureaucratic procedures is to discipline the human components of the bureaucratic machine into the reliable efficiency of machine parts.

Familiarity, and the fading of the memory of a not-yet-totally-bureaucratized social order, dulls our awareness of the extent to which modern life is controlled and disciplined by the bureaucratic state.[2] As David Graeber points out, a graph of the number of times the word 'bureaucracy' appears in books written in English peaks during the 1970s and rapidly declines thereafter.[3] But whether it is a question of health, education, work, or travel, the modern state assigns us a unique identifying number that enables it to regiment our lives into, as Richard Wagner was already observing in 1849, a 'red-tape uniformity' undreamt of in pre-modern times.[4] Max Horkheimer tries to raise our consciousness of this regimentation by contrasting the multiplicity of rules governing the driving of a car on the highway with the freedom of riding a horse over the medieval countryside (p. 33 below).

There are, of course, many bureaucracies that we need to deal with other than those of the state. Booking an airline ticket, struggling to understand one's hospital bill or one's publisher's royalty statements, satisfying the accreditation requirements of one's university, applying for university entrance or a research grant, reviewing an article for a scholarly journal, all require tedious, usually exhausting, and obscurely offensive submission to inflexible bureaucratic procedures. Apart from the state bureaucracy, which he calls 'bureaucratic authority', however, Weber's focus is on the bureaucratization of the workplace which he calls 'management' (FMW 196).

'Management', he says, is the science of the 'rational organization of (formally) free labour' (PE xxxiv). It aims at the 'calculability of the productivity of labour' (ES 150), at, that is, the use of scientific calculation to increase productivity.

What Weber calls 'management' began with the Industrial Revolution. It is discussed already in Adam Smith's 1776 *Wealth of Nations*. Its essence is the move from the craft economy of the workshop in which the craftsman made a whole product – a chair, a bowl or, in Smith's example, a pin[5] – to the economy of the factory in which the individual worker is responsible for only a small part of the productive process.

In discussing management, Weber sometimes defers to the work of his American contemporary, Frederick Taylor (1856–1915) (ES 150), whose *Principles of Management Science* (1911) was the first textbook of management science. 'Taylorism' is the theoretical foundation of 'Fordism', assembly-line manufacture. Taylor saw that by eliminating the time-consuming movement of the worker from one work station to another, and by eliminating the expensive and time-consuming training necessary to produce a worker capable of a skilled task, assembly-line manufacture greatly increased productivity and profitability. His own contribution was the 'time and motion study' which analyses the micro-tasks on the assembly line into the smallest number of bodily movements necessary to their completion. It is worth noting that Fordism was responsible not only for the unprecedented availability of consumer products of all kinds in the 1950s but also for the overwhelming advantage in weaponry that the United States eventually acquired during the Second World War.

Loss of freedom

The industrial division of labour should not be confused with specialization.[6] The medieval sculptor produced the statues, the painter the paintings, each of these specialized tasks being necessary to the completion of the medieval cathedral. As Arendt observes, however (p. 215 below), while each of these specialized tasks produced a satisfying 'end in itself', Fordism reduces work to the mechanical, meaningless drudgery memorably satirized in Charlie Chaplin's *Modern Times* (1936). This was already noted by Adam Smith: the repetitive tedium of work in the pin factory, he observes, infects all aspects of the worker's life with a 'torpor of mind' that makes him 'as stupid and ignorant as it is possible for a human being to become'.[7] (Since the industrial division of labour reduced the worker to low-paid, dazed, 'stupidity', Taylorism predicts and requires the burgeoning of hierarchical levels of corporate management where 'stupidity' decreases and synoptic understanding increases as one ascends the hierarchy.)

The worker is, of course, free to decline to engage in industrial labour. But since the consequence is unemployment and starvation, such freedom is merely, as Weber puts it 'formal' (p. 9 above).[8] In reality, most of us in the modern economy have no option but to engage in meaningless drudgery, if not in the factory then in the office of some corporate bureaucracy. Whereas the pre-modern economy offered the possibility of, in Marx's language, un-'alienated' labour – the kind of work one can imagine pursuing as a hobby – the industrial division of labour offers only 'alienated' labour.

This is Weber's 'loss of freedom' thesis. Most of us have no option but to become work-units in a rationalized, bureaucratized workplace in which we are condemned to spend the majority of our waking lives in mind-numbing, robotic drudgery, drudgery which, though meaningless, is highly disciplined. Required to perform with the reliability of machine parts, we are reduced, as Weber puts it in a famous passage at the end of *The Protestant Ethic and the Spirit of Capitalism*, to a condition of (an oddly mixed metaphor) 'mechanized petrifaction (*mechanisierteVersteinerung*)'. This means that the modern workplace has become an 'iron cage (*stahlhartesGehäuse*)',[9] a cage in which we are denied the freedom to live creative, happy, *human* lives. Weber's word for this unfree cog-in-the-machine is *Berufsmensch*: although the literal translation is 'man of vocation', his ironic use of the term[10] requires its translation into something like 'salary man', Arendt's 'jobholder' (p. 201 below), Horkheimer's 'cell of functional response' (p. 33 below), or simply 'robot'.

Life in the iron cage

The 'iron cage' passage ends with an apocalyptic vision of a dehumanized future that will soon arrive unless there is a radical disruption of current trends. (I shall attend later to the question of the possible agents of such disruption.) In this future, the life of the *Berufsmensch* is

> embellished with a sort of convulsive self-importance. For of the 'last man (*letzter Mensch*)' of this cultural development, it might well be truly said [in

Goethe's words]: 'specialists without spirit, sensualists without heart; this nullity imagines that it has attained a level of humanity never before achieved'.

(PE 124 translation modified)

(The 'last man', here, is the 'last man' of the prologue to Nietzsche's *Thus Spoke Zarathustra*, whose Hegelian 'self-importance', whose blindness to his own condition, is so complete that – laying aside his opium pipe for a moment – he says 'we have invented happiness'.)

The 'specialist without spirit' is, of course, the auto worker or check-out clerk who performs his or her task 'without spirit' (in Adam Smith's phrase, in a 'dull torpor of mind') on account of the 'alienated' nature of their task.[11] By 'sensualism without heart' Weber means sensation without emotion: sex without love or danger without purpose (as in bungee jumping), for instance. It consists in the quest for 'personal experiences (*Erlebnisse*)' which, in the modern age, amount to nothing more than more or less intense 'sensations' (FMW 137). Given the torpor and exhaustion produced by mindless drudgery, all the alienated worker is capable of in his so-called free time is the experience of crude 'sensations'. Already in 1849 Richard Wagner was explaining the decay of nineteenth-century opera in these terms:

> when a prince leaves a heavy dinner, the banker a fatiguing financial operation, the working man a weary day of toil and go to the theatre, what they ask for is rest, distraction, and amusement, and are in no mood for renewed effort and fresh expenditure of energy.[12]

All they demand from opera – all they are capable of receiving – are lush tunes for easy listening.

Loss of meaning

The second of Weber's pathologies of modernity is, in Habermas' phrase, 'loss of meaning'.

As might be expected from a sociologist, Weber is an ethical relativist. The various 'value spheres' of different cultures are, he says, grounded in 'worldviews' that are in irreconcilable conflict with each other (FMW 117). Figuratively speaking, 'the gods struggle with one another now and for ever' (FMW 148). (Weber alludes here to the traditional role of the gods as both paradigms and guardians of their respective 'value spheres': Hera of home and hearth, Zeus of 'manly' power, Eros of love, and Jesus of a different kind of love.) Plato's belief that in addition to 'instrumental rationality (*Zweckrationalität*)' there is also 'value-rationality (*Wertrationalität*)' (ES 24), that reason – 'science' – can establish a single, objectively true morality, is an illusion (FMW 141). On the one hand there is the Sermon on the Mount telling us to turn the other cheek;

on the other the morality of antiquity which sees such behaviour as 'an offence against the dignity of manly conduct' (FMW 148). (Weber's debt to Nietzsche's discussion of 'slave' versus 'master' morality in the *Genealogy of Morals* is obvious.[13])

Although there is no rational adjudication between different moralities, it can happen – 'fate' can bring it about – that one system, one 'god', achieves dominion over the others. This happened in the history of the West during the time in which Christianity 'blinded' us to the truth of value relativism by dethroning 'polytheism' and establishing Christian morality as the single 'godhead'. It did this through 'the compromises and relative judgments which we all know from its history' (FMW 148–9): through, I take this to mean, incorporating paganism into itself by reinterpreting pagan myths and festivals in Christian terms, reinterpreting the myth of Dionysus, for instance, as the myth of the Crucifixion.

Now, however, history has moved on once more, and this 'godhead' has lost its power. The ethical mainstream of our culture has become de-Christianized:

> the ultimate and most sublime values [of Christian ethics] have retreated from public life either into the transcendental realm of mystic life or into the brotherliness of direct and personal human relations.
>
> (FMW 155)

One important mark of this emigration of formerly unifying values from the public to the private sphere is the retreat of art from the 'monumental' to the 'intimate' (the retreat Hegel refers to as 'the death of art'). Formerly the – as Wagner called it – *Gesamtkunstwerk* (collective artwork), the Greek tragic festival or the medieval cathedral, gathered the community into its shared 'godhead',[14] was the occasion of a clarifying re-affirmation of communal ethos. But since the Western ethic has now fragmented, there remains no role for the collective artwork. The result, says Weber, is that 'the attempt to force and to "invent" a monumental style of art', likewise the attempt to 'intellectually construct new religions without a new and genuine prophesy', produces only 'monstrosities' (FMW 155) – monstrosities such as the Nazi state Weber seems here to anticipate, together with its taste for fake *Gesamtkunstwerke* such as the Nuremberg rallies.

The result of this collapse of the Christian 'godhead' is the return of 'polytheism' (FMW 147). As Nietzsche (whom Weber is again paraphrasing) puts it in *The Birth of Tragedy*, the old single, unifying myth is replaced by a 'pandemonium' of individual myths.[15] 'Many old gods rise from their graves', Weber writes, albeit in the demythologized form of 'impersonal forces'. Insofar as there are lives left to live outside the iron cage, some are, in effect, devoted to Eros, some to Jesus, and some (corporate superheroes gripped by the 'will to power') to Zeus. As Nietzsche observes, modernity is a 'motley' world, a world plunged into value chaos. Each individual chooses his or her own 'god' which, from the point of view of a rival value sphere, is a 'demon' (FMW 115). Republicans demonize Democrats, Democrats demonize Republicans.

* * *

If we define 'nihilism' as the *absence* of meaning, then Weber's 'loss of meaning' thesis does not appear to consist in the claim that modern humanity has entered a condition of nihilism. His loss of meaning thesis concerns only the public sphere – as he describes the situation, meaning, the possession of life-defining ethical ideals, is, at least sometimes, preserved in the private sphere. It might, indeed, be more accurate to describe him as affirming a *retreat*-of-meaning rather than *loss*-of-meaning thesis. Given, then, that he does not (at least, not consistently) see us sunk into nihilism, the question arises as to why, and whether, for Weber, our 'loss' or 'retreat' of meaning matters.

Habermas describes Weber's attitude to the disappearance of the Christian 'godhead' from the public sphere as 'oddly ambivalent' (TCA I 350), presumably because, while he seems to regret the disappearance, he notes that its former dominion depended on us being 'blind' (FMW 149) to the 'scientific' truth that there is no objective morality. This strikes me, however, not as ambivalence, but rather as evincing a strong sense – which he shares with Hume – of the dominant contribution to human wellbeing played by institutions, beliefs and practices that lack rational justification. The reason Weber regrets the disappearance of the Christian 'godhead' from the public realm is that its disappearance is also, he says, the disappearance of 'genuine community (*echte Gemeinschaft*)' (FMW 155).

The distinction between *Gesellschaft* (society) and *Gemeinschaft* (community), which will be important throughout this book, has a long history in German thought. Its most thorough scholarly articulation was provided in 1887 by Weber's contemporary sociologist Ferdinand Tönnies.[16] The heart of the distinction is the contrast between a social group based on mutual self-interest (society), and a social group united by a shared conception of the proper way to live (community). The reason the communitarian tradition takes community to be superior to society is that while the members of a society may *tolerate* each other's activities, such tolerance is accompanied, as we will find Heidegger expressing the point, by 'distance and reserve' (p. 128 below). Within a community, on the other hand, within the embrace of shared principles and customs, there exists the possibility of mutual solidarity, mutual care and concern. Expressed in emotional terms, while societies are 'cold' places in which the 'liberty' sought by the French Revolution is the dominant value, communities are 'warm' places in which the 'fraternity' that the Revolution also sought is the dominant value. Weber's regret over the loss of the Christian 'godhead' is regret over the loss of fraternity, over the fact that the modern social order no longer satisfies what, with Rousseau and the French Revolution, he takes to be a basic human need.

Disenchantment and loss of meaning

Why have we lost our shared 'godhead'? According to Weber, the 'fate of our times', the retreat of the 'sublime values' of Christianity from the public sphere, is due to 'rationalization' (FMW 155). Rationalization, then, is responsible not only for our loss of freedom but also for our loss of meaning. While the connection between rationalization and loss of freedom is obvious and straightforward, the connection to loss of meaning is less so.

The crucial point, it seems to me, is that while Weber attributes the loss of freedom to the rationalization of *society*, he attributes the loss of meaning primarily to the rationalization of *nature*. What 'scientific progress' in the control of nature 'means practically', he writes, is

> the conviction that ... in principle, there are no mysterious, incalculable forces that come into play, but rather that one can – in principle – *master* [or 'control'] *all things by calculation*. This, however, means that the world is disenchanted. One need no longer have recourse to magical means in order to master or implore the spirits, as did the savage (*Wilde*), for whom such mysterious powers did exist. Technical means and calculations perform the service.
>
> (FMW 138–9)

Thus, as Weber sees it, rationalization, the 'mastery' of nature facilitated by scientific 'calculation', results in 'disenchantment', the expulsion of all 'mysterious incalculable ... spirits' from our worldview. And since a 'godhead' presupposes, presumably, a God, disenchantment, loss of all gods, results in loss of the godhead. There are thus two connections that require investigation: the connection between rationalization and disenchantment, and the connection between disenchantment and loss of the Christian 'godhead'.

In the past, things happened on account of supernatural (or at least superhuman) causes. Agamemnon has to sacrifice his daughter to get the wind to shift, Siegfried's invincible sword breaks, with fatal consequences for himself, because Fricka convinces Wotan to withdraw his guarantee of its integrity. To get things to go our way in premodern times, we needed (at least sometimes) to resort to means – prayer and sacrifice – which, from the point of view of science, count as 'magic'. Now, however, we have adopted the view that nature is a closed 'causal mechanism' (FMW 350), that things happen always on account of natural causes, never on account of supernatural intervention. And so successful has this presumption proved itself that (given to optimism, or perhaps hubris, as we are) we have concluded that sooner or later we will achieve the intellectual and technological mastery of 'all things' through calculation. And so, we believe, we do not need to appeal to the gods any more, do not, in fact, need the gods at all. Of course, God, or the gods, might exist even if (as both Epicurus and the Deists believe) they do not intervene in worldly affairs. But what the success of natural science 'means practically' (FMW 139) is that we cease to believe in the gods, dismiss them from our worldview. The 'God hypothesis' dies a death of redundancy and the world is 'disenchanted'. 'Positivism' has arrived.

Why, however, does the 'death of God' entail the death of the commanding role of Christian ethics in public life? In providing this diagnosis of the loss of the godhead, Weber is once again following Nietzsche, according to whom the fact that 'the Christian God had become unbelievable' means the collapse of 'our entire European morality'.[17] There is, of course, no *logical* connection between the disenchantment of the world and the loss of the Christian godhead. Many people claim to adhere simultaneously to atheism and Christian ethics, and there is no contradiction in such a claim. Weber's and Nietzsche's claim is, however, not logical, but rather psychological and historical. The fact of the matter, they claim – surely correctly – is that, historically, most people have followed the Christian way only because they have believed in eternal reward and punishment, or, at best, out of reverence for the commands of the heavenly father.

Charisma and change

We face, Weber tells us, a future denuded of both freedom and meaning. We stand in a moment of world-historical crisis, a crisis that can only be resolved by – in Heidegger's language (p. 243 below) – a 'turning' to a new, genuinely post-modern age. The only possibility of such a turning lies, says Weber, in the appearance of 'entirely new prophets' (PE 124), prophets in possession of a 'new and genuine prophesy' (FMW 155). Or, if not prophets of the entirely new, prophets of 'old ideas and ideals' that will be *so* old as to constitute, if realized, a 'great rebirth' (PE 124). (This is a likely allusion to Wagner and the youthful Nietzsche's project of a 'rebirth of Greek tragedy' in the form of the Wagnerian *Gesamtkunstwerk*.)

The importance Weber attaches to the 'prophet' derives from the importance he attaches to 'charismatic leadership' (ES 241–3).[18] In the second of his lectures to the Munich students, 'Politics as a Vocation', he makes clear his view that our best hope of a world-transforming turning lies in the appearance of social and political leaders possessed of 'charismatic authority' (FMW 79–81): authority that is based on the 'exceptional sanctity, heroism or exemplary character of an individual person, and the normative patterns or order revealed or ordained by him' (ES 215; ES 241 provides a fuller definition of 'charisma').

Noting that Hitler came to power little more than a decade after Weber's death, Habermas believes that Weber's call for charismatic leadership makes him a herald of fascism (TCA I 352). For two reasons, this criticism seems to me unwarranted. First, Weber explicitly warns against 'chiliastic prophets' who believe that a noble end justifies any means (FMW 122) and, as we have seen, warns that 'the attempt to force and to "invent" a monumental style of art', likewise the attempt to 'intellectually construct new religions without a new and genuine prophesy', produce only 'monstrosities' (p. 12 above). Second, Weber was an advisor to the framers of the constitution of the Weimar Republic, Germany's one attempt at a form of liberal democracy prior to 1945. Fairly obviously, I think, Weber's call is a call for charismatic leadership *within* the limits of liberal democracy – the charisma of a Churchill or a Martin Luther King Jr – rather than for charismatic leadership *instead of* democracy.

What, however, really offends Habermas – in spite of his considerable admiration for much of Weber's work – is, I believe, the fact that Weber's hope for the leadership of charismatic prophets is a rejection of the idea that we can *reason* our way out of the current crisis. As we shall see, Habermas identifies himself with the project of Enlightenment rationality and believes that the West's current 'pathologies' can be overcome through a rationalization of politics, through rational political action. Since, however, charisma is an essentially non-rational force, the possibility of redemption through rational politics is precisely what Weber rejects: no matter how rational and how effective, no kind of political action is, by itself, capable of resolving the crisis of modernity. And so the question arises as to the grounds of Weber's pessimism about reason. The key to answering this question lies, I think, in the fact that, when he speaks of charisma and prophets, at the front of his mind is not loss of freedom but rather loss of meaning.

By the Christian era, 'charisma' (which comes from the Greek *khárisma*) had come to mean 'gift of divine grace'. Charismatic prophets – the prophets of the Old Testament, for instance – possess a divine gift because it is through them that God – or a god – speaks to the community. The prophet possesses, for us, charismatic authority because we respond to him or her with the reverence due to the god who speaks. (A memory of such reverence survives in the designation of the charismatic opera star as a 'diva', a 'goddess'.) What Weber thinks, I believe, is that our crisis of meaning can be overcome only through a return of communal gods, of gods who not only personify the communal virtues but also *motivate* us to live in imitation of their example. But the gods can motivate ethical action only if we reverence them, only, that is, if we stand in *awe* of them. We can, however, be awed only by that which we cannot fully understand, only by that which is, for us, 'mysterious and incalculable'. And so only the overthrow of the positivist worldview, only the experience of something as beyond reason, as unmasterable by 'calculation', is capable of overcoming our loss of communal meaning. Not reason, but rather a 're-enchantment' of the world is the only force through which we can overcome our loss of meaning.

Weber as transmitter of the Romantic critique of the Enlightenment

The modern age, to repeat, is gripped by the conviction that 'all things can be mastered by calculation'. As such, Weber's description of modernity is identical with Nietzsche's, who takes what he calls 'Socratism' (on account of his fancy that Socrates is its first protagonist) to be the conviction that defines modernity: 'the imperturbable conviction that thought, following the thread of causality, reaches down into the deepest abysses of being, and that it is capable, not simply of understanding existence, but even of *correcting* it'.[19]

Socratism, the youthful Nietzsche believes, is a 'profound *delusion*',[20] an exercise in the Oedipal hubris that harbours its own nemesis. Weber, it is now clear, shares this belief: whatever the benefits of rationalization, it is clear that, in his view, our loss of freedom and meaning reduce them to triviality. Far from being 'corrected', 'existence' has been profoundly damaged by Socratism.

Weber's belief that rationalization has been a disaster places him in the tradition not only of Wagner and the youthful Nietzsche's neo-Romantic critique of the Enlightenment, but also of the critique of the Enlightenment conducted, at the beginning of the Industrial Revolution, by the German Romantics themselves. This is particularly evident with respect to the loss-of-freedom thesis. So, for instance, before the end of the eighteenth century, Novalis (1772–1801) describes the combination of the modern bureaucratic state and capitalist market economy as a 'mill ... without a builder and without a miller, a real *perpetuum mobile*, a mill which grinds itself'. As such, as operating in a manner that is beyond human control, it is a worrying threat to human freedom. This same worry is expressed by Schiller (1759–1805) who complains that in the modern social order 'man fashions himself only as a fragment', a *Berufsmensch*, within 'the monotonous turning of the wheel',[21] and by Schelling (1775–1854), who describes the modern order as 'a machine which ... though built and arranged by human beings ... act[s] ... according to its own laws as if it existed by itself'.[22] And given that he is probably the earliest German critic of the Industrial Revolution, it seems likely that Goethe's resurrection of Lucian's tale of the sorcerer's apprentice – the apprentice uses half-understood magic to make the broom do his work but, because he cannot control the spell, ends up as the broom's slave – is also intended to express the same worry: the fear of a looming reversal of the master–slave relation, the fear of, as these days it is sometimes called, 'the singularity'.

Weber's key significance for modern German philosophy is thus, it seems to me, that of a transmitter: it is through the early Nietzsche's neo-Romanticism that the Romantic critique of Enlightenment rationalization passes to Weber, and primarily through Weber that it passes into twentieth-century German philosophy.

Notes

1 Four months prior to the delivery of the lecture, war-weariness among the general population had caused the Reichstag to pass a 'peace resolution' calling for a negotiated settlement to the war (a resolution that was ignored by both the German high command and the Allies).
2 Among those who retain such an awareness are American 'survivalists' and the Unabomber.
3 Graeber (2015) 3–4.

4 Wagner (1966) vol.1 203–4. Wagner's status as an important social critic, while evident from the fact of his profound, and lasting, influence on Nietzsche, is almost entirely unrecognized by modern scholarship. As I shall have further occasion to note, Weber's account of modernity frequently repeats Wagner's social criticism. And since he quotes a Wagner libretto at atleast one point (PE 63), it seems likely that he was aware of his prose works as well. For a detailed discussion of Wagner's social criticism see Young (2014).

5 Smith (2007) 603.

6 Weber himself seems, in fact, not to be sensitive to this distinction since, as we shall see, he speaks of the assembly-line worker as a 'specialist' (PE 124).

7 Smith (2007) 603.

8 As Tom Morello of the rock group Rage against the Machine puts it, while the 'first freedom' in the 'land of the free' is the freedom to enter a 'subservient role in the workplace', the 'second freedom' is the 'freedom to starve'.

9 A more accurate translation of *stahlhartes Gehäuse* would be 'steel casing', but since the image has become famous I shall generally retain the mistranslation. The image is anticipated in Wagner's description of the modern bureaucratic order as an 'iron harness' whose wearer is denied the freedom of movement and growth required by a living thing (Wagner (1966) vol.1 80).

10 Alluding to his famous thesis that it was the ethics of Calvinism that gave rise to the capitalist entrepreneur (no fun + work = capital), Weber writes that 'The Puritan *wanted* to be a *Berufsmensch*', a man with an economic 'vocation', but 'we *have* to be one' (PE 123; emphases added).

11 A Gallup poll reported, on 3 March 2017, that two thirds of American workers are 'disengaged' from their work.

12 Wagner (1966) vol.1 42–4.

13 Nietzsche (1994) essay II.

14 It also, of course, 'collected' the individual arts into a single artwork. The 'collective artwork' is 'collective' in a double sense – a point missed in the common mistranslation of *Gesamtkunstwerk* as 'total artwork'.

15 Nietzsche (1999a) section23.

16 Tönnies (1988).

17 Nietzsche (2001) section343.

18 Weber's hope for a 'new and genuine prophesy', his search for charismatic prophets of new ways of living, led to an engagement with the Life Reform Movement (*Lebensreformbewegung*) and with, in particular, the 'alternative' commune at Monte Verità, near Ascona on the Swiss–Italian boarder, which engaged, *inter alia*, in socialism, mysticism, environmentalism, vegetarianism, nudism, dance, and free love. Established in 1900 with Tolstoy and Nietzsche as its heroes, it became a magnet for counter-cultural figures in the first decades of the twentieth century: D. H. Lawrence, Carl Jung, Isadora Duncan, Martin Buber, James Joyce, Walter Gropius, Hermann Hesse, and Stefan George, among others. It is to the Life Reform Movement that both the 'hippie' movement of the 1960s and the current environmental movement trace their ancestry. Weber was fascinated, in particular, by the poet Stephan George, the charismatic centre of the 'George Circle'. According to Thomas Karlauf (Karlauf 2007), George was *the* model around which Weber constructed the concept of 'charisma' that I am about to discuss. While this seems to me an exaggeration, it is nonetheless true that Weber mentions George several times in *Economy and Society*, and indeed regards him as a paradigm of charisma in the aesthetic – as opposed to explicitly political – sphere (ES 245, 640, 1157).

19 Nietzsche (1999a) section15.

20 Ibid.

21 Schiller (1845) 22.

22 For the quotations from Novalis and Schelling see Rohrkrämer (2007) 35.

2 Horkheimer and Adorno

The irrationality of reason

The topic of this chapter is the collaborative philosophy of Max Horkheimer (1895–1973) and Theodor Adorno (1903–1969). The emphasis, however, will fall more on Horkheimer, since, as the senior figure, it was he who provided the foundations of the intellectual outlook to which they both subscribed. Each of them, especially Adorno, did important work independently of the other, but this will not be here considered. Together, they produced the two key texts that will be the principal focus of this chapter. The first, the *Dialectic of Enlightenment* (1944), was co-authored by both writers, while the second, *The Eclipse of Reason* (1946), although written by Horkheimer alone, observes in its Preface that 'it would be difficult to say which of the ideas originated in his [Adorno's] mind and which in my own' since 'our philosophy is one' (ER vii). I shall therefore often speak as if both works were co-authored. And since 'Horkheimer and Adorno' is a cumbersome phrase I shall often replace it by 'the authors'.

In 1930, Horkheimer became director of the Institute for Social Research in Frankfurt, and also professor of philosophy at Frankfurt University to which the Institute was attached. The Institute had been founded in 1923 by Felix Weil, the left-wing son of a wealthy Jewish businessman, but attracted no truly major figures prior to Horkheimer's arrival. As director, Horkheimer gathered around him a talented group of social theorists, nearly all of whom were both Jewish and Marxists – albeit orthodox in neither of these affiliations. Apart from Adorno, the most famous of those who were more or less closely connected to this 'first Frankfurt School' of 'critical theory' were Herbert Marcuse, Walter Benjamin, and the psychoanalyst Eric Fromm. (As we shall see in the next chapter, the central figure of the 'second' Frankfurt School is Jürgen Habermas.)

As both Jews and Marxists, the members of the Frankfurt School had two good reasons to emigrate when Hitler came to power in 1933. In 1934 the Institute relocated to New York where it was taken under the wing of Columbia University. In 1948 Horkheimer returned to occupied Germany and in 1950 re-established the Institute in Frankfurt. Adorno returned in 1949.

The Marxist heritage

What did Marx mean to Horkheimer and Adorno? It is clear that neither were orthodox (or as Walter Benjamin puts it 'vulgar') Marxists. They quickly lost their early sympathy for the Russian Revolution: Horkheimer saw that the Leninist claim that the Party is the sole legitimate representative of the interests of the proletariat would inevitably lead to a 'terrorist totalitarian bureaucracy'[1] – essentially Bakunin's point that, since government could not literally be conducted by millions of workers, the so-called 'dictatorship of the proletariat' would inevitably become the dictatorship of a self-serving and self-perpetuating elite. Particularly after their experience of America, more-over, both Horkheimer and Adorno came to doubt the supposed revolutionary potential of the working class, observing that while the unemployed lack the power to organize the employed are organized into unions that effectively co-opt them into corporate membership in the capitalist system (SE vi, ER 147–8).

Two further departures from 'vulgar' Marxism require mention. First, the authors reject, as I shall call it, the 'superstructure thesis', the 'banishing of mind to the far pinnacle of the superstructure' (DE 33), the thesis that the character of 'mind', 'culture', 'psychic life' is determined by underlying eco-nomic conditions.[2] Second, they reject what Horkheimer dubs, satirically, Marx's 'fatalism' (SE 51), the thesis that economic history – and therefore, given the superstructure thesis, all history – is determined by economic laws that, with the inexorability of the laws of nature, will bring about the collapse of capitalism and the arrival of the communist utopia. In affirming economic determinism, the authors declare, 'socialism clung all too desperately to the heritage of bourgeois philosophy' (DE 33) – to the Hegelian account of the history of the West as a 'dialectically' determined *Bildungsroman* terminating in the triumph of 'reason'. Empirically, the authors reject 'fatalism' on the basis of their experience of the American trade unions and the fact that (in 1944) the Russian Revolution of 1917 has failed to repeat itself anywhere else. Philosophically, they reject it on the basis of human freedom, on the grounds that 'individuals and social groups, working and struggling [in freedom], have an effect ... on current economic relationships' (SE 51).

Given, then, these radical divergences from orthodox Marxism, the question arises as to whether there is, in fact, anything in the authors' thinking that can be described as authentically Marxist. The answer, it seems to me, is that there are two central ideas – or, better, perhaps, casts of mind – that they share with Marx. The first is an undying conviction that conflict between the oppressing 'bourgeoisie' and oppressed 'proletariat' lies at the heart of capitalist society, and that the concept of class conflict is therefore an essential tool in social analysis. The second emerges in the authors' – mostly Horkheimer's – answer to the question of what critical theory actually is.

What is critical theory?

The foundation of the 'first' Frankfurt School's conception of critical theory lies, it seems to me, in the eleventh of Marx's *Theses about Feuerbach*, the famous assertion that while '[t]he Philosophers have merely tried to interpret the world in various ways, the point is to change it (Die Philosophen haben die Welt nur verschieden interpretiert; es kommt darauf an, sie zu verändern)'. The authors, as we shall see, reject the 'bourgeois' conception of the task of thought in general, and social thought in particular, as that of providing a neutral analysis of the way things are. To be worth anything, thought must be an attempt to alleviate suffering, an act of 'solidarity' with a suffering humanity.[3] It is the active engagement demanded by Marx's aphorism, the unity of thought and action (SE 228), that seems to me the fundamental impulse behind critical theory.

One thing worth observing about Marx's aphorism is that, technically speaking, it is ambiguous as to whether his own theorizing is to be regarded as post-philosophical or as an exercise in reformed philosophy. This same uncertainty often appears in the manner in which critical theorists talk about themselves: sometimes they say they are doing philosophy, sometimes they prefer the term 'social theory'. And so the question arises: Is critical theory philosophy?

It might seem that given the interdisciplinary character of the first Frankfurt School – it employed economists, psychologists, historians and sociologists as well as philosophers – the answer is that it is not. Philosophy, it might seem, is just one element in an interdisciplinary enterprise. Horkheimer, however, is clear that critical theory *is* philosophy, indeed the only valid form of philosophy: in the 1939 'The Social Function of Philosophy' he writes that, following the example of Socrates, 'the real social function of philosophy lies in its criticism of what is prevalent' (SE 264). While it is true that philosophy must be informed by the natural and social sciences, the business of philosophy is to 'transcend [all] … prevailing forms of scientific activity' (SE 262). This is because philosophy's task with respect to the individual sciences is to 'cancel and negate [the] one-sidedness [of each] in a more comprehensive system of thought, in a system more flexible and better adapted to reality' (SE 265). This conception of philosophy follows from Horkheimer's Hegel-inspired theory of truth. Each of the special sciences constitutes a 'moment of truth',[4] but only a moment, since they each represent a 'one-sided' perspective on reality: 'economic man' is not the whole truth about humanity and neither is 'religious man', 'aesthetic man' nor 'psychoanalytic man'. As Horkheimer conceives it, one of the tasks of philosophy is to synthesize these different perspectives into a unified whole, into, in Wilfrid Sellars' phrase, a 'synoptic vision'. As Nietzsche puts it, 'the more eyes … we bring to bear on the same thing, the more complete will be our "concept" …. our "objectivity"'.[5] The answer to our question, then, is that critical theory *is* philosophy, but philosophy informed by the knowledge produced by the human sciences in particular.

Yet apart from being more informed by empirical research, how does critical theory differ from more traditional ways of practising philosophy? Why do we need a new understanding of the activity of philosophizing about society? Horkheimer's central discussion of this question occurs in a difficult 1937 paper entitled 'Traditional and Critical Theory' in which he sets out to explain his conception of 'critical theory' by contrasting it with 'traditional theory'. A critique of the latter is designed to persuade us of the need for the former.

Traditional theory

Although Horkheimer presents the contrast between the 'critical' and the 'traditional' as a contrast between theor*ies*, it is clear that this is just an abbreviated way of talking about a contrast between types of theor*ists* and the 'social function' (SE 253) of their theorizing.

Traditional social theorists, philosophers for example, pay little explicit attention to the question of the social value of their theorizing – in effect, to the question raised in the title of Weber's lecture of what, if anything, makes the life of science a 'vocation' (p. 7 above). Typically, says Horkheimer, traditional theorists simply 'take for … granted … [their] positive role in a functioning society' (SE 216), take for granted that their society is in reasonably good order and that – somehow or other – their theoretical activity contributes to that good order. If pressed, however, they will justify their activity as adding to the great storehouse of knowledge which society has at its disposal. *In itself*, however, they will emphasize, this activity has no effect on society, either beneficial or harmful. Science, of course, discloses technological possibilities, possibilities for the manipulation of both nature and society, but whether or not these possibilities are realized is entirely a matter for society at large. It is something 'extrinsic' (SE 209) to science itself which must always remain 'objective', 'detached' from practical concerns (SE 222). That it is not the business of science to prescribe social action is reflected in the widespread insistence that it must be value-free, free of 'value judgments' (SE 232, 248).

The scientist may, of course, have strong views about the use of the science he had helped to develop, and may engage in social or political action to put those views into effect. But that is something he does as a concerned citizen, not as a scientist (SE 209). (One might think of the horror and subsequent career of J. Robert Oppenheimer when it came home to him just what he had wrought with the Manhattan Project.)

This distinction between acting as a scientist and as a citizen is a virtually direct (though unattributed) quotation from Weber's lecture discussed in the previous chapter, a lecture in which he warns the students that they should expect neither prophesy nor politics from their professor since 'neither the prophet nor the demagogue belongs on the academic platform' (FMW 146). The professor who feels 'called upon … to intervene in the struggles of worldviews and party opinions may do so outside, in the market place, in the press, in meetings, in associations, wherever he wishes' (FMW 150), but not in the lecture theatre. He may engage in the affairs of the world 'as' a concerned citizen but not 'as (*als*) an academic teacher' (FMW 146), not as a scientist. For all his respect for Weber's work, Horkheimer calls this self-conception 'the false consciousness of the bourgeois savant' (SE 198). Horkheimer has two main arguments to this conclusion, to the self-deluded character of the traditional theorist's self-conception. Both attack the claim that science as such is without social consequence, that, in itself, it is 'suprasocial' (SE 196).

The first of these is contained in the observation that 'bringing hypotheses to bear on facts is an activity that goes on, ultimately, not in the savant's head but in industry'. Research, and to a considerable degree the style of research, is dependent on funding. And capitalist society does not fund what is not to its advantage. So if the scientist thinks he is doing something other than supporting the capitalist social order he is deluded (SE 196). This is pretty obviously true with respect to the natural sciences – medical research, for instance, is notoriously dependent on the pharmaceutical industry. And even so-called 'blue sky' research (the research that produced, for example, the laser), if it manages to get funded, is funded on the assumption that something advantageous to industry will result even if it is not yet clear what that might be.

What, however, about the human 'sciences', philosophy, for instance? How can they be said to promote the current social order? Horkheimer claims that all scientific activity that is not self-consciously critical of the capitalist status quo – even if 'unproductive in the narrower sense' – is part of the 'process of production' (SE 197). 'Even the emptiness of certain areas of university activity as well as all the idle ingenuity … have their social significance' (SE 206). Even they contribute to the 'conservation and continuous renewal of the existing state of affairs' (SE 196). But how so? How exactly do the seemingly 'useless' subjects contribute to the preservation of the status quo?

One answer is provided in Raymond Geuss'*A World without Why?* Recently retired from his position as professor of philosophy at Cambridge, this well known critical theorist bids an amusingly sour farewell to his profession:

> I have always held to be a mildly discreditable day job, that of teaching philosophy at a university. I take it to be discreditable because about 85 percent of my time and energy is devoted to training aspiring young members of the commercial, administrative or governmental elite in the glib manipulation of words, theories and arguments. I thereby help to turn out the pliable, efficient, self-satisfied cadres that our economic and political system uses to produce the ideological carapace which protects it against criticism and change.[6]

What Geuss points out, here, is that mainstream academic philosophy is only *apparently* 'empty'. Beneath the appearance of noble 'uselessness' it *does* play a solid part in the 'process of production'. That, after all, is how we professors, for our sins, try to persuade students to become philosophy majors. At the University of Auckland, it is now (2017) required that *every* course should justify itself in terms of an 'employability' quotient.

A second criticism of the claimed 'suprasocial' status of science focuses on the aping of the methodology of natural science by the social sciences. As noted in the previous chapter, the standard account of scientific explanation is provided by the 'covering law' model. The scientist discovers a law roughly of the form 'If A then B', and, then, given the 'initial condition' of an instance of A, the law retrospectively explains, or prospectively predicts, an instance of B. Social scientists overwhelmingly believe that explanation/prediction in the human sciences must follow this pattern, and so they take their task to be the discovery of 'the eternal law dominating all events' (SE 6), in society as in nature. The effect of this is that, having discovered a regularity in social behaviour, the social theorist presents it as a law, a law that is taken to be a component of an eternal 'human nature' (SE 7, 199).

A second effect of the aping of the natural scientist is that the social scientist thinks of himself [sic] as observing a 'closed causal system' (SE 231) from a 'mathematical point' (SE 209) external to system. This leads him to think that, just as events in nature are unaffected by the scientist's theorizing about them, so, too, society is unaffected by the social scientist's – 'suprasocial' – theorizing. But this is a fallacy. The fact that the social scientist presents himself as describing a timeless, law-governed 'mechanism' (SE 5) has the effect of presenting the current social order as the *only possible* social order. In this, writes Horkheimer, traditional theorists make themselves the successors of Hegel: they 'absolutize' the bourgeois social order as unalterably here to stay, as the 'end of history' (SE 115).[7]

This generates the mistaken belief that there is nothing to be done about the present situation, a belief in the previously mentioned Hegelian 'fatalism' (SE 51, 204). The reason such a belief may well be mistaken is that the social scientist's 'laws' may actually be no more than historically local regularities, regularities produced by, rather than producing, the current social order (SE 5+8). (The exposure of this fallacy, Horkheimer adds, explains the widespread hostility to critical theory among those 'ruled' by the current order: it is the product of 'the unconscious fear that [critically] theoretical thinking might show their painfully won adaptation to reality to be perverse and unnecessary' [SE 232].)

Horkheimer does not given any concrete examples of how traditional social theory presents change as impossible, but I shall venture two illustrations. The first is the routine objection to the possibility of communism: the acquisitive instinct, classical and neo-classical economists assure us, is hardwired into the human being, so that, without the possibility of private property, people would not work and society would collapse. In fact, however, there is no eternal 'acquisitive instinct'. Early peoples, the New Zealand Maori, for instance, had no – not even the conception of – private property, and it is still the case, sometimes, that people who live in kibbutzim and communes live without private property.

A second example is, I think, Freud. Freud holds that 'libidinal' energy is the only source of psychic energy there is, so that, civilization, needing its members to work, must divert – 'sublimate' – that energy from its natural expression into productive work, to which end it imposes its many taboos on natural sexual activity. This causes loss of pleasure, which means that 'discontent' is inseparable from 'civilization'. As we shall see Marcuse arguing, however (pp. 71–2 below), the supposed 'law', 'If energy is expended sexually, production will decline' is – at best – an historically local truth. The reason it is not a law is that the development of modern industry to a point of full automation may obviate the need for work, and hence the need for the diversion of libidinal energy.

Critical theory

So much for what critical theory is not. What now can be said by way of providing a positive account of what it *is*?

Critical theory, writes Horkheimer, thinks in the 'service' of an 'oppressed humanity' and seeks to eliminate 'social injustice' (SE 221, 242). Unlike the 'detached' (SE 222), value-neutral stance of the traditional theorist, the critical theorist takes a 'consciously critical' attitude to the status quo, is hyper-aware of the fact that the bourgeois social order generates the alienation of labour and general wretchedness (SE 203–4). Whereas – to repeat Marx's contrast – traditional theory thinks of itself as simply trying to understand the world, the critical theorist wants to change it, change it so as to bring about 'a future society (*Gesellschaft*) as a community (*Gemeinschaft*) of free men' (SE 217).[8] The aim, then, is liberty, liberation, but also – a point often overlooked – that other battle cry of the French Revolution, fraternity, community.

That the critical theorist's theorizing *is* revolutionary social action means that the traditional theorist's 'Cartesian' split between the self as disengaged (and so, as it were, disembodied) theorist and the self as citizen is abolished: theorist and citizen become one. The critical theorist's 'vocation (*Beruf*)', the meaning of his life, is not theory for its own sake but rather the 'struggle (*Kampf*)' for a better world, 'of which his own thinking is a part, and not something self-sufficient and separable from the struggle' (SE 216).

The critical theorist accepts that there will always be elements in the natural environment that cannot be 'mastered' by the human will. But he rejects the extension of the traditional theorist's supposed 'laws' to situations that 'really depend on [the free choice of] man alone [such as] the relationships of men in their work' (SE 210). What gives the critical theorist the confidence to pursue his or her struggle is the fact that, with respect to the human as opposed to natural sciences, theorizing modifies the theorized. The critical theorist realizes that by clearing away 'false consciousness', by raising our consciousness to an explicit awareness of our oppression, we (the oppressed) are motivated to resist.

This, says Horkheimer, is the 'decisive difference' (SE 210) between the traditional and the critical theorist. Whereas the traditional theorist mistakenly believes his theorizing to be 'suprasocial', devoid of 'social function' or effect, the critical theorist knows that, by focussing on the 'contradictions' (SE 204) within industrial capitalism, on phenomena such as 'class, exploitation ... pauperization and breakdown' (SE 218) that 'contradict' fundamental values (liberty, equality, and fraternity) his audience can be assumed to hold, his theorizing can motivate revolutionary action.

In sum, then, there are two crucial differences between the traditional and the critical theorist. First, whereas both have a social effect, that of the former is conservative while that of the latter is disruptive. Second, whereas the traditional theorist mistakenly thinks that his theorizing has no social function, the critical theorist recognizes the social effect of his theorizing and makes use of that effect.

A question that needs to be raised at this point is this: if the primary aim is to change the world, why should theory, science, knowledge, be the preferred means? Why should one not prefer propaganda? Deeply conscious of Hitler's mastery of 'direct and indirect propaganda which by its nature is indifferent to truth' (SE 290), Horkheimer draws an emphatic distinction between critical theory and propaganda (SE 224, ER 184). Unlike propaganda, critical theory is essentially concerned with *truth*, 'with the intellectual, and eventually practical, effort ... to distinguish the appearance from the essence, to examine the foundation of things, in short really to know them' (SE 270). In *this* respect, then, critical theory is at one with traditional theory, though the truths if focuses on are likely to be different from those of the traditional theorist: truths not about, for instance, the efficient operation of financial markets but about the various modes of social oppression.

The question remains, however: if the aim is to change the world why *should* one prefer truth to lies, knowledge to fiction, science to propaganda? That Horkheimer never provides an answer to this question is a lacuna in his thought. And it might even be made the basis of a challenge to his radical credentials. ('Professors try to change their disciplines, whereas the point', it might unkindly be said, 'is to change the world'.) But perhaps, if pressed on the question of truth versus lies, Horkheimer might appeal to Nietzsche, who remarks that the reason most people tell the truth most of the time is not that they are virtuous but rather that they know they are not clever enough to maintain a lie, that a lie typically ramifies into an ever-expanding bubble that must eventually burst.[9] This, I think, is what Horkheimer ought to say: it is important that one's theory deal in truth because, in the long run, propaganda will be exposed as propaganda. Truth lasts longer.

What, then, are the 'critical' revolutionary-action-motivating truths that critical theory proposes to disclose? In essence, they are elaborations and expansions of Weber's truths: that the rationalization of the modern world has produced the two pathologies, loss of meaning and loss of freedom. The first is the primary focus of Horkheimer's essay 'Means and Ends', and the second, the primary focus of the co-authored 'Concept of Enlightenment'.

Loss of meaning

Typically, philosophers have only a shaky grasp of what they are talking about when they refer (usually approvingly) to 'reason'. 'Means and Ends' attempts to introduce clarity by distinguishing three species of 'reason'. The first is what Horkheimer calls 'formal' reason, 'the abstract functioning of the thinking mechanism' (ER 3). I would call this 'reason' – reasoning – as such. To reason is to think, and thinking as such is 'abstract' in the sense that one can think about any subject matter at all. As Horkheimer says, the rules of inductive and deductive logic (and perhaps of informal logic, too) are the norms that reason follows when it is functioning well (ibid.). To reason well is to reason 'logically'.

Horkheimer's second species – I would say 'use' – of reason is what he calls 'subjective' reason, by which he means reason devoted to the calculation of means to ends that are, or may be, possessed by the 'subject' (ER 3). This – as Horkheimer notes, Weber's *Zweckrationalität* (ER 6 fn.) – is generally referred to as 'instrumental' reason.

The third species or use – Weber's *Wertrationalität* – Horkheimer calls 'objective reason'. Whereas subjective reason calculates means to ends, objective reason determines what those ends should be, determines one's 'destiny' (ER 5, 11), the meaning of one's life. Such reasoning is objective in the double sense of determining the 'objectives' of action and in the sense of determining ends whose normative status is 'objectively' true, true for all human beings irrespective of their subjective desires.

Whether there is such a thing as objective reason is, of course, controversial. Plato, and the seventeenth-century 'rationalists', believed that thought could reveal the essence of the universe, an essence which would determine the good life, the ends that we ought to pursue. Spinoza, for instance, believed that

> insight into the essence of reality, into the harmonious structure of the eternal universe, necessarily awakens love for this universe. For him, ethical conduct is entirely determined by such insight into nature, just as our devotion to a person may be determined by insight into his greatness or genius. Fears and petty passions, alien to the great love of the universe, which is *logos* [reason] itself, will vanish, according to Spinoza, once our understanding of reality is deep enough.[10]

(ER 14)

We moderns, on the other hand, says Horkheimer – we have seen this to be true in the case of Weber – no longer believe in objective reason. This, he says, is the result of the triumph of British empiricism over Continental rationalism. Hume for example – whom Horkheimer calls the 'father of modern positivism' (ER 18) – famously said that 'reason is and ought only to be the slave of the passions', from which he concluded that it is not contrary to any kind of *reason* to prefer the destruction of the whole world to the scratching of one's finger.[11] In other words, the only significance reason has in our practical lives is instrumental. Which ends means are to serve can be determined only by feeling and desire, not by reason.

The rise and fall of objective reason

The idea of objective reason, says Horkheimer, became important to modern thought at the beginning of the Enlightenment. The reason is that reflective thinkers 'aspired to replace traditional religion with methodical philosophical thought' (ER 12). In other words, objective reason became important to the Enlightenment thinkers' attempt to replace the authority of revelation with that of reason as the determinant of the 'human destination' (ER 12), their attempt to replace the *lumen supernaturale* with the *lumen naturale* (ER 15). And initially, they were successful. For the 'pioneers of bourgeois civilization', the leaders of the French and American revolutions, 'wise legislature [sic]' was defined as 'one whose laws conform to reason', objective reason being thought of as a 'spiritual force' dwelling in every human being (ER 9). So, for example, to the framers of the American Declaration of Independence, the rights to life, liberty, and the pursuit of happiness were 'self-evident' to the light of reason (though see p. 206 below for Arendt's alternative reading of 'self-evident').

Why is this conviction no longer with us? Horkheimer's answer is that as soon as reason turns to self-criticism – as soon as we start thinking about thinking – it becomes clear that what the eighteenth-century thinkers were doing was simply projecting a particular cultural heritage onto objective reality. (The Greeks, after all, did not believe in these 'universal rights'.) By the time of Nietzsche's critique of reason it becomes entirely clear that such projection is illegitimate, that 'the structure of the universe cannot be derived from any first principles we discover in our minds' (ER 180–1).[12]

As Horkheimer conceives it, the death of objective value and meaning occurs in two stages. First the Enlightenment says, as it were, 'Don't believe anything that isn't validated by our own reason – but don't worry, our own reason shows that the ideals that gave our lives meaning in the past remain as true today as they ever were.' Soon, however, reason turns to self-criticism and ends up 'liquidat[ing] itself as an agency of ethical, moral, and religious insight' (ER 18).[13]

A way of looking at Horkheimer's narrative is to see it as filling in some of the details in Nietzsche's and Weber's story of the 'death of God' and of

Christian ethics. Nietzsche and Weber say that God 'becomes unbelievable' and as a consequence the Christian 'godhead' dies. This suggests a 'two epoch' narrative: the 'age of faith' in which both God and Christian meaning thrive, followed by the 'age of reason' in which both God and Christian meaning die. Horkheimer, in effect, refines this into an historically more convincing 'three epoch' narrative: the 'age of faith' is followed by an 'age of reason' that preserves Christian meaning, followed by an 'age of reason' devoid of Christian meaning.

The way we are now

The result of the death of objective reason is that the great ideals of Western ethics – though they continue, of course, to receive lip service – have lost their authority over us. The corporation installs disabled access doors while simultaneously 'downsizing' hundreds into poverty and 'outsourcing' to child labour in Indonesia. (Habermas, we shall see, refers to this as the overpowering of 'lifeworld' norms by economic 'system'.) The old ideals no longer truly motivate, so that modern humanity is 'stripped of all aims' (ER 100). More exactly, the modern individual is stripped of all aims save biologically programmed (and presumably pleasant) 'self-preservation'. Self-preservation is not, however, a meaning-giving aim, since meaning (Weberian 'vocation') is what one preserves oneself *for*. What we lack is 'something transcending the subjectivity of self-interest to which the self could ... aspire' (ER 175). We live, therefore, in the age of 'cynical nihilism' (ER 174, 93) – the nihilism which Nietzsche sometimes claims to be the 'normal condition' of the present age and defines in the following entry in his notebooks:

> Nihilism: the aim is lacking: 'Why?' has no answer[.] [W]hat does nihilism mean? – That the highest values devalue themselves.[14]

Two objections to the alleged meaninglessness of modernity

Horkheimer, then, represents modern Western humanity as devoid of the ideals which, in the past, constrained and gave meaning to its use of subjective reason. To this portrait, he anticipates the objection that, while we may have given up on appeals to either religion or objective reason, enculturation into an ethical tradition, the 'reverence for the community in which we live', for its 'founders' and for heroes 'who have given their lives for it', is entirely sufficient to provide us with life-defining ideals and meaning (ER 32–3).

Horkheimer's reply is that, in the past, people extolled 'humility and brotherly love, justice and humanity', not because they belonged to a tradition, but because they believed that the demand that we should live up to those ideals represented 'objective truth', truth guaranteed by '*logos*' whether in the form of God or a transcendental mind or even of nature as an eternal principle'. The very fact that 'tradition' has to be invoked today shows that it has lost its hold on people (ER 33–5).

This seems to me a confused response. That 'tradition' is invoked at the meta-level of a discussion of the alleged nihilism of modernity does not mean that it is invoked in ordinary moral discourse; in, for example, the ethical education and enculturation of children. And plainly, the question 'Why do I have to take the doll back to the shop, mum?' is going to be met not with 'Because, in our tradition, stealing is regarded as wrong,' but rather with 'Because stealing is wrong.' In ordinary discourse, the rightness or wrongness of things is presented as objective truth, even though, at the meta-level, non-philosophers are likely to be unable to present any kind of justification for their moral certainties. It may well be true that the education of children into an ethical tradition is weaker now than in the past, but that, surely, is due, not to the loss of a meta-ethical grounding of moral truth, but to factors such as globalization, immigration, working mothers, the transformation of education into technical training, and the domination of the academy by the resolute nihilism of postmodern deconstructionism. As we shall see, Heidegger, Arendt and Gadamer all regard belonging to an ethical tradition as essential to a flourishing human life, so tradition is a topic to which we shall return on several occasions.

Horkheimer considers one further objection to his loss-of-meaning thesis, in effect, the simple response, 'But I don't find *my life* meaningless'. His reply is to admit that there are

> [o]ld forms of life smouldering under the surface of modern civilization [which] still provide, in many cases, the warmth inherent in any delight, in any love of a thing for its own sake rather than for that of another thing. The pleasure of keeping a garden goes back to ancient times when gardens belonged to the gods and were cultivated for them.
>
> (ER 35–6)

The point, here, I think, is one that is also made by Heidegger. Although a phase of an historical culture has a *dominant* character, historical epochs are never homogeneous but always contain an admixture of the 'early' and the 'late' (PLT 183). If we find meaning in, for instance, cultivating our gardens, then part of the time at least, we live not in the 'now' but in the 'then'. Unconsciously, we live, in Kierkegaard's language, 'in the truth' of a gods-impregnated past.

Loss of freedom

Horkheimer's 'Means and Ends' essay has nothing to say about 'loss of freedom' in the modern age. And, indeed, insofar as its narrative concerns simply the loss of meaning-giving ideals, it offers no reason to think that freedom is under threat. The problem, as the essay presents it, is not that we lack freedom, but rather that we have nothing meaningful to do with it. In fact, however, Horkheimer also believes the modern social order to constitute a serious threat to human freedom. The central discussion of this occurs in 'The Concept of Enlightenment', the work in which Horkheimer and Adorno provide their version of Weber's loss of freedom thesis.

'Enlightenment' is the authors' synonym for 'rationalization'. 'Enlightenment', the essay begins, 'understood in the widest sense as the advancement of thought, has always aimed at liberating human beings from fear and installing them as masters' (DE 1). From the beginning, then, the function of thought has been not only (a) to guarantee our own security, but also (b) to serve the 'patriarchal' (DE 2) goal of making us 'masters' of all we survey. From the beginning, in other words, reason has been in the service, not only of Schopenhauer's 'will to live', but also of Nietzsche's 'will to power'. Unlike Weber, who sees the attempt to master all things by calculation as unique to Western civilization, the authors see it as innate to the human being as such.[15] Thesis (a) is, of course, highly plausible: from an evolutionary point of view the reasoning brain is a survival mechanism. Lacking sharp teeth or claws, the human species has survived only because it became clever at 'calculation'. Thesis (b), however, is much more controversial: is *world-mastery* really part of our biological heritage?

The only evidence offered in support of this claim is a reference to Genesis, in which God says,

> [l]et us make man in our image after our likeness: and let them [sic] have dominion over the fish of the sea, and over the fowl of the air, and over the cattle, and over all the earth, and over every creeping thing that creepeth upon the earth.
>
> (Genesis 1: 26)

The rectitude of the programme of total domination is guaranteed by the fact that, by making man in his own image, God has delegated his dominion over all things to man (DE 6). This, however is relatively weak evidence for thesis (b) given that first, the import of the Hebrew *radah*, translated as 'dominion', is disputed; second, later on in Genesis Noah saves not only the 'clean' but also the 'unclean' (i.e. inedible) animals (6 9–17); third, the evidence concerns only one cultural tradition; and fourth, animal species do not, in general, colonize other animal species, so it is unclear why the biology of the human animal should be different.

Although present from the beginning, the authors claim, the programme made little progress until the Renaissance. Here the key figures are Francis Bacon and Galileo: the former because he initiated the 'totalitarian' project of creating *una scientia universalis* (DE 4), a science that embraces the totality of reality without remainder, the latter because he initiated the mathematization of science, the replacement of descriptive terms by mathematical formulae. For two reasons, mathematization is a crucial step: first, because only when science becomes 'exact' is the exact prediction, and hence control, of nature possible; second, because, only with the homogenization of nature into a single 'mathematical manifold' – the authors borrow the concept from Husserl (see p. 107 below) – is a 'universal science' possible (DE 18–19).

Accompanying the mathematization of descriptive terms, the authors add, is the harnessing of formal logic in the construction of a 'schema' of explanation and prediction: Bacon was satirized for his 'idolized ladder' (DE 4). The 'covering law' model of scientific explanation is, in other words, a harnessing of the logical form of argument known as 'modus ponens' (If A then B, A, therefore B).

Control of nature includes, of course, control of human nature. And so the development of enlightenment includes a drive to incorporate human beings into its calculative 'mould' (DE 9). Scientific method is applied to human society, in particular to the workplace. The 'rationalization and planning' of all aspects of modern life (ER 95) takes the form, in the workplace, of the 'bourgeois division of labour' (DE 23); of, in other words, Taylorism and Fordism. Workers are reduced – 'objectified' (DE 16) or 'reified' (DE 23, ER 39–40) – into mere 'objects of administration' (DE 30). As workers, we are turned into interchangeable, second-order tools, tools for making other tools, and are forced to conform to the requirements of the industrial 'system' (DE 29) as the condition of self-preservation. We are becoming, in short, Weber's *Berufsmenschen*, prisoners of the iron cage. We are losing our freedom. And thus the paradox arises that with every step the scientific-technological system allows us to take away from nature, every step away from a merely animal existence, we become, more and more, just what we sought to escape, mere samples of a species (DE 29). With every step we take away from nature we return, if not to nature, then to a second, pseudo-nature (DE 9, 31). In Chapter 8 we shall find Arendt endorsing this point.

Yet we are not totally passive. A 'smouldering resentment' expresses itself in mental derangement, in seemingly pointless crime, and in expressions of sudden, uncontrollable 'rage' (ER 144). (One might think, here, of Tommy's sudden, occasion-less, rages in Kazuo Ishiguro's *Never Let Me Go*, a novel in which the children slowly realize that they are clones, created as living repositories of spare organs, and doomed to early deaths when they make their 'donations'.) As Freud made clear, 'the more loudly the idea of rationality is proclaimed and acknowledged, the stronger is the growth in the minds of people of conscious or unconscious resentment against civilization and its agency within the individual, the ego' (ER 109).[16]

Of course, there has always been cultural pressure to conform to the social order (ER 144), so Horkheimer concedes that a degree of Freud's 'discontent'[17] is inseparable from 'civilization' as such. Only in modernity, however, has this pressure become total, so that only in modernity has the discontent become acute. In the past, the necessary 'cultural cement' of a shared ethical tradition never produced, nor was intended to produce, a 'completely integrated' society (ER 145). In the past, there was always a region of freedom that allowed for authentic individuality. Now however such freedom-within-limits has disappeared. The modern individual is micro-managed to such a degree that he becomes an 'organic part of the socio-economic system', a 'mere cell of functional response' (ER 145). As noted in the previous chapter, to render vivid the contrast between the 'continual social coercion' (the 'bureaucratization') of modern life and the relative freedom of the past, Horkheimer asks us to compare the 'innumerable laws regulations and directions with which we must comply [in] … driving a car' with the spontaneity of riding a horse over the medieval countryside (ER 98).

The culture industry

It might be objected that the above portrait of modern individuals as a prisoners in the rationalized cage of industrial society applies only to their interactions with the economy and the state. It does not apply, it might be claimed, to our leisure time, and it is here – our lyric cry in the midst of business – that we find our freedom and individuality. Thus even Marx allows that, in industrialized modernity, there remains a 'real life' which 'starts when work ceases – at table, in the bar, in bed'[18] (and also, one might think, in retirement). The authors, however, are at pains to deny this. In what is their most original contribution to the 'loss-of-freedom' thesis, a contribution that is largely the result of their enforced stay in America, they argue that in modern life, so-called 'free' time is not free at all but is rather controlled by a carefully managed extension of the workplace, is regulated in such a way as to complete the disciplining of the individual into a Weberian *Berufsmensch*. The agent of this disciplining is what the authors call 'the culture industry'.

The primary text in which they argue this thesis is the 1944 'The Culture Industry: Enlightenment as Mass Deception' (DE 94–136). A somewhat undisciplined work with little evident structure, the essay operates on the shotgun principle of firing a great many pellets at the 'industry' in the hope that at least some of them will hit the target. It has, moreover, several targets extraneous to the 'deception' announced in its title. The authors object, for instance, to the 'trash' (DE 95) that is modern popular culture (one suspects that the dominant influence, here, is Adorno, more disposed to cultural 'elitism' than Horkheimer), and to the commodification of art, the descent of artworks from the seriousness of the past into today's products of the 'entertainment industry' (DE 112). These lines of criticism are not particularly original: they reproduce the cultural criticism of the nineteenth century, in particular that of Richard Wagner, of whose writings Adorno (himself an aspirant composer) was a close reader. The very phrase 'culture industry' is anticipated and probably inspired by Wagner's description of the world of nineteenth-century opera that he sought to reform as 'the opera industry'.[19] In what follows I shall focus on the 'deception' thesis and largely ignore these less original lines of criticism.

The culture industry is the integrated 'system' of the advertising, news and entertainment industries, everything we receive through 'film, radio, and magazines' (DE 112). In fact, though, the authors' focus is very largely confined to Hollywood. The deception thesis asserts that, under the guise of information and entertainment, the culture industry is designed to discipline modern, mass society into a collection of obedient and efficient productive units (DE 104, 108). The subtext of modern popular culture is, in the authors' Marxist terminology, an 'ideology' (DE viii), subliminal propaganda designed to create acceptance of the status quo, to 'deceive' the masses into 'false', complaisant and compliant, consciousness. Modern liberal societies, of course, guarantee the 'formal freedom' of the individual. Yet, in fact, behind the 'faded foreground' of the Hollywood film, a 'cultural tyranny' is exercised over the individual, a tyranny that, in a phrase the authors borrow from de Tocqueville, 'leaves the body free and operates directly on the soul' (DE 105). One is free to do what one wants, but what one wants is determined by the 'entertainment' arm of the 'gigantic economic machinery' of industrial society (DE 100). Michel Foucault identifies what he calls 'panopticism', 'the gentle efficiency of total surveillance', as modernity's device for 'normalizing' its population.[20] Punishment of lawbreakers becomes largely unnecessary if potential transgressors know their transgressions will be observed. Operating, however, on the soul of the individual so as to extinguish the capacity even to entertain transgressive desires is even more gently efficient.

'The Culture Industry' begins by observing that in the 'sociological view', having lost 'objective religion', society has descended into 'cultural chaos' (DE 94). The reference, here, is clearly to Weber's 'polytheism' thesis, his account of modernity as a 'pandemonium' of rival gods and demons (p. 12 above). But this thesis, the authors say, is evidently false, or at least not the whole story. For in reality, it is clear that the media, 'women's serials' (DE 115), for example, form a 'system' of cultural homogenization (DE 94), a 'mocking fulfilment of Wagner's dream' (DE 97) of a culture unified by a 'collective artwork' (p. 12 above).[21]

In Kant's *Critique of Pure Reason*, the authors observe, a 'secret mechanism in the psyche' has the task of imposing the fundamental concepts of reason onto the raw data of experience, thereby making them intelligible. Now, however, the subject has been denied this 'schematizing' activity since the task has been taken over by industry. The 'secret mechanism' that now operates is the culture industry. The way in which things become intelligible is predetermined because 'the whole world is passed through the filter of the culture industry' (DE 98–9). Of course, with political totalitarianism, the mechanism is hardly hidden at all, but totalitarianism just makes explicit what, in one way or another, happens in Western modernity in general (SE 276–7, 290).

Art, whether high or low, has, of course, always been used to mould feeling and thought. Greek tragedy was used to shore up the principle of masculine domination, medieval portraits of the saints created models to be imitated in life, while representations of the visions of the martyrs were designed to shore up faith in the afterlife. To the objection, however, that the schematizing the authors attribute to the culture industry is nothing new, they respond by appealing to – the phrase is borrowed from their quasi-colleague, Walter Benjamin[22] – the 'mechanical reproducibility of artworks' (DE 100). Thanks to modern communication technology, the same film or radio broadcast can be disseminated throughout society from a single production centre in such a way that it reaches every individual. As distinct from pre-modern times, in which art, language, dialect, and culture was to a great extent local and diverse, modern technology has enabled the culture industry to teach a vast population the same mode of perception and feeling, to produce a homogenized, 'mass' culture. Moreover, the technology is intrinsically authoritarian. Unlike the interactive telephone, the radio dominates its audience, reduces it to the passive recipient of overt or subliminal suggestion (DE 95).

Thus the medium – a mode of, we would now say, 'soft power'. Most crucial, however, is the message the medium is used to convey. What is it about the content of this authoritarian, universal 'ideology' that is designed to reduce us to obedient units of production and consumption? I shall regiment the authors' scattered observations under four headings.

First, the culture industry, the Hollywood film, in particular, operates so as to produce a repertoire of approved social 'stereotypes' (DE 119), which the glamour of the medium 'heroizes' (DE 126) and encourages us to imitate. These role models are all social conformists, and they have a powerful effect, for if one does not conform to what are established as 'average' and approved modes of being (DE 126), one is ostracized as an 'eccentric loner' (DE 106). The authors' examples of such stereotypes are, of course, dated, not to say cringe-worthy – 'the hero's temporary disgrace which he accepts as a "good sport", the wholesome slaps the heroine receives from the strong hand of the male star, his plain-speaking abruptness toward the pampered heiress' (DE 98) – an issue to which I shall return.

The message that we should conform to such 'ready-made clichés' (DE 106) is reinforced by the fact that, in the movies (in the crime drama or the Western) the rule-breaker, the 'outsider', is usually a villain (DE 121). This is the fate of tragedy in the movies. Formerly concerned with the dangerous topic of the individual *versus* society (Antigone versus Creon, Hamlet versus the 'rotten in the state of Denmark'), tragedy, in the cinema, has become an agent of 'moral correction' (DE 123). This is effected by transferring the viewer's empathy from the tragic hero to the society against which he has offended (DE 126). The 'tragic flaw' is turned into criminality and tragedy into a morality play. Individuality, it is true, is sometimes tolerated by Hollywood, but only if the individual's underlying 'wholehearted identity with the universal is beyond question' (DE 124). (One might think of *North By Northwest* [1959]. Cary Grant's seemingly transgressive 'I've got ... two ex-wives and several bartenders that depend upon me, and I don't intend to disappoint them all by getting myself "slightly" killed', is cancelled by the fashionable elegance of his suit, sometimes referred to as 'the most famous suit in movies'.)

The second function of the culture industry is to present the everyday world as the only possible world. Given the drab suffering of everyday life in the industrialized cage, one looks to popular culture, to the cinema, for a brief moment of escape. In the art of the past, escape from the everyday was possible. In Greek tragedy one escaped to the world of the gods and heroes; in Shakespeare, to the world of history or dreams. But in the Hollywood movie, whether comedy or tragedy, one finds oneself simply returned to the 'daily round', returned to the familiar city with its familiar streets (DE 110–11). This is the nature of film – photography – as such. As a medium, it cannot but copy the familiar world and so cannot but deny the imagination the freedom to roam (DE 100). Such denial is important because it extinguishes the capacity to contemplate alternative worlds and thereby the possibility of altering the conditions of the actual world. The consumer of film must 'not for a moment suspect that resistance is possible' (DE 113).

Of course, even if resistance is believed impossible, the desire to resist might still remain as a 'smouldering resentment' (p. 32 above). Thus the third function of the culture industry is, as far as possible, to eradicate that desire by presenting the everyday world as a 'paradise' (DE 113): a paradise of glamorous people, of merriment (the canned laughter of the sit-com *tells* us that the world is a merry place [DE 112–3]) and of sex. The naked torso of the sporting hero and the full breasts beneath the starlet's (Kim Novak's) tight jumper offer the promise of sex. At the same time, however (save in the occasional daring, X-rated movie), we are assured that the sex will never reach consummation. The object of desire is constantly exhibited, but the 'promissory note' of pleasure is always postponed, making Hollywood movies simultaneously 'pornographic and prudish' (DE 111). Since the authors refer to this as the suppression of 'unsublimated pleasure' (ibid.) their point is fairly clearly based on Freud's view that 'civilization' requires the 'sublimation', diversion, of 'libidinal' energy from sex into work.[23] Hence, they suggest, the culture industry must accustom us to a kind of cognitive dissonance: the world is a promise of sex – but actual sex, exciting sex at least, is off the menu.

While the cultural-industrial complex presents the world, as far as possible, as a paradise, there is no getting away from the suffering of life in the iron cage. Suffering has to be acknowledged. Hence the culture industry's fourth function is to reconcile us to suffering:

[t]he emphasis on the heart of gold is society's way of admitting the suffering it creates: everyone knows they are helpless within the system and ideology must take account of this [by] … looking it manfully in the eye and acknowledging it with unflinching composure.

(DE 121–2)

Suffering is inevitable but, we must be made to accept, necessary. We have to be persuaded that life is 'all the more splendid, glorious, the more it is imbued with necessary suffering', that life is 'hard, yet *therefore* so wonderful, so healthy' (DE 122; emphasis added). This seems to be an adaptation of Nietzsche's account of Homer's 'Apollonian' art in *The Birth of Tragedy*. [24] The Greeks 'knew', claims the youthful Nietzsche, the Schopenhauerian truth that life is suffering. But, in Homer's war stories, the splendour of the heroes outweighs the suffering that is inseparable from war, and could not exist without it. By persuading us to a third-person rather than first-person perspective on suffering, Greek art drew a veil of beauty over the 'wisdom of Silenus', the Greeks' knowledge that the best thing is not to be born, and the second best, to die as soon as possible.

* * *

An obvious objection to the authors' account of popular culture in the 1930s and 1940s is that it ignores its *critical* side, ignores, for instance, critical cinema. Because it belongs to the same historical period under discussion, what comes to mind, in particular, is the work of Charlie Chaplin, especially the already mentioned *Modern Times* (1936) and *The Great Dictator* (1940), works which appear to target exactly the same phenomena as Horkheimer and Adorno – industrial rationalization and fascist totalitarianism. Perhaps because his films threaten to undermine their thesis, the authors are particularly hard on Chaplin. Their general thesis concerning the critical potential of film mirrors their thesis that, in the form of trades unions, the economic system co-opts potential antagonists into the system. Those who might wish resist the programme of the culture industry can only survive, they observe, by being incorporated into it (DE 105). The result is that apparently critical works always end up pulling their punches. So, for example, with the 'swaying cornfields' that follow the big, anti-fascist speech about freedom at the end of the *Great Dictator* (Chaplin's satire on Hitler),

nature, in being presented by society's control mechanism as the healing antithesis of society, is itself absorbed into that incurable society and sold off. The solemn pictorial affirmation that the trees are green, the sky is blue, and the clouds are sailing overhead already makes them cryptograms for factory chimneys and gasoline stations.

(119–20)

The dark satanic mills are not so bad because you can always go for a walk in the countryside. No doubt the boy-gets-girl ending of *Modern Times* with the message that love redeems all would also meet with Horkheimer and Adorno's disapproval.

These seem unfair observations.[25] *The Great Dictator*, was, in fact, entirely financed by Chaplin (who was Jewish) himself. It was made and released in the teeth of opposition from the Hollywood establishment, which, worried about its lucrative German market, did everything it could to prevent the film's release. The Hollywood moguls claimed that, as anti-Nazi propaganda, the film's release would violate America's neutrality, which still had nearly two years to run before America's entry into the Second World War. Only, it appears, President Roosevelt's personal intervention secured the film's eventual release. In spite of their distorted view of Chaplin, however, the authors' claim about the movie industry is surely generally valid: Hollywood, in the 1930s and 1940s, was not interested in social criticism.

How dated is Horkheimer and Adorno's critique of the culture industry?

From the perspective of the present, the authors' commentary on the popular culture of the early-to-mid-twentieth century represents a kind of cultural archaeology. It is not to be doubted, I think, that it tells us many sharp truths about the period. But is their critique more than archaeology? Do their observations represent a valid critique of the culture industry of the present (2018), or are they, together with their particular examples, too dated to find any contemporary target?

The most obvious way in which the authors' observations are dated concerns their Benjamin-influenced remarks about the 'totalitarian' nature of the industry's medium. Given the fragmentation of broadcasting produced by cable television, and the further fragmentation of the fragmentation produced by the internet and social media, the days when a couple of studios could exert a totalitarian 'cultural tyranny' over a vast population, the days of the 'mocking fulfilment of Wagner's dream' of a collective artwork, are long gone.

Before, however, celebrating this as the death of a 'tyranny', we should recall that one Wagnerian dreamer was Lord Reith, director-general of the BBC from 1927 to 1938, and creator of the concept of public broadcasting. Fiercely resistant to political pressure, Reith nonetheless insisted on complete state funding of the BBC on the grounds that, otherwise, it would descend to the level of crass commercialism. Since, during his directorship, the BBC had a monopoly over radio broadcasting (there was, as yet, no television), Reith's mission of the 'cultural and intellectual enlightenment of society' amounted to something like a realization of Wagner's collective artwork, a gathering of society into a shared ethos. It is far from clear that we should be celebrating the destruction of Reith's ambition.

For better or worse, however, the days of the dominion of the airwaves by a single broadcaster are gone. But does that mean that the media-induced bovine conformism that both Nietzsche and the authors see as characterizing modernity, our reduction to 'herd animals', has disappeared? Given that we can see things clearly only in hindsight, it is hard to give a definitive answer. Some things, however, can be said.

Despite the existence of 'talk-back' radio, the authors' claim about the intrinsically authoritarian nature of the culture industry's medium, its reduction of its audience to passive consumers surely remains intact. Otherwise there would be no point to the billions of dollars that are invested in commercial and political advertising. It is possible to argue, indeed, that with the deployment of the techniques of behavioural economics (overt and sometimes subliminal 'nudges') it has become even more powerfully tyrannical than in the 1940s.

Turning to the authors' criticisms of the message propagated by American film, the claim that it glamorizes conformist stereotypes seems to be well and truly buried by the outbreak, even the predominance, of films and TV series – *The Wolf of Wall Street, House of Cards, Breaking Bad* – that glamorize bad, even wicked, heroes. But although the prevalence of such films invalidates the use of film in support of the author's loss-of-freedom thesis, this disturbing trend does seem to provide further evidence in support of their loss-of-meaning thesis, further evidence of the ethical polytheism, indeed moral nihilism, of modernity.

The authors' second claim, the claim that due to the nature of the medium, the actual world shows up in the Hollywood film as the only possible world, is obviously vitiated by Adorno's unintelligent contempt for the medium as such. The arrival of computer-generated fantasy films should not, however, be seen as providing a counter-example to the authors' thesis, since such movies are explicitly flagged as 'fantasy', i.e., as set, not in possible variants of the actual world, but precisely, rather, in impossible worlds, worlds that are causally inaccessible from this one.

What does, however, provide a counter-example is the popularity of the dystopian movie genre: *The Hunger Games, Ex Machina, The Handmaid's Tale, Blade Runner 2049*, and so on. Movies such as these depict not only dystopian worlds, but worlds that are projections of possible futures of the actual world. The popularity of such films not only disposes of the claim that Hollywood represents the actual as the only possible world, but also of the claim that it represents the actual world as a 'paradise'. While movies of the 1940s may well have done so, it is clear that modern popular cinema is of a darker hue.

That the culture industry casts a justifying veil of Apollonian glamour over suffering still resonates with respect to the 'women's serials' (p. 34 above) that one finds at the supermarket check-out counter ('Obamas' marriage on the rocks', etc.), but, to repeat, modern popular culture in general is a much darker affair than that of the 1940s.

The irrationality of enlightenment

The process of enlightenment, the limitless development of instrumental reason combined with destruction of the belief in objective reason, the authors have argued, has deprived us of both meaning and freedom. The old ideals that provided society with 'solidarity' and individuals with meaning have been deconstructed. And the application of the methodology of natural science to human behaviour – our 'reification' into 'cells of functional response' – has locked us into the iron cage of the totally 'administered', rationalized, society and thereby deprived us of the freedom to flourish as the unique individuals we potentially are. The Enlightenment, in other words has produced the very opposite of the ideals of liberty, equality, fraternity and the pursuit of happiness that originally animated it. Both enlightenment and the Enlightenment have, in short, auto-destructed. Horkheimer and Adorno sum up this 'eclipse of reason' by reason itself by saying that the society produced by the triumph of reason over revelation has become 'irrational' (DE 72, 98, 120, 162, ER 94, 127 et passim), that it constitutes a 'transformation into stupidity' (ER 56).

Is negation enough?

As remarked in the Introduction, Nietzsche describes the philosopher as the 'doctor of culture', a metaphor which implies not only diagnosis of disease but also prescription of a remedy. 'Only as creators can we destroy', he writes,[26] only if we have something to put in its place do we have the right to attempt the destruction of the current order. The authors' critical theory, however, appears to be entirely confined to the 'diagnostic' phase of the philosopher's task. They 'negate' current social reality (ER 182), rouse us out of false consciousness to an explicit awareness of the suffering it causes, but that, it seems, is all they do. Yet is 'negation' enough, given that the aim is, with Marx, not merely to understand the world, but to change it; to engage in the 'intellectual, and eventually practical, effort' (SE 270) to change the order of things for the better?

Horkheimer is at pains to reject the idea that the critical theorist must be, in Nietzsche's sense, a 'creator'. Philosophy, he says, is not 'propaganda', and neither does it issue 'commands'. Though not irrelevant to the *vita activa*, philosophy belongs to the *vita contemplativa*, so that 'the concentrated energies necessary for reflection must not be drained prematurely into the channels of activistic … programmes'. Thinking cannot be the 'planning' of a new 'social catechism' that responds to current meaninglessness and oppression. For precisely the fact of its being such a response would undermine its authority (ER 184–5). Since, that is, Kant's 'transcendental subject' which preforms all our experience is really current society, any projection of the future is bound to be constrained by present categories of thought (SE 200–4). It follows that any blueprint of the future is almost certain to be anachronistic when the future arrives and the attempt to realize it is likely to be oppressive. A child's conception of paradise is wildly different from an adult's. Philosophy can, then, Horkheimer claims, point to the need for social change, and to that degree motivate it, but it cannot provide any account of the character of the change required.

For at least three reasons this seems unconvincing. First, rigorously thinking through what is involved in negating the causes of current suffering must surely yield, if not a blueprint of utopia, at least some, to borrow Nietzsche's term, 'signposts' to the future. Second, one's 'planning' of a better future might operate at a meta-level, might take the form of an account, not of a better future society, but rather of the procedure by which we might arrive at one. This, we shall see in Chapter 3, is what Habermas does with his notion of the democratic deployment of 'communicative' rationality. And third, one's image of a better future might be contained in an 'archetype' common to all times and cultures and therefore *not* moulded by the 'transcendental subject' of *current* society. This, we shall see in Chapter 4, is Marcuse's response to the 'negativity' of his colleagues.

Is the authors' 'negative' critical theory therefore useless, a betrayal of their neo-Marxist commitment to be engaged in the struggle for social change? That, certainly, is Georg Lukács' view of, in particular Adorno. Alluding to his 'bourgeois' background (his father was a wealthy wine merchant) and to his engagement with music, he describes Adorno as having

> taken up residence in the Grand Hotel Abyss ... a beautiful hotel, equipped with every comfort, on the edge of the abyss of nothingness, of absurdity. And the daily contemplation of the abyss between excellent meals or artistic enter-tainment can only heighten the enjoyment of the subtle comforts offered.[27]

Adorno's critical theory, in other words, is a nothing more than *Schadenfreude* and is devoid of genuine value.

But this, I think, is too harsh, for what it misses is that, even in the absence of a plan for the future of society as a whole, negative critical theory can have a profound impact on individual consciousness by giving articulate voice to one's obscurely felt 'rage' (p. 32 above) against the current order and thereby liberating one from sullen conformism. The value of such liberation from false consciousness is that it can transform us, as individuals, from *Ber-ufsmenschen* into free beings. Possibly this is the only value of negative critical theory – that it constitutes a kind of cathartic therapy for individuals – but possibly, too, in creating outsiders, it creates cells of resistance to the current order, fertile ground out of which a new order may eventually grow. One is reminded of the later Heidegger's similar disavowal of a plan for the future combined with his observation that 'here and now and in little things ... we may foster the saving power in its increase' (QCT 33).

The distorting effect of Marxism

As I have argued, the authors' analysis of modern society is essentially Weber's, reframed as an explicit critique of the Enlightenment and expanded through the 'culture industry' discussion. So it seems that it is Weber rather than Marx who is the real inspiration behind their work. From time to time, however, they recall that they are supposed to be Marxists and so attempt to translate their modernity critique into Marxist categories. So, for example, Horkheimer writes that 'the process of rationalization is no longer the result of anonymous forces of the market but is decided in the consciousness of a planning majority' (ER 98). Here, one can see him determinedly clinging to two Marxist theses: first, that the most fundamental cause of our current distress is capitalism – 'the market'; and second that it is no longer (but apparently once was) 'anonymous' capitalism that causes our loss of meaning and freedom but rather capitalism consciously controlled by an elite class. This claim is clearly intended to preserve the Marxist thesis that 'class conflict' as an essential element in social analysis. It seems to me, however, that both these theses misrepresent the main thrust of the authors' social criticism.

Assuming that I have represented them correctly, the authors' real view is that the fundamental cause of our current distress is rationalization, that is, *technology* in the widest sense of the word. What Horkheimer tries to do is to claim that something else, namely capitalism, is even more fundamental, and is therefore the source and origin of rationalization. But this contradicts their thesis that the drive to rationalize goes back to the beginning of human history, that it is innate in the human being as such (p. 31 above). And it contradicts, too, the fact that rationalization happens in socialist as well as in capitalist economies.

The notion that rationalization is the product of the 'conscious' intention of a 'planning minority' is particularly prominent in the authors' account of the culture industry. The movie producer micro-manages the hem lengths of the female star as carefully as the medieval Church micro-managed representations of the saints and martyrs, they observe (DE 101). But the producer is micro-managed by the 'subjective intention of the board chairman', and he, in turn, by the banks and power corporations on which the movie companies depend for finance (DE 96).

This 'conspiracy theory' analysis of capitalism has, like most conspiracy theories, an air of unreality about it. The bank chairman does, of course, have *a* 'subjective intention' – that of *making a lot of money*. And he may, too, have the conscious intention of doing so by introducing some form of rationalization into this or that region of corporate activity. But that he has the conscious intention of collaborating on the completion of the world-historical process of producing the totally rationalized society stretches credulity. Bank chairmen are not, as a rule, world-historical individuals. They lack the philosophical acumen.

Max Weber's self-deception

The authors provide, then, variations on a theme by Weber. The rationalization of modernity has deprived us of happiness by depriving us of freedom and meaning. Yet while they claim to be *critical* theorists, Weber claims, as we saw (p. 23 above), that it is not for him to pass value judgments on the processes he describes, that one should not look to the scientist qua scientist to provide social or political leadership. But this, surely, is self-deceiving. As the editor's introduction to *The Protestant Ethic* remarks, the 'latent passion' in Weber's description of the iron cage, and of the Nietzschean dystopia we can expect unless something interrupts the progress of rationalization, is unmistakable (PE xviii). Every bit as much as Horkheimer and Adorno, that is, Weber adopts a 'consciously critical' attitude to the status quo. And every bit as much as them, he raises his audience's consciousness to a consciously critical attitude. In short, for all his claims to be a 'traditional' theorist, Weber, at least towards the end of his life, is as much a 'critical' theorist as are Horkheimer and Adorno.

Notes

1 Horkheimer (1980b) 31.
2 Prior to his collaboration with Adorno, Horkheimer seems to have affirmed the superstructure thesis. He writes in 1937 that '[a]lterations in the psychic structure which characterises not only individual cultures but also particular groups within a culture are ... moments in a process the rhythm of which has been dictated by ... economic necessity' (SE 51). It seems that the collaboration with Adorno persuaded him to abandon the superstructure thesis. As we shall see, however, the idea that at least *popular* culture is a function of economic conditions is a version of the superstructure thesis to which both thinkers adhere.
3 Horkheimer (1980b) 32.
4 Horkheimer (1980a) 237.
5 Nietzsche (1994) Essay II section12.
6 Geuss (2014) 231. Presumably the remaining 15 percent was devoted to critical theory. The 'discredit' is thus the difference between 15 and 100.
7 This is the 'Old' or 'Right Hegelian' reading of Hegel, according to which the 'end of history' had already arrived in 1806 in the form of the Prussian state. 'Young' or 'Left' Hegelians such as Marx had an entirely different reading.
8 This is not a casual alternation between *Gesellschaft* and *Gemeinschaft*, since Ferdinand Tönnies' (1988) sociologically weighty distinction is explicitly referred to a few pages earlier (SE 191).
9 Nietzsche (1986) section 54.
10 In Chapter 9 we shall see that, though he would not invoke the word 'reason', the later Heidegger says something remarkably similar about insight into 'nature' as conceived in Rilke's poetry.
11 Hume (1964) 415–16.
12 Horkheimer quotes a passage from *Twilight of the Idols*. More to the point, however, is section 109 of *The Gay Science*: 'The total character of the world ... is, for all eternity, chaos, not in the sense of a lack of necessity, but of a lack of order, organization, form, beauty, wisdom, and whatever else our aesthetic anthropomorphisms are called' (Nietzsche [2001]).
13 A crucial figure in this process – surprisingly not discussed in this context by Horkheimer – is Kant, who, of course, initiated reason's self-critique in *The Critique of Pure Reason*. One consequence of Kant's critique was the transference of God from the realm of knowledge to that of faith. Another, less often noticed, consequence was the transference of morality, of the ends of

human action, from the realm of objective reason to that of formal reason: wrong-doing, Kant attempts to show, is self-contradiction.

14 Nietzsche (1999b) 350, note 9 [35]. The note appears in a rearranged and brushed up form as entry 2 in the first main section of Walter Kaufmann's translation of *The Will to Power* (Nietzsche [1967]), the fraudulent non-book that was fabricated and faked by Nietzsche's fascist and philosophically illiterate sister, Elisabeth.

15 As Jason Baldwin has pointed out to me, it is hard to reconcile this claim with the authors' condemnation of appeals to supposed 'laws' of human nature (pp. 24–5 above).

16 Freud, of course, takes the 'agency within the individual' (the 'garrison within a conquered city') to be the superego rather than the ego. But Horkheimer has not, I think, made a slip of the pen. Rather, his point is that the moulding of the individual by 'administered' modernity is becoming so complete that the distinction between ego and superego is becoming obsolete.

17 See Freud (1989).

18 Marx (1893) 12.

19 Wagner (1988) letter 69. Adorno stands in a paradoxical, not to say disingenuous, relationship to Wagner. On the one hand his (misleadingly titled) *In Search of Wagner* (Adorno [1981]) is a Nietzschean 'assassination', an attempt to destroy Wagner as man, musician, and cultural phenomenon. But, on the other, he adopts a great deal of Wagner's cultural criticism as his own – without, of course, acknowledging its source. See further Young (2014).

20 Foucault (1991) 217.

21 This point is anticipated in Nietzsche's designation of the town that is the object of Zarathustra's love and scorn as 'The Motley Cow'. Beneath the 'motley' surface of things lies bovine conformism.

22 Benjamin (1969).

23 Freud (1989).

24 Nietzsche (1999a) sections 1, 4, 16.

25 The authors' attitude to Chaplin is, moreover, not shared by their colleague Walter Benjamin, who regards Chaplin's films as a genuinely 'progressive' force (Benjamin [1969] 234). Benjamin's attitude to Chaplin reflects his divergent stance to film as such. Whereas Adorno, in particular, regards film as the demise of art, Benjamin – with an eye to the films of the Soviet Union – regards it as a new and potentially revolutionary form of art.

26 Nietzsche (2001) section 58.

27 Lukács (1971) Preface.

3 Habermas

In defence of enlightenment

Born in 1929, Jürgen Habermas, eighty-eight as I complete this chapter, continues a vigorous public life as the unofficial philosopher laureate of the German Federal Republic – of, indeed, the European Union as a whole. Jeremy Waldron describes him as, despite his years, Europe's leading public intellectual.[1] What makes Habermas unique among public intellectuals, however, is the fact that undergirding his public pronouncements is a social philosophy of richness and depth, a philosophy that forms the topic of this chapter.

Habermas' work is profoundly affected by his growing up in Nazi Germany. As a graduate student in the 1950s he was drawn to Heidegger's existential phenomenology. But Heidegger's involvement with Nazism, and in particular his reference to the 'inner truth and greatness of National Socialism' in his 1935 *Introduction to Metaphysics*, led Habermas to turn his back not just on Heidegger, but on the entire post-Kantian German philosophical tradition (Marx excepted) which, he felt, had conspicuously failed in its hour of trial.[2] In its place, he turned his attention to the sociological and philosophical resources of the Anglo-American world. Habermas studied with Horkheimer and Adorno in Frankfurt, but when Horkheimer made unacceptable demands for revisions to Habermas' *Habilitation* (the second Ph.D. the German system requires for a university career), he decided that the Frankfurt School had become paralysed by political scepticism and disdain for modern culture, and completed his thesis in Marburg. In 1964 he left the position Gadamer had found for him in Heidelberg and, with Adorno's support, took over Horkheimer's chair at Frankfurt University together with his directorship of the Institute for Social Research. He and the circle of social theorists he attracted are known as the 'second' Frankfurt School. Although sympathetic to the demands of the student protest movement of the later 1960s, Habermas deplored their militant, extra-legal tactics. Compulsorily retired in 1993, he has continued to write at astonishing speed. This chapter, however, will focus almost exclusively on his magnum opus, the two-volume, thousand-page *Theory of Communicative Action* (TCA) which appeared in 1981. Later developments in Habermas' thought will be touched on only lightly.

* * *

Habermas is a voracious reader. His technique is to develop his own philosophy out of a deep, extensive, critical, but always appreciative, engagement with predecessors he considers important: through an *Auseinandersetzung* with – a 'setting oneself apart from' – those predecessors. (In this respect, at least, in approaching his problems through a history of their discussion, Habermas' methodology remains located in the 'continental' rather than 'analytic' tradition.) And so it is that, after an introductory chapter, *The Theory of Communicative Action* begins with a hundred-page discussion of Weber which covers the ground I covered in my first chapter: the argument that the rationalization of modernity has resulted in the loss of both meaning and freedom. Following this discussion and a discussion of the Marxist philosophy of Georg Lukács, Habermas moves on to discussing his Frankfurt predecessors, Horkheimer and Adorno, who, as we saw in Chapter 2, produced their own version of the Weberian thesis.

Habermas' response to his predecessors

Habermas believes, correctly it seems to me, that by the end of his career, Weber rejects the Enlightenment. Weber holds that something above and beyond reason – charismatic leadership – is needed to rescue us from the arrival of Nietzsche's 'last man'. Habermas also believes, again correctly, I think, that Horkheimer and Adorno end up in the same position, albeit unintentionally. Though they claim to reject 'Weber's pessimism with regard to the possibility of [remedial] rational insight and action' (ER 6 fn.), their view that Enlightenment rationality is intrinsically 'patriarchal' and 'reifying' (pp. 31, 32 above) commits them to the view that any 'rational' response to the predicament of modernity will only result in further dehumanization and domination (TCA I 366–99). Against these intentional and unintentional deniers of the Enlightenment, Habermas thinks of himself, first and foremost, as its defender.

The Enlightenment, he observes, is the 'unfinished project of modernity'.[3] He accepts that the two, as he calls them, 'pathologies' (TCA I 244, II 148 et passim) identified by his predecessors do indeed characterize the modern age and are indeed the product of rationalization. But he also believes that rationalization offers an at least potential remedy for the situation. In other words (although Habermas never puts it quite this baldly), there is 'bad' rationalization but also 'good' rationalization (TCA II 307), and the latter is a potential antidote to the toxic effects of the former. Reason, it is true, has brought us to the unfortunate situation we are in, but reason (rather than the non-reason of Weberian charisma or the rebirth of traditional, religion-based modes of living) can get us out again. Reason, that is – a residual Hegelianism in Habermas' thought – is potentially self-healing. Since the project of the Enlightenment is as yet unfinished, pessimism about reason and about modernity is unwarranted.

Good rationalization

Good rationalization consists in what Habermas calls 'communicative rationality'. Starting in the newspaper columns and coffee houses of the eighteenth century (he might also have mentioned the clubs of the Scottish Enlightenment with members such as Hume, Reid, Hutcheson and Adam Smith), 'bourgeois culture' – Habermas strips the Marxist language of its pejorative connotations – gave rise to the practice of rational 'discourse', a discourse that played an important role in shaping both civil and political opinion.

Communicative rationality is realized to the degree that a discourse approaches – here Habermas acknowledged his debt to the American pragmatist G. H. Mead – the 'ideal speech [or "communication"] situation' (TCA I 22–6, TCA II 28, 58, et passim). The ideal speech situation is one in which all participants exemplify a number of epistemic virtues. They must be 'autonomous', prepared to think for themselves, and intellectually 'responsible', prepared to offer good reasons for the 'validity' of their assertions, prepared to avoid dogmatism. And they must be 'egalitarian', must treat each other as intellectual equals: no one's 'speech act' is regarded as carrying more weight than anyone else's simply because they are who they are. In general, participants must refrain from deploying any mode of 'influence' – bribery, threats, rhetoric, eloquence, charm, charisma – other than that of rational argument. The 'consensus' that terminates the discourse must be produced solely by the 'force of the best argument' (TCA II 145). (Notice that the idea of respecting interlocutors as equals with whom one attempts to secure free agreement solely by offering good reasons, seems to be a paradigm of honouring Kant's injunction to treat human beings always as 'ends in themselves', never merely as means. This I take to be the basis of Habermas' claim that, unlike subjective rationality, and unlike propaganda, communicative rationality is 'non-reifying' [TCA II 329 et passim].)

Discourse ethics

Ideal speech situations can be concerned with extra-moral matters of fact or with morality.[4] Where the topic is the latter what occurs is 'discourse ethics' (TCA I 19, TCA II 77–96) (in later works, 'discourse morality'). Discourse ethics is Habermas' account of how we should – and, in modernity, he thinks, to a considerable degree how we *do* – determine what is, and what is not, a valid 'moral norm'.

Habermas' discussion of moral norms consists in, first, a definition of what a valid moral norm is (moral ontology), and second, a decision procedure for determining whether or not something is a valid moral norm (moral epistemology).

The definition is simple. A valid moral norm is a principle of action that, with respect to 'some matter requiring regulation', 'expresses an interest *common to all* those affected'. The decision procedure which determines whether or not a principle expresses such an interest consists in seeing whether or not the candidate norm is 'capable in principle of meeting with the rationally motivated approval of everyone affected' (TCA I 19). In other words, something counts as a valid moral norm if and only if it could be the 'consensus' of a discussion of its merits by all it potentially affects, a discussion that meets the standards of the ideal speech situation.

Habermas acknowledges a debt to Kant. Discourse ethics is, he says, based on the idea of capturing 'what was intended by the categorical imperative', that is to say, 'the moral standpoint of impartiality' (TCA II 94–5). And he also acknowledges an affinity with his fellow Kantian, John Rawls (TCA II 290).[5] He insists, however, that his position is identical neither with Kant's nor Rawls', since while their decision procedures are 'monological', and as such belong to 'the philosophy of consciousness' (TCA II 95), his own procedure is 'dialogical' (TCA II 12).

What he is referring to is the fact that what both Kant and Rawls ask one to do, in order to determine the rightness of an action or the regulations of a just society, is, in the privacy of one's 'consciousness', to engage in a thought experiment. Kant asks one, roughly, to imagine how one would feel if one were sick and poor in an Ayn Rand society; Rawls asks one to imagine oneself legislating a future society in complete ignorance of one's own position, and hence a society in which one might end up sick and poor.

The trouble with these monological procedures, says Habermas, is that the interests people have, their sense of what is 'worthwhile', are moulded by their cultures, so that, save where the most basic interests are concerned, one cannot, in fact, reliably determine how one would react to a proposed norm were one in the position of the other. One can 'imagine' the other's response in a 'mock dialogue', but cannot reliably 'predict' it (TCA II 95–6). (As we shall see in Chapter 7, Gadamer expresses this point by saying that we cannot entirely transcend the 'horizon' of the 'lifeworld' to which we belong.) So, for instance, we liberal Europeans imagine that Muslim women feel oppressed by the hijab forced on them by a 'patriarchal' society, only to discover that, when we actually ask them, they often seem strangely reluctant to confirm this feeling. In other words, when it comes to determining how a proposed norm would affect the interests of others – especially others in multicultural modernity – there is no substitute for *asking them*. Hence, to avoid cultural imperialism, actual dialogue must replace the thought experiment. A valid moral norm is, then, something that would be approved by all who would be affected by its institution in an actual dialogue meeting the standards of the ideal speech situation.

Problems with discourse ethics

Before proceeding with the exposition of Habermas' social philosophy I want to raise a number of issues concerning discourse ethics. The first of these concerns future generations, children, the mentally impaired or simply uneducated, animals and trees. There are, surely, norms governing our relations with all of them, but since they can never engage in the 'rationality' of the ideal speech situation, there are no proposed norms that can be agreed to by 'all affected'. Habermas' response is that those who cannot participate in communicative rationality must be represented by 'professionalized expert knowledge' (TCA I 340). The problem with this, however, is that Habermas' own objection to 'monological' ethics applies to his notion of professional representation: with respect to, for instance, future generations, we cannot reliably 'predict' what their interests will be (recall Horkheimer's observations about the difficulty of 'planning' for future generations [pp. 40–1 above]). In his later writings, Habermas deplores the 'technocracy', rule by committees of arrogant 'experts', which he thinks is threatening the European Union.[6] Yet it would seem that his own decision procedure for determining moral norms precisely enjoins rule by technocrats.

A second problem consists in the exclusion of all 'influences' from the procedure that determines the validity of moral norms other than rational argumentation, argumentation whose rationality is defined by the rules of inductive, deductive – and informal (TCA I 23) – logic. This is problematic for it is surely the case that, in real-life ethical discussion, an important *and legitimate* role is played by perception rather than reason, narrative rather than argument, emotion rather than intellect, artistry rather than philosophy. As Plato admits, while Socratic dialect was of interest to only a 'small remnant', the title of 'educator of the Greeks' was given to Homer. Later on, the way in which the Greeks worked through their moral dilemmas – family versus state, reason versus revelation, fate versus freedom – was through the *combination* of argument and feeling that was Greek tragedy. Gadamer claims that in excluding everything save rational argumentation from legitimate ethical discussion, Habermas has produced an ethics for 'angels' rather than human beings (HT 287). I would suggest that, rather than angels, he has produced a decision procedure in which those who carry the day are – surprise, surprise – trained analytic philosophers: the reference to the ideal speech situation as a 'ritualized competition' (TCA I 26) cannot but call to mind the Socratic dialectic (which Nietzsche describes as a form of wrestling invented by Socrates because he was too puny to do well at real wrestling). In modelling discourse ethics on the 'ideal philosophy seminar', Habermas seems to have produced one more version of the philosopher-king.

A third problem concerns Habermas' blithe assumption that, if it goes on long enough, discourse ethics will always arrive at a 'consensus' (p. 48). In two ways this is problematic. First, because, as Habermas himself emphasizes, moral views are strongly moulded by culture, so that the possibility of substantial moral agreement within multicultural modernity is fraught with difficulty. One does not have to appeal to cultural difference, however, to make the idea of modern moral consensus a doubtful prospect. As Alasdair

MacIntyre has emphasized – spelling out in his own way, Weber's 'ethical polytheism' thesis – ethical debates within Western modernity (abortion, euthanasia, gay rights, and so on) are distinguished from debates of the past by their 'interminable' character, a fact reflected in the popularity of emotivism and other forms of non-cognitivism in twentieth-century meta-ethics.[7] And so the question arises as to what norms could be agreed on by 'all affected'.

A (somewhat convoluted) formulation of the decision procedure for discourse ethic that appears in Habermas' later work is the following:

> a norm is valid when the foreseeable consequences and side effects of its general observance for the interests and value-orientations of each individual could all be accepted without coercion,[8]

when, in other words, the only force in play is the 'force of the better argument'. (Note the highly questionable implicit assumption that any non-argumentative persuasion is 'coercion'.) This formulation differs from the earlier one in making explicit reference to 'value-orientations'. This reveals what is uppermost in Habermas' mind: his project is to identify social norms that transcend the cultural diversity of modern society, norms that can be agreed upon by Appalachian mountain dwellers, Orthodox Jews, Wahhabi Muslims, and white liberals, norms they would all agree upon if they were to engage in rational discourse. What norms could these be?

The point of the 1948 Universal Declaration of Human Rights (it lists thirty rights), drawn up, it states, by people of different cultural backgrounds 'from all over the world', is precisely the attempt to articulate such norms. And it seems reasonably plausible to say that individuals from at least most cultural backgrounds would agree to (3) 'Everyone has the right to life ... and security of person', and (9) 'No one shall be subject to arbitrary arrest, detention or exile'. Wahhabi Muslims, however, would accept neither (16) 'Men and women are entitled to equal rights in a marriage', nor (17) 'Everyone has the right to own property alone', nor (26) 'Everyone has a right to an education'. So, in fact, at best a very limited subset of the thirty 'rights' will count as moral norms according to discourse ethics. But this is very disconcerting. Sexism, one surely wants to say, is wrong: everyone *does* have a right to education and property ownership, women as well as men. The problem, then, with identifying moral norms as points of intercultural agreement is that it generates far too few moral norms.

Discourse ethics, is then, afflicted with serious problems. Its conception of the 'discourse' that determines morality is a philosophy professor's self-congratulation, and while it claims to generate morality in general, the best it can actually generate is a very small subset of moral norms. This, however, should not disguise the fact that, at the heart of Habermas' conception of morality is a modest core of rather obvious common sense, namely, that it is better to talk about our differences than to fight about them ('Jaw, jaw, is better than war, war', to quote Winston Churchill), and that, occasionally, whatever our cultural background, we should be able to agree on a few rights, rights pertaining to our material survival and freedom from fear. (One might call this common-sense core 'discourse ethics lite'.)

Good rationalization and the lifeworld

Habermas uses his concept of discourse ethics to define 'the lifeworld' or, more exactly, what he calls the 'communication-theoretic' conception of the lifeworld (TCA II 126). He develops this conception by way of a critique of the 'phenomenological' conception, a 'correction' of what he claims to be Husserl's and Heidegger's 'culturalistic abridgment of the concept of the lifeworld' (TCA II 135). (In Chapter 5 I shall discuss 'the lifeworld' in detail, and will argue that Habermas seriously misunderstands Husserl's conception in particular.)

Phenomenologically conceived, the lifeworld is, says Habermas, a 'culturally transmitted and linguistically organized stock of interpretative patterns'. These patterns represent an 'intuitively understood' 'shared horizon' which constitutes the 'familiar' world that, as one grows into adulthood, one finds oneself, in Husserl's phrase always 'already in' (TCA II 124–5, 131). The interpretive patterns that constitute the lifeworld are both ontological (famously, in the lifeworld of the Inuit there is no such thing as what we call 'snow') and ethical. Habermas' focus is almost entirely confined to the latter, so that when he speaks of the norms of the phenomenologists' lifeworld he is speaking of, as Avishai Margalit calls them, the 'thick' set of practices[9] that constitute the ethical tradition of a community.

What is the role of 'communicative action' in the phenomenologically conceived lifeworld? Habermas' one example (in a remarkably example-free book) imagines workers on a German construction site explaining to the new worker that – according to the usually unarticulated norms of their world – it is his duty, as the newcomer, to fetch the beer for the lunch break (TCA II 123ff). (One wonders about the verisimilitude of this example, given the legendary precision of German building construction.) Phenomenologically conceived, writes Habermas, the lifeworld is 'the transcendental site where speaker and hearer meet' (TCA II 126). For the members of a lifeworld, that is, language and culture have a 'transcendental status' with respect to every situation calling for interpretation: the horizon of their experience and action is something they 'always move within … [and] cannot step outside of'. It represents an 'unquestionable' ground of decision and action, a 'social a priori' which 'cannot become controversial' (TCA II 126–31). The lifeworld thus provides the outer limit within which all communicative action occurs. Note that in saying that the norms of the Husserlian lifeworld cannot be questioned, Habermas must be referring to *fundamental* norms. Phenomenologists obviously recognize that low-level norms, norms to do with modes of dress, eating, forms of speech, and the like, change over time.

Habermas claims that this is an 'abridged' conception of the lifeworld because, in reality, and particularly in modernity, lifeworlds inevitably enter phases where they become 'dysfunctional' in ways that require 'repair work' (TCA II 134). It is through these 'orientation crises' (TCA II 140) that lifeworlds change and develop. (One might think of the pressure on established norms exerted from within Western society by gay activists, or pressure exerted from without by Muslim immigration, as examples of such crises.) The way in which these crises should be – and, claims Habermas, to a considerable degree are being – resolved is through communicative action in which the lifeworld's basic norms lose their 'a priori' status and become objects of reflective, interpersonal discourse. 'The reproduction of the lifeworld is no longer merely rooted *through* the medium of communicative action (the brief conversation on the building site) but is saddled [sic] *upon* the interpretative accomplishments of the actors themselves', upon a process of (more or less ideal) discourse ethics in which 'mutual understanding rests in the end on the authority of the better argument' (TCA II 145). *Inherited* social norms are replaced by *achieved* norms, inherited normative consensus by 'achieved consensus' (TCA II 53, 73, 77).

Habermas accepts that, empirically speaking, the phenomenological conception is a relatively accurate description of the traditional lifeworld. As history advances, however, as traditional lifeworlds increasingly mix and mingle, 'the need for consensus' is met less and less by 'traditionally certified interpretations immune from criticism' and 'more and more by ... rationally motivated agreement – be it directly through the interpretative accomplishments of participants', or through the already mentioned 'professionalised expert knowledge' (TCA I 340).

Habermas calls this increasing use of discourse ethics the 'rationalization of the lifeworld' (TCA II 86), a rationalization that also represents the 'linguistification [sic] of the sacred' (TCA II 77), a linguistification through which 'the authority of the holy is replaced by the authority of achieved consensus', the 'rapture and terror' of the sacred 'sublimated into the binding bonding force of criticisable validity claims' (TCA II 77). Notice again, the Hegelian element in Habermas' thought: the rationalization of the lifeworld is *progress*, an emergence from the darkness of the 'age of faith' into the light of the 'age of reason'.

Bad rationalization: system

The increasing rationalization of the lifeworld is, then, 'good' rationalization. The source of 'bad' rationalization is what Habermas calls 'system'. System is the material base of society, the economy together with the subsystems of law and state bureaucracy that support, and to varying degrees, regulate it. System, in modernity, is an instance of rationalization for the reasons outlined by Weber: it is the application of 'calculation' – 'system' – to life in the interests of achieving 'control' over production.

There is nothing wrong, Habermas thinks, with system, with a rationalized economy, as such. Indeed there is nothing wrong (here Habermas makes a decisive break with the neo-Marxism of his Frankfurt predecessors) with capitalist rationalization as such: Habermas criticizes Marx for not seeing that 'the capitalist economy and the modern state administration ... represent a higher and evolutionarily advantageous level of integration in comparison with traditional societies' (TCA II 339). What, however, makes the system we live under 'bad' rationalization, is that it operates, not according to lifeworld norms – which, recall, are expressions of general *human* interests – but 'exclusively' in the interests of 'money and power' (TCA II 154, 259). Since we have no option but to submit to system, most of us are 'steered', i.e. compelled, by the 'non-normative mechanism' (TCA II 115 et passim) of money and power to engage in a form of life that operates not for, but rather *against* human interests. This is the product of two historical phenomena which Habermas calls, respectively, 'uncoupling' and 'colonization'.

Uncoupling

In premodern societies, there is no separation of system from lifeworld. Traditional marriage (as Jane Austen testifies) was both an economic and social transaction, with social customs, 'norms', governing the limits and possibilities of economic exchange (TCA II 163). As society becomes more complex, however, more 'differentiated' into specialized subsystems, there occurs what Habermas calls the 'uncoupling of system and lifeworld' (TCA II 153–97). The economic system becomes detached from the lifeworld, and begins to pursue goals that are not determined by norms of the lifeworld. An example of what Habermas has in mind might be the rise of banking. In medieval Europe, usury was a sin, so that only those on the fringes of society, the Jews, could lend money on interest. In late medieval Italy, however, banks began to appear, banks owned by powerful members of mainstream society such as the Medici. The control of the norms of the Christian lifeworld over system began to loosen.

Colonization

Uncoupling, Habermas thinks, is not necessarily sinister. He emphasizes that, to repeat, he is not opposed to the 'market economy', to rationalized capit- alism, as such. At least in theory, system can separate from lifeworld, operate according to its own imperatives, without the consequences being ultimately harmful. This endorsement of 'the market' is, I assume, based on the idea that the state can rectify the deleterious effects of industrial capitalism through the empowerment of trade unions, a robust welfare system, and redistributive taxation – essentially the programme of the German Social Democratic Party that Habermas has long supported.

What is sinister, however, and what is increasingly happening in modernity, is that system, created in order to serve lifeworld norms, is 'colonizing' its creator, the lifeworld (TCA II 331), is disempowering and threatening to destroy it.[10] As the history of the West has advanced, a 'norm-free sociality' (TCA II 114), has begun to replace the norm-governed sociality of the lifeworld, which begins to shrink into a quaint, 'provincial' sub-system (TCA II 173). Increasingly, the lives of individuals are no longer shaped by lifeworld norms but are rather 'steered' by the requirements of system.

Consequences of colonization

Habermas criticizes Weber for failing to see that, over and above 'system rationality' – Weber's *Zweckrationalität* – there is also 'value-rational[ity]' (TCA II 307) in the form of discourse ethics. But as far as system rationality has manifested itself in modernity, Weber, he accepts, has revealed the truth. We are indeed threatened by the two pathologies, by loss of freedom and loss of meaning. In the rule of system, the workplace *is* becoming an 'iron cage' (TCA II 333, 340), a place of alienated work to further goals we do not support and may even oppose. (One might think of the VW engineers who were forced, as became public knowledge in September 2015, to create pollution-test-deceiving software in order to preserve their livelihoods.) Moreover, since meaning can only come from living according to norms that belong to 'the private and public spheres ... of the lifeworld' (TCA II 319, 323), rule by system means that norm-guided action is being replaced by 'instrumental attitudes' aimed at 'income and advancement' (TCA II 319, 323–4). We are entering a state of nihilism, of joyless 'anomie' (TCA II 93, 386). We are indeed becoming Weber's 'specialists without spirit' and 'sensualists without heart', 'two complementary ways of life that soon become mass phenomena' (TCA II 323).

The result, as Marx pointed out, 'makes a mockery of bourgeois ideals' (TCA II 185), of the founding ideals of the Enlightenment, of liberty, equality and fraternity. In the dominion of system, the effects of Enlightenment rationality have indeed become, as Horkheimer and Adorno put it, 'irrational', 'stupid'. As the German Romantics feared, the broom is becoming the master of the apprentice.

The task

Given this analysis of the way things are, the task is clear. It is one of 'decolonization', of re-establishing the subordination of system to the norms of the lifeworld. This is to be done by reinvigorating the moral-political public sphere of the eighteenth-century coffee houses, by allowing good rationalization to reassert its dominion over bad rationalization. We must, Habermas writes in a later work, pin ... down ... a resistant structure, namely the structure of a rationality which is immanent in everyday communicative practice, and which brings the stubbornness of life-forms into play against the functional demands of autonomized [sic] economic and administrative systems.[11]

Distorted, to be sure, through the hidden manipulation of public opinion by the 'culture industry' (TCA II 380), the lifeworld practice of communicative rationality is still immanent in our culture and so available for reanimation. There is no guarantee of success but, equally, no guarantee of failure. Weber's view that the Enlightenment 'project' has failed is premature because it is, as yet, 'unfinished'.

There is a relatively unusual, and wholly admirable, continuity between Habermas' social philosophy and his life as a public intellectual. The latter is his personal attempt to reanimate the public practice of communicative rationality, to remain true to the Marxist spirit of 'understanding' the world in order to 'change' it. And although, at the time, it called his left-wing credentials into question, his rejection of the extra-legal tactics of elements of the student protest movement in the 1960s, his rejection of 'revolutionary violence', was equally continuous with his philosophy, his insistence on *talk*. All in all, there is a great deal to admire about Habermas as both man and social philosopher. The question remains, however, as to whether he succeeds in his primary mission of identifying a plausible remedy for what both he and his predecessors identify as the two primary pathologies of modernity, of whether he can make it plausible to suppose Enlightenment reason is capable of curing its self-inflicted wounds. I begin with loss of meaning.

Loss of meaning

Can we expect to recover our lost meaning in a Habermasian future, a future in which democratic action has re-established the subordination of system to lifeworld norms?

Let us first recall what, according to Weber, is the 'meaning' that we have lost. What we have lost, he says, is a shared 'godhead', in Hegel's language, a shared 'ethical substance', a shared way of life. What makes this a matter of regret is that it is the loss of 'genuine community' (p. 13 above), the loss of the French Revolution's 'fraternity'. But why, exactly, is this a *loss*?

Ferdinand Tönnies writes that community comes into being where there exists a shared 'consciousness of belonging together and the affirmation of the condition of mutual dependence'.[12] A community exists where there prevails the principle of – as the unofficial motto of the Swiss Federation puts it – 'one for all, and all for one'. What makes ethical substance essential to community is that it defines what it is that one 'belongs' *to*. The sharing of an ethical tradition marks the difference between members and non-members, between, as it were, family and strangers. What makes community a source of meaning is, as Horkheimer puts it, that it provides the individual with a commitment that 'transcends the subjectivity of self-interest' (p. 29 above).

Habermas uses the word 'solidarity' to describe the condition of being in community. But, he claims, social solidarity is *not* something that has been lost, at least not irretrievably so. The solidarity formerly provided by ethical substance can be, and increasingly is being, supplied by communicative rationality. Through discourse ethics we discover a 'substantial unity' in which ethical substance finds its 'argumentative redemption' (TCA I 249). The 'rapture and terror' of the 'holy' that formerly provided ethical substance with its authority is now being 'sublimated into the binding force of criticisable validity claims' (p. 52 above). In this 'achieved', as opposed to 'inherited', moral consensus, we rediscover 'social solidarity' (TCA II 57, 61, et passim), and hence a new path to meaning, to a commitment that transcends the subjectivity of self-interest.

Following Tönnies, Weber says that while a 'communal' relationship is based on 'subjective feeling ... whether affectual or traditional', a 'social' relationship 'rests on a rationally motivated adjustment of interests' (ES 60–1). Habermas' claim, in effect, is that whatever is valuable in a community can be recovered, without loss, in a society based on the 'rational adjustment of interests' through discourse ethics. But is this really so?

Habermas believes that the generation of moral norms through discourse ethics – norms that are at the same time political norms – gives rise to the constitution of a liberal democracy. More exactly, it gives rise to what he calls a 'deliberative democracy': a politics in which legislation and policy are informed by rational debate and deliberation rather than by the simply aggregation of preferences through voting.[13] Earlier I suggested that the requirement of universal agreement among 'all affected' may well preclude Habermas' procedure from generating the basic liberties of a genuine liberal democracy (pp. 50–1 above). But let us put aside such doubts and take it on trust that liberal democracy is indeed generated by discourse ethics, that Habermas' conception of discourse ethics provides liberal democracy with a philosophical justification. Can, then, liberal democracy really secure the 'solidarity' of a traditional community and thereby provide individual lives with self-interest-transcending commitment and meaning?

Surely not. For while a community is defined by a sense of 'belonging together', a liberal democracy is defined – ever increasingly, in multicultural modernity – by a sense of belonging apart. As Charles Larmore observes, political liberalism is the solution to a problem: the problem of how we can live together without harming each other, *given* that we no longer have a shared conception of the good life, a shared ethical substance.[14] While community is based on both respect for and 'fraternity' with the other, liberal democratic society is based on respect alone. In Avishai Margalit's terminology, while society is based on the universal 'morality' that governs one's relations with the *stranger*, community is based on the additional requirements of the 'ethics' that governs relations with the *friend*.[15]

In his later thought, Habermas seems to respond to this objection by suggesting, in effect, that the constitution of the liberal-democratic state can *itself* constitute a shared ethical substance, a shared 'ethics'. Taking over Dolf Sternberger's term 'constitutional patriotism', he puts forward the view that, as Jan-Werner Müller put is, one primary allegiance should – and could – be, not to a national culture but rather to the rules and procedures of a liberal democratic constitution.[16] Given the facts of modern life, liberal democracy is far preferable to any alternative. But no matter how passionate our commitment to it may be, the fact remains that is a recognition of *difference*, of the *lack* of a shared ethical substance, a method of belonging *apart* rather than *together*. Liberal democracy is a method of showing respect for, but not solidarity with, the other.

Both Habermas and Müller put constitutional patriotism forward as the salvation of the European Union, as representing the only way in which one can be expected to care for the 'European idea'. But this seems to me quite mistaken. Nietzsche was the first person to describe himself as a 'good European'. But since he despised both liberalism and democracy, he certainly did not envisage a pan-European liberal-democratic constitution. What he meant was that he felt at least as much at home on the Mediterranean and in the Swiss Alps as he felt in his native Saxony because they all belong to a unitary European history and tradition, to a unitary 'godhead'. Habermas and Müller seem to me to miss the point. The European idea does not depend on the political construction of a pan-national liberal-democratic state. Its strength lies in its 'multiplicity in unity', on the fact that its rich national differences are bound together in an overarching cultural unity.

Loss of freedom

Turning to Habermas' response to the second of the Weberian pathologies, can we expect a Habermasian future, in which lifeworld norms reassert their control over the imperatives of system, to lead to the regaining our lost freedom? Can we expect to recover from our reduction to *Berufsmenschen*? Habermas, we have seen, is not against 'markets'. And so, in the Habermasian lifeworld, industrialized capitalism will remain. In what way, then, can we expect things to be different from the way they are now in, for instance, the United States?

Given Habermas' social-democratic credentials, one can expect the economic order of his future society to show strong similarities to an improved version of the socio-economic model of post-war Germany: worker participation in corporate ownership and in management – 'co-determination (*Mitbestimmung*)' as it is known – shorter working hours, long holidays, paternity as well as maternity leave, the restriction of imports to 'ethical' products, the downsizing of the armaments industry, extensive, universal welfare, and the rapid development of 'green' technology – in my view, all undoubtedly excellent developments. But would such a programme really make a fundamental difference to the pathologies – as opposed to mere stupidities – of modernity, in particular, to our loss of freedom? Surely not. Since industrial capitalism will be retained, work will still be performed in a rationalized workplace, a workplace subject to the basic principles of Taylorism and Fordism. But that will mean that the problem of alienated labour, of the 'spiritless specialist' condemned to drudgery within the iron cage, will still be with us.

Even though it carries with it its own problems – 'the singularity' and the threat of boredom posed by a life without work – the obvious hope for release from the iron cage lies in automation. If (real) machines can take over at least all alienating labour then the possibility exists that only machines will inhabit the iron cage. This makes it very surprising that *The Theory of Communicative Action* contains no discussion at all of the hopes and fears associated with automation. As we shall see, however, the benefits of automation become a central topic in the philosophy of Herbert Marcuse, to whom I now turn.

Notes

1 Waldron (2015).
2 In the 1953 – the first published – edition of the *Introduction to Metaphysics* Heidegger provides an explanation of the reference, and by implication, of his own early enthusiasm for the Nazi movement. The *potential* of the movement was for a 'confrontation between global technology and modern man'. But, he claims, by 1935, it was already clear to him that what had become the more or less official 'philosophy of National Socialism' had 'nothing whatever to do with [this] ... inner truth' (IM 199). For a full account of this confrontation between Habermas and Heidegger see Wolin (1993) 186–97.
3 Habermas (1997).
4 A third possible topic area is aesthetic value which, however, I shall discuss no further.
5 Rawls' famous book is *A Theory of Justice* (Rawls [1978]).
6 Habermas (2015).
7 MacIntyre (1984) Chapter 2.
8 Habermas (1998) 42.
9 Margalit (2017) Preface.
10 Heidegger, too, remarks on what is essentially the phenomenon Habermas calls 'colonization'. Formerly, says Heidegger, the 'self-assertion' of the productive will 'remained incorporated within the embracing structure of the realm of culture and civilization'. Now, however, that containment has been removed, so that nothing remains to impede the 'unconditional self-assertion' of the productive will (PLT 109).
11 Habermas (1992) 155.
12 Tönnies (1988) 69.
13 Habermas (1996) 287–328.
14 Larmore (1996) 54, 122.
15 Margalit (2017) 13, 154–5.
16 Müller (2007), Habermas (1990), (2001).

4   Marcuse

Eros and utopia

Together with Horkheimer and Adorno, Herbert Marcuse (1898–1979) was a member of the first Frankfurt School. Almost entirely ignored by Habermas (he receives only eight glancing references in the thousand pages of *The Theory of Communicative Action*), he is nonetheless an important thinker, one who thinks outside the square that endows Habermas' philosophy with its somewhat quotidian quality. He is also a generous thinker, someone who thinks well of the human capacity for love, and wishes to liberate it in a manner reminiscent of Feuerbach and the 'Young Germany' movement of the 1840s.

Born in 1898 to middle-class Berlin Jews, Marcuse became a Marxist during the turmoil that followed the German defeat of 1918. In 1922 he completed his doctoral thesis, a study of the 'artist-novel', at Freiburg University. Having been thrilled by *Being and Time* when it appeared in 1927, he returned to Freiburg in the same year to study with Heidegger, whose teaching assistant he became. His project during this period was to produce a synthesis between Marxism and Heidegger's existential phenomenology. He completed a second dissertation in 1932, officially under Heidegger's supervision, but in the same year broke off relations with Heidegger on account of the latter's growing enthusiasm for National Socialism. Appointed to the Frankfurt Institute in 1932, he first worked for it in 1934 in New York, after the Nazi accession to power forced both him and the Institute to relocate to the United States. From 1942 to 1951 he was employed in intelligence work in Washington. In 1955 his *Eros and Civilization* (EC) appeared, a work which, as we shall see, attempts a synthesis between Marx and Freud. By now a somewhat scandalous figure – a Marxist at the height of the Cold War who preached sexual liberation – he was nonetheless hired by a progressive president at Brandeis University in 1958. In 1964 he produced his second major work, *One-Dimensional Man* (ODM). Brandeis failed to renew his contract in 1965 – by now, he was too scandalous even for them – but he quickly found an appointment at the University of California in San Diego where he taught until his retirement in 1976. It was during the Californian years that he earned the sobriquet 'guru of the new left' on account of his influence on radical student leaders such as Angela Davis and Abbie Hoffman, both of whom were his students. He died in 1979.

Diagnosis

The Nietzschean philosopher is, to repeat, the physician of culture. This, I think, is how Marcuse conceives his critical theory. Unlike the purely 'negative' work of Horkheimer and Adorno, Marcuse's work contains not only a diagnosis of contemporary Western society's 'diseased' condition, but also a bold prescription of what is to be done to return us to health.

We live, writes Marcuse, in an 'advanced industrial society': the subtitle of *One-Dimensional Man* is 'Studies in the Ideology of Advanced Industrial Society'. An advanced industrial society (hereafter 'AIS') is a society defined by what he calls 'the performance principle'. He introduces this term with an apparent definition: a society ruled by the performance principle is one that is 'stratified according to the competitive economic performances of its members' (EC 44) – as opposed to, for instance, a society stratified by birth, as in feudalism. This, however, will hardly do as a definition of AIS since economic 'stratification' is as applicable to early as to 'advanced' capitalism. The missing ingredient, here – along with his Frankfurt colleagues, Marcuse takes over Weber's term – is 'rationalization' (ODM, EC passim). Unlike early capitalism, AIS stratifies us according to our economic value in a 'rationalized' manner.

As we know, rationalization consists in 'control through calculation'. Treading in Weber's footprints, Marcuse repeats the observation that the rationalization of life consists in applying the methodology of natural science to social phenomena, in 'using the scientific conquest of nature for the scientific conquest of society' (ODM xliv). As the success of the natural sciences depends crucially on the 'mathematization', the 'quantification', of nature, so the rationalization of society consists in the ever-increasing quantification of the social (ODM 148, 150).

As with Weber, the result of the 'rationalization and mechanization of labour' is, first, the reduction of work to 'toil', to alienated labour (EC 93 et passim), and, second, loss of freedom. AIS is essentially a system of 'domination' and 'unfreedom', a society that denies the possibility of the 'free development of human needs and faculties'. Borrowing the phrase from Horkheimer and Adorno, Marcuse sums up this diagnosis of the diseased condition of modernity by saying that the result of the application of reason to life has turned out to be 'irrational'. AIS is 'irrational as a whole' since while we have tried to create an instrument to serve our needs, it has ended up forcing us to serve *its* needs (ODM xl–xli).

Advanced industrial society's methods of self-preservation

Marx believed that, given the alienated and oppressed condition of the masses, revolution was inevitable and industrial capitalism bound to collapse. For Marcuse, as for the first Frankfurt School in general, his experience in

America convinced him that Marx had vastly underestimated industrial capitalism's capacity for self-preservation, so that its collapse was by no means inevitable (this is the so-called 'crisis in Marxism'). Whereas Marx had thought of the overt exercise of repressive violence as the system's response to revolutionary opposition, what he missed was its repertoire of means for preventing oppositional impulses from even arising. Some of the means identified by Marcuse are overt, accessible to ordinary consciousness; others are covert, so that their exposure requires the work of critical theory. I begin with the former.

One of the facts about industrial capitalism not anticipated by Marx is that the introduction of automation has greatly reduced the physical painfulness of labour. Although the extent to which, particularly in the case of semi-automated labour, physical fatigue has simply been replaced by mental fatigue should not be underestimated (ODM 25), it is clear that the prospect of almost total automation diminishes the pain of labour as a revolution-promoting factor.

A second factor stifling opposition that was not anticipated by Marx consists in the fact – also noted by Horkheimer and Adorno – that, at least in America, trade unions, far from representing organized opposition to AIS, function so as to incorporate potential opponents into the system as co-managers of corporate enterprises (ODM 22, 34, 41).

A third factor is the transformation of the 'capitalist bosses' of early capitalism into 'bureaucrats in a corporate machine' (ODM 35). Whereas the top hat and cigar made the early capitalist easy to identify and throw eggs at, with the transformation of small, privately owned enterprises into vast, publicly listed corporations, the source of oppression becomes anonymous, or at least concealed, making it hard to find a target of revolutionary action. (Updating Marcuse's observation, one might suggest that the jeans and t-shirts of the tech billionaire function as a form of camouflage.)

A fourth important reason why the collapse of AIS in not inevitable is that, in a certain sense, it delivers what it promises – affluence and welfare – and thereby lulls the masses into the delusion that there is nothing to protest (ODM 9, 52, 56). Responding to the fact that, by 1958, most Americans were experiencing a level of material wellbeing unprecedented in human history, the economist J. K. Galbraith coined the phrase 'The Affluent Society'[1] – the title of his famous book – a phrase Marcuse adopts (ODM 26). The suggestion is that, as the Roman emperors pacified the plebs with 'bread and circuses', so AIS pacifies the modern masses with 'bread' – the 'circuses' I shall come to shortly.

Soul control: the media

I turn now to the covert means Marcuse identifies as serving to stifle opposition to AIS. As already noted, Marx believed that no matter how oppressive the workplace, there remained, in capitalist modernity, a certain area of 'real life' – the table, bed, or bar – that is beyond its control (p. 33 above). And that, surely, was connected with his belief in the revolutionary potential of the workers: away from the controlling eye of the boss' henchmen, talking with one's comrades in the bar, one was free to criticize and organize. On the basis of his American experience, and again in company with Horkheimer and Adorno, Marcuse thinks that AIS has powerful means of neutralizing this region of potential opposition, of ensuring that, for the masses, there is, in reality, no life at all outside the system. In AIS, so-called 'free time' is, in reality, as much subject to control as work time (ODM 5). This is why every AIS tends to 'totalitarianism' in that 'it determines not only the socially needed occupations but also individual needs and aspirations' (ODM xl). There is, of course, a difference between hard and soft power, but this is a difference in means not ends. In place of the 'terroristic political coordination of society' in the East, what we have in the West is 'total administration' (ODM 5), a 'non-terroristic economic-technical coordination which operates through the manipulation of needs' (ODM 5). Every AIS institutes the 'total mobilization' (ODM 21) of its population (the phrase was coined by Ernst Jünger)[2] for the sake of its self-perpetuation and expansion.

The means adopted by non-terroristic AISs represent various forms of soul-control. The Stoics held that 'stone walls do not a prison make': whatever one's physical circumstances, one's thoughts – the essential self – remain free. But the Stoics were naïve, or at least, pre-modern. For it is precisely this 'inner freedom', says Marcuse, that is abolished by AIS. It achieves this by abolishing the distinction between the 'public' and the 'private' (ODM 12). The public world as determined by the system becomes the private world.[3] This is crucial to AIS's self-preservation because it is in the realm of the private that 'negative', critical, subversive thinking, can occur (ODM 127). (Note this, in Habermas' language, strongly 'monological' conception of criticism. To Habermas' claim that 'criticism' of 'validity claims' is the essence of communicative rationality (p. 52 above), Marcuse would surely point out that since the souls of the participants have already been 'colonized' by AIS, even in an 'ideal speech situation', radical critique of the status quo is precluded from the start.)

A central role in this colonization of the soul is performed by the 'mass media' (ODM 11), the advertising, information, and entertainment industry. As with Horkheimer and Adorno's 'Culture Industry' essay discussed in Chapter 2, Marcuse takes it to be beyond doubt that, beneath the veneer of information and entertainment, the media

> carry with them prescribed attitudes and habits which bind the consumers more or less pleasantly to the producers and through the latter to the whole. The products indoctrinate and manipulate; they promote a false consciousness.
>
> (ODM 14)

One of the ways in which the media create false consciousness is by creating 'false' needs (ODM 7). This, of course, is the *point* of the advertising industry, to persuade us that we 'must' have the product's deluxe version when the standard version does everything we actually need. While it is not difficult to produce examples of obviously 'false' needs, it is not entirely obvious how one is to draw the line between the 'true' and the 'false'. Marcuse's distinction between desires that spring from oneself and those that are 'superimposed on the individual by particular social interests in his repression' (ibid.) is too vague to provide a clear distinction. More helpful is his remark that 'in the last analysis' only individuals themselves can decide on the distinction – 'but only in the last analysis, when they are free to give their own answer' (ODM 8). This suggests the following: a true desire is a desire one would retain even after having become fully aware (through exposure to critical theory) of the degree to which AIS attempts to manipulate one in its own interests. A true desire requires, as one might put it, *'informed* consent'.

Another mode of mind control lies in the promotion of passive 'entertainment', entertainment which 'soothe[s] and prolong[s]' the 'stupefaction' of the workplace (ODM 9) – sitting obesely in front of a TV with a six-pack of beer watching a sitcom in which the canned laughter saves one the trouble of working out where the humour is. Undoubtedly TV and film generate a passive audience, but why is this a form of mind control? Rather than Horkheimer and Adorno's point about the authoritarian nature of the media, Marcuse's point here, I think, is that if consciousness is filled with something – anything – non-subversive, to that extent it is put out of action as a locus of transgressive thinking. If the mind is full of cotton wool, there is no space left for devilry.

Compared with Horkheimer and Adorno's extensive analysis of the culture industry, Marcuse provides little detail of the ways in which popular culture 'prescribes attitudes and habits'. The reason, surely, is that he knows that a great deal of that detail has already been supplied by his Frankfurt colleagues. His own (some would say 'elitist') contribution to the analysis concerns what he calls the 'democratization of culture' (ODM 64), the disappearance of the distinction between popular and high culture, the absorption of all culture into a single, mass-produced entity for mass consumption.

Until the end of the nineteenth century, suggests Marcuse, high culture constituted the remnant of a pre-technological, feudal culture and was, as such, a place of alienation from business, industry and technology. Now, however, this cultural space, a space that used to be reserved for 'outcasts and outsiders', has been lost. It is true that the valuation accorded to high art is as high as ever. What has been lost, however, is its 'subversive force' (ODM 64). The principal cause – Marcuse alludes to Benjamin's 'mechanical reproducibility of artworks' essay (p. 35 above) – is the reproduction of artworks on a massive scale which transforms them into just another kind of commodity on offer within the consumer society: 'the cultural centre has become a fitting part of the shopping centre' (ODM 68); Bach had been transformed from a spiritual journey into 'background music in the kitchen' (ODM 67).

Commodification diminishes the impact of art whatever its content. However, Marcuse has an account of what one might call the 'defanging' of high art that has to do specifically with its content. His focus is on the contrast between current and past treatments of sexual passion. In *Madame Bovary* and *Anna Karenina* (or, one must surely add, *Hedda Gabler*) sexual passion is 'absolute, uncompromising, unconditional'. The denial of passion is 'sublimated' into the 'great refusal' (ODM 80), the absolute negation of tight-laced, stifling, loveless, patriarchal Victorian culture. In a modern treatment of sexual passion, by contrast, in Faulkner, Eugene O'Neill, or the run-of-the-mill Hollywood tragedy, the portrayal of sexual passion is 'desublimated'. Though infinitely more explicit than in the nineteenth century, it is no longer subversive. Certainly one is told a 'sad story' (ODM 65), but it is a story that is 'part and parcel of the society in which it happens' and 'nowhere its negation' (ODM 81). Sexual tragedy, the modern artwork tells us, happens. We need to accept that life is not a perfect paradise. And it is therapeutic to be told, from time to time, a sad story. As Aristotle tells us, through empathy with the tragic hero, we discharge our 'fear and pity', undergo 'catharsis'. But, argues Marcuse, it is precisely catharsis that robs art of its potentially subversive force, allows one to 'enjoy [art] – and forget it' (EC 145). This, he continues, is what his fellow Marxist Berthold Brecht realised. Brecht cultivated the 'estrangement effect' (produced by, for instance, actors stepping out of character to remind the audience that they are merely acting) in order to prevent the audience engaging in 'the willing suspension of disbelief'. The point, observes Marcuse, was 'to teach what the contemporary world really is behind the ideological and material veil, and how it can be changed'. And to that end, as Brecht saw, what was required was precisely *not* empathy, but rather 'distance and reflection' (ODM 69–70).

Summing up this account of the disempowering of tragic art, Marcuse says that nowadays we experience art 'aesthetically' (EC 145). The reference, here, is to the original meaning of 'aesthetic' which is 'feeling or sensation' (see further p. 79 below). Art is no longer a locus of (critical) ideas but a means for the experience and discharge of feelings. As such, it has lost its connection with action and become harmless.

Further methods of soul control

Although its deployment of 'the media' is the principal way in which AIS stifles 'negative' thinking, it is not the only way. Marcuse's view, rather, is that a number of factors conspire to the same end, and it is the purpose of *One-Dimensional Man* to hunt these down. I shall mention three.

The first is the use of psychiatry to defuse alienation from the system. Typically, psychiatric practice operates as a kind of ad hominem: criticism is transformed into neurosis, something to be dealt with by altering not the criticized, but rather the criticizer: all our 'Don Juans, Romeos, Hamlets, Fausts' become cases for the psychiatrist (ODM 74), become, as one might put it, 'suitable cases for treatment'.[4] Marcuse's observations here align him with the 'anti-psychiatry' movement of the 1960s associated with R. D. Laing and David Cooper.

Another factor that helps defuse negative thinking is the incorporation of nature into the system of modern technology:

> when the cities and highways and National Parks replace the villages, valleys, and forests; when motorboats race over the lakes and planes cut through the skies – then these areas lose their character as a qualitatively different reality, an area of contradiction.
>
> (ODM 69)

Marcuse is thinking, here, of poetic nature, the place where the poet experiences the 'other' of the human, the divine. With 80 percent of the world's population living in the darkness of light pollution, the brightness of Van Gogh's 'Night Sky' becomes impossible.

To philosophers, perhaps the most interesting discussion of the ways in which AIS stifles criticism concerns what Marcuse calls 'operationalism'. The term has its origin in American philosophy of science. Inspired by logical positivism – the view that a statement is meaningful only if it is capable of verification or falsification by sense experience – operationalism reduces the meaning of scientific terms to scientific 'operations'. So, for example, to know the meaning of 'length' is to know the operations that would verify or refute the claim that something has a certain length (ODM 14–15).

In fact, though not in name, Marcuse finds operationalism widespread in modern culture. Although perhaps unexceptionable in science, its effect in society at large is to disable negative thinking. Thus, for example, 'free', in politico-journalistic discourse, comes to mean the 'operations' that occur in the 'free world'. It means such things as 'reports in newspapers like the *New York Times* and not like *Pravda*'. So, of course, what the critical theorist wishes to claim – that our society is 'unfree' – becomes, in public discourse, a self-contradiction. Save on minor points of detail, criticism of the status quo becomes impossible (ODM 14–16). Another term that receives a similarly operational definition is 'totalitarian' – hence Marcuse's insistence on applying 'totalitarian' to Western society, too, in the attempt to shock us out of political operationalism.

Marcuse finds that Anglo-American academic philosophy connives at this stifling of radical criticism. J. L. Austin's contempt for alternatives to the common use of words, the chummy use of the 'we' that militates from the beginning against the 'egghead' who wants to say something startlingly different to the 'average' 'John Doe', Wittgenstein's doctrine that 'meaning is [common] use', his explicit assertion that 'philosophy leaves everything as it is', are all instances of philosophy's 'self-humiliation and self-denunciation', of 'the authority of philosophy giv[ing] its blessing to the status quo' (ODM 177–9). This takes us back to the divide between philosophy as 'traditional' theory, philosophy that merely seeks to 'understand' the world, and philosophy as 'critical' theory, philosophy that seeks to 'change' it. For Marcuse, the former is, at best, a waste of time.

One-dimensionality

Marcuse sums up the effectiveness of AIS in stifling radical criticism by saying that it turns the modern, mass individual into, as the title of his book puts it, 'one-dimensional man'. A culture that allows for a distinction between high and popular culture is, he says, a 'two-dimensional' culture (ODM 60). The abolition of that distinction – the abolition of a cultural home for the outcast and rebel – is part of the process of turning the world as we experience it into a 'one-dimensional reality' (ODM 128). An individual who inhabits such a reality is someone whose life represents 'a pattern of *one-dimensional thought and behaviour* in which ideas, aspirations, and objectives that, by their content, transcend the established universe of discourse and action are either repelled or reduced to this universe' (ODM 14).

What, exactly, is 'one-dimensionality'? The notion of a 'dimension' is clearly part of Marcuse's phenomenological heritage – Heidegger often speaks of 'dimensions' (PLT 211–27).[5] It is another word for Husserl's 'horizon', a horizon being something which, in Marcuse's formulation, defines a 'universe of discourse'. A dimension, then, determines the kinds of things that can show up and, as a result, determines the 'aspirations and objectives' that can be properly entertained in the universe in question. (If something shows up as a table, then while sitting at it is a proper goal, jumping on it is not.) A dimension becomes 'closed' (ODM 87) for a given language community when, for that community, it becomes the only way in which things can show up to it. 'Man' becomes 'one-dimensional' when he inhabits a 'closed' dimension.

What is the one dimension that defines Western modernity? It is, evidently, the performance principle, or more exactly the rationalized – and 'reifying' – performance principle. The one-dimensional mass man of modernity is someone for whom things show up solely as producers, products and consumers, and for whom, therefore, his 'aspirations and objectives' are confined to production and consumption. Fairly clearly, then, Marcuse's 'one-dimensionality' thesis is his version of Weber's 'loss of freedom' critique of modernity. To be confined within the 'iron cage' of the performance principle is to be a quasi-robotic *Berufsmensch*, incapable of anything other than production and consumption.

Eros and Civilization: why Freud?

I turn now from the diagnostic to the remedial phase of Marcuse's thought, to his vision of a happier future and his account of how we might get there. This takes us to the earlier of Marcuse's two major books, *Eros and Civilization*. It is this book, it seems to me, that constitutes the 'essential Marcuse'. Whereas Horkheimer and Adorno could have written much of *One-Dimensional Man*, they could have written none of *Eros and Civilization*. The reason is that while they are scornful of 'utopian' thinking, Marcuse (though he sometimes cavils at the word) is unashamedly utopian. It is this inspirational element in his thought that surely accounts for his influence over the student movement of the 1960s, an influence that the purely negative critique of Horkheimer and Adorno – a negativity Marcuse criticises as leading to a paralysis of action (ODM 258) – was never able to achieve.

Given that Marcuse is, in his own way, a Marxist, the subtitle of *Eros and Civilization*, 'A Philosophical Inquiry Into Freud', is what gives rise to the familiar summation of his philosophy as 'Marx meets Freud'. Given, however, that Marxian critical theory is concerned with the *social*, while Freudian psychoanalysis is concerned with the *individual*, the meeting represents something of a surprise. It raises the question: why Freud?

Marcuse's engagement is with the later Freud, with the works written after 1920, above all with *Civilization and Its Discontents*. Following Freud's own practice, he refers to the content of these later works as Freud's 'metapsychology', a somewhat opaque term. What he means to refer to is Freud's speculative account of the fundamental structure of the human psyche – speculative in the sense of being suggested, but by no means established, by evidence gathered in therapeutic practice – and his attempt to derive from it an account of the history and essential nature of civilization.

Freud was a pessimist. He read and, as he conceded, had a natural affinity with Schopenhauer.[6] He claims that civilization depends on the repression of our most basic instincts, and that since their satisfaction is the source of all happiness, civilization – all civilization – mandates unhappiness. As a Marxist, Marcuse believes the point of all worthwhile theoretical activity is to change the world for the better, and so one might imagine that his engagement with Freud is generated by the need to refute his pessimism. But since Marcuse could simply have ignored him, this does not explain the *engagement* with Freud.

The reason for the engagement is Marcuse's belief that Freud got *almost* everything right. He believes, in particular, that Freud got the nature of happiness right. Freud's belief that happiness within civilization is impossible is, however, a mistake. Perhaps it was once true, concedes Marcuse, but it is no longer so. Therefore, purged of this error, Freud's theory can be developed in a way that provides the key to a happy civilization.

What Freud says

According to Freud – as told by Marcuse – all the 'primary' human drives, the instincts, operate according to the 'pleasure principle'. All of them, that is, strive for but one thing – the gaining of pleasure and avoidance of pain (EC 13). All human action, it would seem, is ultimately motivated by pleasure. Freud thus appears to subscribe to the doctrine known as 'psychological hedonism'.

The great trauma in an individual's life – birth – is a confrontation between the pleasure principle and the 'reality principle' (EC 12). This is the social order into which the individual is born, a set of moral, legal, and social norms that determine 'what is useful and useless, good and evil' (EC 142). For obvious reasons, these norms determine that the pleasure principle in the individual cannot be immediately or completely satisfied and demand that it be, to a large degree, repressed. The upholders of the reality principle are parents acting as representatives of society at large. Through parental indoctrination, the reality principle is eventually internalized as the 'superego'. The pleasure principle remains, however, as the unmodified principle of the 'id' (our inner child), the locus of the primary instincts. In the interests of 'self-preservation',[7] the 'ego', which is an outgrowth of the id, then has to reason its way to some compromise between the id's pleasure principle and the superego's reality principle (EC 31), with the result that the immediate satisfaction demanded by the id becomes, at best, seriously modified satisfaction.[8]

An important fact about pleasure is that it is always sexual, or at least erotic, 'libidinal', in character. (Sexual pleasure, writes Freud, is 'the prototype of all happiness'.)[9] So what is really sacrificed in the confrontation with the reality principle is erotic pleasure. In the language of Marcuse's title, Freud's view is that 'civilization' demands the sacrifice of 'Eros'.

According to Freud, the fundamental reason civilization must make this demand is 'economic': the 'struggle for existence' in the face of 'scarcity', the fact that, since bread does not grow on trees (except, it is worth noting, in South Pacific islands), human beings must work to turn the meagre resources provided by a step-motherly nature into the means of human sustenance. This demands that libidinal energy be redirected, 'sublimated', from sexual activity into work (EC 17). Of course, some sexual activity is required for reproduction, but that is all civilization is willing to permit. Hence the multiple taboos with which it surrounds all non-monogamous, non-reproductive sex, the classification of almost anything that is not between 'one man and one woman' as a 'perversion' (EC 49).

The first chapter of Marcuse's book, in which the above exposition occurs, is called 'The Hidden Trend in Psychoanalysis'. This phrase seems to mean that, in spite of Freud's overt pessimism, 'hidden' in his account of the human condition are the seeds of a more optimistic vision of possible forms of civilization. The first of these seeds is 'the identity between freedom and happiness' (EC 51), and the second is the fact that, in spite of oppression, the drive to the realization of the two is preserved in the human psyche. '[T]he freedom and happiness tabooed by the conscious' ego in its confrontation with the reality principle is, Freud holds, 'upheld by the unconscious' id in the form of memory: memory of a time before repression (time in the womb), of a genuinely 'free' time, which finds expression in fantasy, fiction, and dreams. Plato regards the content of dreams as sinister and hence as necessitating repression: in dreams, he writes, 'the wild and animal part' of the soul 'casts off sleep and ... does not hesitate ... to attempt sexual intercourse with a mother or anyone else, man, god, or beast ...' (*Republic* 571c–d). Implicitly rejecting Plato's description, Marcuse regards the testimony of dreams as revealing our deep yearning that the remembered 'paradise' be recreated on the basis of the achievements of civilization. This, he believes, is the hidden optimism implicit in Freud's theory (EC 18–19), the basis, as Douglas Kellner puts it, of a 'revolutionary anthropology'.[10] The triumph of repression is not absolute. Although Marx was mistaken in seeing the working class as an intrinsically revolutionary force, we need not abandon hope, since revolutionary potential is intrinsic to the depth psychology of all individuals.

Freud's mistakes

Freud argues, to repeat, that since the ready-made means of survival offered to us by nature are meagre, civilization demands work. And since work requires repression, the 'sublimation' of libidinal energy into unpleasant activity, civilization necessarily generates unhappiness, the frustration of the pleasure principle.

Marcuse claims that this argument is 'fallacious' because it fails to take account of the fact that

> the prevalent scarcity has, throughout civilization (though in very different modes), been organized in such a way that it has not been distributed collectively in accordance with individual needs ... Instead, the *distribution* of scarcity as well as the effort of overcoming it has been *imposed* on individuals – first by mere violence, subsequently by a more rational utilization of power ... the gradual conquest of scarcity was shaped by the interest of domination.
>
> (EC 36)

The consequence of this historical fact, says Marcuse, is that nearly all historical societies have generated not just the 'basic repression' that is needed for their survival, but also 'surplus repression'. It is Freud's failure to take account of surplus repression that represents a fallacy in his position (EC 35–7).

What is 'surplus repression'? According to the above quotation, surplus repression is *absent* when work is organized 'in accordance with individual needs'. This is a quasi-quotation of Marx's famous definition of the principle of a socialist society as 'From each according to his abilities, to each according to his needs'. Individuals in a socialist society would, then, experience only 'basic repression'. This suggests a definition of surplus repression as follows: an individual suffers surplus repression (repression that results from 'domination') if they suffer a degree of repression over and above that which they would suffer were socialism to be the reality principle of their society. For short, then, surplus repression is 'unjust' repression.

How does the fact that, historically, most repression has been surplus point to a fallacy in Freud's position? If some repression is surplus, man-made rather than imposed by nature, then it is 'artificial', which means, contra Freud, that there is a 'real possibility of [its] ... elimination' (EC 139), elimination by revolutionary action aimed at installing socialism as society's reality principle. Given the current state of technology, a degree of repression will continue to be essential to any society's survival. But, with the installation of the socialist reality principle, it will weigh on the individual in a greatly reduced, 'basic' form. As the proverb tells us, many hands make light work. Hence, insofar as Freud implicitly treats 'discontent' and 'civilization' as omnitemporal constants (see p. 71 below), insofar as he subscribes to Schopenhauer's view that action can change only the form of suffering, never its quantity, he is in error.

* * *

Is, however, revolutionary action possible? What makes this a pressing question for Marcuse is his recognition of the historical fact that 'every revolution' so far, 'from the slave revolts of the ancient world to the socialist revolution [in Russia] ... has ended in establishing a new, "better" system of domination' (EC 90).

Nietzsche (or at least a 'Nietzschean') would say that, since the 'will to power' – which includes power over other people, i.e. 'domination' – is innate and insatiable, every revolution *must* betray itself. But this is not part of either Freud's or Marcuse's position. For them, all that is innate is the pleasure principle. And it is this that is the origin of domination. The first form of domination is that of Freud's 'primal father', a warlord who rules the 'primal horde' with the 'mere violence' referred to above (p. 69).[11] The pleasure principle in the 'father' dictates two things: that 'the sons' be made to do all the (unpleasant) work and that he, the father, grabs all the women, the source of pleasure, for himself. (Perhaps Freud has the *droit de seigneur* in mind as a legacy of the primal father.) The sons eventually rebel, kill, and in fact eat the father, but then, driven by their own pleasure principle, repeat the pattern of domination. And so the depressing pattern continues throughout history. Actually, since the 'sons' are several while the father was one, they have to modify the mode of domination. They need to introduce rules and customs governing their interaction with each other, for otherwise the ruling elite will collapse into internecine warfare. Hence each must repress his own pleasure principle to at least some degree. This, for Freud, represents the birth of civilization (EC 60–8).

The only source of hope in this picture is that what motivates domination is not any intrinsic 'will to domination' but only a 'will to pleasure'. And what this means is that, were the ruling 'father' to have a means to pleasure that did not require getting others to do his work, he would have no motive to inflict surplus repression on 'the sons'. Of course, were the total amount of work required to sustain a society an historical constant – were as much work required now as was required to maintain the primal horde – then there would be no possibility of eliminating the domination of the weak by the strong. In fact, however, Marcuse points out, there is no such historical constant.

This brings us to the second 'fallacy' he finds in Freud. Because Freud thinks biologically rather than historically, he implicitly treats 'scarcity', and hence work, and an omnitemporal 'given' that human society must always confront. In fact, though, it is by no means a given. Science, technology, and the rationalization of economic life have greatly reduced the total amount of work required of humans, and so offer the possibility of reducing, not just surplus repression, but basic repression too. This raises the possibility of a (quasi-Hegelian) self-overcoming of the performance principle: 'The very progress of civilization under the performance principle has attained a level of productivity at which the social demands on instinctual energy to be spent in alienated labour could be considerably reduced' (EC 129), and ultimately abandoned completely (EC 175). What Marcuse has principally in mind here is obviously automation, a topic to which I shall return.

What its technological sophistication means is that AIS has a twofold character. On the one hand, it represents the historical maximum of domination. Concerning the 'domination–rebellion–domination' cycle identified by Freud, Marcuse writes that

> the second domination is not simply a repetition of the first one; the cyclical movement is *progress* in domination. From the primal father to the brother clan to the system of institutional authority characteristic of mature civilization, domination becomes increasingly impersonal, objective, universal, and also increasingly rational, effective, productive. At the end [is] ... the rule of the fully developed [i.e. rationalized] performance principle.
>
> (EC 89)

In Weber's iron cage, in other words, we are much more subject to domination than we were under the primal warlord: domination based on brute force has at least the advantage that it does not enter the soul.

The second fact about AIS, however, is that, on account of its technological power, it offers us the possibility of a repression-reduced, and ultimately a repression-free, society. Modern society presents us, therefore, with the worst and the best: the maximum of unfreedom and unhappiness combined with the maximum opportunity to hope for freedom and happiness.

Aggression, the death instinct, and the Nirvana principle

Marcuse, then, believes that we can move beyond the performance principle. We can move towards, and perhaps one day even arrive at a repression-free society, a society in which the pleasure principle is no longer repressed. (This clearly is Marcuse's version of Hegel's 'end of history', and more specifically, of Engels' 'withering away of the state'.) Since Freud's 'scarcity' argument fails, he says, the possibility of a gradual 'decontrolling' of the instincts has to be taken seriously (EC 133). And the key to this claim, as we have so far understood it, lies in Marcuse's 'automation argument', the argument that since machines are increasingly obviating the need for human labour, the need to divert libidinal energy, the need for 'basic' repression, is getting less and less.

Automation, however, only obviates the economic need for the repression, the sublimation, of sexuality. Yet surely – Marcuse anticipates the objection – there are other, very obvious, grounds for the repression of the instincts, first and foremost the fact that aggression is a central drive in human nature (EC 134). Surely aggression is both innate and intrinsically anti-social, so that repression will have to remain with us *even if* it becomes no longer necessary to divert libidinal energy into work (EC 138).

What is the origin of aggression? Here, I think, we need to start with a distinction – never quite explicitly made by either Freud or Marcuse – between aggression, the infliction of harm or pain on another, as a means and as an end. The former is what we might call (instrumentally) 'rational' aggression, the latter – sadism – 'irrational' aggression.

'Rational' aggression does not, it seem to me, present a difficulty in principle for Marcuse, since it can surely be derived directly from the pleasure principle. This is what we have seen both Freud and Marcuse doing, in effect, with respect to the 'primal father', whose aggression towards the 'sons' is motivated purely by the desire for pleasure and the avoidance of pain. And it is consonant with Marcuse's Marxist view of war and colonization as products of capitalist greed. If aggression is the direct product of the pleasure principle then Marcuse can deal with the need for its repression as he deals with the need for the repression of sexuality, via the 'automation argument': since aggression is produced by the competition for pleasure, as automation and other forms of technology come closer and closer to producing unlimited pleasure for all, the motive for aggression will weaken and eventually disappear.

More problematic for Marcuse is irrational aggression, sadism. Marcuse's discussion of this phenomenon takes us into the darkest and most contentious regions of Freudian thought, his postulation of a 'death instinct', a postulation to which Marcuse gives qualified endorsement.

According to Freud's final metapsychology, life is a battle between Eros, the 'life instinct', and Thanatos, the 'death instinct'. Sadism is, as Marcuse puts Freud's claim, a 'derivative' of the latter (EC 139). (Freud actually posits these two drives as common to all organic life, which gives his final worldview something of the simple grandeur of a Pre-Socratic metaphysics.)[12]

The death instinct, as Freud conceives it, is a response to the trauma of birth. Birth, the emergence into life, is inevitably an emergence from a 'tension'-free condition into tension (EC 25) or 'anxiety' (EC 150), the actual or potential disjunction between desire and reality. Hence, from the start of life there is a (normally unconscious) 'regressive' drive to return to the status quo ante, to the womb-state. This is what Freud (following Barbara Low) calls the 'Nirvana principle'[13] (EC 25 et passim), Nirvana being defined as a condition free of all tension and anxiety.

Given, then, says Marcuse, that the Nirvana principle is 'unshakeable', and that death is the only path to Nirvana, and that aggression is a 'derivative' of the death instinct, it follows, as far as Freud is concerned, that aggression, and hence repression, can never be eliminated (EC 139).

The problem, of course, in understanding Freud's aetiology of aggression is understanding the notion of 'derivation', understanding just what *other*-directed aggression could possibly have to do with the *self*-directed death instinct. The difficulty is, in a word, that of understanding how sadism could possibly be the expression of masochism. Jonathan Lear suggests that there is, in fact, no intelligible connection, and that consequently Freud has no genuine theory of (irrational) aggression.[14]

Freud's suggestion that sadistic aggression is the death instinct deflected outwards is first made in *Beyond the Pleasure Principle*.[15] His account of the genesis of sadism is as follows. The death instinct 'wishes', through death, to enjoy the complete satisfaction of the Nirvana principle. Typically, however, the instinct of self-preservation prevents the natural, direct expression of the death instinct. And so the destructive instinct has to divert itself outwards, has to find a surrogate object on which to vent itself. In other words, although Freud does not put it this way, sadism is a form of sublimation. This seems to me, contra Lear, entirely intelligible.[16] It is simply the reverse of the hypothesis Nietzsche proposes in the *Genealogy of Morals*[17] that the 'sting of conscience' is the introversion of aggression denied outward expression by (in Freud's language) the reality principle, and it seems to me as plausible in one direction as in the other. Common observation tells us that unhappiness produces unhappiness, that self-hate, blocked from recognition of its proper object, transmutes itself into hate for others. The self must remain blameless, so blame and 'punishment' must always be inflicted on the other.

The root of aggression is, then, Marcuse accepts, the death instinct. It follows that if the repression-free society is to be possible, it has to be possible to, as it were, put the death instinct to death.[18] To see that it is possible, it is crucial to observe, says Marcuse, that death is not the end of the death instinct but

merely a means: that the 'objective' of the death instinct 'is not the termination of life but of pain' (EC 234–5). If, then, some alternative means of
satisfying the Nirvana principle[19] can be found, the death instinct can be
weakened and perhaps eliminated.

This is where Eros comes into play. As Freud himself suggests,[20] Eros
operates in the manner suggested by Plato's myth of the whole being as two
halves, torn apart at birth, trying to find each other through love, trying
to reunite. Throughout the realm of organic matter, 'Eros ... endeavours to
impel the separate parts of living matter to one another and to hold them
together'.[21] Eros thus serves the same end as the death instinct: it seeks to
create Nirvana by removing disharmony, tension. It follows that, the more
Eros is allowed free range, the more unrepressed, unsublimated, it becomes,
the closer will become the coincidence between the Nirvana and reality principles and the weaker the death instinct. Freud would, of course, claim that
there can never be such a coincidence on account of scarcity and the consequent need for at least 'basic' repression. But that claim, we have seen, is
refuted by the automation argument. It follows that the death instinct is in
principle eliminable (EC 235).

Fantasy as the vision of a new world

As noted earlier, Marcuse rejects Horkheimer and Adorno's confinement of
critical theory to a purely 'negative' role. If we are to effect a radical transformation in the character of AIS we must have, he says, some conception of 'other
possible ways' of living, radical alternatives to the status quo (ODM xlii).

As Jung recognized, Marcuse continues, fantasy ('phantasy') is the 'mother
of all possibilities' (EC 148). Only fantasy, or 'imagination', can envision
radical alternatives to the status quo. This was recognized, too, by André
Breton, who observed in the first surrealist manifesto, that while 'reason' tells
us what is, 'imagination alone tells [us] what *can* be' (149 fn.). (This is a slightly
odd remark given that surrealism typically deals with the *im*possible. A better
person to quote would have been Nietzsche who, as Heidegger summarizes
his view, holds that 'the creation of possibilities for the will ... is, for
Nietzsche, the essence of art' [QCT 85]).

Freud observed that fantasy – dreams, daydreams, children's games, and
art – is the one area of the psyche uncolonized by the reality principle. It
remains the product of the 'unmodified' pleasure principle (EC 140), that is, of
the id. (Marcuse alludes here to, inter alia, to Freud's theory of dreams as
wish-fulfilment.) Since, however, action is the product of the ego, which has
been colonized by the reality principle, fantasy, for Freud, is powerless to
effect change in the world: it is mere 'play', a vacation from the serious business
of life (EC 141).

This, however, is another aspect of Freud that Marcuse wishes to challenge.
Particularly when presented to consciousness in the form of art, fantasy need

not be powerless. Fantasy can affect the ego. Dreaming (one might call to mind Martin Luther King's 'I have a dream') need not be daydreaming. Fantasy 'looks not only back to an aboriginal golden past but also forward to all still unrealized, but realizable possibilities' (EC 148). And given that it is our only source of radical alternatives to what is, we *have* to attend to fantasy if we are to discover an ideal for the future. Unless we attend to fantasy, all thoughts of change will be confined within AIS's 'one dimension' and can therefore only produce the kind of change which, in Wittgenstein's words, leaves everything as it is.

The content of fantasy

Fantasy, to repeat, is the expression of the id and therefore of the pleasure principle. As Freud tells us, writes Marcuse, fantasy is the imaginative preservation, the 'memory', of a prehistoric past in which 'the life of the individual *was* the life of the genus (emphasis added)'. The content of fantasy is 'the image of the immediate unity between the universal and the particular under the rule of the pleasure principle'. It is, in other words, the normally unconscious memory of the organic unity of the tribe: of a time when the goals of all individuals were in harmony with each other, since the goal of each was determined by his or her functional contribution to the thriving of the tribe as a whole. History, however has consisted in the progressive loss of this 'universal', the progressive fragmentation of social life into an 'antagonistic' individualism, an antagonism harnessed, and greatly exacerbated, by the performance principle. Against such a world, fantasy, writes Marcuse, 'sustains the claim of the whole individual, in union with the genus and with the "archaic" past' (EC 142–3). Fantasy dreams of a recovered harmony, of an overcoming of the 'tension' created by antagonistic individualism. It dreams, in short, of Nirvana.

The principal way in which fantasy presents such a Nirvana is in the form of 'archetypes' which are universal to our species and are raised to explicit consciousness by myth and art (EC 140). Two such archetypes are Orpheus and Narcissus. (In discussing these archetypes, Marcuse is, in the main, no longer expounding Freud but rather striking out on his own.)

The figure of Narcissus has been, Marcuse believes, badly misinterpreted. Authentically understood, his self-love is not autoeroticism but rather, because he sees his beauty in everything, love of all beings. Narcissus has, that is, transcended the *principium individuationis* (Schopenhauer's term for the realm of individuality), inhabits what Freud calls the 'oceanic feeling', the feeling of 'limitless extension and oneness with the universe' (EC 168).

Orpheus (who brought the animals to peace through the magic of his lyre) is important, says Marcuse, in part because, according to the original interpretations, he is gay, and so rejects the tyranny of reproductive sexuality, channelling his erotic energy instead into a form of work that is indistinguishable from play (see pp. 83–4 below for an expansion of these notions).

Principally, however, he is important as an image of Nirvana, the agent of peace, the abolisher of anxiety (EC 159–61).

Marcuse, it seems to me, is here speaking a deep truth. Archetypes such as these – images of peace – *are* a fundamental, inspirational part of the human psyche. His own examples are taken from Greek mythology, but similar images occur throughout the Bible. In the New Testament, the 'glad tidings of great joy' the angels bring to the shepherds are the birth of Christ and, with it, the promise of 'on earth, peace among men' (Luke 2:10–14). In the Old Testament, there occurs the most famous of all images of peace:

> The wolf ... shall dwell with the lamb, and the leopard shall lie down with the kid; and the calf and the young lion and the fatling[22] together; and a little child shall lead them ... and the lion shall eat straw like the ox.
>
> (Isaiah 11:6–7)

Of interest, here, is the vegetarian lion: as we shall see, Marcuse, too, entertains the thought of the 'liberation of nature from its own brutality' (EC 190). *Peaceable Kingdom* (Figure 1) by Edward Hicks (1789–1849), a Pennsylvanian Quaker minister, is a realization of Isaiah's dream.

Figure 1

Notice that, had Orpheus been Christian rather than Greek, he would have fitted quite naturally into this picture as the bringer of peace to the kingdom.

Is Marcuse utopian in a pejorative sense?

Marcuse claims that in the archetypes of Nirvana we find the germ of a new reality principle, an alternative to the performance principle (EC 171), the image of a repression-free society. But of course, he admits, there are going to be many who 'defame' the programme of transferring such a society from fantasy to reality as 'utopian'. And typically, of course, they have a motive for doing so: 'The relegation of real possibilities to the no-man's land of utopia[23] is … an essential element in the ideology of the performance principle' (EC 150). Nonetheless, as Marcuse recognizes, there is a genuine question as to whether 'utopian thinking' is useless thinking, whether, that is, it is *mere* fantasy.

When submarines were invented, they were thought to be the ultimate weapon. Asked what to do about them, Mark Twain suggested raising the temperature of the world's oceans to boiling point so that life in submarines would become impossible. In response to the follow-up question of how that was to be done Twain replied that this was the questioner's problem, not his.[24] The moral of this anecdote is that if utopian thought is to avoid the charge of uselessness, it must provide some account of how to realize the utopia in question – or, at least, of how to proceed in the direction of such a realization. It must, as Marcuse puts it, be able to identify 'liberating tendencies' that are available here and now 'within the established society' (ODM 258).

We can conceive, it seems to me, of two kinds of utopian thinking that are not vulnerable to the charge of uselessness. The first offers a more or less detailed portrait of an ideal society together with an account of steps which, if taken, will eventually result in its – complete – realization. Utopian thought of this kind presents, I shall say, a 'realizable utopia'. The second kind admits that its ideal society can never be fully realized but offers a number of steps which, if taken, will *narrow the gap* between the ideal and the actual. One might call this an 'inspirational utopia': although impossible to realize, the portrait of the ideal may inspire us to effective action somewhat in the way that aiming to throw a ball an unrealistic distance improves one's chances of throwing it a realistic, but difficult, distance.

Does Marcuse wish to offer the repression-free society as a 'realizable' or merely 'inspirational' utopia? Although he oscillates somewhat between the two, it becomes clear that he wants to say that his utopia is *both* – although its full realization will occur, perhaps, only in a very distant 'end of history'.

Closing the gap between here and there

Why believe that the image of a repression-free society is not 'utopian' in the pejorative sense? Why believe is it something other than useless thinking?

What are the practical steps that would at least narrow the gap between here and there?

One thing we could do is attempt to eliminate surplus repression by introducing an equitable distribution of work: by, that is, introducing the socialist principle 'From each according to his abilities, to each according to his needs'. To the charge that human nature renders this impossible, one can cite not only the original communism of the hunter-gatherers, but also that of settled people such as the New Zealand Maori who, to this day, continue to hold tribal land in common. One can also mention the commune movement in general – Marcuse refers approvingly to the movement inspired by Charles Fourier (EC 217–18) – and the kibbutzim, in particular, that continue to supply nearly half of Israel's agricultural produce. It is true that many of the kibbutzim have modified the original socialist ideal – but not all. Some sixty remain true to that ideal.[25]

As things stand, Marcuse notes, even the introduction of a perfect socialism will not really produce 'to each according to his needs', given that, for the foreseeable future, a considerable amount of alienating labour will still be necessary. But with the equable distribution of work and consequent reduction of working hours, one's being will no longer be defined by one's work function: one will no longer be a Weberian *Berufsmensch*.

The overall number of working hours society requires can, moreover, be greatly reduced from the number required by the 'workaholic' status quo. To be sure, this will result in a reduction in the 'standard of living' as it is currently measured, but there is nothing that says that quality of life has to be measured in terms of flat-screen TVs. What we can and must do is start to measure it in terms of true human needs rather than quantity of consumer products. When we do that, when we focus the 'productive apparatus' on the needs of the human individual rather those of AIS, we will see that we can thrive on a great deal less production and hence on a great deal less work (EC 155).

These, then, are realistic steps that, if taken, will significantly alter the balance between the pleasure and reality principles in favour of the former (EC 154). The ideal of a repression-free society is at least 'inspirational', an ideal we can at least move *towards*. But is it also, as Marcuse wishes to claim, a 'realizable' utopia?

Kant, Schiller, and the aesthetic basis of a repression-free society

A genuinely repression-free society would, by definition, be an anarchy in the literal sense of an-archy, 'without a ruler'. But – Marcuse anticipates this objection – surely an an-archy will result in anarchy in the everyday sense. Surely, in other words, a repression-free society is, in fact, *not* a 'realizable' utopia: since humans cannot live together without order, the removal of all repression would 'explode' society (EC 175), reduce it to chaos. This, Marcuse notes, is what Jung believed: he thought that the removal of repression would result in a terrifying 'barbarism' (EC192); as Nietzsche called it, a 'witches brew of sensuality and cruelty'.[26] There is, Marcuse observes, a tradition reaching back from Jung and Nietzsche to Plato, who held that to avoid barbarism, the 'passions' must always be disciplined by 'reason'. Freud, too, of course, belongs to this tradition. His 'superego' is, indeed, essentially Plato's 'reason': both have the function of 'knowing the good', the only difference being that, whereas Plato's 'good' is determined by the forms, Freud's is determined by society.

In outline – I shall attend to the details shortly – Marcuse's answer to the claim that a repression-free society is unrealizable is the classical response of political anarchism: in Proudhon's words, 'anarchy is order' (the meaning of the 'A' within an 'O' that is the anarchist symbol). Marcuse finds the key to arguing this claim in Friedrich Schiller's *Aesthetic Education of Man* (1793) which, in turn, is based on Kant's aesthetic theory in the *Critique of Judgment* (1790).

* * *

As noted earlier, until the mid-eighteenth century 'aesthetic' (because it is derived from the Greek *aisthēsis*) means, 'pertaining to the senses'. But, observes Marcuse, with Alexander Baumgarten (1714–62) and, following him, Kant, its primary meaning changed to 'pertaining to beauty and art' (EC 181). Heidegger sees this change of meaning as confirming Hegel's thesis that great art 'died' at the end of the Middle Ages: it signals the degeneration of art from the site of world-historical truth, as it was in the Greek amphitheatre and medieval cathedral, to a vehicle for pleasurable feelings, art's trivialization into a 'matter for pastry cooks' (IM 131: see, too, PLT 77, N I 77–91). As we have seen (p. 64 above), Marcuse agrees with Heidegger in deploring the 'aestheticization' of modern art. On the other hand, he does not see the eighteenth-century change in the meaning of 'aesthetic' as heralding this trivialization of art.[27] He sees it, not as a downgrading of art to the triviality of the sensuous, but rather the elevation of the sensuous to the level of art and beauty (EC 181).

In German, Marcuse points out, *sinnlich* means both 'sensuous' and 'sensual'. The idea that the *sinnlich* needs to be subject to the firm control of 'reason', that it is inherently lawless and excessive, is based on taking it in the second sense. Yet what he, Schiller, and Kant are interested in is the first sense. And once we get over that confusion, says Marcuse, we become open to Kant's great discovery, which is that the sensuous carries with it its own principle of order (EC 182–5).

Why, asks Kant, do we find things of nature or art beautiful? What makes a Maori tattoo[28] or (my example, not Kant's) a snowflake (Figure 2) beautiful?

Figure 2

Its beauty lies, says Kant, in its form. Artefacts have a form, but their form is created by us and is derived – as with hammers, knives, or saws – from their function. The snowflake, however, was not designed by any human being and its form is not derived from any human function. It is, however, *as if* there is some function the form is designed to fulfil. So what we find in the snowflake or the Maori tattoo is what Kant calls 'purposiveness without a purpose' and 'lawfulness without a law'. There is, one might say, an algorithm at work without any human purpose being responsible for it. And this is what we find beautiful. (Naturally, Kant thinks that this has deep significance for religious belief.) We can, of course, find artefacts beautiful. But if we do, we abstract from their function, their usefulness, and attend to their form *as if* it were purpose-free.

What this shows is that what we find visually beautiful is actually quite law-governed. And this allows Kant to conclude that, just as logic is the science of thought, so 'aesthetics' is the science of the sensuous, a science which uncovers the laws of the sensuous (EC 183), the laws, that is, of the beautiful. And since there seems no reason to suppose that the visually pleasing is any different in this respect from the other sense modalities, it seems reasonable to conclude that the sensuous, the sensuously pleasing in general, is actually quite orderly, law-governed.

* * *

Kant's insight into the lawfulness of the sensuous leads Marcuse to conclude, with Schiller, that we do not need to be afraid of a repression-free society. Sensuousness does not need to be ordered by repressive reason because it is *intrinsically* orderly. This is what Baudelaire understood in picturing a world in which 'There, all is order and beauty, luxury, calm, and sensuousness' (EC 164). And so the thought emerges that we need not fear that the an-archy of a repression-free society will lead to anarchy, since 'sensuousness is rational' (EC 180) ('rational without a reason', as it were). Sensuousness has its own orderliness, and so does not need to have orderliness imposed on it by an oppressive reason.

The orderliness of the sensuous is surely an important insight. Many desires are naturally self-limiting: the pleasure of eating, for instance, turns into the discomfort of satiation if it is over-indulged. Yet it would be hasty to conclude that the pleasure principle as such is self-limiting and orderly, given the other sense of *sinnlich*, the 'sensual'. Even if sensuous desires constitute one part of human nature, that we have a word for it indicates that sensual desires constitute another part. And these, it may be objected, surely, *are* intrinsically disorderly.

The recovery of 'polymorphous sexuality'

The instinct that, above all others, has the reputation of being intrinsically 'disorderly' is, says Marcuse, sexuality (EC 199). And therefore, he antici-pates, it will be objected to the idea of a repression-free society that it must quickly degenerate into a cesspool of specifically sexual 'barbarism' (EC 198). To defeat this objection it needs to be shown that unrepressed sexuality is compatible with, and can in fact promote, 'lasting erotic relations among mature individuals' as well as (since, presumably, no culture can be happy that feels itself stagnating) 'progress towards higher forms of civilized freedom' (EC 199).

Repressive civilization, says Marcuse – reporting Freud – 'desexualizes' the body (EC 199). Prior to the onset of repression, the erogenous ('erotogenetic') zones are not confined to the familiar areas of the child's body. Rather, the entire body is an erogenous zone. All bodily pleasures have the same, erotic character: there is a very close similarity between the pleasures of smell and taste (and presumably touch) and sexual pleasure. In the interests of chan-nelling libidinal energy into work, civilization taboos, not just sexual pleasure, but bodily pleasure in general (EC 38–9). The 'inner-worldly asceticism' Weber observed to belong to the genesis of capitalism (ES 541, PE 53) is something AIS continues to demand of all individuals (EC xiv).

The result is that, under the repression exercised by the performance prin-ciple, libidinal energy finds its only permissible expression 'in the preparation and execution of genital intercourse' (EC 199) – something obviously required for the production of future workers. But even here, as already noted, it must be confined within the bounds of monogamous and lifelong marriage. And even here, it must never be performed for the sake of pleasure:

> The full force of civilized morality [is] mobilized against the use of the body as a mere object, means, instrument of pleasure: such reification was tabooed and remained the ill-reputed privilege of whores, degenerates, and perverts.

Sex has, therefore, to be 'dignified by love', and of course by marriage, since man is no four-footed beast but rather a 'higher being' (EC 200–1). (Sex-for-pleasure is presumably intended to be ruled out by Kant's 'Act that you use humanity, whether in your person or in another, always at the same time as an end, never merely as a means'.)

If we make the transition to the repression-free society, however, the entire body will be resexualized:

> The regression involved in this spread of the libido would first manifest itself in a reactivation of all erotogenic zones and consequently, in a resurgence of pregenital polymorphous sexuality and in a decline of genital supremacy. The body in its entirety would become an object of cathexis [interest], a thing to be enjoyed – an instrument of pleasure.
>
> (EC 201)

But will this not simply result in a society with a *KamaSutra*-like obsession with the varieties of sexual intercourse, and will not this obsession result, in many cases, in sexual violence? Must not the removal of sexual taboos 'lead ... to a society of sex maniacs – that is, to no society' (EC 201), to the destruction of civilization?

Marcuse concedes a certain destructive effect. The freeing up of sexual activity, the abandonment of monogamy as an ethical principle, will indeed destroy traditional institutions such as the 'monogamic and patriarchal family' (EC 201). With 'free love', the family will not survive. But Marcuse regards that as a good thing – he evidently views the nuclear family, from the 'primal father' onwards, as an essentially oppressive structure. (Worthy of note is that Marcuse was an early feminist. In one of his last lectures, 'Marxism and Feminism', delivered at Stanford in 1974, he states his belief that 'the woman's liberation movement is perhaps the most important and potentially the most radical political movement that we have'.[29] Also worth noting is another respect in which the original, socialist kibbutzim, with their communal raising of children, come close to the Marcusean ideal.)

In general, however, the result of the removal of sexual repression will not be a society of violent 'sex maniacs' because that removal will be 'not simply a release but a *transformation* of the libido: from sexuality constrained under genital supremacy to eroticization of the entire personality'. What will happen, that is, will be 'a spread rather than an explosion of libido – a spread over private and societal relations which bridges the gap maintained between them by the repressive reality principle' (EC 201–2).

'Explosion', says Marcuse, is the product, not of free, but rather of *repressed* sexuality. It is the *repressed* libido that manifests itself in the hideous forms of sexual violence known to the history of civilization, 'in the sadistic and masochistic orgies of desperate masses, of "society elites", … of prison and concentration camp guards' (EC 202) – and, Marcuse would surely now add, in priestly paedophilia. (Notice, here, Marcuse's implicit answer to Nietzsche's prediction of a 'witches brew of sensuality and cruelty' [p.79 above]). Marcuse's claim, then, is that what creates violent and violating sexual behaviour is the sudden removal of the lid on libido. Unrepressed, it will express itself, sometimes in civilized forms of sexuality, but more commonly by 'spreading' to non-genital modes of expression.

Marcuse calls this 'eroticization of the entire personality' which follows the release from genital supremacy 'the transformation of sexuality into Eros' (EC 205). Freed from genital tyranny, one's whole life will be transformed into erotic activity. One's sexual, libidinal energy will find *many* rather than only one form of expression, will become 'polymorphous' (EC 201).[30]

Non-repressive sublimation

Odysseus, attempting to sail home to rescue Penelope from the suitors, comes to the island of the lotus eaters. The lotus flowers are so delicious that they drive away every desire other than the desire to lie on the beach eating lotus flowers, with the result that Odysseus has great trouble rousing his crew from their stoned slumber. Does not a similar fate threaten the non-repressive society? Even if we need not fear sexual barbarism, will not the removal of repression, particularly when machines become capable of taking over all labour, turn us into a race of lotus eaters? If so, it would then, of course, constitute the end of anything that distinguishes us from the animals, the death of the distinctively human being.

Marcuse rejects the claim that his utopians will collapse into lotus-eating. The non-repressive society will still be 'culture building' (EC 210), will still engage in art and science, will still engage, he stresses, in the task of overcoming disease and death (EC 157; see further, pp. 86–7 below). To establish this claim, what he needs to show is that, even in the age of automation, we will still work, not because we have to, but because we want to, because we find the work in question pleasurable. In his own language, he needs to show (contra Freud, he suggests [EC 154]) that in addition to enforced sublimation, there is also a 'non-repressive kind of sublimation' of libidinal energy (EC 207), that 'sexuality tends to its own sublimation' (EC 202).

Given the assumption that all psychic energy is libidinal, the existence of what Marcuse calls non-repressive sublimation is, I think, entirely obvious. Any work that is enjoyable counts as such. If there were no such thing as non-repressive sublimation there would be no 'hobbies'. Marcuse makes three claims about such sublimation.

First, unlike a neurosis such as narcissism (in the bad sense) which isolates the individual, the sublimation in question is societal, outgoing. (At least very often) it 'performs socially useful work which is, at the same time, the transparent satisfaction of an individual need (EC 210). At the back of Marcuse's mind, here, is, I suspect, Nietzsche's benevolent egoism. At the beginning of *Thus Spoke Zarathustra*, Zarathustra, who has spent ten years in his cave on the mountain top gathering wisdom, feels like a 'bee that has gathered too much honey'. He *needs* to 'overflow' with the 'gift-giving love', to 'go down' to the world of men to 'discharge' his excess of wisdom. This is the beginning of his Christ-like mission to save the world.

Second, as Plato anticipates in the *Symposium*, Agape is Eros in the sense that it is 'self-sublimating' Eros (EC 222).[31] All human relations are libidinal. However, in the sublimation of libido into friendship, collegiality, mentoring, caring, and sometimes leading, 'sexuality is neither deflected nor blocked from its objective; rather, in attaining its objective it transcends it to others, searching for a fuller gratification' (EC 210–11). In a non-repressive society, one obtains all the sex one needs. But the life of a Don Juan quickly becomes one of tedium. And so the pleasure principle itself dictates that one seek other forms of pleasure, forms which are, in fact, 'fuller' – ultimately better, even more pleasurable. (A list of the 'perfect moments' in one's life would, I think, be unlikely to include many moments of genital pleasure.)

Since it strives for *continuous and uninterrupted* pleasure, the pleasure principle dictates, not only that there be non-sexual human relationships, but also that they be *lasting* relationships. Eros wants to 'eternaliz[e] itself in a permanent *order*' of such relations.[32] It strives for 'community' and the perpetuation of this on an ever-expanding scale (EC 222–4).

Third, there is nothing to say that self-sublimation cannot take spiritual-intellectual as well as material forms: 'spiritual "procreation" is just as much the work of Eros as is corporeal procreation' (EC 211). This is almost a direct quotation from Nietzsche (from whom Freud probably derived the concept of sublimation – Nietzsche calls it 'spiritualization'). 'Making music', Nietzsche writes, 'is another way of making children', so that (the right kind of) '[c]hastity is merely the economy of the artist'.[33] Paraphrasing Plato, Marcuse says that 'the right and true order of the polis is just as much an erotic one as is the right and true order of love' (EC 211). In sum, then, Eros will naturally and *freely* express itself in art and science.[34]

The role of reason in utopia

As with all the Frankfurt theorists, Marcuse has the bad habit of multiplying 'forms' of reason (EC 121, 159, 223) beyond necessity. So we find him saying that in the repression-free society there will no longer be 'aggressive', 'repressive' and 'exploitative' reason, but only 'libidinal rationality' (EC 199), 'post-technological rationality' (ODM 242). This is misleading, for what he really wants to distinguish is not different forms of rationality, but rather different *ends* to which instrumental rationality can be put – different, as one might put it in computer terminology, 'apps'. In this respect, his phrase 'rationality of gratification' (EC x, 224) is less misleading than 'libidinal rationality'.

What Marcuse wants to say is that in the repression-free society, instrumental reason will be devoted not to ever-increasing 'productivity', as in AIS, but to the promotion of the unrepressed pleasure principle, to the life of 'pleasure', of 'joy' (EC xiv).[35]

How, then, will reason still have a role to play in promoting the life of joy? One of its tasks will be to work out a pleasure-promoting 'division of labour', and even a management structure, a 'hierarchy' of authority. Not all authority, Marcuse observes, is repressive; in particular the authority of (genuine) expertise is not: the pilot's authority is not repressive, and neither is the parent's use of authority to prevent the child crossing the street at the wrong moment (EC 224). The role of reason will be to co-ordinate the various forms of expertise into productive units.

Another role for instrumental reason is the repression of repression. Since the manufactured 'need to "relax" in the entertainments provided by the culture industry' is repressive, its repression (through, one assumes, the persuasive power of critical theory rather than force) is a 'step towards freedom' (EC 224).

Non-repressive civilization and nature

In the anthropological literature, notes Marcuse, a 'maternal' and caring stance to nature is contrasted with the 'masculine' stance of aggression and exploitation. The former is always represented as the exclusive preserve of primitive peoples such as the Arapesh of New Guinea who were studied by Margaret Mead. As Mead reports, the Arapesh view the world

> as a garden that must be tilled, not for one's self, not in pride and boasting, not for hoarding and usury [capitalism], but that the yams and the dogs and pigs and most of all the children may grow. From this whole attitude flow many of the Arapesh traits, the lack of conflict between the old and young, the lack of any expectation of jealousy or envy, the emphasis on co-operation.[36]

For the Arapesh, comments Marcuse, nature is taken 'not as an object of domination and exploitation, but as a "garden" which can grow and make human beings grow'. For them, 'man and nature are joined in a non-repressive [but nonetheless] … still functioning order'. Unlike nostalgic anthropologists, however, Marcuse projects this relationship to nature forward to the future of a 'mature civilization'. With release from genital exclusivity, the erotic will embrace not just human beings but entire landscapes, nature as a whole, as is imagined in the Orphic and Narcissistic traditions (EC 216–17).

A likely objection to Marcuse's account of this past and future society is that, unless deluded, one cannot view nature as a lover views the beloved since nature, red in tooth and claw, is ruled by the Darwinian order of cruelty, by survival of the fittest: as Mead sentimentalizes the Arapesh, it may be said, so Marcuse sentimentalizes the future of his 'mature civilization'.

As mentioned earlier, in contrast to Habermas, the measure of Marcuse's willingness to think outside the 'one-dimension' of the current social and intellectual order is his notion that, with technological advance, it might be possible to 'liberate nature from its own brutality' (EC 190), to realize Isaiah's dream of a Nirvana in which, like the ox, the lion eats straw (p.76 above).

Marcuse discusses this idea further in *One-Dimensional Man*. Here, he begins by deploring the glorification of the 'natural' which, he says, 'protects an unnatural society in its struggle against liberation'. The 'defamation of birth control' is, he says, a striking example of this ideological use of 'unnatural'. Against this freezing of nature into a set of eternal laws both descriptive and normative, a joyful, erotic attitude to nature is one of 'mediation', mediation in order to secure 'autonomy' and remove 'contradiction'. And with the advance of technology and the arrival of 'post-technological' ideals of what to do with it, 'civilization produces the means for freeing Nature from its own brutality, its own insufficiency, its own blindness', of bringing to an end the reign of the principle that 'the big fishes eat the little fish' (ODM 242). (As we shall see in Chapter 9, there are affinities here with the later Heidegger's notion of authentic technology as the technology of 'guardianship'.) While this seems an extraordinary ideal, the archetypal status of the Orpheus myth – Isaiah's myth of the 'Peaceful Kingdom' – suggests that it really does lie deep within the human psyche.

The conquest of death

Marcuse's final reflections in *Eros and Civilization* consider what purports to be an 'ontological' objection to the possibility of a repression-free existence:

> [t]he brute fact of death denies once and for all the reality of a non-repressive existence. For death is the final negativity of time but 'joy wants eternity'.[37] Timelessness is the ideal of pleasure.
>
> (EC 231)

Joy, that is, is always accompanied by two things: first, Faust's cry 'stay [for ever], you are so beautiful' (EC 234); and second, the knowledge this can never be. And so joy as we know it is always accompanied – polluted, it might be claimed – by 'anxiety over its [inevitable] passing', by the fact of mortality

(EC 233). This is why, in Christian theology, 'the eternity of joy is reserved for the hereafter' (EC 234).

Marcuse's response to the imperfection of mortal pleasure – the 'repression' of our desire for the eternity of joy – is to assert that we do not have to assume that death is inevitable. (At least unchosen death is not. There is nothing repressive about dying at the right time; what is unconscionable is dying prematurely and in agony [EC 235].) Marcuse deplores the theology and philosophy that 'celebrate death as an existential category' (an allusion, as will become clear, to Heidegger's *Being and Time*). To do this is to 'pervert a biological fact into an ontological essence'. Philosophy that does not work as the handmaid of repression 'responds to the fact of death with the Great Refusal' (EC 236) – does not, in other words, 'go gentle into that good night'. Death is a biological fact that can be approached like any other unwelcome biological fact. Work devoted to the 'conquest of death' (EC 234) and disease is thus an essential component of Marcuse's future society.

Marcuse believes that the conquest of death will complete the conquest of the death instinct. As we know, the goal of the death instinct is Nirvana, to which death presents itself as the only means. It follows that the closer life approaches Nirvana, the weaker becomes the death instinct (p. 74 above). If, then, we can one day conquer death we will have removed the final, ontological (but really biological) barrier to the coincidence of the Nirvana and reality principles (EC 235).

The lineaments of utopia

Let me draw together the threads of the foregoing into a portrait of the repression-free society, of the Marcusean utopia. It has, it seems to me, six salient features.

First, it will be a socialist society organized on the principle 'From each according to his ability, to each according to his needs'.

Second, the nuclear family (together with 'family-values' institutions such as the Catholic Church) will disappear in favour of something like a kibbutz. Since children need to be able to identify, if not parents, at least parent figures, one would think that, like a kibbutz, the basic social unit will be quite small. And this, in fact, is what Marcuse says in his political speeches. He sees 'small groups concentrated on the level of local activities' as the motive force for revolution and also as 'foreshadowing the basic organization of libertarian socialism, namely, councils of manual and intellectual workers'.[38]

Third, authority within these groups will be based on a rational and natural respect for expertise. It will not be based on compulsion, indeed there will be no compulsion of any kind. In particular, there will be no taboos on sexual activity.

Fourth, industrial activity will continue, although all labour that is drudgery will be delegated to machines. There will, however, be a great reduction in production since it will be aimed not at the needs of AIS – ever-increasing consumption – but at the 'true' needs of individuals.

Fifth, our stance to nature will be transformed by Eros from aggressive exploitation to loving stewardship. Our industrial technology will be 'green' technology.

Sixth, we will live as long as we wish.

Hedonism, and the meaning of life

As observed above (p. 68), Freud is a psychological hedonist (and so, too, a 'psychological egoist', since the former doctrine is a species of the latter). The goal of life is one's own 'happiness', and happiness consists in 'the absence of pain and strong feelings of pleasure'. As Mary Midgley points out,[39] this view is the product of 'enlightenment individualism', a view of human nature which regards 'all interpersonal dealings as transactions for private gain', a view that also finds expression in Hobbes' political philosophy (and in Adam Smith's economics). On this view, there is no such thing as a disinterested, other-directed desire: others in general stand to the individual in an essentially 'alien' relation, appearing, mostly, as impediments, at best as means, to pleasure. Hence, for Freud, what might appear as disinterested affection is, in reality, 'exploiting love to produce an inner feeling of happiness'[40] (whatever that might be). Again, in speaking of the origins of the family, Freud observes that in the interests of 'genital satisfaction' on demand, the male had a motive for 'keeping the female, or speaking more generally, *his sexual objects*, near him'.[41]

As Midgley reveals, psychological hedonism is an unattractive doctrine. It pictures the individual as a Cartesian solipsist – his world contains 'objects' but no people – and (a word Freud frequently uses) a narcissist: ultimately, the only object of love is the self. Happiness for the Freudian individual is, more or less literally, masturbation.

Psychological hedonism is not only unattractive, it is also false. Sometimes, Nietzsche is clearly aware of this. Referring to the English Utilitarians, and in particular to Jeremy Bentham, who, like Freud, identified happiness with pleasure, Nietzsche quips:

> If we have our own why in life, we shall get along with almost any how. Man does not strive for pleasure; only the Englishman does that.[42]

A century later, Robert Nozick proposed a thought experiment that provides Nietzsche's aphorism with powerful support. Suppose that there is a machine that will generate nothing but pleasurable experiences. These appear to constitute the real world, but are, in fact, entirely illusory. In reality, one is floating in a tank, attached to electrodes. In Nozick's experiment, one is offered the chance of plugging into the machine, a decision which, once made, is irreversible. Would one accept? Nozick is rightly confident that all, or at least most, of us would reject it.[43] It follow, therefore, that for most of us pleasure is not our highest goal.

Freud's psychological hedonism is both unattractive and false. Yet Marcuse builds his own philosophy on Freudian foundations. The question thus arises as to whether his philosophy, too, is not vitiated by a doctrine that is both unattractive and false.

At first glance, it certainly appears that it is. As Freud says that happiness is the unrestricted satisfaction of the pleasure principle so does Marcuse. Yet how, really, does he understand the 'pleasure principle'? Does he really think that happiness is masturbation?

To live with no restrictions on the pleasure principle (to in live Kierkegaard's 'aesthetic' form of life) is to 'do what one pleases'. It seems natural to follow Freud in parsing 'doing what one pleases' as 'doing what pleases one, gives one pleasure'. But this is not the only possible parsing: 'doing what one wants' is an alternative. The second parsing is different from the first in that, while the object of desire, 'what one wants', may be pleasure, it by no means has to be. 'What I want', the object of desire, may be something other than pleasure, and it may be a state of affairs that pertains to others rather than to oneself.

What do we really want? According to Marcuse's Rousseau-like account of human nature, what we fundamentally want is determined by the 'archetypes' buried in the 'archaic' depths of our psychology (p. 75 above). It is these that, as so located, are normative for us, determine the meaning of our lives. What these archetypes determine as that meaning is Nirvana: not the absolute nothingness of the Freudian death instinct (nor the mystical nothingness of the enlightened Schopenhauerian sage), but rather the Peaceful Kingdom: the kingdom in which individuals live rich, flourishing, diverse lives, yet lives that are contained within 'the unity between universal and particular' (p. 75 above). The task determined by our fundamental desires is that of 'mediating' within both nature and society in order to remove the 'contradiction' between one 'autonomy' and another. Our task is to work towards a Hegelian synthesis between different autonomies, to work towards 'multiplicity in unity'.

Does Marcuse suppose that we want to work towards the Peaceful Kingdom as a means to experiencing a pleasurable sensation, the supposed 'feeling of happiness'? Surely not. As he quotes Mead as saying of the Arapesh, one wants to mediate between beings, to cultivate the garden of life, 'not for oneself, not in pride and boasting' (p. 85 above), not for our own sake, but for its sake, not as a means but as an end. Of course we will take pleasure in the fruits of such cultivation. But we do not, and cannot, cultivate the garden as a means to pleasure, for unless we had an antecedent desire for the Peaceful Kingdom as an end, there would be no pleasure to be derived from its approach or arrival.

Notes

1 Galbraith (1969).
2 Jünger (1930).
3 Marcuse wrote, of course, in the pre-digital age. A number of recent books have discussed the acceleration of this process in the digital age by social media. In the age of the 'selfie', it is argued, the important self becomes the virtual self that is visible to all, while the self that possesses both a body and a private, inner life, shrinks into insignificance. See Edward Mendelson's review of a number of such books in Mendelson (2016).
4 I take this phrase from Karel Reiz's film *Morgan: A Suitable Case for Treatment*, which appeared in 1966, two years after *One-Dimensional Man*. In it, the anarchist son of communist parents ends up in an asylum, partly on account of having been driven through London in an open-toped mini, standing up, in a gorilla suit that is on fire. The movie ends on a rather pleasing note: as the camera gradually zooms out to an aerial perspective, one sees that the flowers Morgan has been planting in his capacity as the asylum's gardener form a hammer and sickle.
5 Heidegger's account of modernity as inhabiting, in Marcuse's language, a 'closed dimension' (the rationalized mode of world-disclosure, we shall see him saying, 'drives out every other possibility of disclosure') occurs most forcibly in 'The Question concerning Technology' (QCT 27). This was published in 1955, nine years before *One-Dimensional Man*. Although, as noted, Marcuse broke with Heidegger in 1932, and intensified the rupture in an angry exchange of letters in 1947 concerning Heidegger's failure to apologize for his involvement with the Nazis (see Wolin [1993] 160–2), it seems to me unlikely that Marcuse did not read Heidegger's seminal essay on technology. Certainly Andrew Feenberg (the leading authority on Marcuse–Heidegger relations) assumes that he did (see Feenberg [2005] xiii).
6 Freud (2009) 63.
7 Freud (2009) 5.
8 Marcuse's use of 'reality principle' is (like Freud's) ambiguous. Sometimes it means the result of the ego's compromise between the two principles (EC 12) and sometimes it means that which necessitates the compromise (EC 34). I shall use it only in this second sense.
9 Freud (1989) 101.
10 Kellner (1984) 162.
11 The discussion Marcuse alludes to occurs in *Moses and Monotheism* (Freud [1939]).
12 Freud is exercised over the question of how the instinct to 'self-preservation' is to be located within this simple 'dualism' (Freud [2009] 67). In an earlier phase of his metapsychology, self-preservation had been viewed as a basic instinct, and the dualism of instincts was then viewed as occurring between self-preservation and the life instinct. In his final view, however, self-preservation is absorbed into Eros by being represented as self-directed, 'narcissistic' love (Freud [2009] 79). An alternative account of self-preservation might have been to represent it, not as a basic instinct, but as a derivative of the life-instinct: obviously, one cannot promote and enhance life unless one preserves oneself in existence. But Freud does not seem to have considered this option.(Freud [2009]).
13 Freud (2009) 71.
14 Lear (2005) 162.
15 Freud (2009) 68–9.
16 Although, on Freud's account, sadism is *caused* by the Nirvana principle, it makes no contribution to its satisfaction and is therefore not rendered *rational* by the principle. Lear's claim that the 'derivation' of aggression from the Nirvana principle is unintelligible is likely based on the assumption that to render a mode of behaviour intelligible is to exhibit it as possessing means–end rationality. But this seems to me a mistake.
17 Nietzsche (1994) Essay II section 16.
18 It is worth noting that Freud's word is *Trieb*, of which 'drive', rather than 'instinct', is actually the correct translation. Since 'instinct' suggests something innate and hence incapable of elimination, 'death drive' is actually more friendly than 'death instinct' to Marcuse's notion that the *Todestrieb* can be eliminated.
19 As Freud states (Freud [2009] 71), the Nirvana principle is really the same principle as the pleasure principle. This, Marcuse points out, is because Freud conceives pleasure as a negative

phenomenon, as the elimination of pain, of 'tension'. Pain is the tension between desire and reality, pleasure is its removal (EC 24–5). Freud almost certainly derives this 'negativity' thesis from Schopenhauer, who writes that 'pain is something positive that automatically makes itself known: satisfaction and pleasures are something *negative*, the mere elimination of the former' (quoted in Young [2005] 214). In fact, however, Schopenhauer points out that the negativity thesis is only a *frequent* truth, more often true than we like to imagine. In reality, there are positive pleasures too – the unexpected scent of blossom on the night air – which, because they are not preceded by a desire, cannot be conceived as the removal of pain or tension. And even when pleasures do consist in the satisfaction of a desire, in addition to the elimination of 'tension', there usually occurs a feeling – albeit brief – of positive pleasure. Marcuse does not, I think, endorse, Freud's negativity thesis. When he uses 'pleasure principle' to express his own views, as distinct from Freud's, 'pleasure' should be understood as embracing positive as well as negative pleasures.

20 Freud (2009) 74–5.
21 Freud (2009) 79.
22 Young animal fattened, normally, for slaughter.
23 A utopia is a *u-topos*, 'no place', hence 'no man's land'.
24 The anecdote is reported in Bertell Ollman's 'The Utopian Vision of the Future (Then and Now): a Marxist Critique', http://monthlyreview.org/2005/07/01/the-utopian-vision-of-the-future-then-a nd-now-a-marxist-critique/ (accessed 14/10/17).
25 Or at least, did so in July 2012. See https://www.theguardian.com/world/2012/jul/23/israel-k ibbutz-movement-comeback (accessed 14/6/16).
26 Nietzsche (1999a) section2.
27 As we saw (p. 63 above), Marcuse sees the trivialization of art as happening, not in the eighteenth, but rather at the end of the nineteenth century.
28 Kant (1931) section16.
29 Marcuse (2005) 165.
30 Marcuse attaches two meanings to 'polymorphous sexuality': the eroticization of 'the body in its entirety' and the eroticization of 'the entire personality' (EC 201). He appears to think that they are equivalent, that, in particular, the first is necessary to the second: the impulse to seek 'pleasure from zones of the body', he writes, 'may extend to seek its objective in lasting and expanding libidinal relations', a notion he uses to ground his claim that, in fact, 'Agape is Eros' (EC 210). The body–personality equivalence seems to me, however, a step too far. The problem is not so much that it renders all friendship as, deep down, 'touchy-feely', but that it fails to accommodate what one might call 'Cartesian' expressions of the erotic. From a Freudian point of view, it is plausible to see the quest for 'sexy' proofs in mathematics as an expression of the erotic. But this seems to have nothing to do with erogenous 'zones of the body'.
31 *This* Plato of course contradicts the Plato who demands *external* repression of the sensuous/sensual part of the soul.
32 Kierkegaard argues that to advance from the life of a Don Juan to the life of marriage one must make the radical transition from the 'aesthetic' life of doing whatever one pleases to the 'ethical' life in which the categories of good and evil determine one's actions. Whether intentionally or not, Marcuse provides a response to this claim: the pleasure principle alone will lead one from DonJuanism to marriage; marriage will be included in Kierkegaard's 'reflective', thoughtful, version of the 'aesthetic' life.
33 Nietzsche (1967) section 800.
34 Marcuse expresses this point by saying that while many of the higher forms of work as we know it will continue, they will be performed in a new spirit, the spirit of, as Schiller wanted, 'free play'. He adds that they will not be subject to 'administration' since 'only alienated labour can be organized and administered by a rational routine' (EC 218). This seems to me a blind alley. Had he reflected on his own intellectual work, he would have been aware of the degree to which, disciplined but, in itself, often tedious research, 'rational routine', is an essential part of almost any creative effort. (Only Schubert could toss off two sublime lieder before breakfast.) And of course, Marcuse's wish to retain the benefits of industrial technology is incompatible with the idea of workers turning up to work only if they are in the mood for 'play'. 'Alienation' pertains to the *goal* of work. A goal can be profoundly un-alienated and yet the process of achieving it involve a great deal of un-pleasure.

35 In AIS, says Marcuse, (instrumental) reason is devoted to the supreme end of maximizing 'pro-
    ductivity' (EC 155). Prometheus is the symbol of this productivity (EC 161), as is Nietzsche's
    'superman', his ideal of (in Weber's phrase) 'inner-worldly asceticism' in service of 'heroic virtues'
    (EC xiv). At first sight, this seems to repeat the error discussed in the previous note, that of
    ignoring the fact that, unless one is Schubert, disciplined tedium is the necessary means to almost
    any 'spiritual' end. In fact, though, I think Marcuse is not discussing the pursuit of ends as such, but
    is rather making the interesting suggestion that Nietzsche's ideal of constant 'self-overcoming' –
    the will to endless 'growth', which is a function of the fact that the 'will to power' that is always
    the will to more power – is not, in fact, intrinsic to human nature as such, but is rather an inter-
    nalization of what Weber calls the 'spirit of capitalism', that this central postulate of Nietzsche's
    philosophy is a projection and product of his Protestant-Prussian upbringing.
36 Marcuse is quoting from Mead's *Sex and Temperament in Three Primitive Societies* (Mead [1952] 100).
    There are, it appears, thirteen genders in the Arapesh language, which suggests an experience of the
    world alive to its rich diversity, the opposite of the homogeneity of a world rationalized into
    'resources'.
37 The quotation is from the 'Intoxicated Song' at the end of Nietzsche's *Thus Spoke Zarathustra*: 'But
    all joy wants eternity / Wants deep, wants deep eternity ...'
38 Marcuse (2005) 27.
39 Midgley (1984) 161–4.
40 Freud (1989) 102.
41 Freud (1989) 99; emphasis added.
42 Nietzsche (2005) X section 12.
43 Nozick (1974) 44–5.

Part II

FREIBURG

5 Husserl

Phenomenology and the crisis of humanity

In this chapter we move from Frankfurt to Freiburg and to a very different kind of philosophy from that which has occupied us so far. Classifying philosophers in terms of Marx's aphorism about understanding and changing, one can say that whereas the Frankfurt thinkers are all 'changers', Husserl returns us to the mould of understanding for its own sake, the mould of Horkheimer's 'traditional theory'. That, at least, is true of much of Husserl's work. Especially in his final years, however, he makes the attempt to show that his life's work *does* have something to say about the existential crises of the modern age, does have something to contribute to the project of changing the world for the better, and it is this aspect of his philosophy I shall be concerned to emphasize.

Edmund Husserl (1859–1938) was born in Prossnitz in Moravia, then part of the Austro-Hungarian Empire, now part of the Czech Republic. Born to Jewish parents, he converted to Protestant Christianity at the age of twenty-seven. Husserl was educated in Vienna, Leipzig and Halle and taught in Göttingen until his appointment in 1916 to a full professorship in Freiburg, a position he held until his retirement in 1928. His final years were over-shadowed by a widening rift between himself and his successor and former assistant, Martin Heidegger, and by the rise of Nazism. Although his first interest was in the philosophy of mathematics, he is now known as the foun-der of phenomenology, which he defines, roughly speaking, as the science of consciousness. Some key works in the development of phenomenology are his *Logical Investigations* (1900–1), the programme-setting 'Philosophy as a Rigorous Science' (1910–11), *Ideas* (1913), *Cartesian Meditations* (1931), and his unfinished final work, *The Crisis in European Sciences and Transcendental Phenomenology* (1954). In the main, this chapter will view Husserl from the perspective of this final book, which he regarded as a comprehensive statement of the nature and full significance of his life's work.

What is phenomenology?

Husserl's philosophy embraces more than can be easily accommodated under the heading 'science of consciousness'. As David Woodruff Smith has emphasized,[1] Husserl has a metaphysics (albeit something of a jungle), an epistemology, a philosophy of mathematics, a philosophy of logic, and an ethics. And central to his final work, we shall see, is a philosophy of science. But since his established position in the history of philosophy is as the founder of phenomenology, I shall begin by trying to determine just what phenomenology is.

Phenomenology, as Smith usefully puts it, is the description of consciousness as experienced from the first-person point of view – as contrasted with neuroscience which studies it from the third-person point of view.[2] In terms of a contrast Husserl uses a great deal, while neuroscience is an 'objective' science – it studies consciousness from the 'outside' – phenomenology is a 'subjective' science – it studies consciousness from the 'inside'. This, however, fails to tell us what is distinctively *philosophical* about phenomenology, since phenomenological description occurs whenever there is first-person description of consciousness. The masters of phenomenological description are, in fact, not philosophers at all, but rather poets and novelists, especially (though not exclusively) those who adopt the 'stream of consciousness' mode of narration. Here, for example, is a passage from Virginia Woolf's *Mrs Dalloway*:

> What a lark! What a plunge! For so it always seemed to me when, with a little squeak of the hinges, which I can hear now, I burst open the French windows and plunged at Bourton into the open air. How fresh, how calm, stiller than this of course, the air was in the early morning; like the flap of a wave; the kiss of a wave; chill and sharp and yet (for a girl of eighteen as I then was) solemn, feeling as I did, standing there at the open window, that something awful was about to happen ...[3]

(Notice the variety of different modes of consciousness Woolf describes: auditory, visual and tactile perceptions, emotions and expectations.) What, then, does Husserl take to distinguish the way phenomenological description occurs in philosophy from the way it occurs in fiction (or in a visit to the doctor or to the psychoanalyst)?

Husserl's answer is that philosophical phenomenology is an 'eidetic' science (in the broad German sense of 'science'), a science, that is, which is solely concerned with 'essences' (Ideas I 3, 8). An 'essence' – or 'idea' – is the 'what-ness' of an entity and is contrasted with its 'is-ness'. (Sartre's famous slogan 'existence before essence' claims that while non-human beings come into existence with pre-established essences – tigers are born and have to be *tigers* – human beings are born essence-less, and are therefore 'condemned to the freedom' of having to choose the 'what-ness' of their lives.) Unlike Virginia Woolf (or the doctor) Husserl has no interest in particular existent states of consciousness (PRS 272). Phenomenology's concern is entirely confined to the essence of consciousness.

Essences ground what, following Kant, Husserl calls 'a priori' knowledge. Such knowledge consists in necessary (but non-trivial) truths that hold of an entity purely in virtue of its being the kind of entity it is. So if we know that something is a Euclidean triangle we know 'a priori' that its angles are equal to 180 degrees, and if we know that something is a physical object we know 'a priori' that it occupies a region of space and time. Turning to consciousness, its eidetic study is thus the study of what can be known about it simply in virtue of the fact that it is consciousness, and about particular states – Husserl calls them 'acts' – of consciousness simply in virtue of them being the kinds of states (memories, hopes, beliefs, and so on) that they are. Philosophical phenomenology thus aims to discern and describe the 'a priori' features of consciousness, aims to discover the framework or structure within which all consciousness must occur. The medieval scholastics applied the term 'transcendental' to properties that apply to – 'transcend' – everything, and Kant adopted the term to refer to the framework features of consciousness. Although Husserl's use of 'transcendental' to identify specifically philosophical phenomenology was a later terminological development, the idea of philosophical phenomenology as the project of acquiring 'transcendental' knowledge about consciousness was clearly present in his conception of phenomenology from the start.

The phenomenological method

Attending to the structural features of consciousness is, Husserl emphasizes, not easy (CS 155). What gets in the way is what he calls 'the natural attitude'. The natural (everyday, common sense) attitude is, of course, 'naively' realist: the world is 'simply there' for me. And my experience of it is immediate. I do not experience an 'object-appearance' and then infer to an object as its probably cause. Rather, 'I directly "know of" objects, a "knowing of"... which involves no conceptual thinking' (Ideas I 27). In the natural attitude, I do not infer from a house-appearance to a house, I simply see – a house. If I know something about cars (this example is Heidegger's), I do not hear 'a sound as of a motor' and infer to a car as its probable cause, I simply hear – 'a Mercedes'. In the natural attitude, my perceptual beliefs are beliefs about objects, not appearances. In ordinary perception, the appearances of things are, as it were, transparent, so that all one sees is the object. Phenomenology, by contrast, seeks to attend to the appearances of objects, to the 'phenomena' – from which phenomenology takes its name. This is because the phenomenologist's interest is focussed, not on *what* we perceive, but rather on *how* we do it.

Husserl's method of overcoming the natural attitude, which he calls, variously, 'epoché' ('suspension' of belief), 'bracketing', and 'the transcendental reduction' is, he makes clear, inspired by Descartes' method of doubt (Ideas I 30–33, CS 155). In his *Meditations on First Philosophy*, Descartes wishes to arrive at absolutely certain beliefs. And since he cannot know for certain that he is awake rather than asleep, he decides that his belief in a world of objects existing independently of his consciousness is not certain, and must be set aside pending further investigation. What he is left with are his thoughts and experiences, his *cogitationes*. Even if he is dreaming (or fooled by an evil god) he still has his *cogitationes*. In a similar manner, the phenomenologist must 'suspend' or 'bracket' his belief in an external world, not in order to *reject* beliefs that fall short of absolute certainty, but rather to isolate the phenomena out of which consciousness of objects is generated. In the natural attitude, we have seen, an independently existing world of objects is 'pregiven' (CS 151), taken for granted. But if I can suspend, 'put out of action' (Ideas I 31), the positing of such a world, then I can attend to *what it is* that I interpret as an independently existing object. Matheson Russell explains the point by means of a partial analogy. If I am paranoid then it is 'pregiven' that my boss is my enemy. But if I am cured, if I can put my paranoia 'out of action', then I can attend to what it is that I have been interpreting as an enemy.[4]

Husserl identifies another difference between the natural and the phenomenological attitude. In the natural attitude, one's stance to the world is engaged, 'interested': entities show up in relation to one's practical desires and goals. If we perform the phenomenological epoché, by contrast, we become 'disinterested spectators' (CS 157). This is necessary, presumably, because it is the demands of practical existence that generate the natural attitude. Creatures disposed to Cartesian doubt, to suspend their belief in an independent world, have (to borrow W. V. Quine's words) the pathetic but praiseworthy habit of dying out before reproducing their kind. The suspension of interest is thus a precondition of our being able to turn our attention from 'world' to 'world consciousness' (CS 151). (Notice that the identification of the phenomenological attitude with 'disinterestedness' – for Kant, Schopenhauer and subsequent thinkers, the defining mark of the 'aesthetic' attitude – points to the already-noted similarity between philosophical and artistic phenomenology.)

The results of phenomenology

As noted, the inspiration behind the phenomenological reduction is Descartes' method of doubt. While acknowledging his debt, however, Husserl observes that Descartes himself was not a good phenomenologist. For while his epoché quite properly led him to the 'ego' as the subject of the *cogitationes*, Descartes' ego, the ego he arrives at via the famous *cogito ergo sum*, is 'empty of content' (CS 155). Had Descartes performed the epoché properly, he would have discovered the rich transcendental structure of the 'pure' or 'transcendental' ego, the a priori structure through which the transformation of phenomenal into objectual experience occurs. What Descartes missed (but Kant saw) is that our experience of a world of external objects is an *achievement*, that it rests on a 'hidden mental accomplishment' (CS 94), a procedure that is disclosed by *fully* attending to what it is that survives the epoché. It is the task of phenomenology to uncover this normally hidden procedure, and thereby unravel the 'mystery' of cognition (CS 5).

Husserl conceived the task of developing such a transcendental 'psychology' (CS 5) as a science that would occupy a community of investigators over many generations, something that would be inter-generational in the manner of natural science. Since the focus of this chapter is on the 'existential' aspects of Husserl's philosophy, I shall confine myself to providing a brief sketch of the results he presents in the first volume of *Ideas*.

From Franz Brentano, his teacher in Vienna, Husserl takes over the idea that the defining feature of consciousness is 'intentionality': in consciousness, we are conscious *of* something (the ubiquitous tree, for example). Acts of consciousness are about, refer to, or 'intend' something beyond themselves. In fact, this is not universally true: a pain or an itch, while 'acts' of consciousness in Husserl's technical sense, are not about anything beyond themselves. It is, however, true that all, as Husserl calls them, 'cognitive' mental states, states that provide information about the outer world, intend something other than themselves, and it is these that are the focus of his attention.

That in virtue of which acts of consciousness are about something Husserl calls their 'noema' (plural 'noemata'), a concept to which I shall return in a moment. There are, however, two other features distinctive of mental acts. The 'noesis' of an act is the kind of act it is: to determine whether an act is one of remembering, hoping, perceiving, imagining, fearing, et cetera, is to determine its 'noesis'. The 'hyle' of an act is its sensory stuff (Ideas I section 85). Not all mental acts have a hyle – acts of mathematical thinking typically do not – but all perceptual acts do. Husserl criticizes the British empiricists for supposing that the immediately given in perceptual experience are sensory 'qualia', 'data' or, as Hume calls them, 'impressions'. That is simply bad phenomenology, an account generated by an implicitly 'objective', third-person, point of view, by a failure to properly adopt the first-person point of view (CS 85–6). (Science tells us that visual perception is the result of light waves generating retinal images, so *of course*, one thinks, the immediate objects of experience must be colour patches and the like.) If we properly adopt the first-person point of view, then it becomes clear that our immediate experiences are not of mere sounds or colour patches but have conceptual content: our immediate experience is not the experience of a red rectangle but rather of a brick house-front. Nonetheless, it is only because the perceptual act contains such 'hyletic data', that it can be the experience of the front of a house. Hume was not wrong to suppose that perceptual experiences *contain* 'sense impressions'; what he missed was that, in normal perception, such impressions always appear in a conceptually interpreted form.

The noema of an act of consciousness is not the same as the object the act intends. If I think of 'the victor of Jena' I intend the same object as when I think of 'the vanquished of Waterloo'. The object is the same – Napoleon – but the manner in which my thought intends the object (the aspect under which it is presented) is different (LI I Investigation I 12). Husserl calls the noema of an act its 'sense (*Sinn*)', which makes it clear that, with respect to consciousness, he is making essentially the same distinction as Gottlob Frege made (in 1892) with respect to language: the distinction between the 'sense (*Sinn*)' of a referring expression and its 'reference (*Bedeutung*)'. (Frege's famous pair of 'senses' are 'the morning star' and 'the evening star', both of which enable a sentence to refer to Venus.)[5] Husserl calls the referent of a mental act the 'core' or 'nucleus' of its noema (Ideas I 91), so, in Husserl's language, Frege's point is that different noema can have the same 'core'.

There are further complexities in Husserl's conception of the noema. As with Hume, the heart of his investigation of the 'mystery' of consciousness is the manner in which different perceptual acts within the stream of consciousness pick out the same object, for it is at this point that consciousness transcends itself, distinguishes between the realm of subjective experience and the realm of objects existing independently of those experiences. Stated briefly, Husserl explains this as follows. In my everyday experience of a given object there is always more to my understanding of that object than is presented in the experience. What I see is the front of a house, but I know – or rather anticipate – that if I alter my perspectives on the object, I will see a side and then a back. The indefinitely large set of implicit assumptions (Ideas I 149) I make as part of a perceptual act constitutes, says Husserl, a 'horizon' (CS 158), a horizon that is contained in the act's noema and determines the range of possible future experiences – 'adumbrations' – of the object in question. Normally, of course, future experiences are consonant with the horizon in question, 'legitimate' the perceptual belief I form on the basis of the perception. But occasionally they 'correct' that belief (PRS 258). Walking into the waxworks museum I see a charming woman on the stairs. Approaching closer, 'she' turns out to be a waxwork figure. My initial perceptual belief 'explodes' and is replaced by a very different one (LI II Investigation 5 27).

There is, of course, a great deal more to the perception of objects than ensuring that visual experiences conform to a given horizon, a great deal more – in the language Husserl takes over from Kant – 'synthesising' that occurs (CS 157–8): visual experiences have to be correlated with auditory, tactile and especially kinaesthetic sensations: it is only relative to my sensations of movement that I conclude that my perspective on a house has changed, so that my current perception of the side of a house is an entirely appropriate 'adumbration' of my former experience of the front of a house (CS 161–4). Husserl's investigation of these modes of synthesis is impressively microscopic, revealing many things that are normally 'anonymous' (CS 111): overlooked not just by the natural attitude but also by philosophers, philosophers such as Descartes. I shall, however, follow these investigations no further.

The lifeworld

The noema which endows us with the capacity to perceive a particular object is contained within a vast range of noemata which, as adult members of a particular culture, we all have at our command. But these noemata are not, of course, independent of each other. Rather, they belong together so as to constitute a systematic whole which – borrowing the term from Georg Simmel – Husserl calls 'the lifeworld'.

The lifeworld is the 'horizon' (CS 159–60) through which reality is made intelligible in daily life. It is the horizon within which things show up as common sense objects, and is contrasted with the 'science world', in which things show up as quarks and black holes. (Wilfrid Sellars, who wrote his master's thesis on Husserl, reproduces something [but not everything] of Husserl's contrast by contrasting the 'manifest image' with the 'scientific image').[6] Thus the horizon belonging to an individual noema is a horizon within a horizon: although it is not normally an object of explicit conscious-ness, 'implied in a particular perception of [a]… thing is a whole "horizon" of non-active and yet co-functioning manners of appearance' (CS 159).

The lifeworld consists in 'the most general features of waking life' (CS 143). It is something that is 'always already there' for us (CS 142). Arriving at adult-hood, we find ourselves already enculturated into a conceptual – 'noematic' – framework, so that all our everyday experience is experienced through the framework of the lifeworld. In terms of the earlier terminology, all normal experience occurs within the 'natural attitude'.

Lifeworld experience is based on sense perception. Everything that shows up in the lifeworld as a 'concrete thing' has, Husserl claims, a bodily aspect (CS 106). A further important feature is that the lifeworld is, in a certain sense, egocentric. All locating of objects within it is relative to one's own position in it, to an 'ego pole' (CS 170–2). Wittgenstein expresses this point – one which he learnt from his study of Schopenhauer – by saying that '[I] am the centre of the world'.[7] All locating of objects in the space of the lifeworld is ultimately indexical, ultimately relative to a 'here' that is determined by my own bodily location, and all locating of objects in time in time relative to a 'now'.

Of course, not all of the entities I experience in the lifeworld are *mere* bodies. It would be closer to the truth to say that none are. For, as already noted, the world of practical life is a world that shows up in terms of our practical 'interests' (CS 142–7).[8] As we shall see Heidegger putting the point, entities normally show up as 'ready-to-hand' rather than 'present-at-hand'. Things show up as 'roads' rather than 'strips of concrete', as 'swimming pools' rather than 'bodies of water'. Of course, not merely practical interests, but also non-prudential values determine the way things present themselves. In the lifeworld, things show up not merely as 'useful', 'attractive' and 'dangerous', but also as 'wicked', 'generous', 'beautiful' and 'sublime'.

A further reason things in the lifeworld do not show up as *mere* bodies is that some of them have 'psychic' and other kinds of 'spiritual qualities' (CS 106). Human and non-human animals (Husserl explicitly includes the animals in this remark) one immediately experiences through 'empathy' as, like one-self, centres of consciousness (Ideas II 12, 46). Other entities have 'cultural' qualities, are 'cultural objects' (CS 106), 'products of the spirit' (CS 297). Under such products Husserl includes not merely the products of art and science, but also such entities as 'the European spirit', 'community spirit', and 'the will of a people' (CS 294).

One further, point about Husserl's use of the term 'lifeworld'. He speaks of both lifeworld*s* and of *the* lifeworld. He speaks, for instance, of 'the European' lifeworld, the world that can be accessed through – and only through – European languages (CS 209–10). Lifeworlds are, then, as multiple and as diverse as there are different cultures. But there is also *the* lifeworld, a universal, transcultural framework that is invariant thorough all particular lifeworlds. This is 'a priori' in the sense that 'no conceivable human being, no matter how different we imagine him to be, could ever experience a world in manners of givenness that differ from … [what] we have delineated in general terms' (CS 165) as the lifeworld. *The* lifeworld – this will turn out to be crucial to the overall argument of *The Crisis of the European Sciences* – is partially defini-tive of what it is to be a human being. It belongs, in Husserl's language of 'essences', to the human essence.

Why is phenomenology important?

What motivates Husserl's philosophical project? What does he take to be the importance of transcendental phenomenology?

One answer might be that phenomenology is a new science and that, as a science, as a contribution to the storehouse of knowledge, it needs no further justification. In his lecture 'The Crisis of European Humanity', Husserl defends the Aristotelian view that a life devoted to pure theory is the highest form of life there is (see pp. 106–7 below). Speaking in this vein, and pointing to Kant's, in his view, inadequate explanation of the genesis of objective from subjective experience, he might say that arriving at a correct and comprehen-sive account of that matter is a fully justifying end in itself. And he might expand on this claim by pointing to the utility of phenomenology in clearing away a lot of bad philosophy – Hume's 'sensationalist' account of the objects of immediate perception and Descartes' account of the 'ego', for instance.

Were Husserl to confine his self-justification to the above defence, he would, of course, type-cast himself as Horkheimer's 'traditional theorist', as someone whose business is to 'understand' the world and leaves the task of 'changing' it to others, or, at least, to himself as citizen rather than as scientist (pp. 22–3 above). In fact, however, Husserl is not content to rest his self-justification on the this defence. Even in his earlier works, he is sensitive to, and concerned to rebut, the charge that his painstakingly fine-grained, jargon-ridden philosophy amounts, in the end, to nothing more than logic-chopping 'scholasticism' (PRS 255, 263). In his final work, the *Crisis*, he returns to this task (spurred on, almost certainly, by the need to show that Heidegger had no monopoly on existential urgency). An untranslated introductory passage indicates that the overriding purpose of the work is to rebut the charge of irrelevance to life, to show that phenomenological philosophy really does have useful things to say to those who correctly see that the world is in need of radical change.[9] Specifically, what he wishes to argue is that there is a crisis in 'European' (Western) civilization to which his philosophy provides the basis of a resolution.

The 'crisis of humanity' and the 'crisis of science'

Husserl spends little time defending the claim that Western civilization is in crisis. In the wake of the First World War, the idea of a crisis was, as he observes, 'much discussed' (CS 269). 'Crisis' was in the air and in the titles of books. Karl Joël's *The Philosophical Crisis of the Present* appeared in 1914, and Arthur Liebert's *The Spiritual Crisis of the Present Age* in 1927. Spengler's *The Decline of the West* appeared in 1918, and Weber's 'Science as a Vocation' – a lecture which, we saw, pictures Western civilization as in quite possibly terminal crisis – was delivered in 1917.

The 'Crisis of European Humanity', as the title of Husserl's 1935 Vienna lecture[10] puts it, is, he explains, a crisis concerning 'meaning', 'values', 'norms'. As early as 1887, Nietzsche had identified nihilism – 'the highest values devalue themselves' (p. 29 above) – as the condition of modern Western society. And so, as Husserl puts it, the question that modern humanity finds 'most pressing' is that of 'the meaning or meaninglessness of the whole of ... human existence' (CS 6). For Nietzsche, it is only the 'highest' values that are in trouble, whereas Husserl's turn of phrase might sometimes seem to suggest that Western humanity has become devoid of values completely, has become exclusively 'fact minded' (CS 6, PRS 141). But that, of course, makes no sense since, as already noted, the lifeworld, any lifeworld, is *permeated* with values that are determined by our practical interests. What, however, is missing, according to both Nietzsche and Husserl, are 'norms of absolute validation', that is, moral as opposed to prudential norms,[11] moral norms that are universally valid. As long as such norms were not 'ridiculed by scepticism' the only question was 'how to satisfy them in practice'. Now, however, when 'every norm is controverted ... and robbed of its ideal validity' all we are left is a clash of 'worldviews' (PRS 140–1). This appears to be a direct reference to Weber: recall that, for Weber, ethical systems are ultimately grounded in 'worldviews', and the confusion and disharmony of modernity consists in the clash of irreconcilable worldviews. It follows that Husserl's 'crisis of humanity'[12] is essentially the same as Weber's ethical 'polytheism' (p. 12 above).

What is the cause of the crisis? According to Husserl's diagnosis, the cause lies in natural science: not natural science itself, but rather a prevalent treatment of the results of modern physics 'as philosophy' (CS 69). It is this 'crisis of the sciences' – more accurately, a crisis in the interpretation of the sciences – that is the cause of the 'crisis of humanity'.

During the nineteenth century, Husserl observes, the position of the natural sciences in social consciousness changed. By the middle of the century the 'prosperity' (CS 6) brought by science-generated technology led to an enormous increase in the prestige of the natural sciences. (Husserl has in mind here such things as the invention of railways, the telegraph, and electric lighting. The fact that he uses the English word 'prosperity' indicates that Anglo-Saxon industrialization is at the front of his mind.) The result of this awesome increase in technological power was the transformation of, in particular, physics, into a worldview, a worldview which Husserl refers to, variously, as 'naturalism', 'objectivism', and 'positivism', and which I shall usually call 'scientism': the epistemological view that our only access to knowledge is through the natural-scientific method, together with its ontological consequence that nothing can be said to exist save the entities recognized as existing by natural science. An important fact about the natural sciences – and the social sciences, too, which ape the natural sciences in this regard – is that they are 'value free': among the entities recognized as existing by science, values (as distinct from valuings) are not to be found. Husserl's claim, as I shall shortly discuss, is that it is the exclusion of values from the realm of the objectively real that results in the onset of nihilism, of ethical polytheism.

Combating irrationalism

Given the dominion of the value-free understanding of science, the universal assumption that science has nothing to say about the 'questions that are decisive for a [meaning-seeking] … humanity', the youth, Husserl observes, have developed a deep hostility to science. 'In our vital need', young people are now convinced, 'science has nothing to say to us' (CS 6). And so, insofar as they turn to philosophy to address those 'vital needs', they are turning to philosophy that takes the form of 'scepticism, irrationalism, and mysticism' (CS 3). This, however, is mere pseudo-philosophy, for genuine philosophy is essentially rationalism, is essentially science, indeed 'rigorous science'.

In the *Crisis*, these remarks are fairly obviously directed against the so-called 'existentialism' of *Being and Time*. Their burden is that Heidegger's student disciples (Arendt and Gadamer, for example), who are hailing him as the 'hidden king' who will rescue German philosophy from triviality and German culture from nihilism (pp. 118, 190 below), are following a false prophet. The insistence that genuine philosophy can only be a science and that all attempts to take it in a non-scientific direction are perversions of the discipline, is not, however, the product of the bitter end of Husserl's career. It reaches, rather, at least as far back as 1910–11's 'Philosophy as a Rigorous Science'. Here Husserl attacks, not 'existentialism' as such, but rather what he calls the newly emerged 'worldview philosophy' (PRS 252 et passim).

'Worldview (*Weltanschauung*)' is a word that was first coined and was much in vogue in early twentieth-century Germany and led to a philosophical movement that culminated in Jaspers' *Psychology of Worldviews* of 1919. Among 'worldview philosophers' Husserl probably has Heinrich Rickert in mind, and possibly Max Weber, who holds, to repeat, that competing ethical systems are grounded in different worldviews between which reason is incapable of adjudicating. The original 'worldview philosopher' was, however, Kierkegaard, who held that in order to avoid 'despair' we must – with Abraham, Kierkegaard's 'knight of faith' – make the 'leap' beyond reason and into the theistic worldview.[13]

As already remarked, Husserl is sensitive to the charge that his philosophy is irrelevant to the 'vital needs' of the times, to the charge that while Heidegger (and the worldviewists) are telling us important things about *Dasein* (being-here) (CS 2) and *Existenz* (CS 298), his own version of phenomenology has nothing to say. (That he uses Heidegger's characteristic terminology confirms that, in the *Crisis*, Heidegger is the 'irrationalist' par excellence.) To this – to the 'existentialism'-enamoured youth – he has three things to say. First, that to turn to 'irrationalism' is a dereliction of duty, a betrayal of the 'eternal ideal' of humanity that is embodied in the spiritual history of the West. We must, that is, do science – and, in particular, practise philosophy as 'rigorous science' – whatever the cost. Second, that it is not science itself, but rather a perversion of the ideal of rigorous science, that has led to the current crisis of humanity, a perversion consisting in the wrong turning taken by the scientific project at the beginning of the modern period. And third, that only science itself, science ultimately grounded in transcendental phenomenology, can correct this wrong turning, can overcome the crisis in the sciences and thereby the crisis of humanity. If Europe is to escape the 'barbarity' that now threatens in the form of philosophical and political irrationalism, he concludes the Vienna lecture, there must be a 'rebirth of Europe from the spirit of philosophy through a heroism of reason that overcomes naturalism [scientism] once and for all' (CS 299). (This talk of 'rebirth' may allude to the youthful Nietzsche's – very different – call for a 'rebirth of Greek tragedy' out of the 'spirit of [Richard Wagner's] music').

The 'telos' of Western history

There is, claims Husserl, a teleology, a telos, to Western history that is determined by the 'entelechy' first laid down by the philosophers in seventh- and sixth-century Greece: by the philosophers, because the spiritual life of the Greeks was determined by philosophy, by philosophy practised as 'universal philosophy', that is, universal 'science' (CS 12, 15).[14]

What is universal science? What, first of all, is 'science'? Taking note of the fact that different cultures had conflicting beliefs concerning both facts and values, the Greek philosophers, observes Husserl, made the distinction between *doxa* (opinion) and *episteme* (knowledge) (CS 285). Their project was the acquisition of 'universal', culture-independent, knowledge. Science, that is to say, aims at truth rather than opinion. This entails, evidently, the abandonment of tradition as a source of knowledge (CS 288), indeed the abandonment of all 'prejudices', all pre-judgments (*Vor-urteile*) (CS 72 et passim). To practise science is to accept as true only that which is given to prejudice-free reason. Husserl accepts, as we are about to see, that, in the modern age, something has gone seriously awry within the Western scientific tradition, so that by the time we reach the so-called 'Age of Enlightenment' we do indeed confront, as the 'irrationalists' claim, a 'misguided rationalism' (CS 290). Nonetheless 'enlightenment' (with a small 'e'), 'enlightenment' as a mode of thought rather than an historical period, is both the essence of Greek science and the Western telos.

Classical Greece, claims Husserl, represented a new form of humanity, a new and unique form of individual and communal life. Other cultures, India and China, for instance, had religious-mythical philosophies, but such 'philosophies' were always geared to pleasing gods and disabling demons – like all worldview 'philosophies', geared to practical needs rather than universal truth. What was unique to the Greeks was the 'theoretical attitude', a form of life dedicated simply to truth, to truth as the highest value. The life of *theoria* took no account of practical interests, was based on pure, 'disinterested spectatorship', on 'wonder (*thaumazein*)', that is, 'curiosity' (CS 285).[15] (Husserl adds, with reference to his own practice of *theoria*, that although it is *unmotivated* by human interests it should not be thought to be *irrelevant* to such interests. For if, as we will see him arguing to be the case, there are absolute, universal truths in the realm of values as well as of facts, truths that can be uncovered by the *theoria* that is phenomenology, then phenomenological science holds the promise of overcoming the crisis of humanity [PRS 287], of overcoming Weber's value 'polytheism'.)

The ethical ideal of science is, then, the exercise of prejudice-free reason in the pursuit of truth, truth whose acceptance is binding on all rational beings (CS 7–10). 'Universal science', philosophy as it was conceived by the Pre-Socratics and then by Plato and Aristotle, is the exercise of this ideal in the pursuit of *comprehensive* truth – of a 'synoptic vision' (in Wilfrid Sellars' phrase), a science that incorporates and integrates the results of all the individual sciences, both natural and human.

This, then, is the 'original founding', the *Urstiftung*, of the spiritual life of Europe, of Western culture. As soon as we become conscious of this founding act, claims Husserl, it becomes normative for us, since every *Urstiftung* is also an *Endstiftung*, the 'founding of a final goal', of a 'telos' (CS 72). (As joining a club commits one to observe its founding rules, Husserl reasons, so to locate oneself in the spiritual life of the West commits one to observing its founding norms.) Of course, the completion of universal science, the achievement of an 'omniscience' (CS 65) that will solve 'all possible problems' (CS 9), will not happen overnight. But as a (quasi-Hegelian) goal, set in the perhaps infinitely distant future (CS 65), contributing to its progressive realization is an ethical requirement on all of us; all of us, at least, who are 'less exhausted' by the cares of practical life (CS 288).

The wrong turning taken by Western science

The 'rebirth' of the spirit of Greece that was the Renaissance was also the rebirth of the ideal of a universal science, an ideal that inspired its natural scientists. In pursuit of this ideal, however, Western science took a wrong turn, a turn that began with Galileo and completed itself in the Age of Enlightenment.

For Nietzsche, it was Galileo's telescope, his Copernicus-confirming observations, that brought about the 'death of God', the death of the medieval worldview and the onset of nihilism. ('What were we doing when we unchained this earth from its sun? ... Where are we moving to? Away from all suns? Are we not continually falling? And backwards, sideways, forwards in all directions? Is there still an up and a down? ...')[16] Husserl, however, makes almost no mention of Galileo's observations. For him, what is decisive about Galileo is the 'mathematization of the world' (CS 66), of nature, the discovery of the power that physics acquires by translating itself into mathematics. Pursuing the ideal of *episteme* – as opposed to *doxa* – Galileo noted, says Husserl, that in the lifeworld, what is used to determine the 'objective' truth about something is measurement. Unfortunately, however, lifeworld objects are incapable of exact measurement. (A gardener measures the area of lawn to be reseeded, but because the lawn is only approximately rectangular, his calculation of the amount of seed needed is only approximately correct.) In the 'ideal' world of geometry, however, objects do have exact measurements. And so what Galileo postulated was that the 'true' world is made up of objects that resemble the objects of geometry in being capable of exact measurement. The advantage of this is that mathematical physics is capable of providing exact predictions, as opposed to the, at best, approximate predictions made on the basis of the general causal 'style' (CS 31) of objects in the lifeworld. Thus, whereas Plato thought of geometry in general as a 'pure' science dealing only with an 'ideal', supra-natural world, Galileo turned geometry, and mathematics in general, into 'applied' geometry (CS 28), a description of the objectively true character of the *natural* world. The trouble with this, however, is that so called 'sensible qualities' are not susceptible to exact measurement. It is true that qualities such as bumpiness and smoothness (and redness) are capable of rough measurement, but only rough: there is no possibility of increased precision. And so they are excluded from the scientific world-description (CS 34). (And, of course, there is the additional problem that the measurement of such qualities varies widely from subject to subject.)

What then happens is that our understanding of the world splits into two (CS 60). On the one hand, there is the world of mathematical physics, on the other, the world of sensible or, in the language of British empiricism, 'secondary', qualities. Husserl's important insight – one which escapes the British empiricists, who think of the distinction between 'primary' and 'secondary' qualities purely in perceptual terms – is that the category of 'secondary' qualities contains *everything* that is distinctively human, everything 'personal' in the sense of pertaining to persons. Not just colours, tastes and sounds, but all descriptions that presuppose aesthetic and moral values, norms of any kind, as well as all reference to spiritual entities such as the aforementioned 'community spirit' or the ideals of a nation (CS 294), are excluded from the world of Galilean science.

We know, however, that there is only one world, and this means that the split in our world understanding becomes intolerable. And so it is resolved in favour of physics. As early as Hobbes, physicalism becomes the order of the day. Reality *is* the completely determined world of physical bodies, some of which are 'psychophysical' in the sense that some events in the physical world (brain events) appear in subjective consciousness as colours, hopes, fears, value judgments, and so on. In reality, however, there is nothing that corresponds to their content. Lifeworld consciousness is reduced to a mere 'annex' of the physical (CS 294), a mere epiphenomenon. The objects and qualities it 'intends' have no being outside consciousness, for all that corresponds to them is a 'mathematical index' (CS 37). And so scientism comes into being – the world is the way mathematical physics say it is, and nothing besides – and, due to the prestige of natural science, gains ever-widening cultural acceptance.

The effect of this 'mathematization' of reality is the 'crisis of humanity'. The spread of positivism, of the scientistic worldview, produces 'scepticism' about values of all kinds. The values and norms of art, religion and morality turn out to be 'so much romanticism and mythology' (CS 294), and so lose their imperative force. (Scientism, of course, recognizes that statements like 'Incest is wrong' and 'One should love one's country' play an important role in human life. But since they cannot be true in the sense of corresponding to reality, positivism analyses them as truth-valueless expressions of emotion: 'Incest – yuk! Love of country – hurrah!') To the extent that we have been taken over by scientism, we live in a depersonalized and de-valued world.

But in such a world, of course, we cannot live a properly human life. Our 'vital need' for 'absolute values', for values that give meaning to the life of individuals and harmony to the life of the community, is denied. And so – the point at which this discussion started – thoughtful people are giving up on science.

Why is scientism mistaken?

The cause of the 'crisis of humanity' is, then, Husserl concludes, the cultural dominion of scientism: in Habermas' language, it is the 'colonization of the lifeworld' by – not 'system' – but rather the science world. Hence, to resolve that crisis, one must defeat scientism. Husserl offers various arguments against scientism, each intended to reveal a way in which it presupposes the reality of the lifeworld so that scientism contradicts itself in excluding the lifeworld from its ontology of the real. I shall discuss these criticisms under three headings.

First, scientism is a pragmatic self-contradiction. Scientism, we know, claims that the furniture of the 'true' world is completely itemized by physics. But the defender of scientism is also a 'teacher and practical reformer' (think Richard Dawkins or Daniel Dennett), 'filled with the aspiration to bring to light scientifically – thus in a way that binds every rational being – that which is genuinely truth'. Yet the content of scientism 'negates precisely what [its proponent] presupposes in his idealistic conduct'. The content of the 'sermon' contradicts the 'preaching', since, while the preaching presupposes the existence of objectively valid norms about what people should and should not believe, the content claims that there are no such norms, that objective reality is 'value free' (PRS 254–5). Science-admirers must thus retreat from scientism. On pain of (pragmatic) self-contradiction, they must concede the existence of entities other than those recognized by mathematical physics. Specifically, since norms belong to the lifeworld, the science admirer must recognize the reality of the lifeworld.

The positivist, however, has a ready reply to this argument. He can respond by saying that he presupposes nothing about what people *ought* to believe. His aim, rather, he may say, is merely to *cause* them to adopt scientism on the grounds that to exit the realm of superstition and folk wisdom will make them happier.

Second, if lifeworld claims are not true then neither are the claims of science. The verification of scientific hypotheses concerning postulated, unobservable entities depends on lifeworld observations of – as Husserl tendentiously puts it – 'the thing itself'. Such observations are our sole source of 'self-evidence'. It follows that if the positivist denies the truth of lifeworld claims he denies the truth of his own scientific claims and is again involved in self-contradiction (CS 127–8).

Once again, this seems to me an inadequate argument. From time immemorial, what has been required of science is that it should 'save the appearances'. What this means is not 'preserving the *truth* of lifeworld observations', but merely 'explaining why there *appear* to be lifeworld objects in given lifeworld states'. What confirms a scientific hypothesis is that things *appear* to be thus and so. The scientist can remain agnostic as to whether they are *really* thus and so.

Third, scientism mistakes a technique of calculation for an ontology. With Galileo and his successors there occurs, writes Husserl, the

> surreptitious substitution of the mathematically substructured world of idealities for the only real world, the one that is actually given through perception, that is ever experienced and experienceable – our everyday lifeworld.
>
> (CS 49)

What, however, naturalism forgets is the genesis of science's own theoretical terms through abstraction from, idealization of, lifeworld objects. (Thus atoms, for instance, stand to billiard balls as Euclidean rectangles stand to garden lawns.) And so it mistakes for 'true being' what is in fact merely a 'method'. It mistakes a 'technique' for improving prediction for an ontology. What naturalism forgets is that the lifeworld is the 'meaning-fundament' of science, that what science is really talking about – 'the only real world' that is available to be talked about – is the lifeworld (CS 48–51). Scientism, therefore, is false: far from the science world being the 'true' world it is, in fact, a fiction.

This amounts to an 'instrumentalist' philosophy of science, to the view that the unobserved entities of scientific theory are merely 'useful fictions': entities which facilitate calculation but which have no more real existence that does, say, 'the perfect market' or 'the rational consumer'. The issue between 'instrumentalism' and 'realism' is a major issue in the philosophy of science. Fortunately, however, we do not need to investigate it, here, since, in order to save the lifeworld, Husserl does not need to go to the instrumentalist extreme of claiming it to be the *only* real world. All he needs to establish is that the lifeworld is *a* real world, a claim that is compatible with allowing that the science world is *a* real world too.

Consider 'Water is H_2O'.[17] This suggests a view of the relation between science and the lifeworld that allows *both* modes of description to apply to reality, a view which holds that the lifeworld stuff one drinks is the very same stuff that scientists describe in terms of its chemical composition. This view can be expressed in terms of Husserl's own phenomenology: it is a matter of two different noemata picking out the same entity (pp. 99–100 above). This account of things (which has its origins in the conception of 'objectivity' put forward in Nietzsche's *Genealogy of Morals*)[18] is what Hubert Dreyfus has called 'plural realism'[19]: there is only one real world, but it is capable of true description in terms of multiple conceptual – noematic – schemes.

Scientism, it seems to me, cannot be decisively refuted. But given plural realism's irenic reconciliation between life and science, given that it allows full reality to the entities the scientist wants to claim to be real, it is hard to think of a reason (other than misanthropy or philosophical confusion) why anyone should want to affirm the unreality of the lifeworld. Scientism appears to be a doctrine without a valid purpose.

How does phenomenology 'solve' the 'crisis of humanity'?

The overarching purpose of Husserl's history and critique of the development of scientism is to rescue the lifeworld. However exactly he is interpreted – whether the lifeworld is *a* reality or the *only* reality – for Husserl, the lifeworld is undoubtedly real, ontologically inescapable. The question we need now to ask is how this securing of the lifeworld is intended to contribute to the

Crisis's central task of pointing to a way of overcoming the 'crisis of humanity', the rise of ethical polytheism.

As noted earlier (p. 102 above), Husserl uses 'lifeworld' sometimes to refer to culturally and historically specific lifeworld*s* and sometimes to refer to a structure that is common to them all, a structure that is partially definitive of what it is to be a human being. In Husserl's language, 'the' lifeworld belongs to the 'essence' of human being.

In part, this common structure is ontological. It is a world of entities in space and time – Ptolemaic rather than Copernican space,[20] Newtonian rather than Einsteinian time – entities which, nearly all of the time, show up in terms of the 'natural attitude', show up in terms of human interests, as roads rather than strips of concrete. Whatever their culture, for all human beings, things have to show up as food, shelter, routes of travel, and so on. (Heidegger's *Being and Time*, we shall see, explores this common structure in much greater detail.) Alongside these kinds of entities, however, the lifeworld also contains people, beings one immediately perceives through empathy (p. 102 above) as, like oneself, subjects of consciousness. Hence there is a fundamental distinction built into the lifeworld between mere things, on the one hand, and people, on the other.

This is an ontological distinction, but it is also an ethical one. A computer one can treat any way one likes. If it annoys one, one can smash it into small pieces. But not a person. If one does not understand this moral distinction one does not understand the ontological distinction either. Husserl observes that

> I am treating a human being as a mere thing ... I do not take him as a person related to the moral ... if I view him as mere matter ... [I view him] not as a member of a community founded on rights, but instead as ... without rights just like a mere thing.
>
> (Ideas II section 51)

People have rights, *mere* things do not. Effectively, therefore, Husserl's point is that, built into the lifeworld is Kant's second formulation of the 'categorical imperative', the principle that we should never treat human beings as 'mere means' but always as 'ends in themselves'. If one does not experience the force of this imperative one is ontologically blind, blind to the difference between people and things.

As David Woodruff Smith points out, in his fragmentary writings on ethics, Husserl actually criticizes Kant for expelling emotion from the 'groundwork' of morality. Ethics, for Husserl, is based on empathy, that is, compassion, so that the highest principle of morality is not the essentially negative imperative of respect but rather the positive, Christian injunction to love one's neighbour as oneself.[21] This principle belongs to the structure of experience that is common to *all* human beings. Hence, as long as we do not allow scientism to alienate us from this common structure – to undermine the lifeworld as the basis of decision and action – we have the basis of a universal morality, a 'monotheistic' rather than 'polytheistic' morality, a renewal of Weber's ethical 'godhead'.

By revealing this common structure, as well as what threatens to destroy it, phenomenological philosophy thus makes a vital contribution to alleviating the 'distress' of our times, to resolving the 'crisis of humanity'. The youth have thus no need to resort to irrationalism: philosophy as 'rigorous science' speaks to our existential needs.

* * *

One thing that emerges from the above discussion is that Habermas either never read the *Crisis*, or else failed to understand it. As we saw in Chapter 3, Habermas claims that Husserl's 'phenomenological conception' of the lifeworld is inadequate. Since for Husserl, he claims, the 'norms' of any lifeworld form a 'social a priori' specific to a particular culture, phenomenology cannot account for the way in which cultures should – and do – deal with the 'orientation crises' that arise when different cultures, different lifeworlds, come into funda-mental moral conflict (p. 52 above). This, as we can now see, misses Husserl's main point: transcending all culturally specific lifeworlds is *the* lifeworld together with the norms embedded in it, norms which are common to all cultures. As Habermas conceives them, therefore, 'orientation crises' never occur. Moral disagreement concerns only the *application* of a universal morality and is, therefore, in principle resolvable through the accumulation of factual information. The question remains, however, as to whether a universal morality really can be grounded in the ontology of the lifeworld.

Can the ontology of the lifeworld really ground a universal morality?

Husserl's grounding of the idea of an intersubjective ethics in an intersubjective world is an important and influential idea. One can see its development in the work of his one-time student, Immanuel Levinas: Levinas' celebrated discus-sion of 'the face' that looks at me saying 'Do not kill me', a face which grounds my 'infinite responsibility' to 'the Other',[22] looks to be a (somewhat hyperbolic) repetition of Husserl's grounding of ethics in the lifeworld experience of immediate empathy. But has Husserl *really* provided a solution to the 'crisis of humanity'? Does phenomenology really disclose the basis of a universal ethics that has the capacity to overcome value polytheism?

One worry lies in the thought that empathy is actually a culturally specific phenomenon. 'Empathy', *Einfühlung*, a term coined in the nineteenth century by the German Romantics, is a matter of 'feeling oneself into' the situation of the other, of inhabiting the other's 'shoes'. It consists in an imaginative change of identity, which is what distinguishes it from the notion of 'sympathy', deployed by eighteenth-century 'sentimentalists' such as David Hume. Smith observes that Husserl's notion of empathy is really an adoption of Wilhelm Dilthey's notion of *Verstehen*, 'understanding'.[23] For Dilthey, empathetic understanding constitutes the 'historical sense', a sense which, if cultivated by a talented historian, allows direct insight into the motivation of an historical actor. As we shall see in Chapter 7, however, Hans-Georg Gadamer mounts a powerful argument that the idea that the historian, no matter how sensitive, can set aside all of the 'pre-judgments' of his own time and culture is mistaken, that Dilthey's 'understanding' is inevitably projection, so that different historians will make different projections. If this argument is correct, then the same will be true of Husserl's 'empathy': the inhabitants of different lifeworlds will arrive at different notions of what it is, in a given situation, to treat someone with respect and love, and so value polytheism will remain.

Another worry concerning Husserl's grounding of ethics in empathy is the charge of 'humanism', in the pejorative sense coined in Heidegger's 'Letter on Humanism'. Since, one might suppose, the possibility of empathetic compassion is confined to other human beings, ethical constraints, for Husserl as for Kant, are confined to one's behaviour towards other *human* beings. As Kant's injunction to treat humanity always as an end, never merely as a means seems to allow and even encourage the treatment of non-human nature as a mere means to human ends, so too, one might think, Husserl's grounding of ethics in the distinction between persons and things is an ethics of human chauvinism. What is missing in Husserl, one might conclude, is the possibility of grounding an environmental ethics, a particularly severe deficiency in the current age.

In one important respect, this criticism is unwarranted. For, somewhat surprisingly, Husserl insists, at length, that animals are, like humans, 'constituted' in empathy as subjects of feeling and cognition (Ideas II especially 45–6). Yet it remains unclear how an ethics based on empathy can be extended to non-sentient nature. Even if Husserl is not a *human* chauvinist, it is unclear how he could avoid the charge of being, as one might put it, a 'sentience chauvinist'.

Is Husserl's diagnosis of the 'crisis of humanity' correct?

Our alienation from values, from universal and commanding values, is, Husserl argues, due to the rise of a worldview according to which nothing exists save material particles in mathematical motion. To the extent that I am captured – 'colonized' – by this view, my world becomes a world of things rather than persons, and this strips it of values and ethical norms.

One objection to this diagnosis lies in the fact that most of us know relatively little about modern physics. And even if we do, we lock it away into a compartment of the mind disconnected from our everyday (in Heidegger's language) being-in-the-world. Even if we 'know' that, in reality, nothing is coloured, we nonetheless stop, without hesitation, when the traffic lights turns red. As Husserl himself shows us, we live not in the science world, but in the lifeworld. Since a similar analysis of lifeworld alienation is provided by Husserl's sometime student Hannah Arendt, I shall return to this issue in Chapter 8.

A further objection to Husserl's diagnosis is that there are other – more plausible – explanations of our alienation from the values and norms of the lifeworld. These explanations speak, not the replacement of the lifeworld by the science world – they acknowledge that we continue to live in a world of solid objects that have colours and textures – but rather of its degradation, its being denuded of ethical value. One such explanation is the neo-Marxist analysis offered by Horkheimer and Adorno: the degradation of lifeworld norms is indeed due to the reduction of people to things, to 'reification', but the things in question are those, not of fundamental physics, but of industrial capitalism, 'commodities'. And, as we shall see in Chapter 9, a related but different account is offered by the later Heidegger: at the most fundamental level, the things to which humans and other beings are being reduced are the things, neither of physics nor of industrial capitalism, but of technological functionality, 'resources'.

Notes

1 Smith (2013) 5.
2 Smith (2013) 180–1.
3 Woolf (2003) 5.
4 Russell (2006) 61: example modified.
5 See 'On Sense and Reference' in Frege (1980) 36–56.
6 See Sellars (1963) 6.
7 Wittgenstein (1969) 80.
8 This is again a point first clearly articulated by Schopenhauer. In many ways it is Schopenhauer rather than Husserl (or Hegel) who deserves to be called the first phenomenologist. Both Husserl and Heidegger ignore him completely, undoubtedly on account of his extremely rude remarks about 'professors of philosophy': Schopenhauer belonged to an age when it was still possible to, as he put it, live *for* rather than *from* philosophy, and he despised those who did the latter (see Young [2005] 46–7).
9 Moran (2012) 40–1.
10 'Philosophy and the Crisis of European Humanity', incorporated into CS as an appendix (269–99).
11 And as opposed, too, to what might be called 'ontological norms', norms that define the being of lifeworld entities (see p. 139 below).
12 A somewhat embarrassing line of thought pursued by Husserl argues that since 'man is a rational animal', and since human reason is properly developed only in the West, the crisis of Western humanity is in fact a crisis of humanity as such. While India and China represent mere biological species of homo sapiens, mere 'anthropological types', European humanity bears within itself the 'absolute idea' of humanity as such (CS 16). Husserl was not merely the victim of racist ideology.
13 Although this is the most explicit version of what Husserl deplores as the height of 'irrationalism', it might actually be described as a different kind of rationalism, as the elevation of instrumental over evidential rationality: according to worldview philosophers such as Kierkegaard and Pascal, we should choose our foundational beliefs – and hence our 'highest values' – not on the basis of evidence for their truth but rather according to the effects of those beliefs on our wellbeing.
14 Without wishing to interrupt the flow of Husserl's argument (hence a mere note), I cannot refrain from observing that his account of the philosophers as the dominant influence on the spiritual life

of the Greeks is certainly false (not to say self-serving). Conspicuously, Husserl excludes the eighth century from the history of Greece, thus cutting out Homer – known, as Plato tells us, as 'the educator of Greece'. And he excludes, too, the fifth century, and hence the great tragedians, who certainly had a far more profound influence of Greek life than the philosophers, given that virtually all citizens attended the tragic festivals. If we take seriously the idea that the 'telos' of the West was established within the spiritual life of Greece, then that telos must turn out to be poetry. Famously, Plato excludes the poets from the ideal Greek state. Similarly motivated, Husserl excludes them from the actual Greek state.

15 Husserl claims *thaumazein* is 'obviously a variant of curiosity' (CS 285). This deflation of the word is no doubt motivated by the desire not to give aid and comfort to those who confuse philosophy with mysticism. In Chapter 9 we will see the later Heidegger providing a very different account of wonder.

16 Nietzsche (2001) section 125.

17 I take this example from Russell (2006) 189. Russell takes the view I am about to outline as Husserl's actual view. I think this is implausible given the claim that the lifeworld is the 'only real world'. But I agree that it is the view Husserl ought to hold.

18 Nietzsche (1994) Essay III section 12.

19 Dreyfus (1991) 277–80.

20 A fragmentary discussion of 1934 is entitled 'The Earth Does not Move' (Moran [2012] 94).

21 Smith (2013) 356–61.

22 See Levinas (1969).

23 Smith (2013) 156.

6 Early Heidegger
Existential phenomenology

Martin Heidegger was born in 1889 into a peasant family in Messkirch, a small town in the Black Forest region of southwest Germany. Save for annual visits to Provence in the 1950s and 1960s, and two visits to Greece, he spent almost his entire life in the region of his birth. In 1928 he was appointed Husserl's successor to the chair of philosophy at the University of Freiburg. Five years later he joined the Nazi Party, and became rector of the university, a position from which, however, he resigned a year later. After the war, the French occupying authorities imposed on him a four-year teaching ban, and he never in fact held a permanent university position again. He died in 1976, and was buried in the graveyard of the Catholic church in Messkirch where his father had been sexton and where he had been baptized.

Two issues are central to coming to terms with Heidegger's philosophy. First, the political question: Was his involvement with Nazism philosophically motivated? If one becomes convinced by some or all of his philosophy will one find oneself committed to fascism? And second, the question of 'the turning': Was there really, as Heidegger himself appears to claim, a radical 'turning' or 'reversal' in his thinking during the 1930s that allows one to speak of two philosophies so divergent that they might almost have been written by two different people?

As the titles of this chapter and Chapter 9 make clear, my own conviction – contrary to a recent trend in Heidegger-research – is that there certainly was a reversal, a claim I shall defend at the beginning of Chapter 9. As to the political question, the only possible way of answering it satisfactorily requires that one first gain a grasp of what Heidegger's philosophy *is* – or, if I am right, what his philosophies *are*. To facilitate such a grasp is the aim of my two Heidegger chapters. By the conclusion of the second, the answer to the political question should, I think, become clear.

Being and Time: the project

Being and Time (1927) is the masterwork of Heidegger's early period,[1] the only 'big book' in the style of the German philosophical tradition that he wrote for publication. It begins with an Introduction which tells us what the project is, as well as the structure of the work in which the project is to be accomplished. Unlike most introductions, *Being and Time*'s appears to have been written before the text it was intended to introduce. This is strongly suggested by the fact that of the two 'Parts' it tells us the text will comprise, each containing three 'divisions', the second Part was never written at all, and, of the first, only two divisions were ever completed. For all of its 437 pages, *Being and Time*, as we have it, is unfinished, the mere torso of the work projected in the Introduction. As I shall discuss at the beginning of Chapter 9, the question of why it was left unfinished – was in fact abandoned – is intimately connected with the question of the 'turning'.

The project, the Introduction tells us, is to answer 'the question of the meaning of being (*die Frage nach dem Sinn von Sein* or, frequently, *nach dem Sinn des Seins*)'. What does it mean for something to be? While this, says Heidegger, was the question that 'provided the stimulus for the researches of Plato and Aristotle' (BT 2),[2] a question they found difficult and disturbing, modern philosophy dismisses it as uninteresting, or as impossible to answer on the grounds that, as the highest genus, 'being' cannot be defined by genus and species. Since the ancients, in fact, the question has been 'forgotten' by philosophy (BT 2, 21). But in reality, claims Heidegger, it is 'the fundamental question of philosophy' (BT 27), indeed of the sciences in general. Each of the 'positive sciences', that is, investigates a particular region of being – 'nature, space, life, … language, and so on' (BT 9) – but, to set their 'ontic'[3] investigations on a firm foundation, to really know what they are talking about, they need an ontology of their own particular science. Kant, for example, in his 'working out of what belongs to any nature whatsoever' provided a trans-cendental framework, an ontology, of the 'area of "being" called nature'. Yet all these regional ontologies remain 'blind and a turning aside (*Vekehrung*) from their innermost aim' unless they have clarified the 'meaning of being' in general (BT 10–11). This is Heidegger's project, a project he calls *'fundamental ontology'*.

Being (*Sein*), says Heidegger, is that which 'determines beings (*Seiend*) as beings'. Crucially, being is not a being (BT 6). It 'transcends' entities; it is, in the language of medieval philosophy, a *transcendens* (BT 14). The clue to understanding this is the above reference to Kant. As Kant sought to reveal the 'transcendental', 'a priori' structure of nature, the structure which any object whatsoever must satisfy to count as a 'natural' object, so fundamental ontology wishes to reveal the 'a priori' (BT 11) structure that any being whatsoever must satisfy in order to count as a being. Being is thus the 'structure' that 'lies beyond every entity and every possible character which a being may possess', is, in fact, *the* transcendens, *'the transcendens pure and simple'* (BT 38).

Being and Time's project is thus importantly similar to Kant's, is an exercise in 'transcendental' philosophy. This makes it appear somewhat specialized, something that is hardly a matter of general interest. Heidegger suggests that without being able to say what 'material being' means, without an ontology of material nature, and hence without a 'fundamental ontology' to tell them what 'being' means, scientists do not really know what they are talking about. But as later Heidegger observes with respect to quantum mechanics, scientists are typically unruffled by 'not knowing what they mean'. As long as their equations produce predictive success they are generally quite happy. So it seems that, really, the 'question of being (*Seinsfrage*)' – as Heidegger often, but perhaps incautiously, abbreviates 'the question of the meaning of being' – is of interest only to philosophers. Even here, however, his claim that it is 'the fundamental question of philosophy' seems odd given that there is no etymological connection between 'being' and 'philosophy'. Etymologically, of course, 'philosophy' means 'love of wisdom', a 'wisdom' that has been understood from antiquity to mean the ability to know – and live – 'the good life'. Not 'being' but rather 'the good' seems to be the true object of philosophy. The question of being seems, in short, to be something that would be of interest only to philosophers with a specialist interest in ontology.

This makes it surprising that the lectures of the 1920s which eventually culminated in *Being and Time* generated the excitement they did (precisely the excitement Weber tells his students they should *not* expect from a professor [pp. 22–3 above]). Hans-Georg Gadamer, for example, reports that he and his fellow students, seeking a way out of the spiritual and political chaos of the Weimar years that followed the German defeat in the First World War, had no time for the 'bloodless academic philosophizing' of the Neo-Kantians that dominated the German university curriculum, so that the entirely different character, the urgency, intensity, and life-transforming implications, of Heidegger's lectures 'work[ed] on us like a magic spell' (PG 8–9). And another student, Hannah Arendt, reports that the spell was so intense as to cause underground rumours to spread throughout Germany of a renaissance of 'passionate philosophy' in the hands of a 'hidden king'.[4] (Arendt alludes here to the ancient myth that, in the hour of greatest need, the Emperor and King Friedrich Barbarossa will emerge from his cave to save the German nation.) But how, one wants to ask, could a philosophy devoted 'the question of being' be other than dry and 'bloodless'?[5] How, indeed, given its Kantian provenance, could it really set Heidegger apart from the Neo-Kantians?

What explains the excitement generated by *Being and Time* is the somewhat strange method Heidegger adopts to answer his 'question of being'. With respect to every genuine question, he observes we can distinguish between what we wish to know by way of an answer (the *Erfragte*) and what we 'interrogate' in order to obtain that answer (the *Befragte*). What fundamental ontology wishes to know, clearly, is 'the meaning of being', but what Heidegger chooses to interrogate is *we ourselves*, or, as he calls us, 'Dasein' – the ordinary German word for 'existence' but divided up into its etymological compoents, 'Sein' and 'Da', it means 'being-there' or 'being-here' (BT 15).[6] He chooses this target because 'the understanding of [the meaning of] being' – albeit an 'average' and inarticulate understanding – 'belongs to Dasein's essential constitution' (BT 8). Hence, in somewhat the way that in Plato's *Meno*, Socrates 'interrogates' the slave boy to get him to articulate the answer to a question of geometry, so Heidegger proposed to interrogate us with regard to being.

Of itself, this choice of a target of interrogation does not explain the excitement generated by *Being and Time*. For although Heidegger calls his methodology 'phenomenology', the idea of turning from high-flown metaphysics to the 'average' and everyday understanding of things in order to solve (or dissolve) philosophical problems is not so far removed from the 'ordinary language' philosophy that was coming into being at about the same time in the Anglo-Saxon world, and was even partly influenced by Heidegger.[7] And, even if ordinary language philosophers might resist the epithet 'bloodless', they would be the first to agree that they were not in the business of resolving spiritual crises, of finding new spiritual directions.

What explains the excitement surrounding *Being and Time* is not the fact that it chooses to interrogate Dasein but rather the manner of interrogation. Heidegger summarized the crucial step that leads to this manner several times throughout the work. It is the following:

> [An answer to] the question of the meaning of being can become possible only if there *is* something like an understanding of being. Understanding of being belongs to the kind of being which the entity called 'Dasein' possesses. The more appropriately and primordially we have succeeded in explicating this being, the surer we are to attain our goal in the further course of working out the problem of fundamental ontology.
>
> (BT 200; see also BT 231)

Since, as the Introduction puts it, a 'pre-ontological understanding of being' belongs to Dasein's essential constitution, '*fundamental ontology* from which alone all other ontologies can take their rise must therefore be sought in the *existential analytic of Dasein*' (BT 13). In plain text, we can only answer the question of the meaning of being by providing a 'primordial' account of Dasein, of us ourselves.

Alexander Pope observes that the proper study of mankind is man. There is nothing we find more urgent or fascinating than ourselves. And, as we quickly discover, *Being and Time*'s account of who we are portrays us as particularly fascinating, not to say troubling, beings. For Dasein, we learn, is that being for whom, uniquely, its own being is an 'issue' (BT 12), the issue being whether to face up to 'anxiety', 'death', 'guilt', and 'the nothing' and become 'authentic', or to evade these phenomena and be 'inauthentic'. Suddenly, the seemingly dry investigation of what we mean when we say that something *is* has transmogrified itself into ultimate Nietzschean and Kierkegaardian questions about the meaning of life. Ontology has become existentialism, 'phenomenology' has become 'existential phenomenology'.

The step by which this transformation is achieved is undoubtedly invalid. To say that to articulate Dasein's understanding of the meaning of 'being' we require a fundamental and comprehensive analysis of Dasein is like saying that Socrates could have extracted from the slave boy the solution to the mathematical problem only by finding out everything fundamental about the slave boy – his attitude to the gods, his sexuality, his feelings about the Athenian polis, about the institution of slavery, and so on. Or, to change the comparison, it is analogous to the NSA claiming that they can monitor terrorist electronic communications only by monitoring all communications. Certainly that is *a* way of doing so, but it is not the only way and is, in fact, a clumsy procedure.

The question of why Heidegger adopted this clumsy approach to the *Seinsfrage*, why he chooses to approach the question of the meaing of being via the question of Dasein's being, is intimately connected with the issue of 'the turning' which I shall discuss at the beginning of Chapter 9. The fact of the matter is, however, that while *Being and Time* provides a deep and fascinating answer to the ostensibly preparatory question of what it is to be a person, it never gets back to the fundamental question of the meaning of 'being'. As we have it, *Being and Time* provides a detailed account of the being of Dasein but never properly returns to the question of 'the meaning of being in general' (BT 436).

Method

Heidegger, we saw, says that we have 'forgotten' the question of being. The reason is that we are captured by a frozen tradition of ontological interpretation that goes back to the Greeks and was perpetuated by the scholastic philosophy of the Middle Ages. The tradition he refers to is what Gadamer calls 'Greek substance ontology' (TM 135). On this view, everything is either a 'substance' or a property of a substance. As Nietzsche observes, this view is enforced by the tyrannical 'governess' of Western grammar.[8] Heidegger adduces Descartes' 'cogito' as an example of this tyranny. Although heralded as a new start in philosophy, the inference from 'there are thoughts' to 'there is a thing that thinks' is simply the old Graeco-Scholastic dogma that wherever there is a 'property' there must be a 'substance' to which it belongs (BT 22). According to this tradition, there is indeed something that 'transcends' all ordinary beings, but since the tradition regards everything that is not a property as a substance, the 'transcendent' is turned into a higher kind of substance, namely God. (The later Heidegger will refer to this disenchantment of the divine as 'onto-theology'). The tyranny of the tradition thus blocks the fundamental insight that *being is not a being*. Hence, to be able to answer the question of being we must 'destroy the history of ontology' (BT 19). Obviously this idea of *Destruktion* is a metaphor: the only thing we can 'destroy' is the hold that tradition has over us. (The idea of 'destruction' as liberation obviously carries over into the work of the French so-called 'deconstructionists'.)

Heidegger says that his method of carrying out his task of liberation is 'phenomenology'. Phenomenology, he emphasizes, is *just* a method, not a 'philosophical "movement"' (BT 38). Although this remark occurs in the course of the genuflection to Husserl that concludes the Introduction (*Being and Time* first appeared in Husserl's series *Jahrbuch für Phänomenologie und phänomenologische Forschung*), it is Heidegger's simultaneous distancing of himself from Husserl's account of phenomenology as a science with, as its own subject field, the objects of first-person consciousness. A 'phenomenon', says Heidegger, is not a particular kind of thing but rather a way of 'treating' things: anything can become a phenomenon; one can have a phenomenology of any subject area. The key terms for understanding Heidegger's notion of the phenomenological method – terms in prima facie tension with each other – are 'description' and 'hermeneutics', that is, 'interpretation'.

Phenomenology does not consist in argument. Rather it describes – 'descriptive phenomenology' is, says Heidegger, a tautology (BT 35). Its aim is to describe the 'phenomena' in which it is interested in such a way as to allow them to 'show themselves' as they are 'in themselves'. In Husserl's slogan, the task is to get 'to the things (or, less misleadingly, "matters [*Sachen*]") themselves'. This is more difficult than it appears since, sometimes by design and sometimes not (BT 36), the phenomena in which philosophers are interested are usually covered up. We have already seen that the frozen ontology of Western thought is one form of cover-up, so that the task here is to free ourselves of ontological 'prejudices'. To borrow Wittgenstein's words, the task is not to 'think' but to 'look', to allow the phenomenon to 'show itself from itself' (BT 16) rather than through the veil of some pregiven theory.

Phenomenology is, then, descriptive. But it is not *mere* description. It is, rather, description with a purpose: that of articulating the meaning of being, the 'structures of being' (BT 25) of which Dasein has implicit knowledge. Hence, the description Heidegger will engage in is selective, a matter of highlighting some phenomena and obscuring others. In Wittgenstein's definition of philosophy, it is a matter of 'assembling reminders for a particular purpose', the purpose of allowing the structure of being to emerge. The description is thus interpretative, 'hermeneutic' (BT 37–8), in somewhat the way in which a selective direction of attention can enable one to see the face in the clouds or the figure in the puzzle picture. Notice that interpretation is not *mere* interpretation, not a *mere* 'reading', but rather interpretation that discloses truth. Agreeing with Husserl to this extent, Heidegger says that phenomenology disclosed 'transcendental truth' (BT 38). What makes such truths difficult to see is that, normally, we are too near to ourselves. As we do not usually notice the glasses we are wearing, so we 'look right through' the 'being of beings' (BT 6). 'Inconspicuousness and obviousness' (BT 121) – inconspicuousness on account of obviousness – can be expected to characterize the structural features disclosed by phenomenology.

Being-in

By a dubious inference, then, Heidegger leaves behind the seemingly 'bloodless' question of being, turning instead to the much less bloodless question of our being, of what it is to be a being like us, a person, so that what *Being and Time* is actually about is, as one may initially put it, the 'ontology of person-hood'. So what is it to be a person? As observed, Dasein is uniquely that being for whom its own being is an 'issue'. Dasein, that is to say, has 'exis-tence (*Existenz*)', in Heidegger's technical use of the term according to which to have 'existence' is for one's being to be an 'issue' for one (BT 42). Dasein can, that is to say, 'either win or lose' itself, can take the difficult and stren-uous path of authenticity or the easier one of inauthenticity. Yet even if it takes the strenuous path, in many respects it still has to live the same kind of life as inauthentic Dasein – still has to go to the bathroom, catch the bus, earn a living, negotiate with other people, and so on. Externally, there may be no visible difference between the authentic and inauthentic life. Heidegger calls this core that is common to both modes of life 'average, everyday' existence (BT 43 et passim). Since personhood is common to both modes, the enquiry into its nature must, says Heidegger, begin with this common core.

What, then, is the ontological constitution of Dasein's average, everyday existence? Heidegger calls the elements that make up this 'structure of being' (BT 59) 'existentials (*existentiale*)'. The question thus becomes: What are the existentials that define Dasein's being?

The most obvious feature of our existence (so obvious as to likely escape our attention) is that we inhabit a world, that we have, or rather *are*, 'being-in-the-world'. Heidegger insists on the hyphens to emphasize that Dasein doesn't have being and then, as an extra feature, location in a world (BT 57). And, phenomenologically speaking, he is surely right: as he says, the idea that man is, 'in the first instance a spiritual thing who subsequently gets displaced (*versetzt*) "into" space' is the result of precisely what good phenomenology avoids, the viewing of experience through the veil of a 'metaphysical' theory (BT 56). (Heidegger is alluding, here, to both Christianity and Descartes, but probably also to Plato's *Phaedrus*, in which the soul's habitation of a body is a result of its 'fall' from the 'rim of the heavens'.) But although being-in-the-world is an essentially 'unitary phenomenon' it has, nonetheless, three distinct aspects: the 'who' of being-in-the-world, the world, and the 'in-ness' relation between them (BT 53). Heidegger begins with the last.

Dasein is not 'in' the world as water is in a glass or a dress in a wardrobe. That is precisely the view that arises from imposing Greek substance metaphysics – and theology – onto the phenomena. Being-in is not a matter of the containment of one 'thing' inside another 'thing' (BT 132). Rather, as 'being in the world of film' or 'the world of music' is a matter of absorbed engagement with the entities of that world – actors, cameras, or musical instruments – so being in the world in general is 'absorption' in that world, a matter of 'concern (*besorgen*)', of Dasein's concernful engagement with the entities with which it shares its world (BT 54–7).

World

The second aspect of being-in-the-world is, rather obviously, 'world'. Famously, Wittgenstein pronounces that 'The world is all that is the case ... the totality of facts not of things'. That, however, is what Heidegger would call an 'ontic' rather than 'ontological' description: it treats the world as a being rather than telling us what makes a world a world, telling us what 'worldhood' (BT 83) consists in. Ontologically, 'world' is not a being but rather the condition of the beings that are in the world being in their world, the condition, as one may put it, of their worldliness. If, therefore, we can discover what it is that constitutes their 'in-the-world-ness' we will have our account of the being of world.

The beings of the world divide into two classes: those that have the nature of Dasein and those that do not. (In Sartre's *Being and Nothingness*, this is the distinction between 'being-for-itself' [us] and 'being-in-itself' [everything else]). In seeking the worldhood of world, Heidegger attends to the latter, makes them, in the language of the Introduction, the *Befragte*, the 'interrogated'.

Being-in, we have seen, is a matter of concernful absorption, of Dasein's being 'taken over (*benommen*)' by its world of concern (BT 61). This means that our basic, everyday relation to the beings with which we share the world is not that of a knowing subject to a perceptual object, but consists, rather, in manipulative concern and use. We are able, of course, to inhabit the 'theoretical attitude' (BT 357) of knowing, but if we do, this is a deliberately created 'deficiency' of the normal, a holding back from the usual stance in favour of a 'just tarrying alongside'.[9] This means that we should try avoid calling the beings with which we are concerned 'things (*Dinge, res*)', for this is liable to give us a world of substance, matter, and mathematical space and time. It is liable to give us the world of what Heidegger calls the 'present-at-hand', the world of science rather than, in Husserl's language, the phenomenologically disclosed 'lifeworld'. What the objects of concernful engagement are, rather, is 'equipment (*Zeug*)', things disclosed as 'ready-to-hand' rather than 'present-at-hand'. Since world is what permits items of equipment to show up *as* equipment, the question thus becomes what it is that allows this to happen.

Heidegger's answer is that it is the 'referential totality' (BT 70) of 'involvement' and 'significance (*Bedeutsamkeit*)' (BT 83). To the being of any item of equipment there belongs a network whose nodal points are constituted by other items of equipment, points connected by 'in-order-to' relations that 'refer' something to something else. Equipment only exists in relation to other equipment. So, for example, in writing *Being and Time*, Heidegger notes that he is making use of 'ink-stand, pen, ink, paper, blotting pad, table, lamp, room' (BT 68). (One might catch an echo, in this account of Heidegger's pen, table, study, and eventually house as an expanding network of 'equipment', of le Corbusier's 1926 assertion that 'a house is a machine for living in'.) Notice that the equipmental network proceeds in two directions: 'vertically' (to use Lee Braver's terminology)[10] the pen is for making marks on paper which are for the printer's setting the type which is for the publication of 'the work (*Werk*)'; 'horizontally', the ink and blotting paper are the collateral equipment needed for the pen to do its job properly.

This gives us the basic idea of world. The world is the bi-directional network of these functional, instrumental, relationships. Heidegger now proceeds to expand on the notion of the functional whole that is the study – or the workshop (true to his rural, working-class roots, his paradigm piece of equipment is the carpenter's hammer) – until it becomes the world as a whole. In addition to the 'domestic' world of the workshop there is also the public world that is available to all. But this too is made up of 'equipment' (the term has clearly expanded beyond its everyday sense)[11], roads, railways, railway platforms, railway platform roofs, and so on (BT 70). As to the natural setting of our lives, the things of nature that show up in the lifeworld show up also as – ready-made – equipment: animals show up as meat and hide, rivers as water power, the wind as 'wind in the sails' (BT 65, 70).

The beings with which Dasein shares its world are, then, items that are 'ready-to-hand' within the network of functional relationships. This, Heidegger insists, is what they are 'in themselves' (BT 87): their instrumental value is not some 'subjective colouring' added to things that are first revealed as 'present-at-hand' (BT 71). That is (a point already made by Husserl – and Schopenhauer), it is *not* the case that one first perceives things of size, weight, shape and so on and then infers to their utility. Rather, as already noted, to perceive them that way one must perform a special act of detachment. In the normal use of equipment what we focus on is the 'work' to be produced, not the tools we use, so much so that, as Heidegger puts it in a later work, the material base without which, of course, the equipment could not be equipment, 'disappears into usefulness' (PLT 46). The writer is not normally conscious of the keyboard that he is writing with, while the pianist who becomes conscious of her keyboard will certainly start to play badly.

If the being of equipment consists in its functionality, what happens when one and the same material object changes its functionality? To slightly fictionalize Marcel Duchamp's provocation, what happens when a urinal is taken out of service and (thoroughly cleaned) set up on a pedestal in an art gallery with a plaque underneath saying 'Fountain'? Given his insistence that the functionality of equipment represents the being it has 'in itself' (BT 84, 106), Heidegger is committed to the view that in spite of the continuity of the present-at-hand material reality, we are, in fact, dealing with two distinct beings. Intuitively, this seems the correct thing to say. Ontological distinctness combined with material continuity is not uncommon – it happens when, for example, the eighteenth-century chamber pot is turned into a flower pot or when the one-time door is set upon two filing cabinets to become a desk top.

Heidegger holds that the functional totality that is 'world' shows up particularly clearly in situations where equipment is broken or missing, where it is, as one might put it, 'un-ready-to-hand'. In such situations – the car won't start or the potato peeler is missing from the kitchen drawer – our normally implicit knowledge of the functional network that defines the being of the equipment becomes explicit, announces itself (a word Heidegger takes over from Husserl) 'thematically' (BT 74–6). It is when a piece of equipment will not do what it is for that we become acutely aware of what it *is* for. (Of course, this does not always happen. The engine's cutting out in the plane I am flying in is likely to produce a state of panic that obliterates all else from consciousness.)

One essential feature of the referential totality that is world has yet to be mentioned. The carpenter wields the hammer to knock in a nail to attach two pieces of wood as part of the project of building a house in order to provide shelter – shelter for *Dasein*. 'In the work-world of the craftsman ... those others for whom the "work" is destined are "encountered (*mitbegegnen*)" too' (BT 117). Instrumental chains, that is, cannot go on for ever. They must have a goal and so a terminus. Heidegger calls the terminus the 'whither' (BT 111) of a chain, its 'on account-of-which (*Worum-willen*)', and says that, in every case, the on-account-of-which is provided by the needs and desires of Dasein: it belongs to Dasein's being that it is 'the sole authentic "on-account-of-which"' (BT 84). (Paul Gorner suggests, correctly, I think, that the idea of Dasein as the sole possessor of intrinsic as opposed to instrumental value derives from Kant's notion that only human beings are 'ends in themselves'.[12] As noted already, Kant's second formulation of the 'categorical imperative' allows that while we can treat everything else as a 'mere means', we must never treat humanity in such a way. In Chapter 9, we shall see that one aspect of the 'turning' is that later Heidegger comes to see this denial of intrinsic value to everything non-human as a reprehensible form of 'humanism'.)

To sum up, then, the world is the 'referential totality' of instrumental relationships where chains of such relationships find their 'whither' in the needs and desires of Dasein. They also, fairly obviously, find their 'whence' in such needs and desires, a matter to which I shall return (pp. 131–2 below).

Being-with-others

The third aspect of being-in-the-world is the question of 'who' has it. Formally speaking the answer is obvious, give that 'being-in-the-world is in each case mine (*jemeinig*)' (BT 43). For every instance of being-in-the-world there is an 'I', in traditional terminology a 'self' or 'subject', who can and must identify it as 'mine'. Heidegger thinks, however, that we need to set aside this formally correct answer since, for at least three reasons, the language of 'subject' is likely to lead us to misconstrue that very subject.

The first of these reasons is that, 'initially (*zunächst*) and for the most part', Dasein is precisely '*not itself*' (116), so that becoming a self is, in an important sense, an achievement rather than a birthright. The reasons for this claim I shall attend to shortly.

The second reason is that, given the tyranny of grammar (the object of Heidegger's *Destruktion*), even if we think we have got over Descartes' 'soul substance' we will still be inclined, like, for example, Kant, to think of the self as an enduring 'thing' and hence will miss the essentially relational character of Dasein's being (BT 114). To think of the self as an 'isolated I' (BT 116) will lead one to think that one can explicate Dasein's being in isolation from everything else, whereas we know already that it can only be understood in the context of world. We will miss in short the fact that 'man's "*substance*" is [dissolves into] *existence*' (BT 117), into, that is, 'issue'-pregnant *being-in-the-world*.

The third reason the formal answer is liable to mislead is that the idea of the self as an 'I' suggests the existence of what philosophers call 'the problem of other minds', a problem of 'getting over' from the 'isolated I' to 'the others'. How do we know we are not alone? Influenced by Descartes, a traditional account holds that we rehearse (below the level of consciousness) what philosophers call 'the argument from analogy': when I feel pain, I behave in a certain way; I see similar behaviour in other bodies, and so I conclude that, in all probability, they are inhabited by consciousnesses too. But this misses the fact that, as we saw in the last section, 'The others are [already] encountered in [any] ready-to-hand, environmental context of equipment' and are not, as the argument from analogy supposes, 'added on in thought to some thing which, in the first instance, is just present-at-hand' (BT 118). So impregnated by 'the others' is the phenomenologically immediate environment that, even when no actual 'other' is present, otherness remains inescapable: when we complain about shoddy materials 'the supplier' has sent us, when we walk around the edge of a field rather than across the middle, and when we refrain from taking the boat lying on the bank for a joyride, although no particular 'others' are present, otherness is (ibid.). There is no problem 'getting over' to 'the others'. If there is a problem at all it is rather, we shall see, getting away from them.

What is particularly misleading about the idea of having to 'get over' to them is that in everyday life, what I understand by 'the others' is not 'everyone except myself' but rather 'those from whom, for the most part, one does *not* distinguish oneself – those among whom one is too' (BT 118). Mostly, that is, I think of myself as a member of a group, as a 'we' – a group of professors, students, New Zealanders or whatever. As we shall see ('we' philosophical thinkers), it is in the expansion of this thought that Heidegger discovers 'the who' of Dasein to be, mostly, not the 'I' but rather 'the we', or, as he puts it, 'the One'. Before getting to that point, however, Heidegger addresses the question of how our being with others is to be distinguished from our being with entities that are ready-to-hand or present-at-hand.

* * *

Being-in-the-world is essentially 'being-with-others (*Mitsein*)'. Other Dasein, we have seen, are encountered, not inferentially, but 'environmentally'. The mode of encounter, however, is other than the mode of encountering equipment. As Husserl observes, to encounter people as people is to accord them rights non-persons do not have (p. 111 above). If you are sitting on the chair I want to sit on I do not pick you up and remove you in the way I might pick up and remove a pile of books. (The cat is an intermediate case.) As we saw (in anticipation of his final claim that the being of Dasein is 'care [*Sorge*]') Heidegger designates our relation to items of equipment as 'concern (*besorgen*)' (p. 123 above). And so, to mark the ontological distinction between dealing with people and dealing with equipment while retaining the idea that all dealings are modes of *Sorge*, he calls our being-towards-persons *Fürsorge*, 'solicitude'.

Solicitude divides into two species, 'deficient' and 'positive'. 'Deficient' solicitude is the manner in which, particularly in modern mass society, Dasein relates to others most of the time: it is a matter of 'passing one another by', of the others not 'mattering' (BT 121). (When, at the age of five, Nietzsche moved from the tiny village of Röcken to, as it seemed to him, the vast city of Naumburg – its actual population was then about 13,000 – he was astonished that its citizens failed to greet each other as they passed by in the streets.)

The modes of positive solicitude form a continuum with a 'leaping in' mode and a 'leaping ahead' mode at the two extremes. 'Leaping in' solicitude, which mainly pertains to problems with equipment (untangling fishing line, filling out tax returns, telling the other the great Scrabble word they are about to miss), takes over the other's 'care' and hands it back to them as a problem solved. This is an exercise of power which tends to make the other 'dominated and dependent' (BT 122). (Since the central, everday meaning of *Fürsorge* is 'care' in the sense of 'welfare', this may be, en passant, the familiar right-wing objection to the welfare state.) 'Leaping ahead' solicitude, rather than taking away the other's 'care', 'leaps ahead of him in his existentiell[13] potentiality-for-being' and 'gives it back to him authentically as such for the first time'. This kind of solicitude, says Heidegger,

> pertains essentially to authentic care – that is, to the existence of the other, not to a '*what*' with which he is concerned; it helps the other to become transparent to himself *in* his care and to become *free for* it.
>
> (BT 122)

Heidegger develops the idea of authentic solicitude by means of the contrast between *Gesellschaft* (society) and *Gemeinschaft* (community) that we have already encountered. If being-with-others is a matter of being 'hired for the same concern' – for a *Gesellschaft* in the sense of a business company – there is, Heidegger observes, no genuine 'solidarity (*Verbundenheit*)', since relations with one's co-employees usually take the form of 'distance and reserve' and often 'thrive on mistrust' (office politics). '*Authentic* solidarity (eigentliche *Verbundenheit*)', on the other hand, arises when individuals give meaning to their lives by 'devot[ing] themselves to some matter (*Sache*) in common', each doing so in their own individual way (BT 122). Only authentic solidarity makes possible the kind of 'grounding in the matter (*rechte Sachlichkeit*) that frees the other in his freedom for himself' (ibid.). Only one who is grounded in authentic solidarity, that is, is capable of engaging in the leaping ahead mode of positive solicitude.

This passage looks forward to the end of *Being and Time* where Heidegger will argue that it is the possession of Hegel's 'ethical substance' (p. 55 above), of a shared 'heritage', as Heidegger calls it, that distinguishes community from mere society (pp. 150–1 below). Since, Heidegger will argue, one's self is *constituted* by one's ethical heritage, to be 'free for yourself' is to live up to the demands of heritage. And so only someone who is himself grounded in ethical tradition can point the other in the direction of his living up to 'himself'. Heidegger is no doubt thinking of his own inspirational teaching as a form of authentic solicitude, and, as we shall see in Chapter 8, Hannah Arendt thinks of teaching in a similar way.

Affectedness and thrownness

We are not, we know, in the world as water is in a glass but rather by way of concernful engagement. In Chapter V of *Being and Time*'s Division I, Heidegger turns to the task of enriching this account of 'being-in' by way of both elucidation and expansion. Unlike a hammer, which does not know that it is in a world, we do. To be in the world in the manner of Dasein is, minimally described, for that world to be revealed, 'disclosed (*erschlossen*)', to one as a structure of functional relations. What we are concerned with now is the enrichment of this account through the discovery of further aspects of disclosure.

The first of these aspects is what Heidegger calls 'affectedness (*Befindlichkeit*)' – 'state of mind' in Macquarrie and Robinson's translation. Affectedness is a matter of 'mood', of the way in which we are 'attuned' to our world. A mood is not a 'psychical condition' of a subject (BT 136).[14] Rather it is the manner in which one's being-in-the-world as a totality is disclosed, what we might call its 'tonality' or 'colour'. In boredom, one's world shows up as flat, stale and unprofitable; in joy it shows up, as it did to Emerson, as a world in which 'all things are friendly and sacred, all events profitable, all days holy'. Disclosure of one's being in the world, Heidegger observes, always has a mood (ibid.). Even the purely theoretical stance of, say, the botanist in the field has its mood – that of 'tranquil tarrying alongside' (BT 138). Disclosure always has an 'atmosphere'. Affectedness, mood, is an *ever-present* dimension of disclosure, is, in other words, an existential – an important phenomenological discovery.

Heidegger is interested in two moods in particular. The first is the mood of involvement, the mood in which the affairs of the world 'matter' to one, the mood in the absence of which there can be no engagement with equipment. This is not a mood one always or necessarily inhabits. In, for example, the Buddhist monk's detached state of 'pure beholding' (BT 137–8), or in the mood of boredom, or of Sartrean 'nausea', worldly affairs precisely do *not* matter.

The second is the 'pallid' *seeming* 'lack of mood' that manifests our 'thrownness *(Geworfenheit)*', the mood in which Dasein recognizes its being as a 'burden', the burden 'that it is and has to be' (BT 134).[15] What makes being-in-the-world a burden is that both its 'whence' and its 'whither' are shrouded in darkness (ibid). Like the small boy in his first days at boarding school, we have no idea of the 'whence' of our being in this world of difficult rules and regulations (BT 267), we know only that it is not of our own voli-tion. The result is that we feel 'handed over' (BT 134), 'abandoned' (BT 141). And as for the 'whither', the 'darkness' that awaits us is the nothingness of death. A crucial part of the awfulness of thrownness is that it is a thrownness into death (BT 252).

Heidegger claims the mood of thrownness reveals a truth about Dasein which is not one that can ever be disclosed by 'theoretical cognition' (BT 136). (That scientific 'method' does not have a prerogative on the disclosure of truth is a point, we shall see, that is central to Gadamer.) What precisely is this 'truth'?

Here, we need to note that, given the thesis that every disclosure has its affectedness, it follows that for any disclosure, we can distinguish between *what* is disclosed, the content, and a *how* it is disclosed, its affectedness. Correspondingly, there can be two kinds of truths associated with any dis-closure: the truth that is its content and the truth about the affectedness that the disclosure brings with it. Heidegger describes *Being and Time*'s account of Dasein, no less than sixty-three times, as an 'existential-ontological' account, without ever precisely explaining the meaning of the conjunction. I should like to suggest that he regards as 'existential' truths about the modes of affectedness that belong to the various significant disclosures he discusses, while he regards as 'ontological' truths about the content of those disclosures.

Thrownness, according to Heidegger, is an existential, an essential part of Dasein's 'being' (BT 284 et passim). This assertion, then, makes two claims. It makes the 'existential' claim that the sense of existence as a 'burden' to which we are 'abandoned' is one that is 'latent' (BT 190) in all Dasein. The 'onto-logical' claim, the ground of the *possibility* of the mood of abandonment, is that the world we are in is one that we are always (in the expression Heidegger takes over from Husserl) 'already in' (BT 192). As we grow up into full Daseinhood we find ourselves, through no volition of our own, unavoidably the creation of a particular historical culture.

The ontological claim contained in the claim that thrownness is an existential is surely correct. One *is* always 'already in', already in a cultural horizon which, if Gadmaer is right, one can never be confident of entirely escaping. Notice, however, that there is nothing inaccessible to 'theoretical cognition' about the ontological claim. Both Husserl and Gadamer discuss the 'already-in-ness' that constitutes the lifeworld at great length but in an entirely 'theoretical' manner. As we shall see in the next chapter, Gadamer even takes over Heidegger's term 'thrownness', but in a manner that completely drains it of the pathos of *Being and Time*.

The existential claim, on the other hand, the claim that resentment concerning the 'whence' of our 'being-here', resentment of our 'abandonment' and anxiety concerning our 'whither', seems to me a dubious one. Hindus know about both their 'whither' and their 'whence', and Christians know at least something about their 'whither'. More importantly for present concerns, later Heidegger, we shall see, insists that, whether or not we 'appropriate' it, 'dwelling', at-homeness – the *opposite* of 'abandonment' – is our fundamental condition. The move from treating not-at-homeness (see further pp. 237–9 below) to treating at-homeness as our fundamental condition represents, I shall suggest, the heart of 'the turning'.

Digression on poetry

In his discussion of language (see further pp. 133–4 below), Heidegger asks how it is that mood enters langauge. His answer is that

> the linguistic indication of the making-known of affectedness that belongs to speech (*Rede*) consists in intonation, modulation, the tempo of the speech, the 'manner of delivery'. The communication of the existential possibilities of affectedness, that is, the disclosure of existence (*Existenz*),[16] can become the innermost aim of the 'word (*Rede*)'.

(BT 162)

When the later Heidegger turns to discussions of poetry as such, the idea that a great poem has and evokes a 'fundamental mood (*Grundstimmung*)' – an idea he takes over from Hölderlin – becomes of central importance.

One of the salent features of the language of *Being and Time* (as it is of the language of the Kierkegaardian texts by which early Heidegger is deeply influenced) is that its key terms – 'thrownness', 'anxiety', 'conscience', 'guilt', 'death', 'the nothing' and 'homelessness' – are all taken from the same affective register. The reason that Heidegger speaks, for example, of 'death' rather than 'finitude' and of 'thrownness' rather than 'already-in-ness' is clear: he wishes to communicate the affectedness of 'anxiety' which he takes to accompany the disclosures of finitude, and the affectedness of 'abandonment' which he takes to accompany already-in-ness. The standard account of Heidegger's development tells us that whereas the langauge of *Being and Time* is 'scientific', that of later Heidegger is 'poetic'. This is a myth. Heidegger was *always* a 'poet', his *Denken* was *always* inseparable from *Dichten*. This, of course, is a major part the secret of the 'magic spell' he cast over his student audience, the reason why, in contrast to the 'bloodless' Neo-Kantians, his students found in his lectures, as Arendt puts it, 'not the old opposition of reason versus the passions' but 'a *passionate* thinking, in which thinking and aliveness became one'.[17]

Passionate thinking is, in my view, what philosophers indeed *should* engage in. But it has its dangers. With respect to thrownness and, as we shall see, the allied notions of conscience and guilt, the language used to denote an onto-logical feature that is indeed universal to all Dasein has attached to it an affectedness which is, in fact, not universal but rather specific to a particular historical mode of consciousness: the confused, potentially nihilistic con-sciousness of the early twentieth century in general, and of the Weimar Republic in particular. Since this would have been the consciousness of most of his students – their *Weltschmerz*, the previous century would have called it – it would have been easy for them to accept the affectedness evoked by Heidegger as universal.

Projection, understanding, and interpretation

In practical activity, as we know, the world is disclosed to Dasein as a referential totality. Practical activity is guided by a 'circumspection (*Umsicht*)' (BT 69), made possible by the fact that Dasein 'understands (*verstehen*)' its world, the fact that it possesses 'understanding (*Verständnis*)'. Understanding is thus an existential. Having introduced the term, Heidegger immediately emphasizes that Dasein's understanding is, as such, a matter of knowing-how rather than knowing-that, practical 'competence' rather than propositional knowledge (BT 143). 'She understands business' means that she is a skilled operator in the business world, not that she has an MBA.

Understanding is always relative to a particular 'on-account-of-which'. 'On-account-of-which' figures in *Being and Time* in two different ways, but the principal function of the term is to refer to social roles that provide partial self-definitions.[18] Somewhat in the way in which Sartre speaks of a 'funda-mental project' that embraces all my individual projects, Heidegger assumes there to be a fundamental on-account-of-which that embraces all my partial self-definitions (BT 123). So, attending for now only to the partial self-definitions, someone who hammers (a lot) is doing so because they occupy the social role of being a carpenter, and because hammering is what carpenters do. Human beings inhabit a large number of such roles, each of which explains a facet of their behaviour: being a Democrat explains my voting behaviour, being a cyclist my recreational behaviour, being a violinist my musical behaviour, and so on. To each such on-account-of-which there belongs a 'point of view' (BT 150) that determines how the referential totality of world shows up to me: certain items of equipment together with their functional connections become salient when I am in my cyclist role, different ones when I am being a violinist.

Being a cyclist, violinist or carpenter is taking out a lien on the future. If I say 'I am a carpenter' (as opposed to 'I've just done a bit of hammering') I give both you and myself warrant to believe that I will still be a carpenter tomorrow and the day after. Heidegger refers to this as 'projection (*Entwurf*)'. In being who I am, father, professor, husband, and so on, I am 'throwing (*werfen*)' an account of myself into the future, a kind of partial plan of my life, although one, Heidegger quickly adds, that may well not have been consciously thought out (BT 145). Projection is thus another element in the structure of Daseinhood, another existential. Since 'thrownness' is also an existential, we can describe Dasein as a 'thrown thrower'.

Projection is a 'pressing forward into possibilities', existence-possibilities, modes of life (BT 145). In pressing forward into some possibilities, Dasein is continually rejecting, 'negating', others. Projection is thus a 'null', or better, 'nullifying', activity (BT 287). The possibilities which have been thrust aside are, however, present in my understanding and so are always liable to exert a 'counter-thrust (*Rückschlag*)' (BT 148), a temptation, or at least nostalgia, towards rejected life-paths. (One thinks of Marlon Brando's famous line in *On the Waterfront*, 'I could have been a contender.') This idea of the counter-thrust – one meaning of *Rückschlag* is 'relapse' – will become important when we come to discussing the difficulty of maintaining oneself in authenticity.

'Possibility' is the key term for understanding what Dasein is. Dasein is, in fact, nothing but possibility. This is the existentialist theme that, unlike a tree, there is no pre-determined 'what' that defines Dasein, that its essence (its so-called 'substance' [p. 126 above]) is nothing but 'existence' (BT 143). Dasein is nothing but a 'pure potentiality for being' (BT 143). Pure, but not, Heidegger quickly adds, unlimited. Although freedom is at the heart of Dasein's being, this freedom is not absolute, not a 'free-floating' 'liberty of indifference' (BT 144). As 'thrown', Dasein is 'already' anchored in a given lifeworld or culture and this determines for it a 'leeway (*Spienraum*)', a delimited space of life options (BT 145). Becoming a hedge fund manager is not a live option for a member of the Arapesh people, but it is for me. Hari Kiri is possible for the Japanese but not for me – though suicide, of course, is.

* * *

Understanding is always 'interpretation (*Auslegung*)' (BT 148). As already noted, in the 'circumspection' that guides our practical dealings with the world we do not see something present-at-hand and then infer that it might have a practical use ('Lo, a heavy metal thing.' Thinks: 'It might be useful for knocking in nails.'). Rather it is immediately present to us *as* a hammer. To see an item of equipment as present-at-hand, to *free* it from the 'as-structure' of equipmentality, requires, we saw, a positive effort. The seeing-as of equipmentality is the 'primordial' mode of seeing; seeing the material thing in which equipmentality is grounded, derivative (BT 149).

The seeing-as that guides practical activity is interpreting-as. Since such activity is normally a know-how that is unaccompanied by knowing-that, the as-structure is usually not grasped 'thematically' (BT 149). But it can be. Somewhat misleadingly, Heidegger reserves the term 'interpretation' for this explicit 'articulation (*gliedern*)' of the as-structure, an 'articulation' that occurs when, for example, we take a watch apart to see how it works. This, however, is not something different from understanding. Rather, it is a 'working out' (or a 'laying out' – *Aus-legen*) of the structural relations implicit in understanding (in a manner, in fact, that mimics the achievement of philosophical phenomenology): 'in interpretation understanding does not become something different but becomes itself' (BT 148). Interpretation as an activity of explicit 'articulation (*gliedern*)' 'articulates (*artikulieren*)' (BT 149) interpretation as an implicit activity.

Assertion

Being and Time is logophobic. It is hostile to its own medium, to 'logos', language. Linguistic 'assertion', the title of section 33 tells us, is a 'derivative mode of interpretation'. Linguistic assertions, to be sure, *also* have a 'meaning (*Sinn*)'. But they do not create it; meaning cannot be defined as that which occurs in a judgment (BT 153). In the first instance, that is, meaning is established by the understanding and interpretation that belongs to practical activity (BT 156), and it is on meaning in this sense that linguistic meaning is parasitic. 'To significations (*Bedeutungen*)', Heidegger writes, 'words *accrue*' (BT 161; my emphasis). Here we confront another aspect of the 'turning', for whereas the post-'turning' Heidegger famously asserts that 'language is the house of being', *Being and Time* goes out of its way to deny this and to affirm, in its place, that *praxis* is the house of being.

An assertion such as 'The hammer is (too) heavy', says Heidegger, really does three things. It 'highlights (*aufzeichnen*)', refers to, a particular entity, predicates something of it, and communicates to others the matter in question. Or rather, it *attempts* to communicate the matter in question: since the truth of things can easily become 'veiled' as assertions get passed on in 'hearsay', linguistic communication is a dubious and uncertain enterprise (BT 155).

From the philosophical point of view, the problem with assertion concerns reference. Reference 'dims down': in referring to, 'highlighting', the hammer we 'dim down' everything else in order to focus in on 'that hammer there'

(BT 155). What this does is to turn something ready-to-hand into a present-at-hand. When we understand something 'as' a hammer in practical activity we implicitly understand its involvement in the referential totality which allows it to be a hammer. But in assertion, although it is still referred to 'as' a hammer (Heidegger calls the 'as' of assertion the 'apophantic "as"' [BT 223]), 'the "as" no longer reaches out into a totality of involvements' (BT 158). Rather than being understood as an entity whose being consists in its role in practical life, the hammer becomes a present-at-hand 'thing' whose nature can be understood without reference to anything else.

As a generalization, this claim seems to me to be based on an overly narrow range of examples and to be, in fact, entirely implausible. I can detect no 'dimming down' in 'Your car is fast', and as for 'Your bishop is about to be taken', the network of involvements becomes, if anything, *more* salient in the apophantic than in the practical – as Heidegger calls it 'hermeneutical' (BT 158) – 'as'. Nonetheless, this perception of the nature of reference is a major contributor to *Being and Time*'s hostility to logos. It is, Heidegger says, very important from the point of view of fundamental ontology to put logos in its place because the ancients took it to be the only medium through which it is possible to grasp 'what really is' and to define the 'being of beings' (BT 154). And it was from such logocentricism that the ontology of the present-at-hand, of substance and accident, was born. To escape it, to do fundamental ontology properly, we must, as we have seen, 'destroy' the tyranny of grammar, destroy Wittgenstein's 'bewitchment of language'.

Truth

Truth, 'being in the truth' (BT 363) (a phrase taken over from Kierkegaard), is, says Heidegger, a fundamental existential (BT 297). But, to raise Pilate's famous question, what is truth?

According to the 'traditional' conception, truth is a property that assertions have just in case they 'correspond', are 'adequate, to' extra-linguistic reality. Contrary to what is often claimed, Heidegger does not wish to *reject* the traditional conception. Rather, he wants to show it to be a 'derivative' conception that is 'founded' on a more 'primordial' kind of truth which he calls truth as *a-letheia* (BT 219, 223).

What happens when I make the true assertion, 'The picture is askew'? Two things: the picture gets 'uncovered (*entdecken*)', that is, 'brought out of hiddenness (*unverborgen*)' *as* a picture; and it gets uncovered as being in a certain state – 'askew'. As one might put it, a 'what' is uncovered and something is said about its 'how'.

Heidegger focuses attention on the 'what', on what the assertion is about (*worüber*), in other words, on its referent. How, he asks, does the hammer get picked out *as* a hammer – rather than as, say, a meaningless lump of iron, a religious icon or a door stop? Only because the hammer is *already* 'disclosed (*erschlossen*)' in Dasein's understanding as a hammer. The 'apophantic "as"' is thus founded on the 'hermeneutical "as"' (BT 223).

This example only deals with reference to items of equipment. How can we generalize it to include present-at-hand things as well – Newtonian bodies, for example? Translated into more accessible langauge, Heidegger's general point is that the possibility of assertions being either true or false depends on reference, and reference depends on a scheme of reference, a prior 'disclosure', 'understanding', or 'interpretation' of the 'being of beings', of the kinds of beings that belong to the domain of discussion. Beings have to be brought out of obscurity – *a-letheia* (BT 222) – as beings of a particular kind for us to be able to make unambiguous reference to them. The referential 'as' depends on a prior understanding of the 'as-ness' of things. This is a point familiar to analytic philosophy. W. V. Quine imagines a translator of a hitherto unknown language noting that every time he points to a rabbit the natives say 'gavagai' and so decides that 'rabbit' is the correct translation. But who knows, muses Quine, but that what the natives actually mean is 'undetached rabbit part',[19] or, perhaps, 'rabbit skin' or, more radically, 'phase of (four-dimensional) rabbit-event'? 'Dimming down' the rest of the world to focus on a particular region of space-time will yield neither reference nor truth unless it is accompanied by an understanding of the being of beings. The truth of assertions, truth as correspondence, is thus dependent on a prior disclosure of beings which Heidegger calls 'truth' *as aletheia*.

Heidegger raises the question of whether this account of truth renders it 'subjective'. In one sense the answer is that it does. He states flatly that before Newton – before he created the theory that makes it possible to refer to things as 'Newtonian bodies' – his laws were not true (or false) (BT 226). So truth is subjective in the sense that it is 'dependent on Dasein'. On the other hand, truth is certainly not subjective if that is taken to mean 'left to the subject's discretion' (BT 227). Earlier in *Being and Time*, Heidegger writes:

> Beings *are* independently of the experience, knowledge, and comprehension through which they are disclosed, uncovered and determined. But being 'is' only in the understanding of that being to whose being something like an understanding of being belongs.
>
> (BT 183)

Being, the 'being of beings', how entities are disclosed to Dasein, depends on Dasein. But being*s* are not thus dependent. Beings, and the structure that comprises their relation to each other, are 'out there' independently of us. Heidegger repeats this point with respect the Newton's laws:

> to say that before Newton his laws were neither true nor false cannot signify that before him there were no such beings as have been uncovered and

pointed out by those laws ... Once beings have been uncovered, they show themselves precisely as the beings which beforehand they already were.

(BT 227)

And in the *Basic Problems of Phenomenology*, a lecture course delivered in 1927, he observes that 'for nature to be as it is it does not need disclosure' (BP 220).[20]

So the basic picture is this. Present-at-hand reality is there independently of us. But it is multi-aspected. Some aspects are revealed by some schemes of reference, others by others. As I noted in the previous chapter, Hubert Drey-fus calls this position, which he, too, attributes to Heidegger, 'plural realism' (p. 110 above). Which scheme of reference is deployed – what things show up *as* – is dependent on Dasein. But what is thereby revealed is not. Ready-to-hand beings are dependent on Dasein, on human practices, for their being. But given that those practices are as they are, the truth or falsehood of assertions about ready-to-hand entities lies beyond linguistic Dasein's 'discre-tion'. If I point my camera in a given direction and have a red and green filters at my disposal, the colour in which things show up depends on me. *What* shows up, however, does not.

* * *

At the beginning of the discussion of 'assertion', I noted Heidegger's para-doxical hostility to logos. Language is at best a second-class citizen: it cannot create meaning but only reflects the non-linguistic meaning pre-established in our dealings with equipment. And it is not, really, a very welcome citizen at all, since it is inclined to lead us into ontological – and, we shall see, existential – error. I noted that this view of *praxis* as the 'house of being' is profoundly different from the later view of langauge as that 'house'.

In fact, however, it seems to me that *Being and Time*'s view of *praxis* as the promordial source of meaning, the view that the meaning of assertions is always derivative from meanings established by praxis, has, at best, very limited application. This can be seen by taking note of Heidegger's own observation that before Newton created his theory of mechanics, before, that is, he created the scheme of reference that allows us to speak of 'Newtonian bodies', it was impossible to make (true or false) assertions about such entities. Notice that Newton's theory is a *linguistic* entity. And so, with respect to Newtonian bodies and theoretical entities in general, *already in Being and Time*, language is, in effect, at least *a* house of being, and has to be since, by definition, insofar as things show up theoretically, they are not disclosed by any non-linguistic praxis. 'All ontical experience of beings', Heidegger writes, 'both circumspective calculation of the ready-to-hand and positive scientific cogni-tion of the present-at-hand ... is based upon projections of the being of the corresponding beings' (BT 324). This seems to me completely correct. The crucial point, however, is that outside the field of equipment, the 'projection' in question has to be done in language. Heidegger basically sees this, but does not seem to have noticed that it is radically inconsistent with the logophobia that leads him to claim that the meaning of language is always derivative.

Care

At the beginning of the concluding chapter of Division I, Heidegger observes that by this stage in the discussion we have discovered quite an array of essential characteristics of Dasein's 'being-in': absorption, concern, circumspection, understanding, affectedness, projection, and thrownness. He wonders whether it is possible to exhibit all these as aspects of a 'unitary phenomenon' (BT 181) somewhat in the manner in which Socrates suggests that all of the virtues – justice, temperance, courage, and so on – are really all aspects of the same thing, namely wisdom. Heidegger's analogue of 'wisdom' is 'care (*Sorge*)'. In ordinary German, 'care' has only a negative meaning as in 'careworn'. Heidegger indicates, however, that like the Latin *cura*, he wishes his use of the term also to embrace, in addition to the negative meaning, the positive meaning of 'caring for' (BT 199). Hubert Dreyfus has reported (in conversation) that Heidegger told him that the English 'care' was better adapted to his purposes than *Sorge*, containing as it does the useful ambiguity.

As we know, Dasein is essentially engaged in a world of beings that are either Daseins or not. In the case of the former, the mode of engagement is *Fürsorge*, solicitude, in the case of the latter *Besorgen*, concern, the two basic modes of *Sorge*. We also know that Dasein's mode of both concern and solicitude is determined by an overall 'on-account-of-which', a self-understanding that embraces all its partial self-definitions (BT 123), one that it 'projects' into the future. And we know, finally, that Dasein's projection always occurs from within a cultural 'thrownness'. These are the elements we need for a definition of 'care' and thereby of Dasein. Dasein is 'care', that is, being 'ahead-of-itself-being-already-in-(the world-) as being-amidst (entities encountered within the world)' either in the mode of concern or of solicitude (BT 192).

One might notice that while 'being already in' corresponds to the past, and 'being ahead' to the future, 'being amidst' pertains to the present. We can thus see that in the analysis of 'care' the stage is being set for a still more fundamental analysis of Dasein in terms that relate to the second word in the book's title, 'time' (see further, pp. 147–52 below).

Inauthenticity and the One

As noted earlier, Heidegger repeatedly speaks of *Being and Time*'s account of being-in-the-world as an 'existential-ontological' analysis. On the whole, however, Division I can be said to be concerned with ontological matters and Division II with existential matters. There are exceptions – inauthenticity, anxiety and the existential, that is, affective, aspect of thrownness are all introduced in Division I – but it makes rough sense to speak of the ontological as 'Division I material' and the existential as 'Division II material'. It is now time to turn our attention fully to the latter.

It will be recalled from the discussion of 'being-with-others' (pp. 126–7 above) that among Heidegger's objections to the 'formal' account of the 'who' of Dasein as the 'I' or 'self' is his claim that, for the most part, Dasein is *not* itself. Mostly, he claims, 'the others' are precisely those from whom one does *not* distinguish oneself. Who or what, then, *is* the 'who' of average, everyday Dasein?

That we mostly do not distinguish ourselves from others is, says Heidegger, grounded in our innate 'distantiality (*Abständigkeit*)', a constant measuring of the distance – *Abstand* – between oneself and social norms, and a 'care' that if one has fallen behind the crowd one should catch up, and if one has got too far ahead one needs to drag oneself back (126).[21]

If one succumbs to distantiality, as we mostly do (the fashion industry would collapse otherwise), one exists in constant 'subjection' to others, which means that 'one's being has been taken away by the others'. 'The others' in question are, however, not definite others. Rather, it is *das Man* to whom one is subject, 'the They' in Macquarrie and Robinson's translation or, in the more literal translation that I prefer, 'the One' (BT 126). In succumbing to *das Man* one does what *one* does.

The effect of the One is to 'level down' one's individuality to an 'averageness'. Heidegger describes such levelling in dramatic (not to say prophetic) terms as 'the dictatorship of the One'. Mostly, he says,

> [w]e take pleasure and enjoy ourselves as *one* takes pleasure; we read see and judge about literature and art as *one* sees and judges; we shrink back from the 'great mass' as *one* shrinks back; we find 'shocking' what *one* finds shocking ... the One prescribes the mode of being of everydayness.
>
> (BT 126–7)

The result of succumbing to this 'dictatorship' is that 'every kind of priority gets noiselessly suppressed' so that the 'public' view of things dominates the way we interpret our world (BT 127). The unique insight of the exceptional, creative individual is levelled down to the clichéd ontological, ethical, and political correctnesses of, in Nietzsche's language, 'the herd'.

A life of submission to the One is what Heidegger refers to as 'inauthenticity', *Uneigentlichkeit*, literally, 'un-ownliness', a failure to 'stand by one's self' (BT 128). Inauthentic Dasein is, indeed, not really a self at all: since its being is 'dispersed (*Zerstreut*) in the One' (BT 129), it fluctuates in accord with the fickle tides of fashion. Lacking the centred solidity of a self, the so-called self is really nothing more than a playground on which conflicting social forces play themselves out, a featureless mirror of the trends of the times, a 'man without qualities'.

The One ('society', 'public opinion') has many techniques for exerting control over the individual ranging from the secret police to the various modes of ostracism: the contemptuous look, the sneer, the cutting remark, the cold shoulder. The extent and visibility of the dominion of the One is, Heidegger observes, historically variable (BT 129). In every case, however, to insist on one's individuality is difficult, so that if one has any tendency to want an 'easy' life, one will accept the One's offer to 'disburden' one of the difficult business of running it (BT 127). By and large, the One is successful in enforcing its norms, in turning its 'subjects' into conformists.

This is Heidegger's answer, then, to the 'who' of being in the world. For average, everyday Dasein,[22] the 'who' is not in fact 'the self' but rather 'the One'. If the 'I' is genuinely to become the 'who' that runs its life, Dasein must reclaim ownership of that life, must become 'authentic (*eigentlich*)'.

So far, it looks as though authenticity is going to be a matter of throwing off our submission to the One and becoming our fully authentic, 'Nietzschean' selves. In fact, however, matters are not that simple, the reason being (as, in fact, Nietzsche knows, too) that we can never entirely 'extract' (BT 169) ourselves from the One. To suppose that we could would presuppose the water-in-a-glass misconception of the self as a present-as-hand, intrinsically world-less entity. All we can do is to 'modify' our relation to it: '*authentic being-one's-self* does not rest upon an exceptional condition of the subject, a condition that has been detached from the One; *it is rather an existentiell modification of the One – the One as an essential existential*' (BT 130).

As we have seen, what the One does is to establish norms of behaviour. Many of these norms are essential to the very existence of a common world. Many norms, that is, are involved in the ontology of world. That something is a hammer rather than a religious icon, a dining table rather than a piece of gym equipment, a church rather than a drinking establishment, determines norms of behaviour with respect to such entities, the general observance of which is essential to one's being-in-the-world. Someone who persistently treats dining tables as gym equipment, bows down before hammers and smokes and drinks in church has fallen into a kind of insanity, has become 'worldless'.

Many norms established by the One are, then, ontologically *constitutive*, constitutive of world, and, as such, preconditions of our being-in-the-world. This is why we conform to them with no more sense of being 'dictated' to than we feel dictated to by the norms constitutive of the game of chess. The norms mentioned in the 'dictatorship' passage are, however, not of this character. They concern seemingly trivial matters such as being required to prefer Proust to Patterson (James), to despise the British lager louts who take their holidays on the Costa del Sol, and to find 'shocking' the latest revelations about the President's sex life. But cumulatively, of course, these norms are far from trivial, for they determine what kind of person one is going to be. To adhere to them is to adopt as one's own the clichéd life 'possibilities' that are sanctioned and approved by the One of one's social 'circle' (BT 298).

Authenticity will, then, consist in a combination of conformity and independence. One will conform, in the main, to world-constituting norms but will exercise one's freedom with respect to the life one lives within the thus-constituted world. To adopt Dreyfus' distinction,[23] an authentic life will be one of conform*ity* but not of conform*ism*.

Idle talk, ambiguity, and curiosity

When language functions so as to disclose the truth, it constitutes what Heidegger calls *Rede* (BT 161), authentic 'speech' ('discourse' in Macquarrie and Robinson's translation). But language can also function as *Gerede*, 'gossip' or 'idle talk'. When it functions in this way it conceals rather than discloses, conceals the 'understanding' of things – things such as death – which, deep down, we all possess. Idle talk is talk that 'serves not so much to keep being-in-the-world open for us as rather to close it off, and cover up the beings within-the-world' (BT 169). (It might seem that, given *Being and Time*'s logophobia, language must *always* obscure rather than conceal. But this cannot be Heidegger's view, for otherwise he could not have written the book. His view must be, I think, that it is the nature of language to make genuine *Rede* difficult, but not impossible. The strangeness of his language and his many neologisms thus appear as demanded by the task of overcoming the clichés of *Gerede*, of producing genuine *Rede*.)

If Dasein lives authentically it will live in the light of the world-'understanding' possessed by all Dasein. But like Plato's cave-dwellers, average, everyday Dasein, Dasein 'mastered' by the One (BT 167), lives in a world of semblances. To maintain this state of affairs is the function of (in fact, not-so-idle) idle talk.

Idle talk constitutes the 'publicness of the One' (BT 167), the public view of things to which everyday Dasein is 'delivered over' (BT 173). Idle talk is always 'right' since it has the authority of the One behind it (BT 169). It is the kind of know-all talk that gets passed on in 'hearsay' (p. 133 above) and in which entities are only understood 'approximately and superficially'. In idle talk we understand each other perfectly well. That, however, is not because we have the same genuine reality in mind but because we have the same linguistic simulacrum in mind (BT 168). So, for example, you and I and can happily agree that 'socialism' is a thoroughly bad thing, but have almost no idea of what socialism is as a political theory or of the differences between its different versions. Idle talk, says Heidegger, can occur in writing as well as speech, and if it does, it amounts to nothing more than a kind of 'scribble' in which one cannot determine what is 'extracted from primary sources and what is just gossip' (BT 169). Almost certainly it is journalism – or as we would now say, the media – that Heidegger has in his sights, here. One might think of Fox News or CNN, and of the observation that the Left and Right in American politics do not even share the same facts any more.

The effect of idle talk is to 'uproot'. One floats in a fog of simulacra with no 'grounding' in extra-linguistic reality. One is cut off from authentic being-in-the-world and from authentic being-with-each-other. (BT 170). Everyone grows up in idle talk to start with. As children we learn by imitation, by mimicking the idle talk and attitudes of our parents and teachers. As authentic Dasein can never extract itself from, but only 'modify', its life in the One, so it can achieve and communicate genuine understanding only by 'modifying' idle talk, by struggling 'in it, out of it, and against it' (BT 169). Dasein cannot invent a new language (though it can do strange things with the existing language), but only engage in guerrilla actions against the 'correctnesses' of idle talk.

Of course everyday speech and writing may sometimes hit upon the real truth as to 'what must be done' (BT 173). The op-ed in the newspaper *might* have something really important to say. But since idle talk *always* presents itself as possessing the authority of expert knowledge, as long as one 'floats' in it, one can never know whether or not it really has such authority. And even if one has an inkling that something important is being said, public attention will have moved on to something different, and have taken one with it, before one can really dwell upon and learn about it. Idle talk is thus, as Heidegger puts it, always 'ambiguous' (BT 173–5). Again, it is the media and the 'attention deficit disorder' they produce, that are in the spotlight.

One of the symptoms of the uprootedness of everyday Dasein is a vague sense of dissatisfaction which expresses itself in 'curiosity', in, that is, the need for 'distraction' (BT 172). Someone who is grounded in a genuine under-standing of matters of importance is concerned with what is close at hand. But lacking such grounding, and obscurely dissatisfied with their 'there', the ungrounded look to the 'alien'. They engage in *looking* at the unfamiliar, looking without understanding, looking for the sake of looking. Heidegger seems to have six-cathedrals-in-seven-days tourism in mind here, which, given that such tourism is impossible in traditional societies, raises the question of whether the discussion of 'curiosity' really picks out something universal, as it is supposed to, or whether it is really a critique specific to modernity. One finds, however, in Plato's *Republic* a similar critique of 'democracy' – it is a social order that is superficially attractive on account of the variety of distractions it offers – and, in any case, Heidegger offers other examples of a 'curiosity' that is symptomatic of alienation from the actual: the attempt to 'synthesize' alien cultures with one's own (yoga, European Buddhism, and so on), and the 'exaggerated self-dissection' in terms of a system of 'characterologies' and 'typologies' (BT 178). This second example seems intended to identify the popularity of Jungian psychoanalysis as a symptom of inauthenticity.

Falling

Idle talk, curiosity, and ambiguity are inescapable aspects of the world in which Dasein finds itself. And on account of distantiality, there is, in all

Dasein, a constant 'temptation' (BT 177) to exist in the uprooted, inauthentic milieu they constitute. That it is so tempted constitutes Dasein's 'falling (*Verfallen*)' nature. Falling, says Heidegger, is an existential. It belongs to Dasein's 'constitution' (BT 176). Falling needs to be distinguished from 'fallenness (*Verfallenheit*)',[24] given that Heidegger offers the latter as his 'definition' of inauthenticity (ibid.) and obviously does not wish to make inauthenticity part of Dasein's *constitution*. 'Inauthenticity', he writes, is a matter of Dasein's having 'fallen away from itself' (BT 175) on account of a complete absorption in a 'being-with-one-another ... guided by idle talk, curiosity, and ambiguity', on account, that is, of its being completely 'taken over (*benommen*)' by the 'world' and by 'being there together with others in the One' (176).

Fallenness is seductive. In addition to distantiality, this is because 'fallen' life receives the full endorsement of the One, the assurance that 'everything is in the best of order'. Life in the One is tempting because it offers a certain 'tranquillity'. Or, if not tranquillity, exactly, a 'tranquilized' existence. What prevents it being true tranquillity is that one also experiences an obscure 'pull (*Zug*)' in the opposite direction (BT 184), towards authenticity, and this creates an inner 'turbulence' (BT 178–9). To understand what it is that creates this counter-movement to falling we need to examine Heidegger's conception of 'anxiety'.

Anxiety

Dasein's fallenness is, says Heidegger, a 'fleeing' that is motivated by 'anxiety (*Angst*)' which is a 'mood' and therefore a mode of affectedness. Anxiety is not the same as fear. Fear is fear in the face of something within the world that is found 'threatening'. Anxiety, too, finds something threatening but it is nothing in the world. The object of anxiety is 'nothing and nowhere'. It is, rather, one's 'being-in-the-world as such'. Anxiety is reflexive: the threatening object is oneself (BT 186).

Anxiety alienates. In anxiety 'the world offers nothing more' and neither does our being-with-others. They become 'of no consequence ... completely lacking significance' (BT 186). The normal mood of having things 'matter' to us (p. 129 above) dissolves. We feel *unheimlich*. Partly, this term expresses the 'uncanniness' (the everyday German meaning of *Unheimlichkeit*) of a mood that comes over us for no identifiable reason (BT 186). More importantly, however, Heidegger uses the word in the sense created by reading its etymological components separately and literally: given that *Heim* means home, *un-heimlich* really means, he suggests, *un-heimisch*, that is, *un-zuhause*, 'not-being-at-home' (BT 188–9).

Notice that we have not yet discovered why, in the state of anxiety, we find our own being 'threatening'. As Heidegger makes explicit (BT 192), this sense of disengagement from a world in which one is not at home is just the already discussed mood of 'thrownness' (pp. 129–30 above), the mood of finding oneself 'abandoned' to a world one did not choose to inhabit. While not, of course, a pleasant mood to inhabit, it does not seem correct to describe it as a state in which one feels threatened. It is rather the mood that both Sartre and Camus describe as 'nausea', the mood in which one finds one's existence, as they put it, 'absurd'. Macquarrie and Robinson respond to this point by suggesting that in many ways 'uneasiness' or 'malaise' might be better translations of *Angst* than 'anxiety' (BT p.227 fn.). While these are not, in fact, possible *translations* – *Angst* essentially involves the idea of a threat (BT 187) – the suggestion does reveal that the mood Heidegger calls 'anxiety' is really a combination of two moods or, perhaps better, a single, dynamically developing, affective condition.

To understand the threatening element in 'anxiety' one needs to attend to something that is, in a sense, positive and which happens in disengagement, in, as it were, the 'negation' of one's everyday being-in-the-world: one is disclosed to oneself, says Heidegger, as a 'worldless' '*solus ipse* (self alone)', plunged into an 'existential "solipsism"' (BT 188).[25] Here, finally, we understand why anxiety contains the experience of a threat, and why it is that it is one's own being-in-the-world that constitutes the threat. For what creates this state of 'solipsism' is the fact that what anxiety reveals in a 'primordial and inescapable (*eindringlich*) manner' is one's 'thrownness into death' (BT 251), a revelation that, as we shall see, is essentially 'individualizing'.

Anxiety, to repeat, is 'always latent' in Dasein: Dasein is anxious 'in the very depths of its being', anxious about death (BT 190). When anxiety comes forth as an occurrent mood, the 'issue' of Dasein's being, whether to be itself or not to be itself, comes to the fore and can receive either a positive or negative response. On the one hand, one may flee quickly back into the 'tranquilizing [but uneasy] security' of being 'of course at-home' in the arms of the One (BT 189). On the other, one may seize the moment, seize upon one's temporary individualization to realize that one's being is an open *possibility*, to realize that there is no *necessity* to follow the 'tasks, rules, standards', and 'urgenc[ies]' (BT 267) that are laid down by the One. In disclosing one's 'freedom', anxiety can have the effect of 'making Dasein free for the freedom of choosing itself' (BT 187–8). Anxiety contains the possibility of extracting oneself from the movement of falling, of turning towards authenticity (BT 191). The turn towards authenticity is, however, a turning towards death. What difference, we now need to ask, does this make to one's being-in-the-world?

Death

What, first of all, 'ontologically' speaking, is death? Heidegger identifies four features: it is a possibility of one's being that is 'ownmost', 'non-relational', 'certain' yet 'indefinite' (BT 258). The meaning of these terms will become clear as we proceed first to describe inauthentic and then authentic being towards death.

The One, Heidegger reminds us, is constituted by the 'public' interpretation of things contained in idle talk. Our everyday, 'idle', way of talking about death is essentially 'fugitive'. While we admit that 'one dies', we avoid both

'I will die' and 'You will die'. We 'comfort' the manifestly dying person with an assurance that he will certainly recover (and of those close to us we say only that they 'passed away'). The most common evasive strategy is to say (mostly to one-self), 'Of course one dies some day – but not yet.' This is a way of seeming to concede the 'certainty' of death without actually doing so. One marks out a domain where death certainly will not occur (a procedure one keeps on repeating) and thereby obscures the 'indefiniteness' of death, the fact that 'it is possible at any moment'. Everyday talk and thought about death is marked by the 'tempta-tion' to seek 'tranquilization', a tranquilization which is at the same time 'aliena-tion' from what one knows to be the truth. That these are the defining marks of 'falling' reaffirms that what falling is a 'fleeing' from is death (BT 252–8).

Authentic being-towards-death, for which Heidegger now introduces the term 'anticipation (*Vorlaufen*)', happens, we know, in preserving the mood of anxiety, in refusing to take cover in idle talk. Heidegger now provides a more detailed phenomenology of the anxious moment. In it, one comes genuinely 'face to face' with the indefinite certainty of death, with the 'nothing' into which one's existence will dissolve (BT 266). In this state of existential solipsism one realizes the 'non-relational' character of death, the fact that death 'lays claim to me *as an individual*', separates me out from 'the others' who will not die with me. It is this confrontation with 'non-relationality' that 'wrenches' me away from the One, brings about the 'individualization' (BT 263) that happens in anxiety. And it is also non-relationality that 'frees' us for the 'freedom of choosing oneself', makes me realize that, whatever kind of being-in-the-world I am to have, it is one that I can and must choose for myself. (Aware of the possibility of authenticity, inauthenticity, too, must be a choice.) Authentic being-towards-death makes one self-governed rather than One-governed, makes one (in my own rather than Heidegger's language) 'autonomous'. This, I think, is why death is my 'ownmost' possibility: it is the possibility which, rightly deployed, makes me my 'own' self.[26]

A second effect of facing up to death is what I shall call 'focus'. In grasping that death is both certain and possible (if not probable) 'at any moment', one realizes that 'there is no time to lose'. This releases one from 'lostness in those possibilities which may accidentally thrust themselves upon one' (BT 264). In authentic being-towards-death I 'run forward', *vor[-]laufen*, 'project', my life to the 'end', and, from that vantage point, look back and decide which are my 'own' possibilities and which I must lay aside as time-wasting irrelevancies. I must decide, that is, what is to be the narrative of my life as a totality, who I am to be. Living in the light of finitude endows life with urgency, intensity, and coherence, with, as I call it, focus.

Conscience and guilt

Authenticity, then, consists in the autonomy and focus that comes to us if we live in the light of authentic being towards, 'anxiety' about, death. Still, the question arises as to why we should bother with what seems to be such an uncomfortable mode of existence. Heidegger's answer is that it is something Dasein demands of itself (BT 267), a demand which, if it can be demonstrated, will verify that there really is the 'pull' in the opposite direction to falling (p. 142 above) and the consequent 'turbulence' it creates. What constitutes this demand is, Heidegger claims, the call of 'conscience'. Although he does not make this explicit, the discussion of 'conscience', and subsequently of 'guilt', seems to me a still more fine-grained phenomenology of the dynamics of anxiety.

Existentially understood, conscience has, initially, nothing to do with the morality of social norms. (When we get to the topic of 'heritage' we will see that ultimately there is a connection.) The call produced by the 'voice' of conscience is, says Heidegger, an 'appeal' from Dasein to itself. The caller is Dasein, yet at the same time something 'above (*über*)' Dasein (BT 275). One might suggest that the caller is really God, but Heidegger rejects this. Or, with Freud, one might suggest that it is a matter of two egos, of the superego calling to the ego. But that is not Heidegger's view either. It is not a matter of two entities but rather two states: Dasein in its 'not-at-homeness' calling to Dasein in its 'lostness in the One' (BT 276–7).

What conscience calls one to do – this much is clued by the everyday conception of conscience – is to recognize and take 'responsibility' for one's 'guilt (*Schuld*)', that is, a certain 'deficit' in one's being (*Schuld* has the dual meaning of 'guilt' and 'debt'). Thrownness, we know, belongs to Dasein's constitution: Dasein in its facticity is the 'thrown basis (*Grund*)' of its self-projection. The kind of being it can be is determined and limited by the possibilities presented by the cultural facticity it is always 'already in'. It has no option but to rest its 'weight' on this basis, yet 'it has not laid that basis itself':

> It is never existent *before* its basis, but only *from* it and *as this basis*. Thus 'being-a-basis' means *never* to have power over one's ownmost being from the ground up. This '*Not* (*Nicht*)' belongs to the existential meaning of 'thrownness'.
>
> (BT 284)

In the myth of Err, discussed at the end of Plato's *Republic*, depending on one's karma, one is given the choice between several future being-in-the-worlds at the termination of one's current earthly existence – rather as one might be given a choice from a row of suits. Existential 'deficit' consists in this *not* being the case. There is no Platonic – or Cartesian – self over and above our being-in-the-world. In the place of such a self there is only a 'nothingness (*Nichtigkeit*)' (BT 283), only, as Sartre would put it, an 'absence'. This nothingness belongs to thrownness in that it is on its account that we experience thrownness as a 'burden' (p. 129 above) that has been thrust upon us (BT 284).

What is one to do about being nothing beyond one's thrownness, about one's thrownness being unchosen, about the salience of the absence of choice?

One possibility that is never mentioned by Heidegger is resignation; suicide, in other words. But given that one rejects that – as nature abhors a vacuum, Heidegger perhaps presupposes an innate repulsion from, as he calls it, 'the Nothing (*das Nichts*)' (BT 285, 302) – then one has no option but to act on the basis of one's thrownness. The realization that I am a 'nullity' over and above my thrownness produces the negative insight that I did not choose my world. But it also produces the positive insight that the 'there', the 'Da' of my Da-sein, is, as it were, the only game in town. That I 'have to be' in the 'Da' is quite literally true because that is the only place where be-ing is possible. Acknowledging one's guilt thus produces the *double movement* that belongs to anxiety: initially it plunges one into the 'existential solipsism' of *unheimlich-keit* but then it throws one back into the world. One is not, however, unmarked by the experience. One returns to the world in a new condition which Heidegger calls 'resoluteness (*Entschlossenheit*)'.

Resoluteness

Resoluteness is essentially a matter of disclosure. Macquarrie and Robinson claim to have discovered one edition of *Being and Time* in which Heidegger hyphenates *Ent-schlossenheit* which, in conjuring the idea of 'un-closedness', brings out the close relation between *Entschlossenheit* and *Erschlossenheit*, disclosedness.[27] Resoluteness is a matter of knowing the 'primordial truth' of one's existence (BT 297), of 'being in the truth', the truth, recall, that belongs to Dasein's constitution (p. 134 above) but is blocked out by inauthentic Dasein. As one could put Heidegger's point, *Entschlossenheit ist eigentliche Erschlossenheit*, resoluteness is authentic disclosure. Being resolutely in the world is being in the world with the living knowledge of one's own individuality and with the critical distance from the norms of the One that such knowledge brings with it. One withdraws from idle talk into 'reticence', an active rather than passive reticence, however, since to be genuinely 'in the truth' is to be already in action (BT 302). As Heidegger puts the point in the 1936 'The Origin of the Work of Art' in a passage that is an explicit commentary on *Being and Time*, 'he who truly knows what is, knows what he wills to do in the midst of what is' (PLT 65).

Repeating once again the point that authentic existence cannot escape, but only 'modify', life in the One, Heidegger emphasizes that resolute existence does not provide one with a new world or new 'circle of others'. One's life still consists in concern with equipment and solicitude towards others. But since one is 'in the truth', since one listens to *Rede* rather than *Gerede*, authentic speech rather than idle talk, this concern and solicitude acquire a radically new character (BT 279–301).

Before exploring this new character I should like to draw attention to the fact that realizing the 'nullity' of one's thrownness into the world is realizing the absoluteness of death. If one never existed 'before' one's thrown 'basis', then there is nothing to exist after it is extinguished. We are just the brief comet-path between one absence and another. Death and 'guilt' are really the same thing, 'the utter nullity of Dasein' (BT 306). This seems to me to make it clear that although Heidegger suggests that *Being and Time* is theologically neutral,[28] it is, in fact, as I pointed out in discussing the mood of abandonment (p. 130 above), the work of an atheist. For *Being and Time* there is no being beyond time, only 'the nothing'. Heidegger's claim, of course, is that phenomenology, as a method, abjures all theoretical constructions, but that cannot really be so since a traditional, believing Christian could not have produced the above account of death. To put the point another way, Heidegger's own atheism is as much a theoretical construction as is theism. This supports the claim I made earlier, that Heidegger's claim to be providing a 'transcendental' account of Dasein as such can only be partially true. While most of Division I can plausibly claim to be an ontology of human being as such, when Heidegger turns to the 'existential', Division II – to the topics of anxiety, conscience, guilt and the nothing – the 'truths' he articulates seem to me to be confined to modern, Western, secular, recently-post-death-of-God, grieving, consciousness.

Temporality as the ontological meaning of care

As we saw (p. 137 above), what Dasein is, ontologically speaking, is 'care': essentially, that is, Dasein is 'ahead of itself', 'already in' a world in which it is 'in the midst (*bei*)' of other beings, some of them Daseins, others not. Fairly obviously, this self-understanding, which all Dasein possesses, is temporal, and so, says Heidegger, temporality is the 'meaning (*Sinn*)' of care, in the sense that this is what we have been talking about all along (BT 301). And so, with perhaps a slight sense of anti-climax, the answer to *Being and Time*'s second most fundamental question emerges: the meaning of Dasein's being is temporality.

Temporality is 'articulated' into three temporal 'ecstasies' (BT 330), three ways in which Dasein 'stands out' from itself: phenomenologically speaking, it extends beyond itself into the past and future, and the present, too, counts as a temporal 'ecstasy' because (a topic I have not explored) Heidegger thinks that the spatiality into which Dasein 'stands out' can be analysed as a mode of temporality (BT 418–21). The past is one's 'already in', one's thrownness, which, Heidegger remarks, 'is the primary existential meaning of facticity' (BT 328), the present is the domain of one's current engagement with other beings, and the future is that which one projects into in choosing the 'on-account-of-which' in terms of which the present shows up to one (BT 329). Since there are two modes of Dasein, inauthentic and authentic (i.e. resolute) there are two kinds of temporality. I begin with authentic temporality.

Being 'authentically futural', we know, consists in 'anticipation'. Rather than evading one's end, one 'runs forward' into, comes 'face to face' with it. In doing so, and in grasping the nullity of that end, one 'takes over' one's thrownness, one's 'having been', as the *totality* of what one is (BT 339). This 'taking over' takes the form of the 'repetition (*Wiederholung*)' of one's cultural past (ibid.), a notion to which I shall return shortly.

Concerning the authentic present, Heidegger says that, in resoluteness, 'the present is ... held in the future and in having been', a contextualization which means that resolute Dasein stands in the 'moment of vision (*Augenblick*)' in which the real 'Situation (*Situation*)' – as opposed to the superficial 'general picture (*allgemeine Lage*)' produced by journalism and other forms of idle talk (BT 297–301) – stands revealed (BT 338). What this means cannot be fully explained until we get to the topic of 'heritage', but, clearly, the idea is that authenticity give one a kind of perspective on the current state of things which inauthentic Dasein lacks: a perspective which, given that Heidegger explicitly relates 'Situation' to Jaspers' 'limit situation (*Grenzsituation*)' (BT 301 n. xv),[29] gives one some kind of decisive, penetrating, and radical insight into 'what must be done'.

Whereas the future is the most important ecstasy for authentic Dasein, for inauthentic Dasein it is the present. Inauthentic Dasein is 'lost in the making present of "today"' (BT 391), it projects its being on what is 'feasible, urgent or indispensable' in today's 'daily business' (BT 337). Of course even inauthentic Dasein projects somewhat into the future – in saying that I am a banker and a Republican, to repeat, I entitle you to expect that I will be these things tomorrow – but, as we know, it evades anticipation of the end. And so, in contrast to the running-forward-all-the-way of authentic Dasein, its stance to the future is one of 'awaiting' (BT 337): awaiting, with hope, the satisfaction of the desires it forms on the basis of the 'conventionalities of the One' (BT 391), and, with repressed dread, the not-to-be-mentioned bad thing from which it is 'fleeing'. As to the past, inauthentic Dasein's relation is one of 'forgetting' (BT 339). Lost as it is in the norms of current political correctness, the past, as a source of norms that might *contradict* those of the current One, is a closed book.

Temporality and historicality

The 'existential meaning' of facticity, recall, is thrownness (p. 147 above). One is thrown into the world of the One. But one is thrown, too – that is, 'born' (BT 373) – into a world with a past, a cultural history. Whether or not one closes oneself off to it, one exists historically, one 'historicizes'. Dasein's 'historicality (*Geschichtlichkeit*)' is the key to answering the question of what difference becoming authentic makes to one's life, the question, that is, of the *content* of the resolute life.

Authenticity, resoluteness, is, in my own language, autonomy plus focus (p. 144 above). That, however, is a purely formal notion. I can be autonomously focussed as an ecologist, a civil rights activist, or a doctor curing malaria in Africa, but, equally, as Kierkegaard's seducer, as a suicide bomber, or as a Ponzi-schemer. So resoluteness seems compatible with any content. Karl Löwith reports that, among his fellow students attending the lectures that culminated in *Being and Time*, a joke circulated consisting in the assertion, 'I am resolved, but towards what I don't know.' Löwith cites this joke in the course of explaining Heidegger's infatuation with Nazism. What *Being and Time* advocates, he suggests, is an 'empty decisionism', a matter of style empty of substance: it does not matter what you do – of necessity, one's fundamental project is a groundless choice – as long as you do it with style. The style required is that of the strong and silent 'hero': decisive, contemptuous of the inauthentic mass, of talk, of explanation, the 'Nietzschean' style of, in short, the jackbooted Nazi SS officer.[30] In fact, however, Heidegger, in effect, anticipates the charge of 'empty decisionism' himself and sets out to rebut it. (Löwith's joke perhaps circulated before Heidegger's lectures had reached this point in *Being and Time*.) 'We must ask', he writes,

> whence ... [authentic] Dasein can draw those possibilities on which it factically projects itself. One's anticipatory projection of oneself on ... death guarantees only the totality and authenticity [focus and autonomy] of one's resoluteness. But these possibilities of existence ... are not to be gathered from death.
>
> (BT 383)

So from where are they to be gathered?

Heritage

One thing that is clear is that we cannot derive our authentic life-defining possibilities of existence from those that '"circulate" in the "average" public way of interpreting Dasein today' since these have 'mostly been made unrecognizable by ambiguity', the ambiguity of idle talk (BT 383). Recall that 'ambiguity' does not mean that everyday talk contains no valid insights into 'what must done', only that, since everything is presented with an air of expert authority, one cannot sort the wheat from the chaff, the fake news from the real news. Hence, although one may, in fact, end up authentically living one of the life-possibilities endorsed by current public opinion, one cannot *derive* it from current public opinion, cannot validate it *as* authentic. One requires, therefore, some other basis against which one can assess the life possibilities on offer within the current One.

The key to discovering this basis lies in Dasein's historicality, in the history into which it is thrown. 'History', here, means neither a record of facts nor their scientific analysis. It is rather history as ethical 'tradition (*Überlieferung*)' or 'heritage (*Erbe*)', the sole source, according to Heidegger, of value, of the 'good' (BT 383).[31] It is history as conceived in Nietzsche's *On the Uses and Disadvantages of History for Life* [32] (Heidegger makes explicit reference to this 'unequivocal and penetrating (*eindeutig-eindringlich*)' work [BT 396]). This is history as it is preserved in the collective consciousness of the community, though it may also be the explicit work of historians. History in this sense is the repository of value, of, more specifically, the virtues. Three features make it such a repository (Heidegger here adopts Nietzsche's tripartite terminology as his own). First, it is 'monumental': it memorializes (that is, partially mythologizes) the lives of certain figures as ethical role models or 'heroes'. Second, it is 'antiquarian' in that it 'reverently preserves' these past lives. The thought, here (pursued, we shall see, by Arendt), principally concerns education. In the initiation of our children into our ethical heritage we teach them to revere the figures that it memorializes. And third, the history in question is 'critical' in that it provides a standard for criticizing the norms of today, for sorting through the 'ambiguous' norms of idle talk and seeing what, if anything, is worth preserving (BT 396).

Resolute Dasein, projecting, in anticipation, on 'the nothing', knows that it is nothing but its thrownness. But it also knows that it is thrown not just into the One of current idle talk, but also into heritage, into, as one might put it, the One of heritage. And so it 'chooses its hero' (BT 385) and 'loyally' follows in its footsteps, 'repeating' an 'existence possibility' that 'has been', because it knows that heritage is the 'sole authority a free existing can have'. Since I am nothing over and above my thrownness, the values of that thrownness are *my* values, so that being true to heritage is being true to myself. In other language, since the self is culturally constructed, the deep values of one's culture are one's own deep values (BT 391). (Notice a second reason why authenticity can only be an 'existential modification' [p. 139 above] of the One.)

So how does heritage govern the content of the authentic life? Heritage is the heritage of a *Gemeinschaft* (community), of a *Volk* (people) (BT 384). The heroes honoured in heritage are those who have provided exceptional service to the community. And so a commitment to heritage is a commitment to service to the community. It follows that being resolutely 'true to' heritage is a matter of 'communication and struggle in and with one's "generation"' in order to 'free' the power of the 'destiny', the proper future, of the community (BT 384–5). Resolute action is that which helps realize the proper future of the community, whether what is most important at present is the community's relations with other communities, or whether it is a matter of internal reordering in order better to live up to the ideal of itself contained in heritage. Because resolute Dasein is 'in the truth' and not 'lost in the making present of "today"', it is able to see the present state of affairs in the light of heritage. Hence it is not bamboozled by the 'general picture' perpetrated by idle talk, but understands the real historical 'Situation'. And to understand that is to be able to project the proper 'destiny' of the community. Resolute Dasein genuinely knows, in general terms, 'what must be done'. But how is it to know what *it* must do?

Dasein is thrown into a world and a heritage. But, Heidegger, emphasizes, one is also 'thrown into one's individualization' (BT 339). One's thrownness is always an *individualized* thrownness. One shares with 'the others' a common One and a common heritage. But one is also, in every case, thrown, into a distinct *individual* facticity which is composed of the strengths and weaknesses that are the produce of one's unique nature and nurture, and by one's position in historical time and cultural space. Every individual, whether it recognizes it or not, constitutes (as Leibniz observes and Arendt emphasizes) a unique perspective on the world, and hence a unique potentiality for action.

One confronts, then, an historical 'Situation', in one's individualized facticity. What should one do? Basically, Heidegger's thought is a fairly commonplace one: one asks oneself, 'What would X [e.g. Jesus] do in this situation?' Obviously some 'heroes' are more relevant to the current 'Situation' than others, and some are more relevant to one's *own* situation within that 'Situation'. And so one 'chooses [as] one's hero', one who will provide a helpful model in the given circumstances. ('Choosing one's hero' has a decisionist ring to it, but this is misleading. There are correct and incorrect choices.) So, to take a somewhat banal example, suppose it becomes clear to me that the policies of the government of my country are tailored to serve, almost exclusively, the interests of the richest 1 percent of the population. I see, further, that the relation of the 1 percent to the 99 percent is an internal analogue of what, in relation to other countries, constitutes colonialism. I further know that, 'independence', freedom from colonialism, is a foundational value of my community, and so I know, in general terms, what must be done. But what should *I* do? A hero of heritage particularly relevant to the resistance to colonialism is Mahatma Ghandi. He is, moreover, particularly relevant to me since (let us suppose) part of my facticity is a certain modest ability to enthuse an audience. And so I conclude that what I must do is found, or at least support, a civil disobedience movement.

* * *

The idea of 'repeating' a pattern of life memorialized in one's cultural heritage might, at first sight, seem extremely conservative, might seem to suggest a society whose 'antiquarian' reverence for the past – for, as it were, 'the ancestors' – has frozen it into the kind of immobility which Plato admired in ancient Egypt and the nineteenth century took to characterize China. To cancel this impression Heidegger says that 'repetition' is not a matter of making 'something that was formerly actual reoccur' but is, rather, a matter of a 'response' (*Erwiderung*) to the past existence-possibility (BT 386). The exploration of the nature of this 'response' is the point at which Gadamer's meditation on 'fusion of horizons' that will be the topic of the next chapter finds its starting point in *Being and Time*.

* * *

And so, with some further mediations on temporality, we reach the end of *Being and Time* as we have it. On its final page it reminds us that although we have read 437 pages, we have still only been dealing with the question of the being of Dasein. The big question to which the answer to this question was only the propaedeutic, the meaning of being in general, is still before us. The only progress we have made towards answering it is to have raised a possible line of inquiry into whether, perhaps, 'time manifests itself as the horizon of being' in general (BT 437), as it has with respect to the being of Dasein,. As we shall see in Chapter 9, however, this is a notion Heidegger will ultimately reject.

Notes

1   Were this a book devoted entirely to Heidegger, I would provide a finer-grained periodization of his philosophy which would identify a very early period prior to *Being and Time*, so that my proposed twofold division would become a threefold division (or actually a fourfold division since I would distinguish 'middle period' (p. 196 below) from genuinely 'late' Heidegger). Here, however, I shall not discuss the works prior to *Being and Time*.

2   Numerals following 'BT' refer to the pagination of the seventh German edition of *Sein und Zeit*, given in the margins of the Macquarrie and Robinson translation.

3   'Ontic' investigations investigate beings, 'ontological' investigations investigate being. An ontic investigation of a kind of being, material bodies, for example, seeks factual information about them such as the laws governing their motion. An ontological investigation asks what it is that constitutes something as a material body, is, in other words, a conceptual investigation. Ontic investigations presuppose that a corresponding ontological investigation has been, or could be, carried out.

4   Y-B 44.

5   In Chapter 9 I shall argue that 'the question of being' is crucially ambiguous so that there is *a* 'question of being' that is certainly not 'bloodless'. *This* question, however, I shall further argue, is not the question that is raised in *Being and Time*. My claim, in short, is that *Being and Time* actually fails to raise the question Heidegger really wants to raise, that *Being and Time, too,* 'forgets' the *real* 'question of being'.

6   Some scholars suggest that 'Dasein' might include institutional and corporate entities in addition to human beings. In the 'Letter on Humanism', however, Heidegger makes clear that, 'as far as our experience shows', only human beings have Dasein. This, however, is a contingent, not a necessary, fact (P 246–8). Being a Dasein – being a person – is a *way* of being which *as far as we know* is exemplified only by those classified biologically as humans, but which *might* one day turn out to be exemplified by non-human beings.

7   I have in mind here the similarity of anti-Cartesian purpose between *Being and Time* and Gilbert Ryle's *The Concept of Mind* (1949) that can be partly explained by the fact that Ryle attended Heidegger's lectures, was a close reader of *Being and Time*, and reviewed it in the journal *Mind* the year after its publication.

8   Nietzsche (2002) section 34.

9   Heidegger thinks this disposed of Cartesian doubt about the external world (BT 202–8). Cartesian doubt consists in a knowing subject wondering whether the object of consciousness also possesses extra-mental existence. But since being a knowing subject is an abstraction from one's normal state which is involvement *with objects*, it follows that the very fact of being in a state of doubt presupposes the existence of what it doubts. This seems to me an invalid piece of reasoning. I, as the doubting subject, may agree that my doubt is an abstraction from *what I normally take to be* my being-in-the-world yet nonetheless intelligibly raise the question of whether my normal self-understanding is true. This 'question' is not, of course, a genuine question, not a genuine questioning, but then it was never intended as such. Descartes was always clear that his doubt was 'hyperbolic', that its purpose was to identify the certain rather than genuinely to question the known but uncertain.

10   Braver (2014) 37.

11   And given that everything other than Dasein is 'equipment' must expand still further to include abstract entities such as constitutions and institutional entities such as universities.

12 Gorner (2000) 70.

13 'Existentials' pertain to Dasein's being, 'Existentiells' pertain to Dasein as *a* being. Being-with-others is an 'existential', being with others as leader of a scout troop is one of the 'existentiell possibilities' in which the existential might find its instantiation.

14 'State-of-mind' is thus a very misleading translation of *Befindlichkeit*. It is important to notice that Heidegger's word for 'mood' is *Stimmung* rather than *Laune*. It is hard to regard the latter – as in *schlechte Laune*, 'bad mood' – as anything but a psychic state of a subject. *Stimmung*, on the other hand, can be entirely detached from subjects, as when one speaks of the *Stimmung* of a room or the *Stimmung* of Spring: in some respects 'atmosphere' would be a better translation than 'mood'.

15 The mood, perhaps, of the beginning of the last movement of Beethoven's last string quartet (opus 135): under the beginning, marked *Grave*, he writes *Muss es sein?* (Must it be?). Then, as the tempo changes to *Allegro*, he writes *Es muss sein* (It must be), the mood, I suggest, of what we will find Heidegger calling 'resoluteness'.

16 Notice, here, the confirmation of my suggestion that the 'existential', that which pertains to *Existenz*, to the 'issue' of Dasein's being, is to be identified with that which is revealed in affectedness.

17 Arendt (1978) 297.

18 As we saw, Heidegger uses 'on-account-of-which' to refer, not just to social roles, but also to the termini of chains of instrumental relations (p. 125 above). The reason I have preferred my 'on-account-of-which' to Macquarrie and Robinson's 'for-the-sake-of-which' as the translation of *Worum-willen* is that it does not make sense to say that the carpenter builds houses 'for the sake of' being a carpenter, as if being a carpenter were some future goal he hopes to achieve. A subsidiary reason is that 'for the sake of' translates *wozu* rather than *worum*, which is normally used to ask what something is 'about'. No translation of *Worum-willen* can really be perfect given that Heidegger uses it to designate *both* the 'whither' and the 'whence' of practical activity. While 'for-the-sake-of-which' indeed makes more sense with respect to the termini of instrumental chains, given that the principal use is with respect to the initiators of such chains, I think that 'on-account-of-which' is the least bad alternative.

19 Quine (1960) Chapter 2.

20 But surely, it may be objected, if Newton's laws are true then they have always been true, so that the *proposition* 'Objects in uniform motion stay in that motion unless acted on by an external force' was true before Newton first asserted the corresponding *sentence*. I think Heidegger would have no objection to this way of expressing his point that Newton merely articulated how the world already was. Heidegger's interest, however, is in *assertion*, in the *grasping* of truth, in Dasein's 'being in the truth', and his point is that being able to assert the truth of Newton's laws requires the 'subjective condition' that one possesses the scheme of disclosure that reveals beings as Newtonian objects, as well as the 'objective' condition that the world 'correspond' to the way Newton's laws claim it to be.

21 Heidegger's definition of distantiality actually says that if one is behind one wants to catch up, whereas if one has a 'priority (*Vorrang*)' over the others one wants to suppress *them* (*sie*). Given that he is about to use distantiality to explain our conformist tendencies this makes little sense, since a concern to *maintain* 'priority', to suppress the others who might catch up, would actually mandate *non*-conformism. What Heidegger is about to say is that, on account of distantiality, we succumb to social pressure so that 'every kind of priority (*Vorrang*) gets noiselessly suppressed' (BT 127). Pretty clearly, I think, the *sie* is a misprint that has gone uncorrected through many editions. It should be *den*, in which case it would be the 'priority' we want to suppress.

22 Heidegger's use of 'average, everyday' is ambiguous. In ontological, 'Division I', discussions, 'average, everyday existence' is the mode of existence that is common to all Dasein. In existential, 'Division II' discussions it refers to inauthentic Dasein, to a Dasein that has 'levelled down' to 'the average'.

23 Dreyfus (1991) 154.

24 Given that *Verfallen* means 'falling', *Verfallenheit* ought to mean 'fallingness'. Heidegger's usage of these words, however, defies grammar.

25 The word 'solipsism' is derived from *solus ipse*.

26 In *Eclipse of Reason* (ER 137), Horkheimer claims that 'man's emergence as an individual' required the invention of the Christian soul. Only subsequently could he be aware of the contrast between

'his [finite] life and that of the seemingly eternal collectivity'. If there is any truth in this claim, then given that inauthenticity is an evasion of individuality, both inauthenticity and authenticity are culturally local, rather than universal, phenomena. Since Horkheimer was a close reader of *Being and Time* (SE 27–8), this is likely the comment he intends to make on section 53, a comment that supports my suggestion that what *Being and Time* really describes is post-death-of-God, 'Weimar' consciousness.

27 BT p.346, fn. The hyphen does not appear in the 'unaltered' eleventh German edition, but whether or not it occurs in *Being and Time* it is certainly sanctioned in the 1936 'Origin of the Work of Art' in which Heidegger writes, 'the resoluteness intended in *Being and Time* is not the deliberate action of a subject but the opening up of human being, out of its captivity in that which is, into the openness of being' (PLT 65); and it appears explicitly in the 1930 'On the Essence of Truth' (P 151).

28 More exactly, he states that the interpretation of Dasein as being-in-the-world is theologically neutral (P 267). The claim, in other words, is that the 'Division I' material (as I call it) is theologically neutral, which it surely is. My claim, however, is that the 'Division II' material presupposes atheism with respect to the Christian God.

29 The *Stanford Encyclopaedia of Philosophy*'s entry for Jaspers (accessed 25/6/17) says that 'limit situations' are 'moments, usually accompanied by experiences of dread, guilt or acute anxiety, in which the human mind confronts the restrictions and pathological narrowness of its existing forms, and allows itself to abandon the securities of its limitedness, and so to enter a new realm of self-consciousness'. Heidegger, we will see, thinks of the limit situation in historical rather than psychological terms as something close to the moment of what Thomas Kuhn calls a 'paradigm shift'.

30 Hans Jonas, Pierre Bourdieu, Habermas, and Richard Wolin also accuse Heidegger of 'decisionism' (see Young [1997] 79–84). Heidegger, I am about to argue, is certainly *not* a decisionist. The philosopher who really is one, however, is Sartre, for whom existential anguish is grounded in the fact that the fundamental project that I am is 'unjustified' since it cannot but be based on radical, reason-less, i.e. 'absurd', choice.

31 '[A]lles "gute" Erbschaft ist...'

32 Nietzsche (1997).

7 Gadamer

Truth versus method

Born in the year of Nietzsche's death, Hans-Georg Gadamer (1900–2002) was a student of Heidegger in Freiburg and Marburg and, in spite of sometimes discouraging criticisms from the master,[1] remained, all his life, in the Heideggerian 'camp'. Unlike Heidegger, he did not join the Nazi Party, but did make enough compromises – he signed a declaration of support for the regime by 'German scientists' – to be allowed to become professor at Leipzig in 1938. After the war he was judged to be sufficiently untainted by Nazism to become rector of his university. Unwilling to live under the East German socialist regime, he moved to Frankfurt in 1947. In 1949 he took over Jaspers' chair in Heidelberg, where he remained for the rest of his life. In 1962 he secured a position at Heidelberg for Habermas, with whom he remained in friendly disagreement for the rest of his life. Gadamer's magnum opus, *Truth and Method* (the German original adds the subtitle, *Basic Features of a Philosophical Hermeneutics*),[2] which appeared in 1960, is the principle exposition of a version of phenomenology commonly referred to as 'hermeneutics'.

What is philosophical hermeneutics?

Hermeneutics is the art of interpretation. It takes its name from Hermes, the messenger of the gods (a somewhat unfortunate provenance, one might think, given Hermes' penchant for deception). The art of interpretation has, of course, existed as long as written texts have existed, but it received a significant reawakening during the Protestant Reformation, for which cutting through centuries of what the reformers took to be Catholic misinterpretation of the Bible to its true and original meaning became a central preoccupation. A crucial figure in the modern development of hermeneutics is Friedrich Schleiermacher (1768–1834) (another unfortunate name, given that it literally means 'maker of veils'), who extended the task of hermeneutics from interpretation of the Bible to interpretation of linguistic texts of all kinds.

The aim of hermeneutics, all practitioners agree, is *Verstehen*, 'understanding', understanding of texts. Modern hermeneuticists, however, extend the scope of hermeneutics to the understanding of all meaningful phenomena.

Not only texts but also 'texts' – human actions and expressions of mind in general – are phenomena that require understanding through interpretation.

Verstehen has a long history of being contrasted with *Erklären*, 'explanation'. The contrast turns on two different kinds of answer to 'Why did X occur?' Consider a man raising and lowering two illuminated orange cones. An explanation could be given in terms of brain stimuli, neurological events and muscular contractions, but this would yield no 'understanding' of the event, no comprehension of its meaning. To understand that, we need to be in implicit possession of what amounts, in fact, to a great deal of background knowledge: knowledge about, not the science world, but rather the lifeworld. To understand that what the actor is doing is guiding a plane to its berth, we need to know about human beings and their needs, about contemporary modes of transport, about planes and airports and so on. Wilhelm Dilthey (1833–1911) made the claim that was influential throughout the twentieth century, that while *Erklären* is the appropriate methodology for the natural sciences (*Naturwissenschaften*) it is inappropriately applied to the human sciences (*Geisteswissenschaften*), since what we want from the latter is understanding. Nature we explain, he argued, but 'psychic life' we understand.

Gadamer is, of course, a philosopher rather than a hermeneuticist (save to the extent that his philosophy requires the interpretation of texts belonging to the history of philosophy). So the common practice of referring to his philosophy as 'hermeneutics' is strictly speaking incorrect. What Gadamer propounds is, rather, as he himself calls it, 'philosophical hermeneutics', or, more clearly, philosophy of hermeneutics. Describing himself as a 'phenomenologist', his aim is thus, in the tradition of Husserl and Heidegger, to reveal the 'transcendental' structure common to all acts of interpretative understanding (TM xxxii–iii). Unlike the hermeneuticists themselves, he emphasizes, he is not concerned to produce a 'manual' of correct hermeneutical procedure analogous to a treatise on poetics or rhetoric, and neither does he seek to 'elaborate a system of rules to describe, let alone direct, the methodological procedures of the human sciences'. 'My real concern', he writes, 'is philosophical: not what we do or ought to do, but what happens to us over and above our wanting and doing' (TM xxv–vi) when we achieve understanding through interpretation. 'I am not proposing a method', he writes, 'I am describing what is the case' (TM 512).

Given that 'understanding' is, in Gilbert Ryle's terminology a 'success word', Gadamer's disavowal of any prescriptive ambition is not unproblematic. For, a fortiori, in describing what happens when the goal of hermeneutics succeeds rather than fails, one is also prescribing how one ought to proceed in one's hermeneutical practice. (To describe the life of Jesus is to prescribe, in outline, the proper life for all Christians.) To a degree, therefore, Gadamer's philosophical hermeneutics *is* prescriptive. It remains true, however, that he is not attempting to write an instruction manual for interpreters, any more than Aristotle's *Poetics*, which describes the basic features of the great tragedies of the century before his own, is an instruction manual for writers of tragedies. The difference lies, I think, in the level of detail. While neither Gadamer's nor Aristotle's work is *irrelevant* to the proper conduct of the practices they discuss, neither is interested in providing a 'technique' for writing tragedies or interpreting historical texts. Although the hermeneuticists themselves traditionally sought to discover one (TM 268), Gadamer in fact rejects the idea that there could be a comprehensive 'technique' of interpretation. The art of interpretation, he believes, contains an ineliminable element of Aristotelian *phronesis*, a practical wisdom that cannot be fully reduced to a set of rules (TM 315 et passim).

Gadamer's motivation

What motivates *Truth and Method*? As noted above (p. 118), Gadamer writes in an autobiographical sketch that in the political and spiritual chaos following the German defeat in 1918, he and his fellow students had no time for the 'bloodless academic philosophizing' of the dominant Neo-Kantian school. What therefore excited him about Heidegger's teaching, was the fact that it dealt with *real* questions whose answers *made a difference* to the lives of real people. He adds that this same thing impressed him about the poet Stefan George, about the 'formative effect' George had on the lives of the members of his 'circle'. Gadamer writes that he 'never completely forgot' the model provided by George as a corrective to the mere 'play with concepts' characteristic of the dominant academic philosophy of his day (PG 5) ('never completely forgot' is typical Gadamerian caution with respect to this ambivalent figure,[3] Gadamer's ingrained habit of preserving a low political profile).

We can infer, then, that Gadamer wishes his philosophy to be, more or less directly, relevant to genuine problems in human life. What, in particular, he wishes it to be relevant to – what he sees as *the* problem of modern life – is the 'growing rationalization of society and of the scientific techniques of administrating it that are more characteristic of our age than the vast progress of modern science' itself, the fact that 'the methodological spirit of [natural] science permeates everything' (TM xxvi). At bottom, then, Gadamer's concerns are, once again, Weber's, the dehumanizing effects of 'rationalization', of the 'control' exercised over human life by scientific 'calculation'.

The 'methodological spirit' underlying the imperialism of science is, says Gadamer, 'positivism' (PG 6), the doctrine that scientific method[4] is the sole path to truth, that only what can be established by scientific method counts as knowledge. Against positivism, against, scientism, Gadamer wishes to show, first, that art and the humanities are sources of knowledge, and, second, that the truth they disclose 'goes beyond the limits of the concept of method as set by modern science expanded to cover further realms of interpretation' (TM xx–xxi). There are, then, to adapt Hamlet's words, more truths in heaven and earth than are dreamt of in positivism's philosophy.

As Gadamer notes, this, of itself, is not a particularly novel claim since it is already part of Dilthey's claim about the human sciences: the human sciences are sources of knowledge but their path to that knowledge is not the method of the natural sciences. But what, then, is that path? Although Dilthey and other philosophers of hermeneutics have attempted to provide an answer, the answer they have given has been fundamentally mistaken. Until, therefore, a correct account of the nature of hermeneutical understanding is provided, the rejection of positivism lacks 'philosophical legitimation' (TM xxi).

Gadamer develops his own account of hermeneutics via a critique of Dilthey and other likeminded theorists. This, however, should not be allowed to obscure the fact that this is a familial dispute, that Dilthey and Gadamer share the same fundamental aim of refuting positivism – the positivism of, for example, Kant. When Gadamer writes that his task is to provide 'the most insistent admonition to scientific consciousness to acknowledge its own limits' (TM xxii), the echo of the *Critique of Pure Reason* is unmistakable. But whereas Gadamer seeks to 'deny' the omniscience of science to make room for other forms of *knowledge*, famously, Kant finds it 'necessary to deny knowledge in order to make room for [mere] faith' (B xxx). As far as Kant is concerned, the limits of science *are* the limits of knowledge.

Notice that if Gadamer's task can be successfully carried out, one practical consequence that follows immediately is that the humanities are essential to higher education. What follows, in other words, is a defence of the *Bildung* (self-formation through education) discussed at the beginning of *Truth and Method* (TM 8–16: see further pp. 182–3 below). If there is knowledge that can be accessed by the humanities but not by science, then an education confined to 'STEM' subjects represents the *cognitive* impoverishment of its victims, their likely reduction to, in Nietzsche's phrase, mere clever animals.

The aestheticization of art

Gadamer's attempt to show that there are forms of knowledge other than science begins with a discussion of art that occupies Part I of *Truth and Method*.

Positivists, clearly, deny that art provides access to truth about reality. Art must be a non-cognitive venture. What, then, does it do? The natural response is to say that it produces pleasant sensations, that it 'expresses' (and so 'evokes') *feelings*. This, as we know (p. 79 above), is what 'aesthetic' originally referred to: the domain of sensation and feeling. (So, for example. the 'Aesthetic' of Kant's *Critique of Pure Reason* deals with the pre-conceptual, and hence pre-cognitive, realm of the mind out of which it manufactures objectual consciousness.)

The exclusion of art from the domain of cognition, its relegation to the realm of feeling, its 'subjectivization' as Gadamer puts it, began with Kant's *Critique of Judgment*. Gadamer notes that the subjective, non-cognitive nature of art is the taken-for-granted starting point of Kant's aesthetics:

positivism is assumed at the outset. The question for Kant is: *Given* that 'aesthetic judgments' do not express knowledge, what is it that they actually do?

Kant's complicated account comes in two parts. The first (briefly discussed in Chapter 4 [pp. 79–80 above]) focuses on the judgments of beauty. In our judgments of beauty, our 'judgments of taste', we express the feeling of beauty which occurs when there is an unexpected harmony between sense and intellect, a harmony which occurs when we discover a conceptual form that has not been conceptually formed. So, as we saw, in the abstract design of a Maori tattoo or the structure of a flower, we find a concept-like unity without there being a concept at work imposing that unity, or at least without our attending to the unifying concept. (So, for example, the unity of a house comes about because it is designed as a 'thing for living in', but in enjoying its beauty one abstracts from its function and enjoys it merely for its form, as if it were an abstract sculpture.) The feeling of beauty expressed by the judgment of taste occurs when we discover a 'purposiveness without a purpose'.

This theory of beauty applies to both nature and art. But art (*die schöne Künste*, 'the beautiful arts' in German) surely, has something to offer that is not offered by nature, something to offer in addition to beauty. This, says Kant, is due to genius. What the genius who produces the great artwork does is to present us with the 'aesthetic ideas' (TM 80), the ideas of 'first and last things' such as heaven, hell, freedom, and the immortal soul. Such ideas exceed what can be grasped in conceptual thought, and hence demand 'genius' for their representation, a capacity distinguished from mere crafts-manship by the fact that it 'cannot be reduced to a rule'. There is no algo-rithm that can be followed to produce a great work of art and neither therefore is there any algorithm for grasping its content. A great artwork generates 'more thought' than can ever be fully captured in a paraphrase of its meaning (TM 46).

It is clear that the account of judgments of beauty as expressions of plea-surable 'harmony between the faculties' renders such judgments non-cognitive in the sense that they do not report facts about the external world. But why does Kant regard his account of art as the presentation of the aesthetic ideas as excluding it from the domain of knowledge? First, because were art to convey any kind of knowledge it would not be knowledge about *this* world – the only world science claims as its exclusive preserve – but rather about a supernatural world. Second, however, art does not convey knowledge about a supernatural world either since, according to Kant, nothing can provide such knowledge. The 'aesthetic' ideas, that is, correspond to the 'ideas of reason', ideas which, according to the 'Dialectic' of the *Critique of Pure Reason*, while inevitable objects of thought, and even 'presuppositions of practical [moral] reason', can never be objects of knowledge.

* * *

The Kantian theory of genius, Gadamer observes, became the foundation of the account of art provided by nineteenth-century Romanticism. The reason artistic creation cannot be 'reduced to a rule' is that the great artist produces unconsciously and so cannot say how he has done what he has done, or even, very clearly, what it is that he has done. The genius is treated as a 'somnambulist' (TM 61). (Richard Wagner uses this very word to describes Beethoven's creative genius: Beethoven created out of a 'somnambulistic clairvoyance'.)[5] This is because the great artist has had a profound *Erlebnis*, has 'lived through' (*erlebt*) an 'experience' marked by infinity and totality. It is this experience that is expressed in the work and reproduced in the mind of the spectator. For Kant, who maintained an eighteenth-century concern for decorum, 'taste provides the rule to genius': in a genuine artwork, the expression of genius is conditioned by the formal rules of beauty. But in the age of *Sturm-und-Drang* Romanticism taste goes by the board. All that matters is sincerity and intensity, 'genuineness of the experience and the intensity of its expression' (TM 62).

The 'cult of genius' in nineteenth-century aesthetics is, observes Gadamer, the cult of 'irrationalism' (TM 52). It represents a lyric demand for freedom in the midst of the ugly business of living, a protest against the industrialized unfreedom of Enlightenment rationalization. So, for example, in Schiller's *Aesthetic Education of Man* (which Gadamer reads rather differently than Marcuse does) we are enjoined to 'live aesthetically', to 'alienate' ourselves from the world as it is and live in the world as it ought to be. This is a matter of a kind of 'inner emigration', of spending one's time in galleries and concert halls, of living in 'cultured society', and averting one's gaze from the ugliness of life elsewhere. (Or listening to music: according to Schubert's 'To Music', music is *'the* blessed art' because it 'transports' us from the 'grey hours' of earthly life and into 'a better world'.) Art becomes the art of 'aesthetic differentiation': in attending to the artwork, we seek a purely 'aesthetic consciousness', to which end we 'disregard everything in which the work is rooted (its original context of life and the religious or secular function that gave it significance)' (TM 74).[6] So, for example, in attending to the elegance of a pastor's rhetoric but not his message, or in listening to a Bach cantata but not to the meaning of its words, one adopts the 'aesthetic attitude'.

The need for 'aesthetic differentiation', for purifying the 'aesthetic' content of the work of everything else, exists mainly with respect to pre-nineteenth-century artworks. From the nineteenthcentury onwards, however, artworks are largely theory-driven, specifically made to measure up to the specifications of the aesthetic theory, as is the artworld in which they are housed. They present themselves as, as it were, already 'differentiated'. As one wanders from the gallery's Medieval room, through the Renaissance room, into the Impressionist room and on to the Twentieth Century, one does not have the dizzying effect of moving rapidly from one world to another because each artwork, decontextualized by its frame and by the blankness of the museum wall, presents itself as a prepackaged moment for an 'aesthetic experience'. According to the theory, it is because we can thus separate out the 'pure art-work' from inessential, contextual features, that great art is, as we say, 'timeless' (TM 119). Since the *Erlebnis* that absorbs us raises us above place and time, since it is supratemporal, it is also onmitemporal, capable of appeal in all ages. Moreover, as art is abstracted from its life-context, so too is the artist. The cult of the 'bohemian' comes into being, the cult of the artist as free-spirited exile (TM 76). Formerly almost all art was commissioned, commissioned for a particular site – in church, town square, or palace – and for a particular worldly purpose. But under the influence of the aesthetic theory, the artwork becomes site-less and functionless, the 'free creation' of a free spirit, a moment of timeless communication from one free, alienated, spirit to another.

Symptomatic of the aesthetic theory is the denigration of allegory. In the eighteenth century 'allegory' and 'symbol' were treated as synonyms. Both were sensible signs of something that, at least currently, is not present to sense perception. As the aesthetic theory develops, however, allegory is rejected, since the intervention of cold, hard reason, of logos, is required in order to understand its meaning. With the symbol, on the other hand, no such intervention is required, since the symbol *is* the symbolized. (So, for example, the bread and wine 'is' the body and blood of Christ, the statue of the virgin 'is' Mary and is endowed with her magical powers, the flag 'is' the country so that in defending the flag one is defending one's country.) The indefiniteness of the symbol is well adapted to the 'indefiniteness' of the symbolized (TM 61–70).

* * *

What, according to Gadamer, is wrong with the aesthetic theory? One of his criticisms, which he directs against the 'Kantian' position of Richard Haman, a former student of Dilthey (TM 77–8), seems to consist in the claim that 'aesthetic differentiation' is impossible since, as Husserl has shown us, all seeing is intellectual, all seeing is a seeing-as. Even if we do not dwell on the haystack as an object with a particular function, in 'reading' the Monet painting of the wheat field at harvest time we have to recognize the haystack as a haystack. It follows that 'pure seeing and pure hearing are dogmatic abstractions that artificially reduce phenomena' since 'perception always includes meaning' (TM 80). An artwork cannot, in fact, be 'differentiated' from the world out of which it arises.

For at least three reasons, this criticism seems misconceived. First, although to 'read' the painting we do indeed need to recognize the haystack as a haystack, it is possible for the aesthetic theorist to say that one can, in Husserl's language, 'bracket' the 'reading' stage and experience a 'pure seeing' of the work as a non-representational, two dimensional mosaic of colour and light. (Standard art school exercises train one in such a pure seeing in order to liberate one from the tired clichés of everyday perception.) Second – a rather obvious point – some paintings are entirely 'abstract' so that they do not need, indeed cannot be, 'read' for representational content. Third, there is the phenomenon of, as Richard Wagner called it, 'absolute', purely instrumental music. Gadamer addresses this last phenomenon: even though absolute music is 'a kind of auditory mathematics'[7] where there is no content with an objective meaning' we must still 'understand' it, understand its musical structure, before we can receive it as an artwork (TM 79). While this is to some degree true, it is surely irrelevant. In claiming that there is no 'pure seeing or hearing' Gadamer means to be claiming that there is no absolute 'differentiation' of the artwork from its world. The claim therefore has to be that every artwork has *world-representing* meaning. That every artwork has to have at least *formal* 'meaning' is irrelevant. Gadamer appears to have been deceived, here, by the vagueness of the word 'meaning'.

Gadamer's second criticism of the aesthetic theory is more straightforward and more substantial. Rather than denying that the aesthetic theory accommodates *any* art – a losing battle since, on his own showing, a great deal of both Romantic and post-Romantic art is created specifically to instantiate the theory – Gadamer points out, following Heidegger, that there is a great deal of art it does not accommodate. Conspicuously, it does not accommodate the art of antiquity and of the Middle Ages which, since it had profound extra-aesthetic – religious, civic and moral – functions, was deeply integrated into its world. A clue to this lies in the fact that, prior to modern times, 'art (*Kunst*)' embraced 'all transformation of nature for human use' (TM 71). (As Heidegger points out, in ancient Greece there was no special word for 'fine art': together with philosophy, science, and the manufacture of tools and utensils, it was all simply *techne*, 'bringing forth' (QCT 13; see further pp. 246–7 below).) To the extent, then, that fifth-century Greece is represented as a – or even *the* – highpoint of Western civilization and art, the suggestion arises that the aesthetic theory accounts, at best, for art in a condition of decay, the art of a sick, alienated culture. We are thus fully motivated to seek for an alternative account of the nature of art, an alternative 'ontology of the artwork'.

Play as the clue to the ontology of the artwork

Gadamer begins the process of trying to say what kind of thing an artwork is in a surprising place: he starts talking about sport, or 'play' (*Spiel* means both 'play' and 'game') which at first sight seems completely irrelevant to the topic of art.

What is a game? What, for example, is the (soccer) World Cup Final? It involves first of all the players between whom there is a 'backwards and forwards' motion, a kind of 'dance', the kind of motion that also occurs when we speak of the 'play' of light on the waves, or the 'play' in the gear lever (TM 104). Second, it involves the spectators. Spectators are not neutral 'observers' but are actively, usually passionately, involved in the event. They are, says Gadamer, not subjects who relate to the game as object, but are themselves elements constitutive of the event that is the game. The game is 'the whole comprising players and spectators' (TM 109). (That, save in exceptional circumstances, it has 'spectators', is definitive of what it is to be a 'spectator sport'.) Third, while the game constitutes a 'closed world' in which aims and rules have no connection to real life aims and rules, it nonetheless has its own kind of seriousness. Both players and spectators take the proceedings on the pitch with the utmost seriousness. So, to conclude: the World Cup Final – or any kind of sporting 'festival' (TM 121–2) – is an 'in principle repeatable' event (in analytic-philosophy jargon, an 'event type') (TM 110) whose constituent elements (in addition to a place or stadium) are players and spectators, an event that constitutes a closed world, yet a world in which goals are seriously pursued.

And now, via an illuminating pun, the connection with art suddenly dawns. For the theatrical presentation of a drama (a *Schauspiel* – literally a 'viewing-play') is also designated by the word 'play'.

And when one thinks about it, it becomes clear that there are a great many ontological similarities between drama and sport.[8] Thus a performance of *As You Like It* involves, first, 'players' ('All the world's a stage, And all the men and women merely players...') between whom there is a back and forth motion. Second, it involves spectators who are not neutral observers but engaged participants, elements in the 'whole' event of which players and spectators are both constitutive (TM 109). Third, while the play is a 'closed world' (ibid.), while the aims and fates of the characters in the play are disconnected from real life, everyone involved in the event, players and spectators alike, treat those aims with the utmost seriousness. And so *As You Like It*, too, is a repeatable event whose constituent elements are players – between whom there is movement back and forth – and spectators, an event-type that constitutes a world closed off from life, and yet a world in which goals are treated with absolute seriousness.

There are, of course, literary works written in dialogue form that neither receive, nor are intended for, performance. But these are not genuine plays, but rather works for silent reading that mimic the form of the script of a play. (Seneca's turgidly undramatic tragedies are sometimes thought to be of this character.) The telos of a play is thus performance: dramatic and also musical artworks 'acquire their real existence only in being played' (TM 309).

Analogies, of course, do not need to be exact to be illuminating. The most salient disanalogy between sport and drama is that while the 'plot' of, say, a soccer game is not predetermined, the plot of a drama is: its 'winners' and 'losers', as one might put it, are predetermined. (An exception is improvised drama, referred to, appropriately, as 'theatre sports'.)This fixed nature is, I think, what Gadamer has in mind when he says that when play becomes art it is 'transform[ed] into structure (*Gebilde*)' (TM 110). The predetermined plot and cast of characters represent a permanent structure that is re-presented in different performances by different players in different places. This structure, he says, constitutes a 'meaningful whole' (TM 116): it 'says' something complete in the way in which a sentence does but a word does not.

And now, finally, we come to the question of truth, truth in art, to the phenomenon that is excluded by the aesthetic theory. In contradiction to that theory, serious drama is not, claims Gadamer, a 'bewitchment' (TM 112). It does not transport us from the world as it is to the world as the Romantics think it ought to be. Serious drama is about *this* world, is about *life*. And if it is a great work, what we experience is, not exactly pleasure, but rather the 'joy of recognition' – recognition of *truth*. 'Yes indeed', we say reflectively, 'that is how things are' (TM 112).

What is it that grounds this recognition of truth? What grounds the great drama's truth to life, its 'verisimilitude'? Since the Greeks, art has been recognized as mimesis. One account of mimesis (suggested by its standard translation as 'imitation') is that it consists in copying. In praising an artwork as true to life we might be thinking of it as an accurate copy. But that, obviously, is not what we mean. ('Art,' as the depressed Virginia Woolf once remarked, 'is not a copy of the real world. One of the damn things is enough.') The actor does not *copy* Richard III (and *cannot* copy the ghost of Hamlet's father), rather, if he is any good, he 'is' Richard III.[9] In the dramatic play of children they 'are' their characters, and become upset if one discloses their status as actors with insensitive remarks such as 'You really looked like the wicked witch' (TM 111). 'Art does not stand like a copy next to the real world but it [presents] that world in the heightened truth of its being' (TM 132). Recognition of truth in drama is recognition of the 'familiar', but not the *merely* familiar. Rather, great art distils the 'essence' of the familiar, separates it out from the obscuring effect of contingent circumstances. Homer's Achilles is *more* than the original, 'more authentically "here"' (*eigentlicher ins Da gekommen*)' than in life (TM 114). (As Picasso once said of his famous goat sculpture, 'she's more like a goat than a real goat, don't you think?')[10]

The performance of a great dramatic artwork is, then, an event in which an audience takes part in a disclosure of truth. That the audience is an essential part of the event lies in the origin of dramatic art in the Dionysian festivals of the Greeks. As in the religious festival, the audience in the tragic festival is better described as a congregation than as a group of spectators. As a member of the congregation, one is 'claimed' by the work, so that, in a state of *ekstasis* (TM 127), one 'stands out' from one's everyday self. And then, through the disclosure of the essential truth of one's religious and moral world, one is restored to oneself in the wholeness of one's being (TM 119–124).

In bringing the audience and its response to the drama into the very definition of tragedy, claims Gadamer, Aristotle understood both the essentially cognitive character of drama and the ontologically constitutive status of the audience. 'Tragedy', according to the famous definition in Aristotle's lecture notes, is the representation of a serious and complete action, which has magnitude, [is] in embellished speech, with each of its elements used separately and in the various parts of the play; [and is] represented by people acting and not by narration; accomplishing by means of *eleos* and *phobos* the catharsis of such emotions.

(*Poetics* 1449b 25-9)

Gadamer suggests that the tradition of translating *eleos* and *phobos* as 'pity' and 'fear' is too subjectivist. Properly understood, *eleos* and *phobos* should not be treated as subjective feelings but should be understood in essentially cognitive terms, as modes of *ekstasis*, modes of standing out from the everyday into the fragile finitude of life. Catharsis, tragic 'purification', is not the discharge of emotions but rather the 'tragic pensiveness' in which one acknowledges fate, acknowledges the fact that the world is not a moral order in which everyone gets their just deserts, but in which one continues, nonetheless, to affirm life.[11]

* * *

A dramatic artwork is, then, a repeatable, truth-disclosing event-type such that to perform the work is (again in jargon) to produce a 'token' of that type. Every performance is, perforce, an interpretation of the work. Given, however, that the work is truth-disclosing, it follows that there is a distinction between correct and incorrect interpretations. Not just anything goes: treating the work as an occasion for 'arbitrary and ad-lib effects' (as happens in the tiresomely fashionable 'deconstructive' productions of canonical works) simply fails to produce a performance of *the work*. That a performance uses some or all of the work's text does not guarantee that it is a performance of work it purports to perform. There is an 'obligatoriness' the work places us under – the obligation, as one might put it, to be truthful, true to the truth of the work. Nonetheless, for at least two reasons, there is no limit to the number or range of valid performances. First, the truth of a great work is multi-aspected, so that, in the succession of different productions, its 'own possibilities of being ... emerge as the work explicates itself, as it were, in the variety of its aspects'. The richness of the truth contained in *Hamlet* (or a Beethoven symphony) means that any given performance must render one or more aspect salient while obscuring others.[12] Second, the manner of presentation must change through time (and culture) so that it can speak to its particular audience without alienating through quaintness. 'Authentic' performances of old music on old instruments (Bach with Bach bows and no vibrato) produce not a living experience but a museum piece. Shakespeare delivered in the declamatory style of the nineteenth century would empty the theatre (TM 117–19).

It is because it licences this endless variety of valid interpretations, says Gadamer – and *not* because it communicates an omnitemporal-because-supratemporal experience, as the Romantics suppose – that we regard the great dramatic artwork as 'timeless' in the sense of being 'contemporaneous with every age' (TM 119). Gadamer calls the unfinished sequence of the varying performances of the artwork its 'temporality', the manner in which it occupies time (TM 120).

Novels and paintings

A performance artwork is, then, an event-type that essentially involves both actors and audience in a disclosure of truth, whose being is fully realized[13] only in the unfinished temporal sequence of the necessarily varying event-tokens that are its legitimate performances. Gadamer wishes to claim that this 'ontological perspective' (TM 153) – the account of the ontology of the performance artwork that now stands before us – is, in fact, the ontology of artworks in general. But when we come to works of literature that are intended for silent reading, novels and poems, the claim appears to meet an insuperable obstacle: there is, it seems, no such thing as the 'performance' of this kind of artwork, so that the idea of its 'temporality' as being realized in a sequence of necessarily varying interpretive performances seems to find no application. To be sure, there are public recitations of poems and there can even be public reading of novels (usually on radio), but this is unusual and no part of the essence of what it is to be a poem or novel, no part of its 'ontology'.

Gadamer's response to this objection is to insist that to read a novel or poem is, in fact, to perform it. Silent reading of such works is essentially the same as their public recitation, save that the audience is reduced to one. One 'performs' the work for oneself:

> there is obviously no sharp differentiation between reciting and silent reading. Reading with understanding is always a kind of reproduction, performance and interpretation. Emphasis, rhythmic ordering, and the like are parts of silent reading too. Meaning and the understanding of it are so closely connected with the corporality of language that understanding always involves an inner speaking as well.
>
> (TM 153)

And, of course, to readers of the classics that are handed down from generation to generation, the 'performance' in which the work becomes meaningful to a later generation will necessarily differ from its performance for an earlier generation.[14]

What, however, of the plastic arts? Surely, at this point, the claimed universality of the 'performance' ontology finally crashes to earth? Gadamer insists that this is not so, but a great deal of his discussion of the matter (TM 130–52), is discursive to the point that it certainly loses sight of the thread of the argument. Even Jean Grondin, that most devoted of Gadamerians, admits that, when it comes to the non-performance arts 'it is not at all certain' that he answers the questions he should be answering.[15] Insofar, however, as Gadamer does answer the crucial question of how the performance ontology can be applied to sculpture or painting only a small part of the discussion seems relevant. In it, his answer to the question of how the performance ontology can be applied to the plastic arts seems to me to be the same as the answer he provided with respect to novels:

> Essential to dramatic or musical works ... is that their performance at different times and on different occasions is, and must be, different. Now it is important to see that, mutatis mutandis, the same is true of the plastic arts. It is not the case that the work of art exists 'an sich' and only the effect varies: it is the work of art itself that displays itself under various conditions. The viewer of today not only sees things in a different way, he sees different things ... the work of art determines itself anew from occasion to occasion.
>
> (TM 141)

So, for example, whereas a seventeenth-century Dutchman might see in a Rembrandt self-portrait an affirmation of solid, successful, bourgeois respectability, commensurate with the multi-aspected 'truth' it contains, I might see it as – *that is, 'perform' it for myself as* – a man anxiously preoccupied by the affairs of the world. Thus the painting, too, is a truth-disclosing event-type whose 'temporality', whose 'real existence' (TM 309) in time, consists in a sequence of necessarily varying performances.

But this surely, it may be objected, is a 'category mistake', for, quite obviously, the painting is not an event but a substance. This, however, is precisely what Gadamer wishes to deny. The *material base* of the painting (its 'thingly character' as Heidegger calls it),[16] that about it which is salient for the chemist or furniture mover, is indeed a substance. But the *artwork* is not the same as its material base. The artwork is, rather, the temporal sequence of interpretations, of 'performances', that share the same material base.

Romantic hermeneutics

Hermeneutics, we know, is the discipline concerned with the interpretation and understanding of texts. But some of these texts are artworks. Indeed, on Gadamer's approach, all artworks are either literal or figurative texts, entities whose understanding requires interpretation that necessarily varies over time. Hence, he writes, 'aesthetics has to be absorbed into [philosophical] hermeneutics' (TM 157). It follows that, without Gadamer making this explicit, Part I of *Truth and Method* is, in fact, a case study in the practice and presuppositions of hermeneutics, so that his account of interpretation in general is intended to mirror his account of the interpretation of artworks.

As already remarked, the extension of the topic of hermeneutics from the Bible to texts of all kind occurred towards the end of the eighteenth century in the work of Friedrich Schleiermacher. The impetus for self-conscious reflection on the nature of interpretation was, says Gadamer, the rise of 'historical consciousness', the awareness that history divides into different epochs, each one shaped by a distinctive (in Hegel's language) 'shape of consciousness', a distinctive worldview. Schleiermacher's achievement of turning an aggregate of useful observations into a 'universal' art was, he observes, based on the premise (which, as we shall see, Gadamer himself only partially endorses) that understanding an historical text is a *problem* and a *task*, that not understanding but rather *mis*understanding is the default position (TM 185). In the case of historical texts, the task is to avoid anachronism, the projection of the interpreter's 'shape of consciousness' onto the interpreted (as, in the case of the understanding of other contemporary cultures, the task is to avoid ethnocentrism).

Gadamer identifies two basic ways in which the attempt to understand historical texts has been attempted: 'reconstruction' and 'integration'. The first requires that we imaginatively transport ourselves into the historical world of the text and thereby 'reconstruct' the meaning it had for its original audience and author, the second requires a 'thoughtful mediation' between the past and contemporary life (TM 157–61). Reconstruction is the approach of Schleiermacher, which was followed by the historians Leopold von Ranke (1795–1886) and Johann Droysen (1808–1884), and then by Dilthey. Gadamer refers to this as 'Romantic hermeneutics', in part because Schleiermacher belonged to the Romantic movement – he was a friend of the Schlegel brothers – and in part because he subscribed to the 'somnambulist' theory of genius discussed in connection with the 'aesthetic' theory of art (p. 160 above), a theory endorsed by both the Romantics and by neo-Romantics such as Richard Wagner. The 'integration' approach, Gadamer ascribes to Schleiermacher's almost exact contemporary, G. W. F. Hegel (1770–1831) and is the theory he himself favours: favours to such an extent that he regards his own account of the successful understanding of the alien in terms of 'fusion of horizons' (TM 304–5) as 'retrac[ing] the path of Hegel's phenomenology of mind' (TM 301). (Later on in this chapter, however, I shall be concerned to argue that Gadamer overestimates his debt to Hegel, that he has, in fact, *two* accounts of fusion, only one of which is indebted to Hegel.)

As indicated above, Gadamer defines and defends his own account of hermeneutical understanding via a critique of his Romantic predecessors. Schleiermacher's recommended method for understanding an historical text is that one should imaginatively transport oneself into, in his own words, 'the whole framework of the author', the framework of his audience, and indeed his entire historical world, so that eventually, one comes to understand the 'inner origin' of the work, an understanding which enables one to perform a 're-creation of the creative act' that first brought the work into being. One does this by 'as it were, transforming oneself into the other', something made possible by the alleged fact that 'everyone carries a tiny bit of everyone else within him',[17] so that 'divination is stimulated by comparison with oneself' (TM 186).

By the 'inner origin' of the work, says Gadamer, Schleiermacher understood the meaning-determining authorial intention, 'what the author meant and expressed'. A certain complication is introduced here by the fact of Schleiermacher's subscription to the 'somnambulist' theory of genius: since the genius works unconsciously, the interpreter understands the authorial intention behind a work of genius 'better than [the author] understands himself' (as the learner of a foreign language understands the rules unconsciously followed by the native speaker better than the native speaker does) (TM 191).

A later phase of Romantic hermeneutics is represented by Dilthey, who combined Schleiermacher's approach to hermeneutics with the approach to history represented by the 'historical school' of philosophically reflective historians such as von Ranke and Droysen.

Dilthey postulates an 'historical sense', a sensibility that can be cultivated in a way that allows one to transcend the prejudices of one's own times, to become capable of (in Gadamer's gently satirical words) a kind of 'epic self-forgetfulness' consisting in 'universal sympathy' or 'empathy'. Since human nature is at least somewhat homogeneous, as suggested by Schleiermacher, sympathy – not the active force that motivates moral action but rather the 'ripe, detached wisdom of old age' – can allow us to transcend our own sub-jectivity and achieve objective knowledge of an author's intentions or of the motivation of an historical actor, 'objectivity' being, for Dilthey, the essential condition of all science. Such objectivity is more easily obtained, Dilthey observes, if the interpreter belongs to the same 'great object' as his subject. As a Lutheran, for instance, von Ranke has an especially empathetic under-standing of Luther, while Thucydides, as a fellow member of the Athenian polis, had a special insight into Pericles. Like von Ranke, Dilthey regards it as belonging to an 'historian's dignity' to cultivate the historical sense, a culti-vation which requires a mode of self-knowledge: only if one can identify one's own historical and cultural prejudices does one have the ability to transcend them (TM 225–7).

Gadamer's critique of Romantic hermeneutics

Gadamer's fundamental criticism of, not just Dilthey, but of the entire tradition of Romantic hermeneutics is simple: since, he claims, all consciousness is 'historically effected', historically and culturally conditioned, there is no such thing as unconditioned, 'objective', 'absolute' knowledge (TM 224) with respect to the hermeneutical object. Despite thinking of himself as an opponent of the Enlightenment positivism, Dilthey, in attempting to introduce into hermeneutics the Enlightenment notion of prejudice-free objectivity, is, in fact, its captive (TM 227–35). That such objectivity is a Fata Morgana, the 'historicity' of all consciousness, is a thesis Gadamer takes over from Heidegger.

Gadamer observes that in *Being and Time* (sections 31–2), Heidegger, building on the work of Husserl, transforms the entire subject of hermeneutics by showing that hermeneutical understanding – understanding through interpretation – is not just something that happens with respect to historical texts but characterizes our entire being-in-the-world. For what we are, Heidegger shows, is 'thrown projection' (TM 254). We see, interpret, the world always from within the 'horizon' of the particular 'lifeworld' into which we are 'thrown' (pp. 129–30 above). This as we have seen, determines the range of life possibilities that make sense for us, the possibilities into which we can project ourselves. Becoming a witch doctor is a live option in certain African cultures, being an exorcist was a live option in the medieval world, but neither is an option for me. (Note, here, the interdependence of possibilities of projection and ontology: only if the ontology of a world allows for demons is the notion of exorcism intelligible.)

Given, then, that there is no escaping the 'horizon' of the lifeworld one is always 'already in', it follow, says Gadamer, that the imaginative transport postulated by Romantic hermeneutics is a myth. The question thus becomes: How should hermeneutics proceed *given* the historicity, the conditioned nature, of all understanding? Is there any sense in which one interpretation can be said to be more 'objective', and therefore better, than another, given that the aspiration to 'scientific' objectivity[18] must be abandoned? The key, says Gadamer, as Heidegger has once more shown us, lies in the 'hermeneutical circle'.

The hermeneutical circle

The 'circularity' of the hermeneutical circle consists in understanding parts from the whole to which they belong, and also understanding the whole from the parts. The most obvious manifestation of the use of the circle is in the manner in which one goes about translating a text written in a language that one understands only imperfectly: one seeks to understand the meaning of the whole from the meaning of the words one does understand, and seeks to understand the words one does not understand from a hypothesized meaning of the text as a whole, adjusting one's meaning hypothesis if it turns out to conflict with the meaning of further, already understood, words (TM 189).

The circle was always important to hermeneuticists. In Dilthey, for instance, interpretation is a matter of circling back and forth between the individual text, other works by the same author, his audience, and ultimately his entire historical world, in order to reconstruct the authorial intention. For Heidegger and Gadamer, however, the circling occurs not *within* an historical world but rather *between* the interpreter and the object of interpretation (TM 388–9).

As Heidegger shows, says Gadamer, the hermeneutical circle is virtuous rather than vicious, a method rather than a problem.[19] So suppose that we are trying to understand an historical text, let us say a section of Nietzsche's *The Gay Science*. We begin with what Heidegger calls a 'fore-projection' of the meaning of the text as a whole, a fore-projection based on our initial expectations of the text. According to Gadamer, such presuppositions include the expectation that it has a 'complete', self-consistent meaning[20] and, crucially, the expectation that what the author says is *true* (TM 294). (In the analytic philosophy of, for instance, Quine, Davidson and Dennett this presupposition is known as the 'principle of charity'.) The reason for this 'regulative principle' (as Kant would call it), is that, as in reading a letter or a newspaper report, our primary interest in a text is in the subject matter rather than the author, and our assumption is that the author is likely to be better informed on that subject matter than we are. And so we work away, circling back and forth between our meaning-and-truth hypothesis and the details of the text, likely rendering our initial hypothesis richer and more nuanced as we proceed. Only if we fail to find an hypothesis that accommodates all the details do we finally relinquish the 'charitable' assumption and treat the text as a record of the author's – false – opinion (ibid.). If we are forced to do this, however, the text will become less interesting. We read Nietzsche because we want to *learn* something from him, something about the subject matter that is true. If all we learn is something about Nietzsche's psychology (isolated passages in his final works do, in fact, provide evidence of his advancing madness) the text may be biographically interesting, but it will not have the interest that originally drew us to it.

So let us suppose that we do finally come up with a meaning-and-truth hypothesis that accommodates all the details of the text. This, says Gadamer, and not historical empathy, not the Romantics' notional periscope into the mind of the author, is the only kind of 'objectivity' that can be attained by hermeneutics (TM 270).

Understanding is never final

To understand a text in the above manner is, says Gadamer, to 'reach an understanding' with it concerning the truth about its subject matter. The purpose of hermeneutics is, we know, understanding, the assignment of meaning to a text. But given the constraint placed on meaning-hypotheses by the principle of charity, it follows, claims Gadamer, that the primary form of understanding (*Verstehen*) is 'agreement' (*Verständnis*) (TM 292). Since, however, every age represents an unique historical situation, every age has to understand a transmitted text anew, has to search again for an account of the meaning of the text that says something true and important about its own times. It follows that 'the real meaning of a text, as it speaks to the interpreter', its meaning for us, is not identical with either the authorial intention or the manner in which the original audience would have understood the text, but is 'co-determined also by the historical situation of the interpreter' (TM

296). And from this it follows that 'the discovery of the true meaning of a text or work of art is never finished; it is in fact an infinite process' (TM 298).

As this reference to art makes explicit, Gadamer is, at this point, merging his account of the interpretation of a canonical historical text with his account of the meaning of art. As a performance artwork is reinterpreted in each performance with the result that 'the meaning' of *Hamlet* is an indefinitely long temporal sequence of meanings, so 'the meaning' of any historical text is an indefinitely long temporal sequence. Each age must 're-perform' the meaning of the text for itself.

The rehabilitation of prejudice and the authority of tradition

One of the ways in which Gadamer expresses the 'historicity' of all understanding that requires each age to reappropriate a text for itself (an important, 'canonical' text), is by pointing to a disjunction between the 'horizons' of the present and the past. The term 'horizon', he says, he uses in Husserl's sense as that which determines a 'lifeworld' (TM 239; see further pp. 174–7 below). Moved by a polemical motive, Gadamer expresses the idea of a disjunction between present and past lifeworlds as a disjunction between different historical 'prejudices (*Vorurteile*)' (TM 305). 'Prejudice' claims Gadamer, did not acquire a pejorative meaning until the Enlightenment. Before that, as its etymology – *Vor[-]urteil* – suggests, the word simply meant a *praejudicum*, a preliminary judgment (a 'decree nisi', for instance) that preceded a final one (a 'decree absolute').[21] The Enlightenment's fundamental conviction – its fundamental 'prejudice', as Gadamer provocatively puts it – was its 'prejudice against prejudices' of all kinds. After the Enlightenment, 'prejudice' comes to mean simply 'unfounded judgment' (TM 273).

To understand Gadamer's defence of prejudice – or less provocatively 'prejudgment' – we need to distinguish between those prejudices that are due to over-hastiness in judgment and those due to respect for authority. For the former, he holds no brief. The prejudices that were the Enlightenment's principle target, however, were those based on authority, in particular, those based on the authority of the European religious-moral tradition. This antagonism appears in the motto of Kant's famous essay 'What Is Enlightenment?': 'Have the courage to use your own understanding' where the stress is on the word 'own'. One is enjoined to believe nothing that one has not worked out *oneself*, either from direct observation or from self-evident first principles. Paradigmatically, says Gadamer, the injunction is to believe nothing one has not first passed through the scrutiny of Cartesian doubt. To do otherwise the Enlightenment saw as 'blind obedience', 'diametrically opposed to reason and freedom', freedom in the sense of self-governing autonomy (TM 180–1).

In fact, however, claims Gadamer, this is not necessarily the nature of authority-based belief at all. With respect to the authority of persons (the eyewitness to the crime, or the climate scientist's assertions about global warming) such belief may be the acknowledgment of the other's epistemic superiority, of the other as 'superior in judgment and insight' (a point Marcuse makes too [p. 85 above]). 'True' authority is not 'authoritarian' (TM 374 fn. 22) but is something earned. And so to base a belief on authority may well be an act of *reason*, an act based on the knowledge of one's own limitations. The essence of authority is thus immune to the – in fact irrational – 'extremism' of the Enlightenment (TM 281).[22]

* * *

It is noteworthy, writes Gadamer, that there are no ethics in Descartes; no ethics, at least, in his official philosophy. And the ethical observations in his letters to Princess Elizabeth are thoroughly conventional, certainly not beliefs that have been put through the fire of Cartesian doubt. This is symptomatic of the fact that ethics cannot consist in, or be derived from, first principles that are immune to doubt (TM 279–80). Rather, '[t]he real force of morals is [and can only be] based on tradition' (TM 282), an assertion I take to mean that the sole rational authority of morals lies in ethical tradition.

This, says Gadamer, is something we presuppose when we socialize our children into our culture (TM 381). In educating them, we assume the correctness of our moral and political tradition (an observation central to Arendt's discussion of tradition, as we shall see in the next chapter). We do so, presumably, because, having stood the test of time (Gadamer's affinity with Edmund Burke manifests itself at this point), we attribute to tradition the same kind of epistemic authority we attribute to individuals who are 'superior in judgment and insight'. This does not, however, entail a slavish attitude to tradition. Although one's initial grasp of morals is 'by no means created by free insight or grounded in reasons', on attaining adulthood, one can and should determine whether tradition, as handed down, really is grounded in superior insight (TM 282).[23] How one might do this is a matter to which I shall return.

Text and tradition

To date, Gadamer seems to have been running two parallel discussions, one concerning the understanding of texts, the other the authority of tradition. In fact, however, he wishes to treat these as two strands in a single discussion. The reason for this returns us to Heidegger's demonstration that 'understanding' is not just something we achieve with respect to the specialist activity of interpreting historical texts, but is a defining condition of our being-in-the-world. In particular, it is on the basis of tradition, of that which has been 'handed down to us' (Heidegger's 'heritage' [pp. 149–52 above]), that we project our future, project the person we are to be. Our self-projection is thus based on an understanding of what tradition means in the current context. In other words, in living our lives in the light of tradition we are performing the same kind of hermeneutical act as we perform in understanding an historical text. Metaphorically, and in part literally, tradition is a 'text' which we understand in the same way we understand literal texts (TM 297).

Fusion of horizons

As noted, a 'horizon' is the normally inarticulate set of ontological and normative 'prejudgments' (as Gadamer calls them) that determine a lifeworld. A horizon or lifeworld, is, as Husserl tells us, something we are always 'already in'. This, says Gadamer (the absence of a 'view from nowhere'), is the epistemic aspect of human finitude (TM 366). As the critique of Romantic hermeneutics reveals, we cannot simply remove our horizontal 'spectacles' and replace them with those of an historical world (and neither can we do without 'spectacles' completely). Does it not then follow that the interpretation of an historical text must inevitably be anachronistic, a projection of the mentality of the interpreter onto the interpreted, an exercise in spiritual colonization? Not so, says Gadamer. For what happens if and when genuine understanding is achieved is that the old and the new horizons 'fuse' with each other in a way that allows the interpreter to learn something new, to 'expand his horizon' (TM 304–5).

Gadamer's phrase 'fusion of horizons' has attracted a great deal of commentary, at least in part, on account of the irenic, if somewhat fuzzy, feeling it generates. Although Gadamer himself is interested only in fusion between present and past lifeworlds, recent interest has been mostly directed towards the possibility of fusion between different contemporary lifeworlds as a path to overcoming the fissures in multicultural modernity. But what actually *is* fusion?

Gadamer states, we have seen, that the task of philosophical hermeneutics is to 'retrace the path of Hegel's phenomenology of mind' (p. 168 above), Hegel's history of the West as a dialectical succession of 'sublations (*Aufhebungen*)' in which, paradigmatically, 'thesis' and 'antithesis' are sublated into a 'synthesis' that supersedes both while preserving what is worthwhile ('rational') in each. It is in these Hegelian terms that Gadamer first introduces the notion of fusion: when fusion between two horizons occurs he says, a 'higher universality' is achieved which overcomes the 'particularity' of each (TM 304).

Described in this manner, there is no doubt, I think, that fusion is a genuine historical phenomenon, a phenomenon testified to by the number of double-barrelled names that populate our moral and political discourse: 'Judeo-Christian', 'left-liberal', 'compassionate conservativism', 'democratic socialism', and so on. Thus consider 'liberal democracy'. The principle of liberalism, of the individual as possessor of inalienable rights and liberties goes back to the natural right theorists of the seventeenth century. But not until the French Revolution does the idea of democracy become a historical force in the modern world. In the nineteenth century de Tocqueville and others observe the tension between democracy and liberalism caused by the threat of the former to become a 'tyranny of the majority', until finally, in the twentieth century, the 'higher universality' of liberal democracy overcomes, as Hegel would puts it, the 'one-sidedness' of each principle.

It is this Hegelian understanding of productive encounters between present and past lifeworlds which generates the metaphor of 'fusion'. (If a welder 'fuses' shaft to head so that they become a hammer, shaft and head 'sublate' their individual identities into the 'higher universality' that is the hammer.) The trouble, however, with Gadamer's notion of fusion is that what dominates most of the discussion is not this Hegelian conception which gives rise to the metaphor but rather a different notion based on what happens in legal hermeneutics.

Legal hermeneutics, the interpretation, principally, of legal texts inherited from the past, is, says Gadamer, 'exemplary' of how fusion works (TM 321). So let imagine, for example, a case brought before the U.S. Supreme Court by the American Civil Liberties Union asserting that the death penalty is a 'cruel and unusual punishment' and is consequently 'unconstitutional'. Conservative 'originalists' on the Court, let us imagine, reject the argument out of hand on the ground that it is the intention of the founding fathers that determines the meaning of the Constitution and that, in the eighteenth century, there was nothing cruel or unusual about executing murderers. (Note that this kind of originalism is just a version of the Romantic hermeneutics that Gadamer attacks, an attack which has made him a figure of interest in contemporary jurisprudence.) Liberal members of the Court might, however, be persuaded by the following argument. Death in the eighteenth century was a point of transition from this world to the next world, a world in which most people still firmly believed. In the age of modern materialism, however, death counts as absolute extinction. And that is a punishment that should be inflicted on no one; is, in other words, 'cruel and unusual'. (That in Western modernity the death penalty is at least 'unusual' is a statistical truth.)

Suppose that the majority of justices accept this argument and the ACLU wins its case. Then what has happened in this encounter between the two 'worlds' is that, as Gadamer calls it, the 'application' (TM 305) of the term 'cruel and unusual' has expanded, which is to say that there has been a change in what linguists call its 'extension'.

As there is no doubt that fusion conceived in the Hegelian manner is a real historical phenomenon, there is no doubt that fusion conceived on the model of legal hermeneutics is also a real historical phenomenon. The trouble, however, is that the two notions of fusion are quite different from each other. For while in the Hegelian case there are *two* principles involves, in the legal case there is only *one*. The *question*, that is, to which 'fusion' provides the answer is different in the two cases. In the Hegelian case the question to be answered is: How can the tension between two principles, each of which has partial, but not total, authority over us, be resolved? In the legal case the question is: What does this principle inherited from the past – a principle which has unconditional authority over us – *mean* in the conditions of modernity? Hegel speaks of the sublation of two principles into a 'higher universality' as 'reconciliation'. The business of legal hermeneutics as Gadamer discusses it, however, is not 'reconciliation' but rather updating, modernization, or what I shall call 'renewal'.

In my judgment, none of the secondary literature devoted to 'fusion of horizons' manages to explain clearly what fusion is. The reason, I suggest, is that neither Gadamer nor his commentators have achieved a clear grasp of the fact that the notion is fundamentally ambiguous, ambiguous between, as I shall say, 'fusion as reconciliation' and 'fusion as renewal'.

Fusion and ethical tradition

Ethics, as we have seen, cannot be derived from first principles that are immune to doubt. There is, Gadamer holds, no 'God's eye' view of ethical truth, no basis for ethics external to all traditions. Traditions, however, cannot survive unless they are 'cultivated' (TM 282). Living traditions are 'always in motion' (TM 303), always responding to new circumstances through processes of fusion. Only by being thus 'affirmed and embraced' (TM 282) can a tradition achieve 'preservation amid the ruin of time' (TM 286–91).

That this language of 'cultivation', 'affirmation', and 'embracing' fits so naturally the 'exemplary' work of a constitutional court, suggests that when Gadamer focuses specifically on the way in which ethical traditions change and develop so as to preserve themselves 'amidst the ruin of time', the only process he recognizes is fusion as renewal. It suggests that he implicitly thinks of an ethical tradition as an unwritten 'ethical constitution' which can be modernized – 'renewed' – in a way that allows it to speak to the current situation, but can itself never be altered. But this is an incomplete view of how ethical traditions change and yet survive. While a tradition's 'orientation crises', as Habermas calls them (p. 52 above), may often be resolved through fusion as renewal – the recognition of gay marriage, we come to see, is required by the principle of equality before the law – the more profound crises can only be resolved through fusion as reconciliation. When, for instance, at the end of the *Orestia*, Athena's deciding vote acquits Orestes of the charge of matricide she (or rather Aeschylus) introduces a *new principle* into Greek ethical discourse: that one has duties to the state that override all others. (Orestes has killed his mother because she has killed Agamemnon, but he has done so, not just because Agamemnon is his father, but, more importantly, because he is the king.) This was a direct challenge to the family-first morality of the pre-Olympian age which produced an orientation crisis that could only be resolved through (as Sophocles'*Antigone* points out) the difficult process of fusion as reconciliation. And when Jesus preached the 'soft' virtues of love and forgiveness this was a direct challenge to the 'hard' morality of the Old Testament that initiated an orientation crisis that, again, could only be resolved by reconciliation, the reconciliation we refer to when we speak of the 'Judeo-Christian tradition'.

Heidegger, as we saw (p. 151 above), emphasizes that while authentic Dasein's living in the light of tradition is a matter of 'repeating' a past existence possibility, this is not a matter of slavishly binding the present to the past (in the manner of the 'originalists'), but rather of making a creative 'response' to the past in the light of the present. Fusion is Gadamer's elaboration of this 'response'. The question thus arises as to whether Heidegger, too, is committed to the inadequate view that the development of ethical tradition happens solely through fusion as renewal. Given the brevity of Heidegger's discussion, one cannot be certain of the answer. But that he speaks only of a 'repetition' of tradition, and never of its response to challenges from initially alien ethical principles, suggests that he, too, ignores the role of Hegelian fusion in its historical development.

Criticisms

In order to gain a deeper understanding of Gadamer's philosophical hermeneutics I want to test it against a number of critical questions that have been raised against it. They are the following:

1 By asserting the historically conditioned nature of all consciousness, does not Gadamer's theory undermine itself since it, too, becomes the product of historical conditioning?
2 Given that empathy is a fact, is not the 'historical sense' of Romantic hermeneutics something more than the dogmatic fiction Gadamer claims it to be?
3 Does not Gadamer confuse the meaning of a text with its reconstruction, and is not the former, in fact, determined by authorial intention, as the Romantic hermeneuticists claim?
4 Does not Gadamer confuse 'thrownness' with 'tradition'? Even granted that all consciousness is culturally and linguistically conditioned, does that really imply that all human beings are thrown into an action-guiding, *ethical* tradition?
5 Is not Gadamer's hermeneutics too conservative, incapable of providing a proper critique of 'ideologies', of *oppressive* traditions?

Self-refutation?

Gadamer affirms, we have seen, the 'historicity' of all consciousness, claims that all consciousness is 'historically affected'. Call this thesis 'T.0'. But if T.0

is true, is it not *itself* 'historically affected'? How then can Gadamer assert, as he does, that T.0 is 'absolutely and unconditionally true'? Surely – Gadamer anticipates the objection – this involves him in a 'contradiction' (TM 445).

Gadamer regards this objection as a sophism, indeed as following a pattern first formulated by the Sophists themselves (TM 340). His response is the following. T.0 is indeed an absolute truth. But 'reflective philosophy' deals in propositions that are on a different 'logical level' to propositions expressing 'life-relationships (*Lebensverhältnisse*)' (TM 445), so that what is true of propositions on one 'level' need not be true of those on another. Gadamer's response to the charge of self-contradiction consists, therefore, in introducing a distinction between first order (or 'level') propositions that are true *in* particular lifeworlds and second order philosophical meta-statements *about* lifeworlds. The former lack absolute truth – 'There are demons and angels', 'Homosexuality is a mortal sin', are true in the medieval but not the modern lifeworld – but the latter are absolutely true, true period. Hence, Gadamer concludes, there is no contradiction in his position. What thesis T.0 entails is only that all *first order* propositions lack absolute truth.

Michael N. Forster formulates Gadamer's thesis as follows: 'all knowledge is historically relative'.[24] Call this thesis 'T.1'. Forster calls Gadamer's response to the charge of self-contradiction 'naïve and unconvincing',[25] which is itself rather unconvincing since, Gadamer is effectively deploying the 'Theory of Types' response to paradoxes of self-reference first formulated by that acme of logical sophistication, Bertrand Russell. The main point I wish to make about T.1, however, is that it is *not a thesis to which Gadamer subscribes* – even though, when worrying about the apparent problem of self-contradiction, he thinks that, absent the distinction between 'logical levels', he does. My claim, in other words, is that, distracted by the worry about self-reference, *Gadamer misunderstands his own theory*.

Thesis T.1 is a thesis about knowledge, and hence about truth. It is the thesis that there are no 'absolute' truths, that all truth is relative to particular historical lifeworlds. But this, surely, is *not* what Gadamer holds. For consider his fundamental motivation: as we saw (pp. 157–8 above), his fundamental project is to show that there are *truths* about reality that cannot be accessed by the methods of natural science, but can be by the humanities. Hence the very *title* of *Truth and Method*: 'truth', as I have parsed it, *versus* scientific 'method'. And recall the foundational discussion of art in Part I of the book. There is nothing relative about the *truth* of the great artwork. On the contrary, as we saw (p. 165 above), that a performance of a performance artwork remains true to the truth of the work is a condition of its legitimacy, to its counting as a performance *of that work*. In short, so I suggest, panicked by the issue of self-contradiction, Gadamer momentarily loses sight of his own fundamental thesis, the thesis that *what is relative to lifeworlds is not truth, but rather modes of representing or accessing that truth*. The basic point can be illustrated by deploying, once again, Frege's distinction between sense and reference. 'The Morning Star is a planet' and 'The Evening Star is a planet' are different modes of accessing a truth, but the (absolute) truth that they access is the same.

Gadamer's confusion about his own – essentially Heideggerian – position is one that Heidegger himself never falls into. Referring to his own reading of Nietzsche he writes that 'while a right elucidation never understands a text better than the author understood it, it does surely understand it differently. Yet this difference must be of such a kind as to touch upon the Same towards which the elucidated text is thinking' (QCT 58) – 'the Same' truth in other words.

The historical sense

A crucial step, we saw, in Gadamer's argument towards his conclusion that understanding historical texts consists in (one of the forms of) fusion of horizons is his claim that the 'historical sense' postulated by Romantic hermeneutics – the idea that we understand an historical text or action by empathetically projecting ourselves into the shoes of the author and thereby 'divining' the intention behind the text or action – is a myth. It is a myth, he claims, because Heidegger has shown that since 'thrownness' is a transcendental, a priori feature of our being-in-the-world, we know that such acts of 'epic self-forgetfulness' are impossible (p. 169 above). But this, it might be objected, is mere *assertion*, a mere appeal to authority (not unexpected, it might be added, in a writer for whom authority looms so large). And given that empathy between contemporaries is clearly a real phenomenon, it might be continued, the appeal is a vain one since, if empathy can operate 'sideways', it can surely also operate 'backwards'. As any biographer of an historical figure knows, the more one discovers about the life and times of one's hero, the more one engages imaginative time travel, in a vanishing from the present and reappearance in the past. And when one does that, is it not frequently the case that layers of anachronistic misinterpretation are stripped away (as one might remove layers of unscholarly 'restoration' from an old painting) to reveal the real meaning of the text or action beneath?

Gadamer's response must be that although the biographer's sense of time travel is, of course, a genuine phenomenon, the idea that one *becomes* the historical author is a delusion. What happens, rather, is that one transport one's *self*, complete with the inescapable prejudgments that define the perspective of the present, into the past. One does not become the other but remains oneself in, as it were, the other's shoes. This, however, is a *mere* claim. Granted that the prejudgments of the present – as Heidegger would put it – 'initially and for the most part' limit one's being, it remains the case that we are given no reason for accepting that they are *absolutely* inescapable, that there can *never* be real (albeit rare and difficult) acts of historical empathy.

Although Gadamer does not make his response clear, this objection, while making a valid point, misses, I think, the real character of his project. Gadamer's main point, it seems to me, does not require him to assert the absolute impossibility of at least occasional acts of 'epic self-forgetfulness'. His principal thesis, rather, is that a hermeneutics based on such acts is not – to employ one of his favourite terms – 'productive' (TM 296 et passim). His negative stance towards, as it were, 'musical originalism', the performance of old music on 'original' instruments (TM 117–19), is instructive on this point. As we have seen, his view is that what one does in such performances is to produce a museum piece. To appropriate the musical (and other) riches of the past in a meaningful way, one needs, not to transport oneself into the past, but rather to transport the past into the present, and that means reinterpreting the old music in terms of the musical language of the present. Heidegger makes this same point in terms of translation. Productive translation, he says (referring obliquely to the alleged 'violence' of his readings of Sophocles and Hölderlin) is not a 'trans-lation' of oneself into the mind of the foreign but rather a bringing back from one's encounter with the foreign something that enriches one's own understanding of the world (I 65–6; cf. QCT 58) – in short, a 'fusion' (of one kind or the other) between the domestic and the foreign 'horizon'. Gadamer employs a similar metaphor of journeying:

> if, by entering foreign language-worlds, we overcome the prejudices and limitations of our previous experience of the world, this does not mean that we leave and negate our own world. Like travellers we return home with new experiences.
>
> (TM 464, 445)[26]

The essence of productive understanding is homecoming.

Does Gadamer confuse interpretation with reconstruction?

On the face of things, it seems uncontroversial to say that understanding a text is a matter of understanding 'the' meaning that it has. But given that there is such a unique meaning, the conclusion seems inescapable that what determines it is the author's intention (even if that intention might be partially unconscious). But, claims Emilio Betti, impressed by the fact that the interpretation of texts varies over time, Gadamer denies that there is any such thing as 'the' meaning of a text. But this is confusion. What Gadamer should do is to distinguish between the 'cognitive' meaning of a text, the author's meaning, and the 'reproductive' meaning, the most vivid approximation to that meaning that can be provided for a contemporary audience.[27] A similar criticism is made by E. D. Hirsch: what Gadamer should be doing is distinguishing between the 'meaning' of a text which is determined by 'what the author meant' and its 'significance', the significance it has for a later point in time which is to be determined by 'criticism'.[28]

Does Gadamer really want to deny anything Betti and Hirsch want to assert? Although given to incautious flights of rhetoric – 'the true meaning of a text or work of art is never finished; it is in fact an infinite process' (p. 172 above) – which might suggest him to be a 'death of the author' theorist, the answer, surely, is that he does not. To return to legal hermeneutics, he does not, for example, wish to deny that the prohibition of 'cruel and unusual punishments' is part of 'the meaning' of the Constitution, nor that the fact that there is such a prohibition is determined by the intentions of its authors. What he wishes to say, however, is that 'the meaning of a text as it speaks to an interpreter' is not determined by authorial intention alone, but is rather a 'co-determination' (p. 172 above) in which both author and interpreter play a role. The founding fathers articulate the moral and legal truth that cruel and unusual punishments are forbidden, the interpreters decide whether, in the facticity of the *current* lifeworld, the death penalty for example (p. 175 above), counts as 'cruel and unusual'. What, Gadamer does, in effect, is to distinguish between meaning as authorial intention and meaning as 'application' (TM 306–10). Betti and Hirsch thus miss the point that the distinction they say should be in Gadamer *is* in Gadamer.

Does Gadamer confuse 'thrownness' with 'tradition'?

According to Gadamer, to repeat, all consciousness, all thought, is histori-cally conditioned. In Heidegger's terminology, we are always 'already in' a cultural thrownness, in other words, in a 'tradition', on the basis of which we 'project' ourselves into the future. The claim that we always find ourselves in a particular cultural thrownness, a particular lifeworld, is surely correct. As we grow to adulthood we grow into a particular way of making reality intel-ligible, a particular ontology. Ontologies, moreover, carry with them certain norms. As already observed, to be in a world of tables is to be in a world of things for sitting at but not jumping on, to be in a world of angels and demons is to be in a world where there are things to be revered and things to be exorcized. But do the norms of a world necessarily amount to an ethical 'tradition', a basis and guide for projecting the definition of one's life as a whole? Is the 'in other words' between 'thrownness' and 'tradition' in the second sentence of this paragraph justified?

On reason to pause before accepting the equivalence is that although, as Gadamer claims, Heidegger indeed says that we are 'thrown projection' (TM 254), it is only *authentic* Dasein that projects on the basis of ethical tradition. Inauthentic Dasein projects on the basis of the conventions and pseudo-'urgencies' of current public opinion, so that its relation to tradition, to 'heritage', is one of 'forgetting' (p. 148 above). But if individual Dasein can 'forget' tradition, might not an entire culture? Might not an entire lifeworld be 'tradition-less', and might not the diminished, modern Western lifeworld be an example of such a world?

In third and final part of *Truth and Method*, Gadamer argues, as was first argued by Wilhelm von Humboldt in the early nineteenth century, that different languages determine different 'worldviews', that lifeworlds are 'verbal' through and through (TM 445). 'Language', says Gadamer, 'encompasses simply everything' (PG 25). (This aligns him with later Heidegger's 'language is the house of being' (P 254) and with a rejection of *Being and Time*'s logophobia.) And so he holds, of course, that language is the bearer of tradition. His thought is that, in acquiring language, in becoming an adult human, one simultaneously and inevitably acquires an ethical heritage. This same assumption is made by the English Hegelian F. H. Bradley. As a child learns to speak, Bradley asserts,

> he appropriates the common heritage of his race, the tongue that he makes his own is his country's language ... the same the others speak, and it carries into his mind the ideas and sentiments of the race ... and stamps them indelibly. He grows up in an atmosphere of example and general custom ... the soul within him is saturated ... [29]

To learn one's native language, Gadamer holds, is to internalize a repertoire of 'models' of action (TM 290), ethical exemplars who, as belonging to tradition, have 'authority' over one. But this seems to have something of an antiquated ring to it. In the age of multiculturalism, of two working parents, of the dying of the humanities, of the academy's 'deconstructive' contempt for the moral heroes of the past, of the Internet's destruction of the need to internalize a picture of the past, of the reduction of language to computer-speak, it seems to me no longer true that to learn one's native language is to come under the authority of an ethical tradition.

As earlier noted, Gadamer begins *Truth and Method* by talking about *Bildung*, self-formation (TM 8–16). It is in *Bildung* that one first acquires an ethical tradition: the *Bild* (picture, image) in *Bildung*, he suggests, refers both to a *Nachbild*, an 'after-image' of a figure from the past, and a *Vorbild*, a 'model' (one might almost say 'precedent') for future action. It is in the *Bildung* provided by home, school and perhaps church, that one first becomes properly human. Through *Bildung*, says Gadamer, the individual 'raises himself out of his natural being to the spiritual [in that he] finds in the language, customs and institution of his people (*Volk*) a pre-given body of [ethical] material which, as he learns to speak, he makes his own' (TM 13). The unity of *Bildung* within a society establishes, Gadamer continues (borrowing the term from the Roman Stoics), a *sensus communis*, a largely intuitive 'common sense', a common sense of the proper way of doing things, a shared understanding, which 'founds community' (TM 19).[30]

Gadamer's notion that one always inhabits an ethical tradition[31] amounts to the notion that *Bildung* – and hence entry into 'community' – belongs to the socialization of all individuals. What he does, in other words, is, in the language of *Being and Time*, to transform *Bildung* into an 'existential', an a priori feature of human existence. But while this may have been true for much of Western history, it is highly doubtful that it remains true any longer. It seems to me, in short, that *Truth and Method* mistakes a noble ideal for an ontological inevitability.

In later reflections on the topic, Gadamer seems to accept this. There is, he accepts in the 1971 'Reply to my Critics', an 'erosion' of the 'power of tradition'. The modern period *is* a 'break with tradition'. Nonetheless, he says, 'the fundamental presupposition of the hermeneutical project, a presupposition which no one wants to acknowledge and which I am attempting to restore, has always been the [need for] appropriation of a dominant meaning', of, in other words, an ethical heritage. 'I am not', Gadamer continues, 'being especially original in asserting the hermeneutical productivity of temporal distance' nor in asserting that hermeneutics 'finds its real legitimisation in the experience of history' (HT 284–5). Gadamer finally admits, in other words, that modern humanity is becoming increasingly 'history'-less and thereby 'tradition'-less. Increasingly, we fail to find in the past a guide to the future because the historical dimension of our being is disappearing. Gadamer deplores this and hopes that his work will help restore a sense of the importance of tradition, the importance, that is, of education as *Bildung*. Nonetheless, in the end, he agrees that ethical tradition is *not* an a priori feature of human 'thrownness'. The world we find ourselves 'already in' may be a world with no effective ethical tradition (no shared 'godhead' as Weber puts it); it may be a 'nihilistic' lifeworld. It *ought* to be part of our thrownness, and we ought to try to make it a part, because without it we become a diminished form of humanity. But what ought to be is, unfortunately, not necessarily so.

Is Gadamer's hermeneutical philosophy too conservative, incapable of criticizing oppressive ideologies?

In dealing with this question, I am entering into a long, complex, and sometimes fuzzy debate between Gadamer and Habermas, the central texts of which are a review of the second (1965) edition of *Truth and Method* that Habermas wrote in 1970 (HT 213–44), and Gadamer's reply to Habermas and other critics the following year.[32] I shall ignore the twists and turns of the debate and try to isolate the main points.

Habermas claims that, because, for Gadamer, tradition always has authority over one, Gadamerian hermeneutics has no way of allowing the possibility of criticizing one's tradition *as a whole*. And that means that he has no way of determining whether it might not be, in Marx's sense, an 'ideology', a belief-system designed by those with money and power to keep the rest of us in docile submission. To conduct such a critique we need to step outside tradition and set it in the context of labour and power. Only 'by grasping the genesis of tradition', writes Habermas (i.e. grasping it in the manner of Nietzsche's 'genealogical method of refutation'), do we have the capacity to 'shake the dogmatism of life-practices' (HT 236). This, however, is something hermeneutics cannot do, given that its sole mode of criticism is intra-traditional. For the hermeneuticist, we remain forever confined within the 'walls of the traditional framework' that is 'handed down' to us (HT 239). What we need, therefore, to be able to expose a tradition as ideology, is to advance beyond Gadamer's hermeneutics to (such is the implication) Habermas' own critical theory.

It is not difficult to see the force of this criticism. For insofar as Gadamer thinks of ethical tradition as an implicit ethical 'constitution' which is subject to fusion as 'renewal' but never as 'reconciliation' – as, I have argued, in *Truth and Method* he largely does – then he does indeed picture tradition as a set of 'walls' within which we are confined.

Replying to Habermas' criticism a decade after *Truth and Method* first appeared, Gadamer denies that one has to move beyond hermeneutics in order to engage in critical reflection upon one's own tradition. Hermeneutical reflection, he says, renders 'every ideology suspect in that it makes prejudices conscious' (HT 283).

The primary point of 'understanding' an historical text, we have seen, is 'agreement', agreement about truth (p. 171 above). The truth on which we and the text agree may be something we already know. But the more exciting possibility is that it is not; that, as *Truth and Method* puts it, we are 'pulled up short' by the text's 'alterity' (TM 270–1), by a clash between the truth-claims of the text and our own prejudgments. The clash may, of course, be resolved by our rejection of the prejudices of the text, as when we reject the antisemitism in Shakespeare's *Merchant of Venice*. But, again, the more exciting possibility is that the clash is resolved by our modifying our own prejudices. 'The hermeneutical experience' says Gadamer, 'forces he who understands to place his [own] prejudices at stake' (HT 292), and hence exposes him to the possibility that it is they rather than the alien prejudices that must be modified.

Effectively, what Gadamer is talking about here is Hegelian fusion, fusion as reconciliation. Prompted by Habermas' criticism, Gadamer has finally realized that there are two kinds of fusion through which ethical tradition can develop, that it can develop through 'reconciliation' as well as 'renewal'. It is on account of the former, on account of the fact that one can look at one's tradition from the point of view of an alien tradition, that enables one to subject it to radical criticism.

Notes

1   See the 'Gadamer' entry in the online *Stanford Encyclopedia of Philosophy* (accessed 23/7/17).
2   There are three versions of the identical translation by Joel Weinsheimer and Donald Marshall of the 'second, revised edition' of *Truth and Method*, two published by Continuum in, respectively,

2000 and 2004, and a Bloomsbury edition published in 2013. Annoyingly, they all have different pagination. My references are all to the 2004 Continuum edition.

3 As observed in Chapter I (fn. 18), George, who died in 1933, was a partial model for Weber's conception of 'charismatic leadership'. He preached a conservative 'secret Germany' of the future which should be the goal of national self-renewal. Some members of his circle saw the Nazi Party as the herald of their secret Germany while others came to see it as its antithesis. One of these was Claus von Stauffenberg, who was executed for his attempt to assassinate Hitler in July 1944.

4 Scientific method, writes Gadamer, consists in the 'grasping of the concrete phenomenon as an instance of a universal rule' (TM 4) – the 'covering law model', in other words – plus the rule that an observation that is claimed to confirm (or disconfirm) a scientific law must be interpersonally 'repeatable' (TM 342).

5 Wagner (1966) vol. 5 69.

6 Walter Pater's 'all art aspires to the condition of music' thus expresses the essence of the appropriately named 'aesthetic movement' that he helped found.

7 This repetition of Leibniz's implausible formalism, his claim that 'music is the pleasure of counting when the mind does not know that it is counting', suggests that, like Leibniz and Heidegger, Gadamer has very little sensitivity to music.

8 A similarity not recorded by Gadamer is that sport and drama originally happened in the same kind of place – the amphitheatre.

9 What is the sense of 'is', here? One's natural inclination is to say that it rests on empathy: Lawrence Olivier 'is' Richard III because he has temporarily exited his normal identity and 'become' the character he is playing. 'Method' acting is a particularly intense form of such 'becoming one's character'. This, however, creates something of a problem for Gadamer who, as we shall see (pp. 169–70 below), seems to deny the possibility of empathy as I have described it.

10 The Romantic theorists of the nineteenth century were, of course, not the first to exclude art from the realm of truth. Famously, Book X of the *Republic* settles the 'ancient quarrel between philosophy and poetry' in philosophy's favour by confining the artists to the realm of illusion, and consequently banning them from the ideal state. Access to truth is reserved for philosophers, who alone have access to the universal 'forms'. Though he does not stress the point, Gadamer's observation that art reveals the 'essences' of things is essentially a repetition of Aristotle's rebuttal of Plato's claim that art has nothing to do with truth. Gadamer acknowledges this repetition indirectly by quoting Aristotle's remark that 'poetry is more philosophical than history' and is hence a matter of vital importance (TM 114). (Whereas [narrative] history merely presents us with a succession of facts, Aristotle observes, poetic drama deals in universal essences.)

11 Gadamer is here adopting a contested position in the long-running debate as to the meaning of Aristotelian 'catharsis'. Specifically, he is rejecting the so-called 'psychological interpretation' of catharsis proposed by Edward Bernays, Freud and others. Equally, he rejects the 'metaphysical interpretation' of the early Nietzsche, Hölderlin, and others. Aristotelian catharsis, he claims, in not Dionysian 'intoxication' (TM 128) in which we are temporarily swept away into another world. (In *The Birth of Tragedy* Nietzsche *does*, of course, think of tragic 'intoxication' as truth-revealing – the truth of the Kantian-Schopenhauerian 'thing in itself' relative to which this world of sin and pain is mere illusion. But, to repeat, when Gadamer speaks of art as truth-revealing he always means truth about *this* world.) In place of these psychological and metaphysical interpretations, Gadamer is effectively insisting on the 'cognitive interpretation' proposed by Leo Goldman, G. F. Else and others. (For a detailed discussion of these three interpretations see Young [2013], chapter 2.) Notice that Gadamer does not, in fact, need to insist on the 'cognitivist' interpretation of catharsis to establish that tragic drama is truth-disclosing, since, as mentioned in the previous endnote, he has already quoted Aristotle's observation that (in full) 'poetry is a more philosophical and more serious thing than history: poetry tends to speak of universals, history of particulars' (*Poetics* 1451b 6–8). Tragic drama can, that is, *both* be essentially cognitive, reveal universal and profound truths about life, *and* discharge suppressed emotional states of fear and pity. As I read him, that, indeed, is Aristotle's position.

12 It follows that Gadamer should not have attempted to offer an account of 'the' meaning of Geek tragedy as we have just seen him do.

13 Gadamer says several times that while being a 'repeatable' entity (TM 110), a performance art-work 'exists only in being played' (TM 116). This raises the question of the status of the artwork before its first performance, the status, for example, of Beethoven's late quartets, which, when first published, were considered unplayable. One thing we do not want to say is that Beethoven's quartets did not 'exist' until after his death. I think that my type-token distinction comes to the rescue here. Before its first performance, a performance artwork 'exists' as a type but not as a token. Of course, only after it has been performed does it realise its telos, which is presumably what Gadamer has in mind when he says that only in performance does a work achieve its 'real existence' (TM 309). I would prefer to say 'full' existence, since there is nothing 'unreal' about the yet-to-be-performed Beethoven quartet. For the artwork to exist 'fully' is for it to exist as both type and token.

14 Something that lends support to Gadamer's argument is the familiar phenomenon of disappoint-ment when re-watching a film that one had cherished one or more decades ago. The clothes, turns of phrase, the cars, the general style of the environment, alienate through quaintness. The source of the disappointment is, of course, that one's memory has unconsciously 're-performed' the film so as to make it at home in the current context.

15 Grondin (2003) 49.

16 See 'The Origin of the Work of Art' in Heidegger (2002) 1–56, 3. Gadamer's entire discussion of art has an evident and enormous debt to this work. It might, indeed, be described as, a second 'performance' of Heidegger's seminal work, thirty years after its first 'performance'.

17 An idea that plays a role in Schopenhauer's account of portraiture as, for the viewer, a mode of self-discovery (Schopenhauer [1969] vol. I 230–2). Schopenhauer is generally very rude about Schleiermacher, as he is about all his immediate predecessors, yet he owes him a certain debt.

18 *Supposedly* scientific objectivity. Gadamer actually believes that Enlightenment objectivity is a Fata Morgana with respect to the natural sciences as well, that natural science, too, is moulded by 'historically effected consciousness'. It is no surprise, he observes, that most of the fundamental positions of modern physics are anticipated in pre-Socratic philosophy, since modern physics is profoundly moulded by Greek metaphysics (TM 549). Moreover, as Thomas Kuhn has shown with his notion of a prevailing 'paradigm', the direction of scientific research, the kinds of questions that are put to nature, are deeply moulded by the needs, tastes and proprieties of the age in which they occur. The historicity of fashion also affects the natural sciences (PG 28).

19 The reference is to BT 152–3.

20 Deconstructionists, presumably, have the opposite expectation.

21 The same etymology applies to the English 'pre[-]judice'. The English word, however, already had a pejorative meaning in the thirteenth century, which somewhat weakens Gadamer's historical claim.

22 Gadamer's point about the epistemic superiority of the expert is correct as far as it goes. But it is very easy to postulate expertise in domains where, in fact, no expertise is possible. Are there *really* ethical experts (as is implied by the existence of 'ethics committees'), do moral philosophers really make better moral judgments than the rest of us? As we saw in Chapter 3 (p. 49 above), Habermas' notion that there can be 'professionalized expert knowledge' with respect to the interests of sub-cultures, future generations, children, and so on, is both dubious and potentially oppressive.

23 Notice Gadamer's implicit answer to the 'why be moral?' question: the moral tradition of a com-munity is that which time has shown to promote its survival and flourishing. Note, too, the rela-tivistic character of this answer: what has promoted the flourishing of one community may not promote the flourishing of another.

24 Forster (2007) 63.

25 Forster (2007) 65.

26 Notice that this applies also to the 'productive' use of historical empathy. If, by exercising the 'historical sense', I strip away generations of anachronistic misinterpretation of a text and gain access to the author's original meaning, to make 'productive' use of that access I must still 'fuse' that meaning with and into the horizon that defines my own being-in-the-world.

27 See HT 159–97. Gadamer replies to this criticism at TM 308–9.

28 Hirsch (1967) 42, 254 ff.

29 Bradley (1962) 171–2.

30 In these passages Gadamer is actually summarises first Hegel and then Vico. There is, however, no suggestion that he is doing anything other than endorsing the views expressed.

31 Which early Heidegger shares. Although inauthentic Dasein 'forgets' tradition, the possibility of authenticity, resoluteness, and hence the possibility of 'remembering' it, is always there.

32 HT273–97. A helpful commentary on the details of this debate is to be found in Warnke (1987) chapter 4.

8   Arendt

The *human* condition

Apart from Simone de Beauvoir and perhaps Iris Murdoch, Hannah Arendt (1906–75) is the only really famous dead woman philosopher, certainly the only famous dead woman political philosopher. It is no surprise, therefore, that she has attracted a great deal of secondary literature, much of it written by women. Arendt herself, however, had no interest in being a hero of the women's movement, indeed she *opposed* feminism, holding that women's issues should be subsumed under wider political struggles (EIU 68, Y-B 96–7). She actively opposed – in, as she was aware, positively Victorian terms – equality of opportunity between the sexes,[1] and was greatly annoyed at being congratulated on being the first woman invited to deliver the Christian Gauss Seminars at Princeton (Y-B 272). To the end of her career, her writing remained resolutely attached to 'he' and 'man'.

Arendt's anti-feminism is, I think, of some significance. The prevailing fashion in Arendt scholarship is to read her as, while critical of some of its aspects, fundamentally a defender of the modern, post-Enlightenment social order, regarding it as representing genuine progress over pre-Enlightenment, traditional society. So, for example, the Habermasian critical theorist Seyla Benhabib asserts that Arendt was 'no philosopher of antimodernity': although in some respects 'a reluctant modernist', she was 'a modernist, nonetheless'.[2] In the same vein, Margaret Canovan, alluding to the familiar contrast between the supposed warmth of pre-modern *Gemeinschaft* (community) and the supposed coldness of modern *Gesellschaft* (society), claims that Arendt is 'blessedly free from romantic nostalgia for *Gemeinschaft*', a claim to which I shall return.[3] It is entirely understandable that, as women, Benhabib and Canovan should wish to claim Arendt as a fellow defender of a social order which, for the first time, values gender equality. What Arendt's anti-feminism suggests, however, is that in the effort to appropriate her to their cause, they have failed to do justice to her 'otherness', an otherness springing from her rootedness in a different time, language, nation, and philosophical tradition. In this chapter I shall be concerned to validate this suggestion of hermeneutical failure: to argue that Arendt is indeed a 'philosopher of antimodernity', which is also to say that she is a philosopher not of the decayed modernism that passes itself off as 'postmodernism', but of a genuine post-modernity.

* * *

Arendt studied with Husserl and Heidegger, and completed her doctoral dissertation in 1929 with Heidegger's then-friend, the existentialist philosopher-psychologist Karl Jaspers. Heidegger was, from 1925 to 1928, her lover, and remained a lifelong friend. Being both Jewish and clear-sighted,[4] Arendt fled Germany when Hitler came to power in 1933, and, after many adventures, ended up in 1941 in New York, which became her home for the rest of her life. Eventually she secured a permanent position as professor of political philosophy at the New School for Social Research. Although she never lived in Germany again, she made frequent visits after the war, principally to see Heidegger.

In 1951 she published *The Origins of Totalitarianism*, which, since it is a work of political theory rather than philosophy, I am not going to discuss. In 1958 she published *The Human Condition* which is the focus of this chapter. In 1961 she attended the trial in Jerusalem of Adolf Eichmann, the principal organizer of the logistics of the Holocaust, and reported on the trial in a series of articles for the *New Yorker* magazine. She collected the articles together as a book entitled *Eichmann in Jerusalem: A Report on the Banality of Evil*. This continues to this day to be a source of controversy within Jewish circles, partly on account of its suggestion that Eichmann was just an ordinary bureaucrat, so that, far from the perpetrators of the Holocaust being uniquely monstrous, the crime was something which, given the right incentives, ordinary people of all nationalities might well commit. (Recent research has shown Arendt's account of Eichmann as an ideology-free bureaucrat to be factually false. Philosophically and psychologically, however, the figure she constructs contains the important insight that a great deal of modern evil is the result of deference to inhuman, bureaucratic authority rather than moral monstrousness as such. It is worth noting that the famous Milgram experiment, begun at Yale in 1961, was also a response to the Eichmann trial. In the experiment, volunteers were asked by men in white coats to give – actually fake – electric shocks to a subject – who was an actor – in the interests of developing a conditioned learning programme. The results showed that two-thirds of the subjects were willing to administer shocks up to a level deemed potentially fatal. Stanley Milgram, also Jewish, commented that Arendt's view of the Holocaust 'comes closer to the truth than one might imagine'. Milgram, too, has been subject to criticism, but his results have been supported by Philip Zimbardo's 'prison experiment' at Stanford in 1971.)

It was in Arendt's nature (as it was in Foucault's) to resent and resist classification. Sometimes she denied that she was a philosopher, and sometimes that she was a political theorist. In a 1963 letter to Gershom Scholem who, in the midst of the Eichmann controversy had described her as 'one of the intellectuals who came from the German Left' (as, in other words, a 'modernist'), she replied

> I am not one of the intellectuals who came from the German Left. ... If I can be said to come from anywhere it is from the tradition of German philosophy.
>
> (Y-B 104)

A remark to a student specifies in which part of the tradition she locates herself: 'I am a sort of phenomenologist, but ach, not in Hegel's way – or Husserl's' (Y-B 405). Notice that she does not say, 'not in Heidegger's way'. As noted in Chapter 6, Arendt belonged to the cohort of students for whom Heidegger's rediscovery of 'passionate thinking' made him the 'hidden king of German philosophy' (Y-B 44). Together with their life-long friendship, this strongly suggests that Arendt is, above all, a Heideggerian, and that, as a political philosopher, she takes herself to be working out the political implications of Heideggerian phenomenology – an inconvenient truth for her 'modernist' interpreters.

The *human* condition

The Human Condition (HC) is not, Arendt insists, a study of human *nature*. The reason is that there is no such thing as human nature (and even if there were, she suggests, a study of it would alter its character). While we can speak of a 'nature' common to all members of a non-human species – the nature of 'the tiger' or 'the daffodil' – we cannot speak of 'the human' in the same way. This is because, uniquely among animal species, human beings are essentially 'plural', radically diverse in their characters and unpredictable in their actions. The earth, she emphasizes, is inhabited by 'men, not Man' (HC 7). This, of course, is another way of asserting existential freedom, the Heideggerian and Sartrean theme that one's 'existence' does not come with a pre-determined 'essence' (p. 96 above).

There is, nonetheless, something common to all human beings, a common set of 'conditions' under which 'life on earth had been given to man'. It is these conditions, insofar as they concern the *vita activa* as opposed to the *vita contemplativa*, the active as opposed to contemplative life, that constitute the topic of Arendt's book. (An unfinished later work, *The Life of the Mind*, deals with the *vita contemplativa*.) Along with 'plurality', these conditions are 'natality', 'mortality', 'earth', and 'world'. Life is something we are born into, and is given to us to be lived on earth, among others, in a world, and in the face of mortality (HC 4).

Given Arendt's closeness to Heidegger, it is tempting to view her project, here, as a rewriting of *Being and Time*, an attempt to enumerate the 'existentials' of human existence, the 'a priori' template of our 'being-here (*Dasein*)'. But this cannot quite be her project since she holds that modern man characteristically seeks to escape the conditions under which life is granted, and is sometimes *successful*, albeit to his detriment, indeed to a diminishing of his status as a human being.

What motivates Arendt's project, that is, is the fact that modern man has initiated what she calls a 'Promethean revolt' (HC 139) against the human condition. The Sputnik, the first man-made object to escape the earth's gravity, launched as she was completing *The Human Condition*, she views as a symbol of modern humanity's desire to escape the earth, to transcend the limits placed on all natural beings (HC 1). Like Nietzsche, who sees modern man as seeking to take the place of the God he has 'murdered', Arendt sees him as seeking godlike omnipotence, as seeking to become the 'lord and master of all things' (HC 157), able to remake anything, including himself, in any way he wants. Unlike Nietzsche, who sometimes seems to endorse the project, Arendt regards this as a fatal kind of hubris that threatens us with nemesis. This nemesis is taking two basic forms. The remaking of nature by modern science – the creation and manipulation of forces which, in nature, occur only on the sun – threatens us with the nuclear holocaust (she might now choose to emphasize the climatic holocaust), while the rise of the 'mass society' of 'consumers' threatens to reduce us to mere 'specimens' of a biological species (HC 118, 212) – the claim we have already encountered in Horkheimer and Adorno's modernity critique (p. 32 above).

Unlike the 'existentials' of *Being and Time*, then, Arendt's 'conditions' of human existence do not have 'a priori' status. We can override, transgress, at least some of them. But to do so threatens disaster. And so, while not a priori conditions of human existence as such, they are a priori conditions of *thriving* human existence, 'quasi-existentials', one might say. To put it in the Aristotelian manner characteristic of Arendt's thinking, they are conditions of our being fully *human* beings, and as such they represent the properly *human* condition. The moral of the book is thus that life is given to us on certain 'conditions' which we ignore at our peril.

As Margaret Canovan remarks, this has a religious ring to it. In *The Origins of Totalitarianism*, Arendt identifies resentment against the limits of human existence as the primary impetus to the totalitarian attempt to remake both man and world. Rather than resentment, Arendt holds, the proper attitude to the world is 'gratitude'; gratitude for a life that is granted by, in some sense, God, whose existence, Canovan says, Arendt never doubted.[5] Speaking of the later Heidegger in *The Life of the Mind*, Arendt observes that, for him, the proper attitude to being is 'thanking' (see p. 234 below), which he identifies with Plato's *thaumazein* (LM II 185). In *The Human Condition* she makes clear that this is her own attitude too: the proper attitude to life, she says, is the Greek *thaumazein*, that is, 'wonder at everything that is as it is' (HC 275).[6]

'Conservative' has different meanings, but its root meaning is, of course, 'to conserve'. In this sense, at least, Arendt is evidently a 'conservative' thinker. Unlike, for instance, Nietzsche who constantly yearns for 'new horizons', to stand in grateful wonder at everything 'as it is' is to conserve and cherish the horizons that are given to us – given to us by, as Canovan suggests, some form of the divine. To the extent that Nietzsche is the paradigm of the 'modern', Arendt is 'antimodern'.

Labour

Arendt holds that life, the *vita activa*, divides into three fundamental forms: labour, work, and (in a special sense) action (HC 7). Although an individual's life may contain elements of all three, ultimately one of the three determines its overall form. At the end of the day, the story of one's life will be one of labour, work, or action. These three modes of being form a hierarchy. A life confined to mere 'labour' hardly differs from that of the non-human animals. 'Work' is somewhat more dignified, but human excellence is realized only when one ascends to 'action', by which Arendt centrally means, in the broadest possible sense of the word, 'political' action. In the ancient world, and in her own view, 'action' is the 'highest possibility of human existence' (HC 64) – of, at least, the *vita activa*. I shall discuss Arendt's three forms of life in their ascending order, beginning with labour.

Labour, Arendt quotes Marx as saying, is 'man's metabolism with nature' (HC 98). It is the process by which the human animal incorporates parts of nature into its existence in order to sustain life and reproduction. As a labourer, the human being is simply a part of organic nature, no different from the other animals that live on earth. Paradigmatically, labour is performed with the whole body, unlike 'work' which is performed with the hands – Arendt quotes Locke's distinction between 'the labour of our bodies and the work of our hands' (HC 79).

Leaving aside the arrival of robots, labour is something the human animal *must* do. It is essential to our bodily survival and so belongs to the realm of 'necessity'. It is necessary, that is, that at least many people labour. As Marx observes, one of the characteristics of human labour is 'productivity', its tendency to produce a surplus, which enables some – the citizens of ancient Athens, for instance – to escape the realm of necessity, to have their material needs taken care of by others, their slaves (HC 88).

Although necessary, labour is essentially toil, drudgery. This is reflected in the word 'laborious', and in 'travail' which comes from the French '*travail*' ('labour' or 'work') which, in turn, comes from the Latin '*tripalium*' which refers to an instrument of torture (HC 48). As this etymology suggests, labour is paradigmatically not only boring but also painful (ibid.) (Note, en passant, the masculine tenor of Arendt's thought. Leaving aside 'labour pains', there is nothing painful about such 'women's work' as sewing or washing dishes. The picture she has in mind the peasant scything the wheat field or the road worker wielding a pick-axe.) Labour is, also, in a sense, solitary (HC 22). Labourers, of course, often work together in gangs, but here they relate to each other rhythmically rather than discursively, as parts of a machine rather than as human beings – hence the development of labour songs (HC 145–6 fn.). Arendt does not explicitly make this point, but there is a strong connection between pain and solitude. As severe pain restricts the limits of one's world to one's body, so to the extent that labour really is painful, it confines the labourer's world to his body together with its prosthetic extension, his tool.

Not only is labour painful, it is also meaningless. As a labourer, man partakes in 'the eternal recurrence of the life process' that reigns throughout non-human nature. Unlike the 'work' of the craftsman which produces a durable object as a satisfying 'end in itself' (the potter's pot), labour has no such end and hence yields no creative satisfaction. It is, rather, 'futile', 'circular' (HC 46–8): one labours in order to preserve life, but that life has nothing to show for itself other than the capacity for further labour. (As Nietzsche would put it, 'Why?' has no answer.)

Arendt admits that there are certain pleasures associated with the life of labour, positive pleasures rather than the merely negative pleasure of the cessation of pain at the end of the day's work. She identifies at least two: joy in the rhythmic unification of man, tool, and nature, and the more spiritual joy of merging one's identity with the great cycle of birth and rebirth (HC 106–7, 120, 145) – in both cases one may think of Levin's epiphany in *Anna Karenina* as he scythes the wheat alongside his serfs.

Whatever these compensations, however, they are always exceptions to the rule (for otherwise 'laborious' would not have the meaning it does). And in any case, says Arendt – debunking Marx's romanticizing of labour – labour is beneath human dignity since it is a merely animal life, the life of a mere '*animal laborans*'. This is why, in the ancient world, labour was assigned to slaves (and, of course, women) who were regarded by Aristotle as not fully human (HC 11–13). (One can see, here, the origin of the charge of 'elitism', the charge that, like Nietzsche, Arendt confines the possibility of human excellence to the few.)

Work

Like labour, 'work' is a solitary, 'isolat[ed]' activity (HC 161). (The potter or painter, concentrating on the wheel or canvas, can spare neither the time nor attention to chat.) But whereas labour produces mere commodities for consumption (wheat, coal, meat), work produces *things*, things which collectively, as we shall see, make up a 'world'. Arendt's paradigm worker is the craftsman – '*homo faber*', the 'fabricator', she calls him – whom she understands in a thoroughly Platonic way. The craftsman (the demiurge of the *Timeus* or the bed-maker of the *Republic*) has in the 'eye of the mind' a 'blueprint' (HC 161) of what is to be produced, and then operates on the earth's raw materials to realize an instance of what is represented in the blueprint. The worker, that is, 'reifies' (HC 139): his activity produces a durable 'thing (*res*)'. Even though it does not always consist in the transformation of natural materials, Arendt generalizes the notion of 'work' to cover not only manual activity but also 'intellectual', 'artist[ic]' and 'spiritual' activity (HC 91–3): one can 'craft' not only pots but also paintings, legal codes, and the 'works' of philosophy and theology. (Heidegger calls philosophy 'the craft of thinking'.)[7]

Work, claims Arendt, is essentially violent, a violation of the earth. In contrast to labour which is Sisyphean (Camus calls Sisyphus 'the proletarian of the gods'), work is Promethean: 'violation and violence is present in all fabrication' (HC 139), inevitably so, since it is possible to 'erect a man-made world only after destroying part of God-created nature' (HC 89). While the *animal laborans* values the earth as the source of all good things, *homo faber* regards it and its materials as intrinsically valueless. Locke's observation that only when materials are worked do they acquire value thus represents the outlook of *homo faber*, the dominant outlook of the early modern period in which he wrote. And it survives into the later modern period in which, as we have seen, man 'conducts himself as lord and master of the whole earth' (HC 157).[8]

Homo faber's consciousness of his violence gives him 'the most elemental[9] feeling of human strength' (there is an echo here of Nietzsche's 'feeling of power'), a feeling which is something like the opposite of the Tolstoyan 'joys of labour' mentioned above (HC 140).

Difficulties in the work–labour distinction

Arendt's distinction between unskilled labour and skilled 'fabrication' makes intuitive sense. Yet she herself raises prima facie difficulties for it. For a start, it might be objected that her basic paradigm of labour, farming, *does* produce a durable 'thing', namely the farm. Her response is that this is not 'true reification', does not produce something that is 'secured once and for all', since without constant tilling the soil will revert to nature (HC 138–9). This however, does not meet the objection, since, for instance, the medieval cathedral – a paradigm product of 'work' – also needs constant labour, needs maintenance, to remain a cathedral. (In Cologne, the cathedral is referred to as 'God's eternal construction site'.) The correct response, I think is that if the farm is truly to be a 'thing', it will require more than tilling the land. It will require buildings and at least rudimentary economic planning, both products of work rather than labour. In short, for the farm to become a durable entity the farmer must graduate from being a mere labourer to being an agricultural *homo faber*.

A further prima facie difficulty with the work–labour distinction is the idea that whereas labour produces commodities for consumption, work produces things for use. (The distinction between mass nouns and count nouns seems to lie behind Arendt's distinction between the products of labour and the products of work.) Is it not the case, Arendt herself asks, that there is really no genuine distinction, that use, the use of clothes or shoes, for instance, is just slow consumption? Not so, she replies. Even if things for use do wear out, there is a valid distinction between destruction as a collateral effect of the use of a thing and destruction through consumption as the designated end of a commodity. Even though they may wear out over time, use-things such as shoes have a substantiality, an independent existence, of their own (HC 137–8). (One of the effects of great still life paintings, Cézanne's for example, is to eternalize the substantiality of knives, clocks and glasses, by presenting them as belonging to a world without users.)

Arendt is in a slightly tricky position concerning the substantiality of use-things, for, as we shall see, she wants to argue that in the modern consumer – and, one might add, 'throwaway' – economy, apparent things are really only pseudo-things. And one can see her point with respect to cheap fashion, for instance, where the point of an H&M dress is to wear it exactly once and then discard it. What she should be saying, a point she should have learnt from *Being and Time*, is that a thing for use – a 'ready-to-hand' item of 'equipment' – may be *visually* indistinguishable from an object of consumption. Ultimately, which ontological category an entity belongs to is a matter, not of how it looks, but of how it figures in human practices.

Difficulties in Arendt's account of work

The difficulties in distinguishing between 'work' and 'labour' can, then, I suggest, be overcome. There are, however, other difficulties in her conception of 'work', one of which concerns her account of art and the artist. Artists, it is clear, she regards as *homines fabri*, and so the question arises as to whether the artworks they create count as the 'things of use' that all *homines fabri* are supposed to produce. Arendt begins her discussion of this issue by saying that 'proper intercourse' with a work of art is certainly not 'using' it, not, at least, in the ordinary sense. This, she says, gives them an 'outstanding permanence' since they are 'almost untouched by the corroding effects' of use (HC 167). What artworks do, she continues, is to 'transform' and 'transfigure' their subject matter, make it 'shine'. In doing so, 'the permanence of art'[10] contributes like nothing else to the 'worldly stability' that constitutes a 'non-mortal home for mortal beings' (HC 167–8). What I think she is discussing in this oracular passage is the role of artworks in preserving the ethical 'tradition' which, for her, as for Gadamer, is the essential 'groundwork' of a world that can be a 'home' for mortal man (pp. 000 below.) As with Heidegger's 'heritage', we shall see that for Arendt an ethical tradition is preserved in the memorialized lives of ethical heroes, moral exemplars. But the preservation of their lives depends on works of artists and historians – historians as artists rather than scientists (pp. 000 below). If we understand the term correctly, therefore, artworks *are* things of use. In the final pages of *The Human Condition* Arendt returns to the topic of art. Only the 'charlatan', she says, talks of self-expression: 'expressionist art' is a self-contradiction. Genuine art is essentially 'worldly' (HC 323 fn.), by which she means 'world building and preserving'. In memorializing the bearers of 'tradition', authentic artworks are 'things of use', albeit spiritual rather than material use, essentially the point we saw Gadamer making in his critique of the Romantic theory of art.

* * *

The most problematic aspect of Arendt's account of work is the claim that it is essentially 'violent'. What is problematic can be presented in terms of Arendt's relation to Heidegger.

In 1953, Heidegger published for the first time his *Introduction to Metaphysics* (the work savaged by Habermas [p. 000 above]), originally presented as a lecture series in 1935. Arendt, having by now resumed her close personal relationship with him, possessed a copy and, as is clear from her heavy underlinings, read it closely.[11]

The *Introduction to Metaphysics* belongs to Heidegger's middle period. The works of this period are replete with the rhetoric of heroic violence. Heidegger repeatedly quotes Heraclitus's 'War is the father of all things', and, in the 1935–36 'Origin of the Work of Art', he discovers that the great artwork reveals the essential 'strife' between 'world' (and so the fabricator of world, *homo faber*) and 'earth'. In the *Introduction* itself man is *defined* as 'the violent one', violent because he must use violence to shape 'the place and scene of history' (i.e. 'world') in the face of 'the overpowering', a hostile and terrifying nature (IM 150, 53). Even language, poetry, is violent, a 'taming and ordering' of the 'overpowering' (IM 157). (This idea of poetry as a 'violent' ordering feeds into Heidegger's involvement with Nazism, his attempt to 'lead the leader'. For, as he writes in 1934, it is 'the poet' [Hölderlin] who opens up the new order of existence that is to be created, 'the thinker' [Heidegger] who interprets, 'grasps and orders', the poet's words, and the 'state-founder' [Hitler] who [of course, violently] gives concrete reality to the blueprint thus revealed [GA 39 144].)

The account of *homo faber*'s creation of durable things is thus consonant with, and evidently heavily influenced by, Heidegger's middle period account. What is puzzling, however, is that by 1953, as Arendt certainly knew (Y-B 304), having completed his 'turning' against both his early and middle-period philosophy, in essays such as 'The Question Concerning Technology' Heidegger provides a quite different, violence-free account of, as one might call it, authentic fabrication, and relegates the middle-period account to the level of inauthenticity: an inauthenticity that, to be sure, characterizes modern technological practice, but by no means characterizes technological activity as such. In brief (because this will be the topic of Chapter 9), far from viewing authentic technology – the *techne* of the archaic Greeks, for instance – as a violation, later Heidegger views it as the essentially gentle and respectful activity of 'bringing-forth' that which is already implicit in nature, a notion preserved in, for example, Michelangelo's description of himself as 'setting free' the figure imprisoned in the marble, and in the advice to the gardener in the *Sakutei-ki* (the classic eleventh-century Japanese gardening manual), to 'listen to the request made by the land'.

In her introduction to *The Human Condition*, Canovan correctly summarizes Arendt's account of *homo faber*'s fabrication by saying that 'a craftsman ... [makes something] by forcing raw material to conform to his model. The raw material has no say in the process' (HC xi). But, while this is indeed an accurate account of, say, the stamping out of car bodies from sheets of rolled steel, it obscures the way in which the model – the 'blueprint' – that is realized by Heidegger's authentic technologist is not imposed on nature but is provided by nature herself.

Arendt, as I noted, was certainly aware of this 'turn' in Heidegger's thinking about the activity of *homo faber*. The puzzle is why she choose to ignore it. The answer, I believe, has to do with her focal interest in politics and in the violating violence of twentieth-century totalitarianism. As we shall see, her explanation of such violence is that it is the product of a tradition of political thinking reaching back to Plato, according to which significant political action (the action of a Heideggerian 'state-founder') is the action of a *homo faber*, that is, a matter of possessing a 'blueprint' of human wellbeing (the blond, blue-eyed Aryan, for example) and then applying creative violence to the human 'material' at one's disposal that is needed to realize it. (One might think here of Nietzsche's apparent eulogy to the 'artists of violence' who were the creators of states.)[12] Her conclusion is that the entire tradition must be rejected and an alternative account of political action discovered.

The reason, I suggest, then, that Arendt ignores the possibility of a non-violent *homo faber* is that such an account is of no service in explaining political violence. While Arendt's explanation of totalitarian violence is undoubtedly illuminating, I shall argue later on that a certain incoherence in her alternative account of political action could have been avoided had she attended to the possibility of a non-violent *homo faber*.

World

Homo faber's creative activity – creative violence according to Arendt – results in the creation of a 'world'. *Homo faber* is 'the builder of the world'. A world is, above all, a home for human dwelling:

> If nature and the earth generally constitute the conditions of human *life*, then the world and the things of the world constitute the condition under which this specifically human life can be at home on earth.

'Without being at home in the midst of things', Arendt continues, 'this life would never be human' (HC 134–5). While not a Heideggerian 'existential', 'world', and thus 'home', are, as I put is quasi-existentials, conditions of *thriving* human existence.

In the first instance, a world is made up of the durable material objects that are produced by craftsmen. These are 'things that are used' (HC 134) – houses, temples, roads, bridges, city walls, and the like – with which are associated characteristic human practices.[13] Importantly, however, as already noted, the durables of a world that are the products of intellectual and spiritual *homines fabri* are abstract as well as material. They include, for instance, the political, legal and economic institutions that help constitute the infrastructure of social life. And, as we have seen, the artworks of a world are particularly significant on account of their exceptional capacity to 'hand down' the essence of a world from one generation the next.

A world, then, is the kind of thing that can be studied by archaeologists and historians. It is what all who belong to a given culture have in common (HC 6). An expository question that emerges is whether, in Arendt's conception, natural objects are included in a world. Finn Bowring suggests that they cannot be – and that an Arendtian 'world' is therefore not the same as a phenomenologically conceived 'lifeworld' – because she views world as entirely 'unnatural', something 'artificial' (HC 7) that is constructed in the teeth of an, in itself, worthless and hostile nature.[14] And it is true that, echoing Heidegger's talk of the 'overpowering' (p. 196 above), Arendt indeed speaks of 'untouched nature' as a 'sublime[ly] indifferen[t] … overwhelming elemental[15] force' (HC 136). Nonetheless, Bowring's reading seems to me a misinterpretation. We know, as Canovan records,[16] that Arendt's account of 'world' is strongly influenced by Heidegger's account of the same concept in *Being and Time*. And as we know, what happens in *Being and Time* is that nature is included as an aspect of world, but only as refracted through human practices. The cow shows up within a world but only as ready-made hide, the forest shows up, but only as a supply of timber, the mountain as a quarry of rock, and so on (p. 124 above).[17] This seems to me Arendt's understanding of the nature–world relation: as with the lifeworld that is set forth in *Being and Time*, world is not entirely an 'artifice'. Natural things do show up in it – but only insofar as they are 'ready-to-hand'. This, I think, is what Arendt means when she says that 'only we who have erected the objectivity of a world … can look on nature as something "objective"' (HC 137). And it is certainly the understanding of world that she *needs*, for without it she is open to the serious objection of rendering nomadic peoples, the Australian Aborigines and American Indians, 'worldless'. Nomads, that is, do not, typically, wander idly from place to place. Rather, they move around, generally according to the seasons, within a bounded homeland, whose dimensions are established by natural objects. Arendt needs to allow a world to nomads because it is surely not true that 'humanity' first began with settlement – nomads, after all, have both artefacts and art. Arendt's treatment of nomads – she speaks of the 'wandering of nomad tribes' as 'floating, futile and vain' (HC 204) – somewhat thoughtlessly confuses 'nomads' with 'wanderers' (which many of us now are, as we 'float' – or rather 'surf' – 'futilely' from one Internet site to another).

World as a precondition of individuality

As we have seen, it is with the appearance of world that humanity first appears as distinctively human. Without a world that provides it with a home, *homo sapiens* might exist as a biological species but, in the full sense of the word, 'would never be human'. The reason for this is that one of the conditions under which 'life on earth has been given to man' is that we have in common something which 'gathers and separates us at the same time' (HC 53).

We can begin trying to understand this by examining the claim that a society[18] composed purely of *animal laborans* is 'worldlessness'. This is a condition we shall see Arendt explicitly attributing to mass, consumer society (HC 116, 257). Such a collectivity, she claims, is merely a 'mass' made up of clone-like 'specimens' of a species, not a society of genuine individuals (HC 7). The claim, in short, is that world is a precondition of individuality. Why should this be so?

Developing Hume's observation that we find in consciousness no 'impression' of a self, Kant argues in the *Critique of Pure Reason*'s 'First Analogy' that a distinction between subject and object can only be derived from the contrast between the flux of subjective experience and the 'substantiality' of objective reality, from the durability of objects through time. Arendt rehearses this line of thought. If everything were in constant, Heraclitean flux (HC 137) (if the totality of our experience were as if seen through the window of a fast-moving train) we would have no sense of our own identity through time: 'human beings can retrieve their sameness, that is, their identity [through time], only by being related to the same chair and the same table' (ibid.).

The trouble with this line of thought is that, in this sense of 'identity', neither we nor the hunter-gatherers (supposing them to be wanderers rather than nomads) have any problem. Since we have no difficulty in reidentifying ourselves through time, 'worldless' though we may be, the excursion into Kantianism seems a red herring.

The problem, I think, is that Arendt is actually operating with two senses of 'individuality': a psychological sense in which to be an individual is merely to be able to reidentify oneself through time, and what I shall call a 'spiritual' sense. I take the word 'spiritual' from the Prologue to *The Human Condition* in which Arendt laments modernity's lack of a 'political' and 'spiritual' 'aristocracy' (HC 5; see further pp. 200–1 below). To belong to a spiritual aristocracy is to separate oneself from the 'herdlike' mass (HC 160). This use of a term famously coined by Nietzsche surely reveals Arendt's inspiration at this point. To become an individual in Arendt's spiritual sense is to become, as Nietzsche puts it in *The Gay Science*, 'new, unique, [and] incomparable'.[19] What distinguishes individuality in the spiritual sense from individuality in the psychological sense is spiritual uniqueness.

Why might uniqueness require a world? This cannot be fully discussed until we have elaborated Arendt's concept of 'action', but, to anticipate, let us note that in creating a world, *homo faber* (and here it must be intellectual and spiritual *homines fabri* who come to the fore) also create a 'public realm' (HC 52): an arena in which men emerge from the privacy of family and household to deal with the *res publica*, matters of public concern such as administration, morality, and justice. Speaking of the Athenian polis, and again emphasizing exactly what Nietzsche emphasizes, Arendt says that the public realm of the polis

> was permeated by a fiercely agonal[20] spirit where everyone had constantly to distinguish himself from all the others, to show through unique deeds or achievements that he was the best of all ...The public realm, in other words, was reserved for individuality; it was the only place where men could show who they really and inexchangeably were.

> (HC 41)

Action

Arendt's special sense of 'action' takes its inception from its Greek root, *archein*, which, she points out, means 'to begin', to initiate, and 'to lead' (HC 177). To perform an 'action' is to be, in a philosophical sense, spontaneous, to be, that is (at least from the phenomenological point of view),[21] a 'first cause', a 'new beginning' (HC 184). An 'action', she says, always appears as a 'miracle' (HC 178). Most actions are thus not 'actions': flying to the moon was an 'action', flying to Winston-Salem is not.

Action (until further notice, I shall take the scare quotes to be understood) is the 'highest possibility' (HC 64) of the *vita activa*. Who is capable of it?

In the Prologue to *The Human Condition*, Arendt says that since, in modernity, everyone is levelled down to the circular life of labour and consumption, modern society is 'egalitarian' in a very bad sense. What we need, she says, is a reanimation of 'class', the re-creation of the 'political' and 'spiritual' 'aristocracy' referred to earlier, from which 'a restoration of the other capacities of man could start anew' (HC 5). (Arendt created a furore with her 1959 'Reflections on Little Rock' by arguing that, while there should be no legal barriers to racial integration, social discrimination was a good thing as a barrier against 'mass society' [Y-B 311].)

Fairly clearly, this is a repetition of Nietzsche's famous (or infamous) argument that 'expansions of distance within the soul', the striving for 'self-overcoming', can only happen in an 'aristocratic society ... which believes in a long ladder of rank-order and differences in worth between men'[22] – can only happen, that is, if social inequality provides a model from which one can derive the idea of higher and lower states of the soul. This repetition enhances the suspicion that Arendt is a 'Nietzschean elitist', that she holds that only a few, exceptional types are capable of action.

In fact, however, this is not exactly her view, since she writes that 'men' – not 'some men' – 'are not born to die but to begin' (HC 34). Even more explicitly, she says that although most do not live up to their capacity for action, '*all* men are capable of deed and word' (HC 27; emphasis added). We should recall, moreover, that her book is a discussion, not of the 'condition' of a few outstanding individuals, but of 'the human' condition. Since 'natality' is common to us all, and natality is the capacity for a 'new beginning inherent in birth' (HC 9), we all have the capacity for action. Hence, unlike Nietzsche, who believes that some human beings are intrinsically more excellent, have more 'worth' than others, Arendt seems to hold that all human beings have the capacity to become elite, to become members of her spiritual aristocracy. At the same, time, however, she appears entirely certain that most people will succumb to levelling forces and fail to realize their potentiality for action. Though all men are capable of action, 'most of them – like the slaves in the ancient world ... like the labourer or craftsman prior to the modern age, the jobholder or businessman in our world' will not inhabit 'the space of deed and action' (HC 199).

What seems to follow is that the ideal, Arendtian society will resemble the Platonic pyramid.[23] At the bottom are the labourers who are provided with a home by the middle layer of *homines fabri*, while at the apex are the shining men of action through whom the labourers and the workers are redeemed from the 'meaninglessness' that would otherwise accrue to their lives. I shall discuss this issue of 'meaning' later on (p. 217 below), but, to anticipate, Arendt's thoughts on meaning are contained in the question 'What is the use of use?'. *Homo faber* scurries around building bridges, roads, and constitutions, aided, usually, by the menial activity of *animal laborans*, but, Arendt believes, they both need an answer to the question 'What is it all for?' As she puts it, an 'in order to' stands in need of a 'for the sake of' (HC 154).

There is, it seems to me, no escaping the fact that Arendt is a 'social elitist'. Any decent society will be – de facto, if not de jure – a pyramid in which the meaning of the whole is determined by, and only by, the men of action.

The political

Arendt claims that the highest form of action is 'political' action (HC 64). This seems to sit uncomfortably with the claim that her topic is a capacity which all human beings in principle possess, given that we do not all possess the skills required of successful politicians. In fact, however, the sense she attaches to 'political' is not the usual one. The arena of authentic politics (which for reasons we shall come to she calls 'the space of appearance'), she says, comes into being whenever men are gathered together in the manner of speech and action, and therefore *predates and precedes* all formal constitution of the public realm and the various forms of government, that is, the various forms in which the public realm can be organized.

(HC 199; my emphasis)

She points out that while, in ancient Athens, only citizens could discuss the affairs of the polis, the framing of laws could be delegated to foreigners (HC 63, 194). Lawmaking was not the 'content of' (HC 63) political action but merely created the 'space' (HC 194) in which it could occur (an observation which casts a revealing light on the current media habit of referring to politicians as 'lawmakers'). In relation to the usual understanding of 'politics', political action as understood in *The Human Condition* thus belongs to the realm of what she later calls the 'pre-political'. And as we shall see (pp. 223–5 below), all of us, especially in our roles as parents and teachers, can engage in politics in this sense, in shaping the climate of opinion that provides the parameters within which politics in the usual sense occurs.

It has often been suggested that politics, in Arendt's sense, is, first and foremost, poetry. Shelley famously claimed that 'poets are the unacknowledged legislators of the world' (in 'A Defence of Poetry'), and Heidegger, following Hölderlin's notion that poetry establishes a 'fundamental mood', claims that 'poetry is "politics" in the highest and most authentic sense' (GA 39 214). Arendt, too, accepts that poetry can be 'politics', arguing that on account of the 'political function' of his shining examples of human excellence, Homer really was (contrary to Plato's claim that he was a fake educator) 'the educator of all Hellas' (HC 197).

The fragility of human affairs

Unlike both labour and work, which, recall, are (or at least can be) conducted in solitude, action is essentially communal: as work cannot happen without materials to work with, so action requires 'the surrounding presence of others', requires what *Being and Time* calls *Mitsein*, 'being-with-others'. Robinson Crusoe performs both labour and work, but until Man Friday arrives, he cannot 'act'. Action is an attempt to influence the affairs of men, and since men, far from constituting inert material, are each capable of expressing their freedom in independent action and reaction, it follows that action requires what Aristotle (following Aeschylus) calls 'persuasion' and identifies as the specifically political mode of speech (HC 26 fn.9). Action, that is, requires one to secure the voluntary co-operation of others: the idea of the strong, isolated leader is a myth (HC 189) (even the dictator needs his cronies). But since such co-operation can never be guaranteed, it follows that the consequences of action are radically 'unpredictable' (HC 232). (As the Yorkshire proverb has it, 'There's nowt as queer as folk'.) Impatience with such unpredictability, with the 'fragility' (HC 196) of the results of political action, leads to either Epicurean world-withdrawal or to yielding to the totalitarian temptation to become a political *homo faber*, to visit violence and terror on one's human material in the attempt to mould it to the desired shape. But in the end, all such attempts fail. History is full of examples of the failure of would-be leaders who did not know how to enlist the voluntary 'co-acting' of their fellow men (HC 189).

One of the consequences of the unpredictability of action is that, in reality, 'action reveals itself fully only to the storyteller, that is, to the backward glance of the historian who indeed knows better than the participants what it was all about' (HC 192). The result is that action is merely the initiation of a process in which the actor 'never quite knows what he does' (HC 233) ('The owl of Minerva', as Hegel remarks, 'flies only at dusk'.)

Arendt has, I think, two kinds of 'unpredictability' in mind without, however, distinguishing between them. The first is the problem of unintended consequences, unintended 'outcome[s]' of action (HC 192). When the second President Bush invaded Iraq his action was, unbeknownst to him, 'the creation of ISIS'. The unforeseen consequences of actions, that is, generate new, and often unwelcome, redescriptions of the action in question. The second kind of unpredictability lies in the capacity of later generations to reinterpret, to place a new 'spin' on the actions of earlier generations. So, for example, the Catholic use of sculpture as an aid to devotion became, with the Reformation, 'idol worship'. And in 2016, students at Oxford demanded the removal of the statue of Cecil Rhodes because what was salient in the light of their sensibilities was not his beneficence towards Oriel College, but the exploitation of Africans that provided the means of such beneficence. Notice that while both cases can be described as the retrospective 'storyteller' knowing better than the actor 'what he does', the second kind of unpredictability is not necessarily a matter of new consequences of action coming to light but rather of different aspects of action becoming salient in the light of changing perspectives.

A further consequence of the unpredictability of action – here, I think, Arendt has the problem of unintended consequences exclusively in mind – is the fact that action is *dangerous*. It is the actions of modern scientists (Arendt explicitly acknowledges 'the use of scientific experiment to take command of nature' as an instance of 'action' [HC 233]) that release forces which, in nature, occur only on the sun, that threaten us with nuclear extinction (HC 231). (One might think of J. Roger Oppenheimer's eventual realization of the appalling danger he had released by leading the Manhattan Project as the slow dawning of Arendtian wisdom concerning the unpredictability of action.)

In the political arena, too, action is dangerous. So, for example, the French Revolution led to the Terror and the Bolshevik Revolution to Stalinism. In the face of the potential 'chaos' generated by action (HC 237), however, we have two, at least partial, remedies, remedies that can create an 'island of security' in the 'sea of uncertainty' (HC 237).

The first is promise-making, the commitment, for example, to observe a constitution, a commitment that introduces a measure of predictability to human affairs. The value of promise-making was well understood by the Roman legal system: its insistence on the inviolability of agreements and treaties was what kept the 'public space' in existence (HC 244–5) – recall that it is lawmakers who create the 'space' in which authentic politics can occur.

The second antidote to chaos is forgiveness. Unknown in the ancient world (and, according to Teddy Kollek, to Judaism), the practice, and its status as a virtue, was first discovered by Jesus. Although recognizing it as a moral virtue, Arendt is more interested in it as a political virtue. Its political importance is that it breaks the 'chain reaction' of offence and revenge, the vendetta (HC 239–41). So, for example, one might think of South Africa's post-apartheid Truth and Reconciliation Commission as institutionalized forgiveness. Since, however, Arendt acknowledges legal punishment as an 'alternative' to forgiveness (HC 241) (the invention of the jury trial is celebrated at the end of Aeschylus's *Oresteia* precisely because it ends the vendetta within the House of Atreus) it is not entirely clear why she considers it so important as a *political* virtue.[24]

The motive for action

What motivates people to perform 'actions'? For us humans, writes Arendt, 'appearance constitutes reality'. Being seen and heard in the 'public realm', showing up in the 'space of appearance', constitutes our 'reality'. The 'passions of the heart' have only a shadowy existence until they are 'shaped for public appearance'. 'Growing old', she adds, quoting Goethe, is 'gradually receding from appearance', a gentle pre-echo of death. (HC 50–1).

Arendt takes delight, here, in playing transgressively with philosophers' favourite distinction. What she obviously does not mean is that the first Christians who, being 'worldless', lacked a 'space of appearances' (HC 54–5), were merely fictional beings. And neither does she believe that the 'worldless' members of modern, mass society are mere fictions. Moreover, she does not really think that *all* the passions of the heart fail to be fully real unless they appear in public, since she says that, for example, love is essentially private and is extinguished the moment it appears in public (HC 51). What she is really doing, I think, is rehearsing Hegel's notion of 'recognition', his thesis that my identity as the person I take myself to be depends on that identity being 'recognized' by appropriate others. Even in its own eyes, a nation does not count as a nation unless it receives 'diplomatic recognition' from established nations; even in my own eyes, I do not count as a doctor unless I am recognized as such by the Medical Council. In general, I do not count, even in my own eyes, as instantiating my self-image unless I am recognized as doing so by others. This Hegelian thought is memorably expressed in Sartre's assertion that 'the other holds the secret of my being'.[25]

It is part of the human condition, Arendt believes, to wish to be in this sense 'real'; to be acknowledged as a (real) philosopher or a (real) philanthropist, to be, as we say, a 'player' in the world, or sub-world, that is important to us. What one seeks is not merely the temporary mark of a five-minute celebrity. One seeks, rather, to make a permanent, indelible mark on the memory of one's community. That, at least, was the manifest desire of citizens of those flourishing civilizations of the past, in particular, of the Roman Republic. The ground of this quest was the desire to overcome 'the futility of individual life' (HC 56), the 'vanity' (as 'the melancholy Ecclesiastes' calls it) of a life of which there is no 'remembrance' (HC 204), a life in which 'even [one's] name is forgotten' (Ecclesiastes 9:5). It is for this reason that in the ancient world, the private was essentially 'privative' (HC 8): to be excluded from 'appearance' in the public realm (by exile, for example) was for one's life to be rendered 'futile'.

What does Arendt mean by 'futility' and how does she understand 'vanity'? Why exactly is the desire that motivates action a desire to overcome? Arendt attaches futility to the 'mortal[ity]' of life, so that the desire in question is a desire to achieve – not, certainly, the supernatural 'eternity' promised by Christianity – but rather 'worldly immortality'. Men of action want 'something of their own' to become immortal (HC 55–6), which requires, of course, the immortality (or at least durability) of one's world: 'if one was convinced that the world would end shortly after one's death it would lose all reality [importance] for one', as it did for the early Christians (HC 120).

There are, of course, those whose names are remembered with disgust and horror. (Andreas Lubitz, who crashed his plane into the French Alps on 24 March 2015, killing himself and 149 other people, wanted, he told his former girlfriend, 'to do something … [so] that all will know my name and remember it'.) But unless one is very sick, this is not how one wants one's name to be remembered. One wants, rather, to be held in *glorious* memory, one wants one's name to '*shine* through the centuries' (HC 55; emphasis added). As Machiavelli observed, 'the criterion of political action is glory' (HC 77).

The quest for 'glory', for 'immortal fame' (HC 193), might sound like 'ego-tripping'. But to be remembered as an ego-tripper, as a 'narcissist', is to be remembered with contempt and, in fact, soon forgotten. To be held in hallowed memory, the story of one's life must be one not one of self-aggrandisement, but of contribution to the common good. As Canovan points out, Machiavelli's 'virtú' to which glory accrues *is* public spirit,[26] having the good of the *res publica* rather than the self as one's goal.

Authentic politics

We have understood something, by now, of Arendt's conception of 'action', and something of the motive for engaging in its 'highest possibility', 'political' action. But what of the practice of politics? What is it for politics to be practised *well*? What, as I shall put the question, is 'authentic' politics?

Authentic politics, we have seen, is not 'lawmaking'. The arena of politics is, rather, something prior to lawmaking. Arendt's guiding insight about this arena is that it is a place where *many* individuals disclose their unique individuality. Since they all have their unique perspective on how things are and how they ought to be, authentic politics is the politics of 'plurality' (HC 7) and 'diversity' (HC 16). It follows that, far from the quiet orderliness of court, church, lecture theatre (or, one might add, the 'ideal speech situation'), authentic politics is essentially *messy* – noisy, argumentative, disruptive, rude, polemical, rhetorical, unpredictable, democratic – a messiness which, as noted, generates the totalitarian impatience that seeks to replace free-range plurality with the work of a political *homo faber*.

As this implies, authentic politics is essentially a matter of 'speech' between 'equals' (HC 32). Governing, in the sense of *ruling*, while the norm in the private household of the Athenian citizen, has no place in the arena of authentic politics. And the use of force, of violence, has no place either. As Pericles knew, the sublimation into speech and action of the violence that occurred within the space of appearances that was the Homeric battlefield was the birth of the polis (HC 197). Instead of force, authentic politics generates a 'power' that is essentially plural (HC 199), the power, I take Arendt to mean, of public opinion.

Does this mean that authentic politics is nothing more than arriving at consensus on matters of common concern by any means short of violence? Not so. There are, Arendt believes, better and worse ways of doing so.

One way of arriving at consensus on a matter of common concern is logical argumentation, the valid derivation of conclusions from agreed premises. When it comes to politics, however, this procedure is, says Arendt, unavailable. As Aristotle notes, the 'persuasion' that constitutes political discourse is essentially different from 'philosophical' argument (HC 26 fn). The reason for this, as Arendt makes clear in a later work, 'Truth and Politics', is that, contra Plato and political *homines fabri* in general, politics is not a realm of truth, of facts, but rather of opinion. Of course, facts are not irrelevant to politics – as Clemenceau observed, however much historians rewrite the history of the First World War, no one (except, perhaps, the 45th president of the United States) will ever claim that Belgium invaded Germany. 'Brute' facts such as these, however, can never determine political decisions, since historians can incorporate them into any number of different stories that provide radically different interpretations (BPF 234–5) – the 'spin' referred to earlier as an aspect of the unpredictability of action (p. 203 above). This is what Jefferson understood in saying not 'these truths are …' but rather 'we hold these truths to be …' Unlike Plato, he understood that 'all men are created equal' is not a provable philosophical truth but rather an opinion requiring agreement and consent (BPF 242).

The problem of political consensus is, then, a matter, not of proving truths, but of reconciling opinions. How is this to be done? Arendt answers this question by giving an account of how, as an individual, one ought to arrive at a political judgment, an account which, she says (BPF 243), is a model for interpersonal dialogue. She calls this 'representative thinking' and acknowledges Kant's *Critique of Judgment* (section 40) as its inspiration.

Representative thinking is a matter of achieving what Kant calls an 'enlarged mentality'. It is a matter of

> considering an issue from different viewpoints, by making present to my mind the standpoints of those who are absent: that is, I represent them ... The more people's standpoints I have present in my mind ... the better I can imagine what I would feel and think if I were in their place, the stronger will be my capacity for representative thinking and the more valid my final conclusions, my opinion... the only condition for this exertion of the imagination is disinterestedness, the liberation from one's own private interests.
>
> (BPF 237)

The question to be asked, here, is what exactly Arendt means by 'valid', specifically, what does this 'validity' come to in interpersonal dialogue?

* * *

Habermas claims that it means for Arendt essentially what it means for him. Although he concedes that her language is different (the word 'rationality' occurs exactly once in *The Human Condition*), what she means by 'representative thinking' is essentially what he means by 'communicative rationality' as exemplified in 'discourse ethics'. Both of them, moreover, he continues, are aware that the possibility of such thinking depends on 'radical equality', and both are aware of the need for 'unimpaired intersubjectivity': for an open society that does not, as does totalitarianism, isolate individuals from each other in order to render them a docile, unitary mass.[27]

This attempt to extricate Arendt from Freiburg and claim her for Frankfurt and the Enlightenment involves at least two errors. The first is that whereas Habermas, as we saw, is concerned with the determination of 'moral norms', Arendt is concerned, not with morality – that, we shall see, comes from 'tradition' – but rather with politics, not with moral but rather political consensus. The second error is that whereas Habermas is concerned with establishing truth – if something is a moral norm it is *true* that it represents a 'common interest' – Arendt is concerned merely with reconciling *opinions*. With respect to political consensus, that is, there is *no* truth of the matter. The problem is not finding out the truth but reconciling perspectives that are as necessarily divergent as are spatial perspectives (HC 57). Since there is no truth of the matter, it follows that, while in Habermas' 'ideal philosophy seminar' only the 'force of the best argument' wins, Arendt, as we saw, specifically distinguishes the Aristotelian 'persuasion' she takes to be the mode of communication that occurs in authentic politics from 'philosophical speech'. (I shall have further comments to make on Arendt's relationship to Habermas later on.)

* * *

But if not the product of 'communicative rationality', what then does Arendt mean by 'valid' political judgment? *How* does 'representative' discourse produce political consensus, that is, integrate necessarily divergent perspectives? Clearly while less than establishing truth it is more than counting heads. What she has in mind, I think, is essentially Hegel's notion of 'reconciliation' discussed in the previous chapter. We, the audience, 'representing' to ourselves Creon's point of view, see the force of his insistence on the primacy of the state, of the general interest, but representing to ourselves Antigone's point of view, see, too, the force of her insistence on the primacy of family. As we reflect on the tragedy a 'synthesis' between the competing demands slowly emerges, a combination of some of the demands of the family and some of the demands of the state into a consistent whole.

Arendt's critique of modernity

What we have been examining, to date, is Arendt's account of the 'human condition' in the sense of the *ideal* human condition. Ideal humanity lives on the earth, in a world, a world that provides a public, plural space in which men can overcome the 'futility', the 'weightless irrelevance', of a 'private life centred on nothing but itself' (BPF 3). They do so through original, community-enhancing 'action', action that realizes the potential given to them in their 'natality', and thereby provides a solution to the problem we all face in the form of 'mortality'. For all its faults – slavery and, Arendt believes, an overly rampant individualism that eventually destroyed it – the Athenian polis was the nearest approach to such a paradigm. Modernity, however, falls – a vast distance – short of this ideal. As to how and why it does so, Arendt has a lot to say. Her critique is summed up in the phrase 'world alienation' (HC 248), the title of the first section of the final part of *The Human Condition*. What, then, is 'world alienation', and why is it problematic?

World alienation

Insofar as Arendt has a tendency to identify 'world' with 'public realm' and 'public realm' with the 'space of appearance', and that in turn with 'politics', the loss of world means the loss of authentic politics. Really, however, this equivalence between 'world' and 'arena of authentic politics' does not withstand serious examination. From the discussion to date, it is clear that authentic politics is, for Arendt, in some sense 'liberal' and in some sense 'democratic'. If then, liberalism and democracy are necessary conditions of authentic politics (but for Arendt, not, I shall argue, sufficient conditions [pp. 220–1 below]), in the time between the ancient and modern worlds there was really no authentic politics at all. Moreover, as Arendt herself points out, what concerned men in the Middle Ages was, not the 'worldly immortality' that is the motive for authentic politics, but rather 'eternal' life in another world (HC 34, 74). Yet, almost tautologically, the medieval world was a 'world'.

Really, it seems to me, the basis of Arendt's notion of world is something even more fundamental than politics: the idea of 'home', a term that occurs no less than forty-two times in *The Human Condition*. 'Without being at home in the midst of things', we have seen, 'this life would never be human' (HC 134–5). Heidegger, as we shall see, notes that this identity between being human and having a home is rooted in the German language: '*bin*', the first person singular of the verb 'to be', derives from '*buan*', to be at home, 'to dwell' (p. 238 below).

Arendt's splendid biographer, Elizabeth Young-Bruehl, observes that, as a Jew in a gentile world, forced to flee her native land and for many years a stateless person, Arendt constantly experienced her own condition as one of 'alienation', 'estrangement', 'homelessness' (Y-B 90), and had thus a corresponding yearning for 'homeland' (Y-B 86).[28] This, I think, expresses a deep human truth. As Schopenhauer observes – his example is health – one needs to be deprived of something to realize its true value.

What does being at home – 'dwelling' as opposed to temporarily 'staying' or 'lodging' somewhere – require? It requires a dwelling *place* – and hence (save for genuine nomads [pp. 198–9 above]) *homo faber*'s activity of 'building'. The basis of a dwelling place is one's 'immediate earthly surroundings', surroundings in which, and out of which, *homo faber* fashions things of use. For one to have 'immediate' surroundings, for some things to be 'close at hand', there has to be a distinction between what is near and what is not. There has to be, that is, a more or less sharp boundary – in the ancient world it was the city wall (HC 194, 197) – that distinguishes one's dwelling place from places where one does not dwell. (As Heidegger observes, a boundary is not where something stops but where it starts [PLT 152].) Without a boundary, dwelling is impossible: there is no such thing, says Arendt (a thought repeated by Theresa May in her 2016 debut speech as British prime minister), as a 'citizen of the world' (HC 257).

Arendt observes that within the public space of the homeland there is also the private space that is defined by the four walls of the family home (BPF 183). This suggests that we could think of the dwelling place as four walls contained within four walls – although writing as a grateful immigrant in a land of immigrants, Arendt would certainly wish to see multiple points of entry through the outermost walls. (It may be no accident that the emphasis on 'four', here, reflects later Heidegger's account of the dwelling place as 'the fourfold' [pp. 247–8 below].)

This, then, is the fundamental notion of a world – and pretty clearly, the emphasis on 'home', on the traditional rather than modern lifeworld, is another barrier to Habermas' attempt to claim Arendt for Frankfurt. We in modernity, however, at least many of us, have become 'worldless', have developed a 'worldless mentality' (HC 257). This 'world alienation' represents a point of affinity between modernity and medieval Christianity (HC 53–4) (though whereas the medievals had at least the consolation of an *eventual* place of dwelling, we do not).

Modernity has, then, Arendt claims, deprived us of the conditions of living a fully human life. She identifies four causes of this state of affairs – science, scepticism, capitalism, and technology – which I shall now discuss in that order.

Modern science and world alienation

Arendt's worries about modern science centre on Galileo's telescope. Before his observations revealed, *inter alia*, that Jupiter's moons revolved around Jupiter rather than around the earth as they were supposed to, Copernicus' heliocentric alternative to geocentric astronomy was just a theory. Galileo's observations, however, turned it into fact, so that with early modernity's acceptance of the new astronomy, the earth lost its privileged status and became just one among an infinity of 'stars' (sic). This, says Arendt, constituted the 'alienation of man from his immediate earthly surroundings' (HC 251). It condemned us to a 'centerless' existence (HC 263), deprived us of a place where we can feel 'centred', feel, that is, at home. Why should it have done this?

The object of Arendt's attention is the collapse of the medieval worldview, the geocentric view medieval Europe inherited from the Greeks. On this view, as portrayed on medieval maps, the cosmos consists of the seven planets circling the earth together with, beyond the 'seventh sphere', God and the angels looking down with loving concern on the affairs of men. On this picture, the cosmos is a small, intimate, even cosy, place. As one looks up into the night sky at the 'dome of the heavens' one sees the world's boundary a few miles away. This, Arendt seems to lament, is what science has deprived us of.

The medieval worldview is not only spiritually comforting, it is also confirmed by sense perception: from one's position on earth one *sees* the sun rise in the east and sink in the west. The heliocentric view, by contrast, cannot be confirmed by terrestrial sense perception. To confirm it, to see – or to imagine oneself as seeing – the rotation of the earth around the sun, one has to imagine oneself as no longer standing on the earth but rather at a point outside the solar system. And to imagine oneself as observing the solar system within the wider context of the universe, one has to imagine oneself as standing outside of the universe at an 'Archimedean point' (HC 257), a point of view which allows a 'view from nowhere' in particular. And the consequence of this is that we become 'centerless' beings. The medieval map of the universe came supplied, always, with a 'we-are-here' arrow. It showed us our dwelling place. The modern map has no such arrow. Modern science has destroyed our dwelling place, has rendered us 'homeless'.

The problem with this account of world alienation (as with Husserl's [pp. 107–8 above] by which it is probably influenced) is that it fails to take adequate account of the fact that we live not in the science world but in the lifeworld (albeit a world in which people and other beings may have been degraded, 'reified', into 'commodities' or 'resources' [pp. 113–4 above]). Most of us know little about modern science, and even if we do, we lock it away in a compartment of the mind divorced from everyday life. Unable to convince himself of the existence of mind-independent objects, David Hume none-theless had no problem in 'consorting with modest women and playing backgammon' once he shut the study door behind him. Arendt assumes the expulsion of the geocentric view from modern science is a fortiori its expulsion from 'our worldview'. The astronomers and the scientifically minded philo-sophers of early modernity have, she claims, 'abolished' the 'dichotomy' between the 'earth' on which, and the 'sky' under which, we live (HC 258). But this is manifestly not the case. Although science tells us that nothing has colour and that the earth revolves around the sun, we carry on stopping at red lights and enjoying the sunrise and sunset.

Arendt's anxiety about the de-centring effect of Galilean science is a close paraphrase of the famous 'death of God' passage in Nietzsche's *The Gay Science*. By abolishing the medieval map of the universe, the map that pro-vides a clear and simple account of the relation of God to man, we have, 'the madman' tells us, 'murdered' God. What on earth, he continues,

> were we doing when we [i.e. Galileo] unchained this earth from its sun? Whither is it moving now? Whither are we moving? Away from all suns? Are we not plunging continually? Backward, sideward, forward, in all directions? Is there still any up and down? Are we not straying through an infinite nothing? Do we not feel the breath of empty space? Has it not become colder? ....
>
> (p. 107 above)

This passage seems to me to commit the same error as does Arendt. It pro-jects the anguish of the study onto life in general, thus ignoring the fact that, in the midst of his nomadic existence, even Nietzsche felt himself centred on the Alpine paradise where he wished to be buried, Sils Maria.

Scepticism, Cartesian doubt, and world alienation

Arendt sees world alienation through 'scepticism' as another effect of modern science. Pre-modern science was contemplative, satisfied with cataloguing the regularities of phenomenologically given nature. (Some impressive achievements were based on such catalogues: Polynesian peoples were able to traverse the Pacific long before Europeans traversed the Atlantic, basing their navigation on such things as wave patterns and patterns in the flight of birds.) Modern science, by contrast, is not content to describe the given. It *constructs* a thought picture of the mechanism hidden behind the scenes and then experiments on – as it were, torments – nature until it finds a thought picture that achieves predictive success (Weber's 'control through calculation'). This, says Arendt, is another long-term effect of Galileo's telescope: since the senses are mistaken about the earth–sun relation they can no longer be trusted to put us in touch with an independent reality. 'Cartesian doubt' is 'logically ... and chronologically the most immediate consequence of Galileo's discovery' (HC 287). And with the contradiction of the very laws of thought by quantum mechanics (Schrödinger's cat is both alive and dead) it follow that science's ultimate message is that thought is no more capable of putting us in touch with reality than are the senses. We are locked into the Cartesian prison of the mind. We have theories that allow us to predict future *experiences*, but as to whether they correspond to reality we have no idea. We do not even know that there is anything behind the experiences (maybe, as Berkeley and Derrida think, there are just minds and the void). The result, as Werner Heisenberg puts it, is that, so far as we know, 'man encounters only himself' (HC 261–2).[29] We thus come to think of ourselves as Cartesian minds, disconnected from our bodies and so from earth and world.

Once again, it seems to me, this aetiology of alienation fails properly to take account of the fact that we live in the lifeworld, not the science world. We respond to colours, untroubled by Galileo's assurance that they are not real. And as to Cartesian solipsism, the notion that outside the mind there is only the void, Schopenhauer is surely correct that metaphysical 'realism' belongs to the 'original disposition of the human intellect'[30], is, that is, a product of biology; as Quine says, creatures disposed to sceptical doubts about the existence of trains and tigers have the habit of dying out before reproducing their kind.[31]

Capitalism and world alienation

My, to date, critical stance towards Arendt's attempted aetiology of modern world-alienation might seem to suggest that I acknowledge no such phenomenon. But this is not at all the case. And when we come to her identification of early modern capitalism as a contributing cause her point is, I think, a valid one.

Proudhon's famous quip that 'property is theft' has, observes Arendt, a solid basis in the origins of modern capitalism (HC 67). Capitalism began (as Weber argues) with the Reformation: with the expropriation of Church land, and with the enclosure of common land that began shortly thereafter. Deprived of their property, and so of the world in which their property had rooted them, the peasants became literally homeless. With the birth of capitalism began the depopulation of the countryside, the migration of the peasants to join the worldless mass in the city (a process now, of course, vastly accelerated by the mechanized mega-farming of the agribusiness).

Underlying and motivating this process was a conceptual shift. Traditionally, one's property was simply the place where one's family had lived for many generations and was no more the kind of thing that could be bought or sold than was the family who lived there. In the early modern period the distinction between 'immobile' and 'mobile' property (in German, a real estate agent is still referred to as an *Immobilienmakler*) began to disappear as both were transformed into 'wealth'. Property in the sense of land belonging to one's family became simply a temporarily frozen form of wealth. This 'liquidation' (HC 61) of property contributed to world-alienation since property ceased to provide one with a tangible worldly place of one's own (HC 39).

Notice that Arendt is speaking, here, of two forms of homelessness: the physical homelessness of the peasant, and the spiritual homelessness of the capitalist, who regards his home – or house – as nothing more than a temporarily illiquid form of money.

Technology and world alienation

Thanks to modern transport technology, writes Arendt, 'men now live in an earthwide continuous whole' in which speed has 'conquered distance'. The result of this 'shrinkage of the globe' is loss of dwelling. If nothing is distant then, as already remarked, nothing is near, so that we are 'alienat[ed] from our immediate earthly surroundings' (HC 250–1).

Much greater shrinkage, however, is causes by the 'surveying capacity' of the human mind. The exploration of the early modern period that enabled us to chart the entire globe uprooted us from our dwelling place because, in surveying the entire globe, one surveys it from a point outside the globe, from an Archimedean point (HC 251).

Arendt is strangely insensitive to the central role played by electronic technology in the deracination of modern humanity – unlike, in particular, Heidegger: already in 1955, appalled by the forest of TV aerials suddenly sprouting from the medieval roofs of his native Messkirch (DT 48), he speaks of the 'uniform distancelessness' of modern life in which 'everything is equally far and equally near' (PLT 166). Were she to be writing now, Arendt would surely focus, not, as she does, on early modern map-making, but rather on the 'surveying capacity' of the Internet. The shrinkage of distance by transport technology is, she says, limited by the fact that one cannot be in two places at the same time (HC 250). If, however, she had known about cell phones she would surely have revised this judgment. According to the sociologist Sherry Turkle, we check our cell phones on average 221 times per day. One of the consequences of this addiction to the virtual, she observes, is that our capacity for conversation, and other forms of direct human interaction, is withering, among other reasons, because we only half attend to our immediate company.[32]

The rise of 'society'

Modernity, Arendt claims, has become 'worldless' and consequently homeless: our lives resemble the 'futile … wanderings of nomad tribes' (HC 28) (but, on nomads, see pp. 198–9 above). What, then, has replaced the world we have lost? Her answer is: 'the social'.

In the modern age we live, says Arendt, in 'society'. Although this looks like the Aristotelian truism that man is a social animal Arendt is in fact using 'society' in a special and pejorative way to mean, roughly, a collectivity bound together by nothing save a shared concern for economic wellbeing. In this sense, she says, neither the Greek polis nor the Roman Republic were 'societies'.

For the Greeks and the Romans, economics, concern with the material necessities of life, belonged to the private realm of family and household. It had nothing at all to do with the public realm of the political, other than being a precondition of the freedom to engage in political 'action': that one was free to concern oneself with the *res publica* depended on the fact that one's slaves (and womenfolk) took care of the realm of 'necessity'. The idea, however, that politics has something to do with economics would have struck the ancient world as absurd: 'political economy' would have seemed a self-contradiction (HC 29).

The 'emergence of society' is 'the rise of housekeeping[33] from the shadow interior of the household into the light of the public sphere' (HC 38). It consists in matters formerly confined to the household becoming a 'collective' concern (HC 28).

With the collapse of the Roman Empire, all that were left were private households belonging to the king and feudal nobles (HC 40). The early modern period witnessed the coalescence of these household economies into loose federations, whose spokesmen came to demand the creation of a public authority to protect both their acquired wealth and their ability to acquire more. By the eighteenth century the 'commonwealth' exists for, and only for, the protection of the common *wealth* (or rather the common pursuit of wealth), and so we arrive at the modern state in which activities 'formerly banished to the privacy of the household' are 'permitted to take over the public realm' (HC 68). Marx looked forward to the withering away of the state, but what he failed to realize was that it had already happened in its transformation into 'national housekeeping' (HC 45).

The way we are now

The final stage in the growth of the 'social' – our stage – is where states and governments give way to pure administration (HC 44–5); to government no longer by a king or a parliament, but rather by 'nobody', rule by pure 'bureau-cracy' (HC 40). (Notice that unlike her Frankfurt School contemporaries Arendt has no disposition to speak of 'capitalist elites'. Although modernity's rule by 'nobody' may turn out to be the 'cruellest', most oppressive there has been [ibid.], it is rule by anonymous social technology, not by capitalist bosses.)

A 'society', we have seen, is – to put Arendt's conception in Habermas' language – a society in which the lifeworld has been colonized, 'taken over', by the economy. But clearly there can be different kinds of 'societies'. Arendt's reference to bureaucracy shows that Max Weber (to whom *The Human Con-dition* refers numerous times) is very much on her mind. What distinguishes modern from early modern 'society' is Weber's 'bureaucratization'. Like Weber (pp. 9–10 above), Arendt focuses on the bureaucratized, rationalized workplace. And like him she attends to the industrial division of labour into a multitude of meaningless micro-tasks (HC 121–4). Unlike him, however, she draws a dis-tinction between the industrial division of labour and 'specialization' – recall that Weber refers to the inhabitants of the iron cage as 'specialists without spirit' (pp. 10–11 above). Specialization, she says, characterized the activity of *homo faber*. The painter and sculptor who worked on the medieval cathedral (to recycle the example used in Chapter 1) each performed a specialist task, but it was a satisfying task since it had an 'end in itself' (the icon or statue). Since, however, the industrial division of labour produces no such end, the modern worker is not a *homo faber* but rather an *animal laborans* (HC 47–8): modern 'society' is 'the victory of the *animal laborans*' (HC 320).

Modernity is the realm of *animal laborans* not merely because the modern worker incorporates materials that come, ultimately, from nature into the life process without thereby producing a thing of use, but also because the work-er's life has the circularity of animal life. In that the life pattern in the modern 'consumer economy' is work–consume–work, the modern worker reproduces the Sisyphean rhythms of animal life.[34] And so, as Horkheimer and Adorno observed a decade earlier (p. 32 above), modern 'society' represents a curious return to the beginnings of *homo sapiens*. One inhabits a kind of 'pseudo' nature made up of machines (HC 152), an 'unnatural growth, so to speak, of the natural' (HC 47).[35]

Of course, the labour-saving effects of automation might change the Sisyphean patterns of work somewhat, although, so far, its main effect has been promotion from meaningless blue collar labour to meaningless white collar labour (HC 121–2). But even if automation abolished labour completely (as in the Marcusean utopia), we would still be a labouring society – a 'society of labourers without labour' (HC 5, 129–33), a society of pure consumers.

What is wrong with the way we are?

Modern society is distressing, we have seen, because we are 'worldless' and so 'homeless'. Why, however, should we be distressed specifically by the fact that it is a 'society', that modernity is the non-world of *animal laborans*? One of Arendt's grounds of distress is Aristotelian: the life of *animal laborans*, and in fact of *homo faber* too, fails to possess the 'dignity' of 'an autonomous and authentically human way of life' (HC 13). Arendt's critique of modernity does not, however, rely upon one sharing her Aristotelian sensibilities. She has other strings to her bow, which, to a considerable extent, mirror Weber's critique: life in 'society' represents both loss of freedom and loss of meaning.

Loss of freedom

Weber, we know, views our rationalized, industrial economy as an 'iron cage (*stahlhartes Gehaüse*)' in which we suffer 'mechanized petrifaction' into semi-robotic *Berufsmenschen* (p. 10 above). On the question of freedom, Arendt actually quotes Weber, without mentioning him by name. With the rationalized 'administration' of the workplace we are reduced to a society of 'jobholders' – Arendt's translation of *Berufsmenschen* – a society which demands of its members an 'automatic functioning' that results in a 'dazed', 'tranquilized' loss of individuality. The result of this may well be 'the deadliest, most sterile passivity in history' as human bodies (Foucault's 'docile bodies') gradually become covered with 'shells of steel' (HC 322–3). As noted earlier, 'shell of steel' is an accurate translation of Weber's *stahlhartes Gehaüse*.

The emancipation of the worker from the Dickensian factory, from the dark, satanic mills of the nineteenth century, has, Arendt observes, certainly led to a decrease in violence suffered by the worker. But it has not led to 'progress in the direction of freedom' (HC 129). On the contrary – here Arendt's observations become indistinguishable from those of her Frankfurt School contemporaries – modern society is the most 'tyrannical' (HC 40) there has been. And the trade unions, far from being the liberating force of early socialist hopes, merely serve to incorporate workers into the system. In terms of freedom, there is no fundamental difference between the Western and totalitarian societies, save for the fact that while the latter employ terror, the former construct the iron cage (HC 215–16).

A consequence of the iron cage of rationalization – here again Arendt echoes the Frankfurt theorists – is the destruction of the private sphere. In the ancient world, although the private sphere was 'privative' (p. 205 above), it was still a place of authentic human connection. The Romans preserved the 'warmth of the hearth'. As, however, the lifeworld becomes ever more colonized by the economic system, as civil society crumbles and disappears (as the dating that used to happen in church, bowling club, or dance hall goes online), the whole of life becomes absorbed into the iron cage. And since, as we saw, labour (and work, too) is essentially solitary, the iron cage is a lonely place. The modern human being becomes the 'lonely mass man' – Arendt quotes David Reisman's 1950 *The Lonely Crowd* to this effect (HC 59, 257).

Loss of meaning

Like Weber, Arendt views modern society as inhabiting a condition in which there is (in Nietzsche's language) a 'devaluation of all values' (HC 236), that is, a condition of 'nihilism' (HC 261) – of, 'futility', 'vanity' (HC 204), 'meaninglessness' (HC 236). The reason for this is that the rise of 'society' has destroyed the public realm as effectively as it has destroyed the private. We no longer possess a 'common world', which makes us resemble people at a séance from whom the table has been removed (HC 52–3).

The modern industrialized economy is incredibly productive. We are outstandingly good at producing things cheaply and efficiently. But all we do with these things is consume them, as we must, in order to prevent the system breaking down. But what we never do is to ask what the point is of all the wealth we produce, we never even raise the question of the ends to which it should be devoted. And that is because the public space of 'speech and action', of authentic politics, has disappeared, dismissed as 'idle uselessness' (HC 220). The fear of the Greeks that the agora would be reduced to a mere marketplace has been realized (HC 160). Only things that have use are regarded as valuable, but the question 'What is the use of use?' (p. 201 above) is never raised.

How would the rebirth of authentic politics redeem the situation? By producing 'meaningful stories' (HC 236), says Arendt. As I shall argue in a moment, the reference here is to the need for an ethical 'tradition' which, like Heidegger's 'heritage', is embodied in the narratives of the lives of ethical exemplars. It is the ideals that are embodied by these 'heroes' (pp. 149–52 above) – heroes who, memorialized by artists and historians, achieve 'worldly immortality' – that establish the ultimate ends of a society, create the possibility of meaning. But – this, I think, is Arendt's claim – the reduction of politics to economic management has led to the exclusion of ethics, of ethical tradition, from public life, and hence from life in general.

Gesellschaft versus *Gemeinschaft*

Since the word 'society' is, in its normal usage, emotively neutral, Arendt's entirely pejorative use of the term sounds, to Anglo-Saxon ears, odd. And so the question arises as to why she indulges in this odd usage.

I have had several occasions already to note imperfections in Arendt's command of English (notes 9, 15, and 20). She herself was conscious of never being entirely at home in the language: 'I write in English, but I have never lost a feeling of distance from it' she confessed in an interview; 'I still speak with a heavy accent and I often speak unidiomatically' (EIU 13). Thus the hypothesis suggests itself that, at least with regard to her use of 'society', though Arendt writes in English, she thinks in German. And, of course, the German word for 'society' is *Gesellschaft*, so that, as a matter of linguistic necessity, her critique of 'society' is, in German, a *Gesellschaftskritik*.

As I have already remarked, in the tradition of German, communitarian thought, *Gesellschaft* is contrasted unfavourably with *Gemeinschaft*, 'community'. To recapitulate Tönnies' classic statement of the contrast (p. 13 above), while traditional 'communities' are small, rural, warm, and collectivist, the modern 'societies' that have replaced them are large, urban, cold and individualistic. Conceptually, however, the crucial contrast turns on a question of means and ends. A *Gesellschaft* is a social organization the purpose of which is to maximize the promotion of individual interests – hence a business 'company' is, in German, a *Gesellschaft* – whereas a *Gemeinschaft* is a social organization in which the ultimate purpose of individual life is the promotion of the good of the community as a whole. So, for example, Wagner, who, as we saw, wished there to once again be a 'collective artwork' that would gather people into community (p. 12 above), defined a community as a society in which everyone 'recognizes individual want in collective want or finds it based thereon'.[36] What it is that constitutes the good of the community as a whole, its 'collective want', is determined by its – as Gadamer emphasizes, always evolving – ethical tradition. Since historical experience reveals which virtues are important to the surviving and thriving of the community, making the communal good the purpose of one's life is a matter of living up to the values of heritage.

A *Gemeinschaft* is, then, the paradigm of a meaning-giving society. In a *Gemeinschaft* one knows the meaning of one's life to be, in one's own individual way, the promotion of the communal good by living in the light of ethical tradition. Given, then, that one of Arendt's central criticisms of modern 'society' concerns its nihilistic lack of meaning, it becomes plausible to suppose that for Arendt, human beings can live up to the human condition only in a *Gemeinschaft* – that she is to be regarded, along with Heidegger and Gadamer, as, above all, a communitarian thinker.

Canovan's interpretation

Mainly because the Nazis hijacked the language of community – their propaganda was peppered with references to *das Volk* (the people) and the *Volksgemeinschaft* – communitarianism is unpopular with contemporary German thinkers such as Habermas, and, for similar reasons, with most Anglo-Saxon Arendt scholars. As already noted, Margaret Canovan is quick to reject the idea that Arendt is a friend of *Gemeinschaft*, quick to claim that she is 'is blessedly free from romantic nostalgia for *Gemeinschaft*' (p. 188 above). (This, to repeat, is the essential message of Seyla Benhabib's *The Reluctant Modernism of Hannah Arendt*: although 'reluctant' allows a little more nostalgia that does Canovan, that Arendt is an affirmer of 'modernism' remains Benhabib's essential message.) It is true, Canovan concedes, that Arendt is no friend of *Gesellschaft* as conceived by communitarian thinkers. But that does not make her a communitarian, since there is a third alternative, Arendt's own version of 'republicanism'.[37] Arendt, she holds, is properly understood as belonging to a tradition of 'classical republicanism' which embraces both Machiavelli and the French Revolution.[38]

Canovan asserts that Arendt rejects liberal democracy as a complete political theory on the grounds that

> [l]iberal democracy is... a 'thin' theory of democracy, one whose democratic values are prudential and thus provisional, optional and conditional – means to exclusively individualistic and private ends. From this precarious foundation no firm conception of citizenship can be based on a body politic the only function of which is to promote individual interests. From this precarious foundation no theory of citizenship, participation, public good or civic virtue can be expected to arise.[39]

What a thriving society needs according to Arendt's republicanism, Canovan continues, is, in addition to the 'thin' framework of liberal democracy, a kind of 'patriotism' that consists in 'setting the public interest above [one's] own private concerns, even at the cost of profound personal sacrifice'. Traditional republicanism, that of Machiavelli,[40] for instance, which developed during the time in which a city state was an oasis of peace and freedom in a chaotic world, emphasized the need to be willing to sacrifice one's life in defence of the republic. Arendt talks less dramatically of jury service. Jury service, as Canovan reads Arendt, is not a case of enlightened self-interest. Rather, the public realm has 'interests of its own' which the patriotic, self-sacrificing good citizen is willing to serve.[41]

At first glance one might think that this is precisely the conception of *Gemeinschaft* as earlier defined. Why then, we need to ask, does Canovan take Arendt's alleged 'republicanism' to be something other than a defence of *Gemeinschaft* as essential to the fully *human* condition? It differs, she says, because what determines the public interest of an Arendtian republic is the – current – political interaction of its citizens. (Although Canovan appears not to have read him, this sounds very like Habermas' 'discourse ethics'.) There is nothing, that is, that transcends political negotiation. Arendt's admired Romans, for example, never felt 'the need of a source outside politics to legitimize their laws'.[42] So whereas a *Gemeinschaft* acknowledges ethical tradition as the highest authority, Arendtian republicanism does not.

What, then, does, republican 'patriotism' amount to? Since the patriot has no set of commitments above or other than those determined by some agreed procedure of political negotiation, it can consist only in a commitment to that procedure itself – to, for example, a constitution and to the legal system of which jury service is a part. The republican patriot, that is, 'sacrifices' himself not for any particular conception of the public good but rather for a way of reaching consensus, at any point in time, on what might constitute the public good. In other words, the republicanism Canovan attributes to Arendt is what

Michael Sandel calls 'procedural republicanism'[43] and Habermas, as we have seen, 'constitutional patriotism' (p. 57 above). If Canovan is right the distance between Arendt and Habermas becomes vanishingly small, and Arendt will turn out, after all, to belong at least as much to Frankfurt as to Freiburg.

I want to argue, however, that Canovan's account of Arendt is a deep misrepresentation, the result of viewing her through the distorting lens of Anglo-Saxon political theory rather than, as Arendt herself says she should be viewed (p. 190 above), from the perspective of the German philosophical tradition.

Tradition

To find out where Arendt really stands with respect to the question of *Gemeinschaft* one needs to turn to *Between Past and Future* (BPF), a collection of essays written within a few years either side of *The Human Condition*. (Notice, en passant, that the work's very title, even if not evincing 'romantic nostalgia', at least suggests that Arendt considers the past to be an important guide to the continuation of life into the future.)

What unifies the work's constituent essays is that, together, they provide a more or less continuous discussion of what, like Heidegger and Gadamer, Arendt calls 'tradition'. The possession of an authoritative ethical tradition is, says Arendt (mixing her metaphors, somewhat), the 'unshakeable cornerstone', the indispensable 'groundwork of the world'. The loss of tradition is the loss of 'world' (BPF 95). Given, then, that one cannot live up to the *human* condition without a world, it follows that to be without a tradition is to be a less than fully flourishing human being. Modern, mass humanity lives in a desolate, 'worldless' condition, above all because it has lost the meaning-giving authority of ethical tradition.

Although its importance was anticipated by Plato, tradition, writes Arendt, was first made a living reality by the Romans. Unlike most German philosophers, who generally regard Rome as a vulgarization of Greece, Arendt takes Rome as her paradigmatic *Gemeinschaft*. Rome, she says, represented 'the un-Greek experience of the sanctity of house and hearth', so that it was 'not the Greeks, but the Romans, [who] were really rooted in the soil, and the word *patria* derives its full meaning from Roman history'. Whereas, observes Arendt, the Greeks could happily emigrate and found new cities, for the Romans, 'home' was always the eternal city (as was England for the imperial English) (BPF 120).

Roman ethical tradition was, Arendt claims (somewhat dubiously), preserved by the Roman Church (BPF 125). It survived in an at least attenuated form until the twentieth century. Although it 'wor[e] thinner and thinner as the modern age progressed', it was not until the horrors of totalitarianism that the 'thread of tradition finally broke' (BPF 13). But now that it is broken it follows, as de Tocqueville anticipated, that 'since the past has ceased to throw light on the future, the mind of man wanders in obscurity' (BPF 6). Since the past no longer tells us how to live (to live, of course, into the future), we live in the state of 'nihilism' referred to above (p. 217). Since our public realm contains no ethical 'ends', we have nothing to give meaning and purpose to our busily productive lives, no answer to the question of the 'use of use'.

How does Arendt conceive of tradition, this 'groundwork of the world' and 'cornerstone' of any fully flourishing society? Tradition is not the past. It is, rather, a 'guiding thread through the past' (BPF 25), a canon which 'selects and names' and thereby indicates 'where the treasures are' (BPF 5). These 'treasures' are the 'ancestors' whose life stories, as preserved by artists and historians, are 'guiding examples' (BPF 190) for us, 'examples of greatness for each successive generation' (BPF 119). In Rome, 'the deeds of the ancestors [in Roman mythology, the first ancestors were the Trojans] and the usage that grew out of them was always binding' (BPF 123). That she identifies ethical exemplars as the bearers of tradition makes it clear that Arendt's notion of tradition is essentially that which Heidegger articulates in *Being and Time* and which Gadamer tries elaborate upon.

Arendt says that the ethical exemplars are the men of action. 'Action', the highest form of the *vita activa*, we have seen, is motivated by the desire to achieve (the right kind of) 'worldly immortality' (p. 205 above). To achieve such immortality is to become, oneself, one of the figures 'named' in tradition, to join the eternal pantheon of ethical 'greatness'. As one approaches the end of an exemplary life, one becomes, oneself, 'already, almost an ancestor', a 'model for living' and 'authority for others' (BPF 190). 'As long as tradition was uninterrupted', writes Arendt, 'to act without … tradition, without accepted time honoured standards and models, without the help and wisdom of the founding fathers, was inconceivable' (BPF 124).[44]

Authority

An ethical tradition at a given time has a given content, a set of ethical ideals embodied in the stories of the lives of ethical exemplars. But also, if it is to 'hold [people] together' (BPF 191) as a community, it needs to be *effective*, to 'bind' (BPF 120) them in such a way as to shape the character of private, and more importantly public, life. It must be a *living* tradition rather than an object of mere academic study ('the Gothic tradition') or something to which people pretend to subscribe but in reality pay only lip service. Arendt puts this by saying that a tradition must possess 'authority'. This is the topic of her essay 'What Is Authority?', an essay which might, she says, have been better titled 'What *Was* Authority', given that ethical authority has vanished from the modern world (BPF 91). What then is ethical authority – what was it in Rome, the place of its paradigmatic manifestation?

Authority is not, says Arendt, force: 'where force is used authority has failed' (BPF 92). Authority implies, rather, 'an obedience in which men retain their freedom' (BPF 105). One can disregard an ethical authority without fear of (external) punishment. And neither is it 'power': as Cicero said, 'while power resides in the people authority rests with the senate' (BPF 122). (As earlier remarked, I take 'power' here to mean the 'soft' power of public opinion.) Authority is not rational 'persuasion'. For persuasion

> presupposes equality and works through argumentation. Where arguments are used, authority is left in abeyance. Against the egalitarian order of persuasion stands the authoritarian order, which is always hierarchical.
>
> (BPF 92-3)[45]

Recall, here, Arendt's Nietzschean lament for the disappearance of hierarchy from modern society (p. 201 above). And notice the decisive break with the Habermas–Canovan notion that the ends of a society are to be determined by nothing but rational negotiation. Although Arendt's 'representative thinking' might look somewhat like 'discourse ethics', it seems clear that in a flourishing society representative thinking will occur, for Arendt, within parameters of ethical tradition.

Authority, says Arendt, is 'more than advice and less than command' (BPF 122). A way of putting the authority–command distinction is to say that the authority of tradition is based on respect rather than fear, respect for 'the founding fathers'. In Rome, this respect was 'religious' in character, religious in the pre-Christian sense of *religare*, 'tied back, obligated, to the enormous, almost superhuman and hence always legendary effort to lay the foundations' (BPF 121).

Arendt reports such reverence as simply a fact about Rome, but one can raise the question of what really motivates such 'ancestor worship'. Here, Nietzsche provides a relevant comment in the course of discussing what it is that constitutes a *healthy* religion. A thriving tribe, he suggests, feels that it exists only because of the efforts of the founders who continue to exist as guardian spirits. And so the motive for revering the ancestors is gratitude.[46] If I feel privileged to belong to, let us say a club, then I experience gratitude towards its founders and am happy to observe the rules they have created.

Our loss of tradition

A thriving humanity requires, then, a unifying ethical tradition, requires, that is, a *Gemeinschaft*. But we moderns have lost the 'thread' of tradition. Modern society is no longer 'held together by tradition' (BPF 191). We live in a mere *Gesellschaft*. The reason the thread is broken is that 'authority has vanished from the modern world' (BPF 91). We confuse authority with power and violence, which makes us terrified of anything that might seem remotely 'authoritarian'. The result is that, even in 'child-rearing and education where authority ... has always been accepted as a natural necessity', we shy away from it (BPF 92). (Recall that Arendt is writing on the cusp of the 'swinging sixties', the age of the permissive paediatrics of Dr Spock and of the so-called 'progressive' education that she scorns [BPF 175].) The result, as we have seen, is that we live in an age of nihilism, and age in which, to repeat de Tocqueville's observation, 'the mind of man wanders in obscurity' because 'the past has ceased to throw its light on the future'. The 'silence of tradition' results in an 'ominous silence that still answers us whenever we dare to ask, not "What are we fighting *against?*" but "What are we fighting *for?*"' (BPF 27). We construct nothing, every change we undertake (feminism, gay marriage, multiculturalism, gender voluntarism, libertarianism) is a *de*construction which we refer to as 'progress'.

What is to be done?

We live, then, in 'dark times' (the title of one of Arendt's later works is *Men in Dark Times*). And so the question arises as to how we can lighten our darkness. The nearest Arendt comes to providing an answer is in her essay 'The Crisis in Education'.

The purpose of education, she writes, is to introduce the newcomer to the world. Education is therefore essentially 'conservative', conservative in a double sense of protecting the new against the old and the old against the new: it protects the newness of the child against the world, and protects the continuity of the world from the potentially destructive novelty that is the child. The reason we must protect the new from being stifled by the old is that, like all human artefacts, the world 'wears out', is subject to the 'ruin of time'. For each new generation the times are – thankfully – always 'out of joint' and only the novelty of the newcomer can put them right. Only the newcomer can produce the creative 'augmentations' (BPF 121)[47] that are required for the preservation of tradition in a changing environment (BPF 188–9).

The goal of education is thus not merely to impart knowledge. It is rather the 'renewal of a common world' (BPF 193), of the tradition that is its 'ground-work', by the absorption of new energies into it. Although one cannot educate without teaching, one can all too easily teach without educating: like Heidegger and Jaspers in the 1920s, Arendt deplores the ever increasing pressure to reduce the modern university to a place of mere 'professional training' (BPF 192). (Arendt's distinction, here, between 'teaching' and 'educating' – between *Erziehung* and *Bildung* – reveals, once again, the depth of her roots in the German philosophical tradition. For the elevation of *Bildung* over *Erziehung* is an endorsement of the 'Humboldt model' of the university established in the early nineteenth century by Wilhelm von Humboldt. According to this model [the model Gadamer defends], the aim of higher education is, first and foremost, *Bildung*: the 'cultivation', 'development' or 'formation' of excellent human beings, future leaders of society, through their immersion in the 'treasures' of the Western ethical tradition, its highest and most inspirational 'examples of greatness'.)

A good educator has a 'natural' authority (BPF 92) which arises from the asymmetric relation between teacher and student. Knowledge of the lifeworld to which the newcomer is being introduced is part, but not the whole, of that authority. Principally, rather, '[h]is authority rests on the assumption of responsibility for that world', so that 'it is as though he were representative of all adult inhabitants, pointing out the details and saying to the child: this is our world' (BPF 186). The educator's authority is that of a host welcoming guests to the family house.

As mediator between the old and the new, the educator's profession 'requires of him an extraordinary respect for the past' (BPF 190). One cannot welcome someone into one's home unless one treasures what is inside it. During the Roman period there was nothing remarkable about this attitude, since reverence for the past, the past as the repository of all 'greatness', was the essence of what it was to be a Roman. This acceptance of the authority of tradition was, as already noted, preserved by the Roman Church, which, according to Arendt, augmented rather than abandoning the ethical tradition of Rome. Until present times, reverence for tradition was routine. But with modernity's 'crisis of authority' – the lack of a living tradition that is part of our world-'estrangement' (BPF 191) – comes the 'crisis in education'. The predicament of the modern educator is acute. For how, asks Arendt, can one be an educator when the profession 'by its very nature cannot forgo either authority or tradition, and yet must proceed in a world that is neither structured by authority nor held together by tradition?' (BPF 191).

Arendt's response to the 'crisis in education'

Arendt replies that not just educators, but all of us as 'members of the pre-political realms of family and school' (BPF 187) must,

> insofar as we live in one world together with our children and with young people ... take towards them an attitude radically different from the one we take towards one another. We must decisively divorce the realm of education from the others, most of all from the realm of public, political life, in order to apply to it alone a concept of authority and an attitude towards the past which are appropriate to it but must not claim a general validity in the world of grown-ups.
>
> (BPF 191–2)

Modern politics, in other words, politics in *animal laborans'* consumer society, is confined to questions of economic efficiency, so that appeals to ethical tradition (in the manner, perhaps, of Bernie Sanders' appeal to the forgotten value of equality in his 2016 campaign for the Democratic presidential nomination) will be dismissed by the political establishment (the Democratic National Committee) as 'idle uselessness' (HC 220). That is the way things are, and we have no direct means of altering the situation.

Yet we are not powerless. For as educators and parents, and simply as concerned human beings, we can play our small parts in communicating to the 'newcomers' the deep values of the Western ethical tradition through an appropriation of the past. To do this we must sequester our interactions with the newcomers – our hopes for the future – from the public world of modernity. This, however, should not be done in a spirit of 'alienation' but rather out of a deep world-affirming love:

> Education is the point at which we decide whether we love the world enough to assume responsibility for it and by the same token save it from that ruin which, except for renewal, except for the coming of the new and the young, would be inevitable.
>
> (BPF 193)

Note that since one cannot love a non-existent entity, Arendt's assumption must be that although we in modernity have a 'worldless mentality', our Western 'world' (together with the individual worlds it embraces) is not, in fact, dead, but merely dormant. Buried in the depths of our collective cultural memory, the Western ethical tradition is still, somehow, intact. (For Arendt, what preserves, above all, is language. So for example, she writes that as long as we use the word 'politics', 'the Greek *polis* will continue to exist at the bottom of our political existence' – at the bottom of the 'sea' of memory [IB 49].) Since tradition is preserved, it is available for reanimation, reanimation by, above all, educators, each acting in their own small area of responsibility. It is, I think, no accident that Heidegger's words are appropriate here. As educators, we can 'here and now, and in little things, foster the saving power in its increase' (QCT 33).

The irreparability of the 'thread of tradition'

It is important to notice that, in her discussion of education, Arendt does not say that the educator's task is to create a new world, with a new ethical tradition, but rather to 'renew' (BPF 193) a world that, although at present in 'default' (to use a Heideggerian word; PLT 89), is not dead. This makes it puzzling that, in the introduction to Walter Benjamin's *Illuminations*, she writes that

> insofar as the past has been transmitted as tradition it possesses authority ... Walter Benjamin knew that the break in tradition and loss of authority that occurred in his lifetime were irreparable and concluded that he had to find a new way of dealing with the past.
>
> (IB 38)

In *The Life of the Mind*, Arendt repeats this view, this time as her own rather than Benjamin's. Given the horrors of twentieth-century totalitarianism, she writes,

> the thread of tradition is broken and we shall not be able to renew it. Histori-cally speaking what has actually broken down is the Roman trinity that for thousands of years united religion, authority and tradition.
>
> (LM I 212)

So it appears that, on the one hand, as parents and educators, we are charged with the task of renewing the thread of tradition but, on the other, are told that it is impossible to do so.

On the basis of the 'irreparability of the thread' remarks, Michael Gottsegen concludes that, although Arendt 'never directly spells out' how it is to be done, she believes that what we need to do is to 'invent' a 'new' ethical tra-dition.[48] To flourish, humanity needs an ethical tradition, but the old tradi-tion is bankrupt, so we need to invent a new one. This attributes to Arendt a radical-discontinuity view that echoes Adorno's hyperbolic 'After Auschwitz, poetry is no longer possible': the view that the Holocaust constitutes a '*Stunde Null* (Zero Hour)' from which German and European life and morals must begin again, free of all reference to the past. Since the Holocaust 'refutes' Western ethics we need a new ethics.

In contrast to Gottsegen's generally sensitive understanding of Arendt's com-munitarianism, this seems to me a jarring misrepresentation. For one thing, she explicitly and scornfully rejects it in the Preface to *Between Past and Future*: 'Least of all', she writes, does she seek to 'invent some newfangled surrogates with which to fill the gap between past and future'. And she had good reason to reject the notion of inventing a new tradition since that is precisely the activity of her ultimate bête noire, a political *homo faber*, a Pol Pot or a Mao Tse-Tung.

What I think one should hold onto is that, for Arendt, it is not the *content* of the Western ethical tradition that has broken down in the sense of having been somehow 'refuted'. As Gottsegen and others note, Arendt always identifies the 'break' in the (already frayed) thread of tradition with the 'unprecedented criminality' (BPF 133) of the totalitarian regimes. Were those crimes to have been somehow *sanctioned* by the Western tradition then the tradition would indeed have been 'refuted'.[49] But Arendt insists that what constitutes the criminality the Nazi crimes is their *contravention* of the Western ethical tradition: 'The totalitarian rulers', she writes in 1971,

> reverse[d] the basic commandments of Western morality – 'Thou shalt not kill', in the case of Hitler's Germany, 'Thou shalt not bear false witness', in the case of Stalin's Russia.[50]

Far from a rejection, this, clearly, is an *affirmation* of the Western ethical tradition, and affirmation to which Arendt is, in any case, clearly committed in virtue of her counting both love and forgiveness (p. 204 above) as ethical virtues.

What has broken down, therefore, is not the content of the tradition but rather its *authority*. As already observed, this did not happen overnight. The crimes of the totalitarians were made possible by the fact that, through the long process of 'secularization', Western morality's loss of its religious foundations, the authority of tradition had been slowly eroding for centuries (BPF 133).

Ethical tradition versus Hegelian tradition

But, to repeat the question, why cannot we renew the broken thread, work towards re-establishing the authority of the Western ethical tradition in private, but more particularly, in public life? Why does Arendt tell us both that we must renew the thread of tradition and that we cannot do so? Although it is not entirely clear what the answer to this question is, my hypothesis is that the source of the obscurity is an ambiguity in Arendt's use of 'tradition'.

Tradition, says Arendt, is that which had been 'handed down' (IB 42). But many things are (or were) handed down between generations. Two in particular concern us. The first is ethical tradition as we have been discussing it, a relatively consistent, though evolving, set of virtues that embodies an ideal of both individual life and the life of society as a whole. The second is an account of the past as the *progressive realization* of these ideals: what I shall call (speaking loosely) a 'Hegelian' narrative of the past. Historically speaking, most cultures have educated their 'newcomers' into a 'Hegelian' account of their own past. In England, for instance (before, at least, the academy caught the virus of deconstructionism), one was brought up on a 'Whig' view of history, an account of English history as the progressive realization of security, freedom, and justice.

Arendt writes – obscurely – that given that the 'thread of tradition' is irreparably broken, it follows that 'metaphysics' must somehow be 'dismantled': that it is, in other words, refuted (LM 212). My hypothesis is that by 'metaphysics', she means 'Hegelian' metaphysics, that is to say, 'Hegelian' narratives of the past. Given this assumption, it makes sense to say that the horrors of twentieth-century totalitarianism have, once and for all, made all narrations of the history of the West as a history of unquestionable moral progress untenable. What I suggest, therefore, is that it is not the *ethical* tradition of the West that is somehow refuted by totalitarianism and the Holocaust but rather the *Hegelian* tradition of the West, its habit of congratulating itself on its ever-increasing ethical perfection. Arendt is *not*, in short, I suggest, a *Stunde Null* thinker. Our task is not the creation of a new ethical tradition but rather the reanimation – the reestablishment of the authority of – the dormant, but not yet dead, ethical tradition that we already have.

One final point. As we have seen (p. 202 above), central to Arendt's thinking is the insight that the consequences of action are profoundly unpredictable (an insight that, at the time of writing [2017], finds confirmation almost every day) – her insight that, in the field of politics, 'chaos theory', as it were, applies. Like Heidegger (and unlike Habermas), Arendt believes in the need for a radical 'turning' (a turning that will also be a re-turning), a turning away from the advancing threats of 'nihilism' and nuclear self-destruction that confront the present age. And she uses her unpredictability thesis as an antidote to pessimism about the possibility of such a turning. 'On human freedom', she writes, 'on man's ability to fend off the disaster which advances like an auto-maton and seems therefore inevitable, on man's ability to implement the "infinitely improbable" and transform it into a reality',[51] depends the possi-bility of a turning to a better future. We live in 'dark times'. But the unpre-dictability thesis allows us to live and act in the hope that one day the darkness will dissipate.

The thesis, then, that whatever probabilities we might acknowledge, the future remains radically unknowable is, to repeat, central to Arendt's thought. It follows that were she to claim to know that, whatever future generations might be like, they will *never* be able to repair the thread of the Western ethical tradition, she would introduce a contradiction into her thought. She would be claiming definitive negative insight into the future, claiming to know something of the 'mysteries of the whole historical process' (OT 469) for which she rightly criticizes Hegelian and Marxist political *homines fabri*.

We should not, then, I suggest, read Arendt as claiming that the thread that cannot be repaired is that of the Western ethical tradition. The thread in question is, rather, the 'Hegelian' account of the history of the West up to the present moment as the progressive *realization* of its ethical tradition.[52] Notice that since *that* claim is concerned only with the past, it is entirely consistent with the thesis that the future is radically unpredictable.

The West must, then, give up its habit of moral self-congratulation. How-ever, the ethical, meaning-giving ideal of which we have fallen lamentably short remains, available for reanimation. Our task, each of us in our own small way, is to educate ourselves and the newcomers into that tradition in the hope that, one day, its authority will be restored.

Notes

1   Asked in an interview about 'women's emancipation', Arendt replied that she was actually rather old fashioned. 'I always thought that there are certain occupations that are improper for women, that do not become them, if I may put it that way. It just doesn't look good when a woman gives orders. She should not try to get into such a situation if she wants to remain feminine' (EIU 3). This is part of, as we shall see, her quasi-Platonic view that 'discrimination', hierarchy and defined social roles, are of the essence of a healthy society: 'in society everybody must answer the question of *what* he is – as distinct from who he is' (I 3).

2   Benhabib (2000) 138.

3   Canovan (1992) 120–1.

4   Jaspers and his Jewish wife, who were far less clear-sighted, declined several opportunities to leave Germany and spent the war years is a state of constant terror.

5 Canovan (1992) 104. For 'gratitude' Canovan cites *The Burden of Our Time* (the British title of the first edition of *The Origin of Totalitarianism*), 438.
6 For further discussion of 'wonder' see Arendt (1974/5) 186.
7 Wolin (1993) 187.
8 A wrinkle in Arendt's classification of early modernity as the age of *homo faber* and later modernity as (as we shall see) the age of the return of *animal laborans*, is that the feeling of lordship over all things is said to characterise both ages, while being, at the same time, distinctive of *homo faber*. But the contradiction is, I think, more apparent than real, for what she really holds is that while the masses in late modernity are 'labourers' with the outlook of labourers, the outlook of *homo faber* belongs to the demonic movers and shakers of the twentieth century, scientists and totalitarians who have determined its world-historical character.
9 Arendt actually writes 'elementary', an example of her fluent, but never quite perfect, English.
10 Notice the double meaning of 'permanence'. Artworks are permanent in the sense that they are almost immune to wearing out, but also in the sense that a great work of art speaks not merely to the artist's contemporaries but to each succeeding generation.
11 See Yaqoob (2014) endnote 19.
12 Nietzsche (1994) II 18.
13 Arendt says that the durables 'give rise to the familiarity of world, its customs and habits of intercourse between men and things as well as between men and men' (HC 94). While there is truth in the idea that the products of technology sometimes 'give rise' to profound changes in human practices – one only has to think of cars or cell phones – the more important point is that without human needs and practices, the durable things would not be 'things' in the first place. As I argued (p. 195 above), it is ultimately only by appealing to the manner in which they figure in human practices that Arendt can establish her crucial distinction between commodities for consumption and things for use.
14 Bowring (2011) 18.
15 Once again, what Arendt actually writes is 'elementary'.
16 Canovan (1992) 106 fn. 26.
17 Notice how this is essentially *homo faber*'s conception of nature as, in itself, worthless material. Heidegger's middle-period conception of work as essentially violent is already implicit in the dominant conception of 'world' in *Being and Time*.
18 As we shall see, Arendt attaches to the word 'society' the pejorative sense that it acquires through the contrast between it and 'community'. I shall rely on context to determine whether the word is used, as here, with the usual, neutral meaning, or whether it is used in Arendt's pejorative sense.
19 Nietzsche (2001) section 335.
20 That is, 'agonistic': another slip in Arendt's never-perfect English.
21 The question of scientific determinism is, I think, irrelevant to Arendt's project. Whatever its truth, for the lifeworld – the world of Arendt's concern – it is axiomatic that some actions are uncaused causes.
22 Nietzsche (2002) section 257.
23 'Discrimination', writes Arendt, 'present opinion to the contrary, is a constituent element of the social realm' because 'in society everybody must answer the question of *what* he is – as distinct from *who* he is – which is his role and function' (MDT 154). Since this is a virtual quotation from Plato's *Republic*, one would expect Arendt to have some sympathy for Plato's definition of social 'justice' as everyone fulfilling a given social role and not attempting to usurp the role of another.
24 Arendt thinks of forgiveness as a free relinquishing of one's right to punish – as when one forgives a debt. From this equivalence she draws the conclusion – some three years before covering the Eichmann trial – that we cannot forgive what we cannot punish. With respect to 'radical evil', 'willed evil' of an 'extreme' nature of which there is very little comprehension, even by 'us who have been exposed to one of [its] rare outbursts onto the public scene' (the Holocaust of course), there can be neither punishment nor forgiveness (HC 241). Arendt certainly did not regard all evil as 'banal', and neither did she regard all evil perpetrated by the Nazis as 'banal'.
25 Sartre (1956) 363.
26 Canovan (1992) 203.

27 Habermas (1977).
28 After the war, Arendt worked for the establishment of a Jewish homeland, for the creation of Israel. But she wanted it to be a homeland for both Jews and Palestinians and became progressively alienated from the actuality of the Jewish state. After the Eichmann furore the breach was complete, with many leading Jews declaring her an enemy of Israel.
29 Heidegger discusses Heisenberg's remark in a more subtle way at QCT 27.
30 Schopenhauer (1969) I xxiii.
31 A further at least prima facie difficulty with Arendt's claim that science leads to scepticism, and thence to world alienation, lies in her claim that what was world-transforming about Galileo's telescope was that his observations established the new worldview 'with the certainty of sense perception' (HC 260). So it seems that, as Husserl claims, to get a grip, the new science actually presupposes the reliability of some sense perception. To overcome this difficulty Arendt would need to talk, with Wittgenstein, about 'throwing away the ladder after one has climbed up'.
32 Turkle (2015).
33 'Economy' derives from the Greek *oikonomia*, 'household management', which is derived from *oikos* (house) and *nemein* (manage). The current sense of the word dates from the seventeenth century. The *Wirt* of the German *Wirtschaft* ('economy') is the host of a tavern or head of a household.
34 Not only is the life of the worker circular, the system itself is: it produces for the sake of consumption and consumes for the sake of production. The problem for the modern economy is that the durability of use things diminishes the need for labour and hence the supply of consumers. And so, as noted earlier (pp. 194–5 above), the system turns durables into consumables (HC 124–5). Hence (as Marcuse also notes) waste is inseparable from the modern economy (HC 134).
35 According to Young-Bruehl, Arendt 'was never sympathetic to the Frankfurt School Marxists on intellectual grounds' and had a personal antipathy to Adorno (Y-B 80). It is clear, however, that she read and learnt from them.
36 Wagner (1966) vol. I 75–6.
37 Canovan (1992) 201–52.
38 Canovan (1992) 202.
39 Ibid. The words Canovan quotes with approval are actually those of Benjamin Barber.
40 Canovan takes Machiavelli to be an Arendtian hero. But what Arendt actually says about Machiavelli is that, together with the French revolutionaries, he made the 'tragic' mistake of thinking of violence as necessary to state-founding and as therefore justified (BPF 138–9). In other words, Machiavelli is an example of the political *homo faber* whom, we know, she detests.
41 Canovan (1992) 204–5.
42 Canovan (1992) 220. As we will shortly see, this is an extraordinary claim which might prompt one to wonder how carefully Canovan read Arendt's central works, how carefully she read, in particular, the essay 'What Is Authority?' that I am about to discuss.
43 Sandel (1984).
44 Arendt says that the successive examples of greatness 'constantly augment ... the foundation' of ethical tradition (BPF 121) which indicates that her notion of augmentation is intended to address the same question Gadamer's 'fusion of horizons' tries to address, the question of the ways in which tradition changes and develops over time. And that raises the question of whether she thinks of augmentation purely as, in my terminology (p. 176 above), the 'renewal' of tradition, or whether she includes those who challenge tradition and thereby initiate a process of 'reconciliation' between it with some originally alien element. Since Arendt says almost nothing by way of articulating the concept of augmentation, it is not possible to give a definite answer to this question. Her language of 'time-honoured standards', however – standards created by the first 'ancestors' who 'laid the foundation for all things to come' (BPF 121) suggests that, like Gadamer, she thinks of tradition in terms of an implicit ethical 'constitution' which can and must be renewed to continue to speak to a changing world, but does not incorporate alien elements into itself. As I argued, this failure to acknowledge 'fusion as reconciliation' seems to me to result in an incomplete account of the way in which ethical traditions develop over time.
45 Arendt is clearly using 'persuasion' here in a sense different from the Aristotelian sense we saw her using in *The Human Condition* (p. 207 above).
46 Nietzsche (1994) II 19.

47 See note 44 above.

48 Gottsegen (1994) 126–8.

49 One might plausibly speak of an ethical tradition that promotes or allows honour killings or female genital mutilation as 'refuted'.

50 Arendt (1971) 436.

51 Arendt (1961) 216–17.

52 Arendt compares her own mode of thought to 'pearl diving'. Although, in place of the 'Hegelian' narrative, we now have to deal with a 'fragmented' past, the 'pearls' that are the models of ethical 'greatness' are still present within it (LM I 212).

9   Later Heidegger
Re-enchantment

The reason one speaks of 'early Heidegger' and 'later Heidegger' is that Heidegger himself did. Beginning in 1930 but with a second, crucial change of direction in 1936, there occurred, he says, a 'turning' in both the 'what' and the 'how' of his thinking (P 250 fn.). Since his word for 'turning' is *Kehre* rather than *Wende*, what he attributes to himself is a U-turn rather than a gentle curve, a fact that has led some translators to translate *Kehre* as 'reversal'. The idea that the turning was indeed radical is further supported by a letter to William Richardson in which Heidegger endorses the legitimacy of Richardson's distinction between a Heidegger I and a Heidegger II, although he adds the provision that 'only by way of I does one gain access to II' (R xxii).[1] If we are to understand the character of Heidegger's later philosophy, therefore, the first order of business is to gain some understanding of the nature of Heidegger's turning.

Truth and the turning

Although it has several aspects, at its foundation the turning[2] is, as Heidegger says, a turning in his thinking about 'being' (P 249–50). One of his important statements about being is that it constitutes the 'hidden essence of truth' (DT 83). This suggests that an investigation of the development in Heidegger's philosophy of truth will be a fruitful way of investigating the development of his philosophy of being. Since he states that the turning began in his 1930 essay 'On the Essence of Truth' (P 250), we need to determine what advances over the conception of truth presented in section 44 of *Being and Time* occur in that essay.

According the *Being and Time*, we saw (pp. 134–7 above), the essence of truth, its 'enabling ground' (P 136), is *a-letheia*, 'dis[-]closure' or 'un[-]concealment'. A presupposition of propositional truth, truth as correspondence, is reference, and reference requires the disambiguation of reality. If you say, pointing to the river (for the moment you are Heraclitus) 'You'll never bathe in that again', and I am to assign a truth-value to your assertion, I need to know the background ontology of your claim, to know whether you are talking about common-sense entities such as rivers, or about the 'stuffs' those objects are made of.

The 'Essence of Truth' essay accepts that the essence of truth is disclosure. The new insight, however, is the realization that *disclosure is simultaneously concealment* (P 148). *Being and Time* has occasional and partial glimpses of this – 'the botanist's plants', it notes, 'are not the flowers of the hedgerow' (BT 70) – but such glimpses are not developed and do not find their way into the account of truth in section 44.[3] Thus, if I am to refer to, and make true remarks about, entities such as rivers, I need to 'conceal', put out of action ('bracket' Husserl would say) the, as Heidegger calls it, 'horizon' of disclosure (DT 63) in which reality shows up in terms of 'stuffs' rather than entities, not to mention the horizon in which it shows up in terms of quarks and black holes. When we take into account the possibility that future generations will experience the world in ways that are unimaginable by us, not to mention the possibility of non-human knowers, we realize that there is no limit to the number of potential horizons of disclosure that are concealed by the horizon – the 'being of beings', as *Being and Time* calls it – that constitutes our life-world. This 'unexperienced domain of being' is the 'non-essence of truth' (P 143) and is as inseparable from the essence of truth as is (an image of Rilke's that Heidegger finds useful) the dark side of the moon from its illuminated side (PLT 121). Heidegger calls this unexperienced domain simply 'the mystery' (P 148). And since it is unlimited in extent it is, as with all things we cannot fathom, profoundly 'awesome' (PLT 65).

The second phase of the turning, which, he says, began in 1936,[4] starts with the reflection that, as the 1946 'Letter on Humanism' puts it, the 'projection' of world described in *Being and Time* is not an 'achievement of subjectivity' (P 249). The key to understanding this remark lies, I believe, in taking note of the fact that Heidegger is presenting his account of the relation between ourselves and our world 'by way of contrast' to the account presented by Jean-Paul Sartre (P 250–1). (The 'Letter on Humanism' as a whole was written as a critique – not to say demolition – of Sartre's 1945 lecture, 'Existentialism Is a Humanism'.)

Famously, Sartre sums up his existentialism with the slogan, 'existence precedes essence'. I exist as a bare (Cartesian) self endowed with nothing but the power of absolute, unrestricted, choice. Everything else about me is a product of that choice, including the world I inhabit. 'My world', Sartre writes in *Being and Nothingness*, 'is the image of my free choice of myself'.[5] Partly he means that what one might call the *mood* (*Being and Time*'s 'affectedness') in which the world shows up depends on my choice of myself. If I choose the 'victim' personality for myself then the rape I suffered was yet another example of the unconquerable tyranny of men, while if I choose the 'hero' personality the event was a sharp stimulus to revolutionary action. Since I choose my world there are, says Sartre, 'no excuses'.[6] *How* things show up in my world is the product of my freedom, but Sartre also thinks that *what* shows up is the product of my free choice of myself. That the world shows up as 'ready-to-hand' is a product of my choice to live some version of the of the *vita activa* rather than the *vita contemplativa*. Even the date and place of my birth, the date of my emergence from the impersonal 'in-itself' as a self-conscious 'for-itself', is, he suggests, the product of my free choice.[7]

Heidegger observes that this mode of thinking 'has nothing in common ... with *Being and Time*' (P 250). Less politely put, his point is that, despite its subtitle, 'An Essay in Phenomenological Ontology', *Being and Nothingness*'s existentialism represents a complete failure to understand the phenomenological tradition to which it claims to belong. For what it misses is the foundational truth of thrownness, the fact that the lifeworld is something that, always, we find ourselves 'already in' (pp. 129–30 above).

Although, then, the disclosure of world – or, as Heidegger increasingly prefers to say, 'the clearing' of intelligibility – happens through human *activity*, it does not, cannot, happen through human *choice*, because the capacity to make choices of any kind presupposes a world that is *already* intelligible to one. World-disclosure, rather, is something we *receive*, receive from out of 'the mystery'. 'The Essence of Truth' established the awesomeness of the mystery. From 1936 onwards, however, Heidegger engages in an ever-deepening meditation on its generative character, on the fact that the clearing is not man-made, not a human 'achievement', but rather a *self*-clearing; the fact that intelligibility is something 'sent to' us. Inspired, however, by a simultaneously deepening engagement with Hölderlin's 'thinking poetry' (PLT 93), Heidegger sees that the clearing is not merely 'sent', but is, rather, 'gifted' to us. To engage in the 'meditative thinking' (DT 46–7) that properly thinks through the nature of truth and being is to be overcome by wonder, 'wonder that around us a world worlds, that there is something rather than nothing, that there are things, and we ourselves are in their midst' (GA 52 64). To be in this state of wonder at the miracle of intelligibility is to share in the 'fundamental mood (*Grundstimmung*)' of Hölderlin's poetry (GA 39 82–3), a deep and festive 'gratitude (*Danken*)' for the 'favour (*Gunst*) that has been bestowed on us' (GA 9 310), for the privilege of being in such a wonderful world. 'Thinking (*denken*)', writes Heidegger, 'is thanking (*Danken*)': 'insofar as we think in the most serious way, we give thanks' (GA 8 149–52). (One encounters this thought, almost word for word, in the religious writings of the Catholic thinker, G. K. Chesterton. 'Thanks', Chesterton writes, 'are the highest form of thought and ... gratitude is happiness doubled by wonder.')[8]

Heidegger calls this thanks-giving experience of wonder the '*Ereignis* experience'. It is an experience, he says, of 'transport and enchantment'. Enchanted, captivated, by the 'lighting-concealing' that is the 'ground and essence of truth' (GA 65 70), one is transported – in a manner to which I shall return – out of one's mundane identity and into that of the mystery itself. It is on account of this self-transcendence that Heidegger calls the *Ereignis* the 'event of appropriation' (TB 19). In the *Ereignis* experience, one is captivated, 'appropriated (*er-eignet, aneignet*)', made its 'own (*eigen*)' by the mystery. As thus appropriated, we shall see, one's being-in-the-world becomes a reciprocal appropriation of the mystery.

This, then, is the turning. What seems clear from the above account is that, although, in Heidegger's case, the turning is occasioned by prolonged meditation upon being and truth, it is, at heart, spiritual rather than technical in character, a turning from a kind of spiritual sickness (*Unheil*) to health (*Heil*) (P 267). One need do no more than attend to the emotional register of *Being and Time*'s key words – 'anxiety', 'care', 'guilt', 'nullity', 'death', 'thrown-ness', 'abandonment', 'homelessness' – to see that the 'fundamental mood', the prevailing 'affectedness', of at least Division II of that work is one of post-death-of-God anguish. Profoundly influenced by Kierkegaard, *Being and Time* is Kierkegaardian despair *minus* the redemptive, Kierkegaardian God. The turning is Heidegger's redemption – an exemplary redemption – from anguish. 'As soon as man gives *thought* to his homelessness', later Heidegger tells us, reflecting on his own path of thinking, 'it is a misery no longer' (PLT 159). Through Hölderlin, he discovers not exactly Kierkegaard's Christian God, and certainly not the personal, omnipotent, transcendent, self-causing 'god of the philosophers' (QCT 26), but rather the God of the 'mystery', Hölderlin's 'unknown god' whose 'qualities' are immanent in the 'face of the sky' and in the sight of 'the things that are familiar to man' (PLT 223).

The axis around which the turning turns is 'the nothing'. In *Being and Time* the nothing is an absolute 'empty', 'abysmal' (PLT 149, BT 152), desolating nothing, a nothing that throws us back into the world, not out of love for it, but because it is the only alternative to the abyss (p. 146 above). After the completion of the turning, while the 'non-essence of truth' remains 'nothing', nothing graspable by conceptual thought, it is far from empty. Rather than desolating, it is gift-giving.

Metaphysics

To make the turning, as described above, is, says Heidegger, to stand in the 'truth of being' (P 243), 'the truth of being as a whole' (P 152). Sometimes he describes the turning as a matter of grasping one's 'ek-sistence', one's (as the word tells us, ecstatic) 'standing out into' the truth of being (P 254). To fail to stand in the truth of being is to be engulfed by what he calls 'metaphysics'. This is a crucial term in later Heidegger because he regards it as not merely a philosopher's error, but as the fundamental cause of the desolation of modern culture as a whole. It is important, therefore, to be clear as to the meaning of this – always pejorative – term.

In part, Heidegger's use of the term 'metaphysics' is the same as everyone else's. The essence of metaphysics is, he says, ontology. Its concern is to discover the 'being of beings' (P 246), the 'most universal traits' which all beings, as beings, have (P 287). So, for instance, Descartes thinks everything is either material or mental substance, Berkeley eliminates the material, materialists eliminate the mental, Schopenhauer thinks that everything is 'will to live', Nietzsche that everything is 'will to power', and so on. Metaphysics in this sense becomes 'metaphysics' in Heidegger's pejorative sense through a kind of naïve arrogance: it becomes 'metaphysics' when it 'drives out every other possibility of disclosure' (QCT 27), when, as I shall put it, it 'absolutizes' itself into *the one and only correct representation* of the fundamental nature of reality.[9] The classic absolutizing gesture is the sting in the tail of Nietzsche's claim in *Beyond Good and Evil* that 'the world is "will to power", *and nothing besides*',[10] a gesture which leads Heidegger to call him is 'the last metaphysician of the West' (N III 8).[11]

What is intellectually mistaken and spiritually crippling about metaphysics is that it denies 'the mystery' and thereby the *Ereignis*. Metaphysics, says Heidegger, 'thinks the being of beings [b]ut it does not think being as such' (P 246). It is 'oblivious' of 'being as such' (ibid.) in somewhat the way in which a mariner who mistakes an iceberg for an ice floe is oblivious of the iceberg.

Metaphysics and 'oblivion of being' are thus one and the same thing. Or rather, metaphysics and 'forgetfulness of being' – this is the literal translation of *Seinsvergessenheit* (P 262–3, QCT 41) – are one and the same. (Since one can only 'forget' what one once knew, the literal translation has the virtue of making clear that Heidegger's analysis of *Seinsvergessenheit* in terms of being and truth is, in fact, an analysis of the historical process, the progressive, in Weber's language, 'disenchantment' of our worldview.)

What leads metaphysics into blindness to 'the mystery' is that it conceals 'its own fundamental characteristic, namely disclosure as such' (QCT 27). What it misses, that is, is *the horizonal character* its own horizon of disclosure, the fact that it is just *one horizon among indefinitely many alternative horizons*. Imagine that one sees the world only through very strong microscopic glasses so that it shows up as nothing but strange molecular structures. Suppose, now, that one 'forgets' that one is wearing the glasses. Then one thinks that the reason the world shows up as nothing but strange molecular structures is that the world *is* nothing but strange molecular structures. Metaphysics thus represents a *double* concealment: it conceals the mystery, and does so because it conceals its own mode of disclosure *as* a mode of disclosure. It is on account of this second concealment that Heidegger says that the error of metaphysics is the same as the error of thinking that there is nothing more to truth than correspondence. Both errors miss the fact that the essence, the 'enabling ground', of truth is disclosure (P 280).

An important question is whether, from the perspective of later Heidegger, *Being and Time*, which sets out, its first sentence tells us, to overcome forgetfulness of being, itself succumbs to that very condition. This is what seems to be suggested by Heidegger's retrospective remark that in *Being and Time*, 'a metaphysics is still dominant' (P 256). It is certainly true that in the discussion of truth in section 44, in achieving the insight that truth depends on disclosure, early Heidegger takes the first crucial step away from metaphysics.

But on the other hand, as earlier remarked, save for isolated glimpses, *Being and Time* does not take the second step of seeing that disclosure is always concealment. And in fact, the existential *Angst* before the 'nothing' that dominates Division II is precisely a denial that there *is* anything that is concealed. Reality, for *Being and Time*, is material things showing up, mostly, as equipment – 'and nothing besides'. Later Heidegger's remark is thus, it seems to me, the truth of the matter: save for isolated moments, *Being and Time* does succumb to the 'metaphysics' it set out to overcome, is itself a case of 'forgetfulness of being'.

The historicizing of being

The 'turning' is, then, a turning in Heidegger's thinking about being and truth. A second aspect is that it is, in a certain limited way, a turning from Kant to Hegel. *Being and Time* aims, in the manner of both Kant and Husserl, to articulate a transcendental structure. It aims to provide the a priori structure of human being as such, of all human beings at all times and places. Later Heidegger, on the other hand, recognizes that, within that highly abstract, transcendental structure, history is made up of radically different epochs, where each epoch is defined by a different, foundational disclosure of the 'being of beings', a different, in Hegel's language, 'shape of consciousness'. I shall not attend to the details of Heidegger's 'history of being'; suffice it to say that in Weber's terminology, Heidegger's history is a history of ever-increasing 'rationalization', and thus 'disenchantment', forgetfulness of 'the mystery'.

One result of this 'historicizing' of his thought is to bring Heidegger's later philosophy explicitly under the rubric 'modernity critique' – even 'critical theory' – and hence bring him into closer contact with the other thinkers who figure in this book and with issues specific to modern life. In a way I shall attempt to bring out, the later thought has more to say than the earlier thought about specifically *us*.

Homelessness

We live, the 'Letter on Humanism' observes, in a time of 'world crisis' (P 276), a surprising observation to make in 1946, given that the Second World War had just *concluded*. In Hölderlin's words (of 1801), we live 'in a desolate time (*dürftiger Zeit*)', in the age in the world's 'night' (PLT 89). The reason the times are desolate lies in 'the homelessness of contemporary man' (P 258). (Note, here, the depth of the gulf between the later thought and *Being and Time*. Whereas *Being and Time* sees homelessness [*Unheimlichkeit*] as the condition of human beings *as such* [p. 142 above], for later Heidegger it is a condition specific to the *modern* human being – the condition of, for instance, the author of *Being and Time*.) Contemporary homelessness is, says Heidegger, a phenomenon grasped with considerable insight in Marx's conception of 'alienation' (ibid.) as the modern condition, but is thought through in unrivalled depth by Hölderlin. As he regards all of his later philosophy, Heidegger's discussion of homelessness is conceived as an 'Elucidation of Hölderlin's Poetry' – the title of volume 4 in the collected edition (*Gesamtausgabe*) of Heidegger's works. (Note that since Hölderlin is *the* poet of German Romanticism, Heidegger's unqualified deference to him situates his later philosophy squarely within the Romantic tradition.)

Homelessness consists in the lack of what Heidegger calls 'dwelling', our failure to be in the world as in a 'homeland (*Heimat*)' (P 257). What makes it fundamental to the 'plight' of modernity (PLT 159) is that dwelling is the human essence: 'to be a human being[12] means ... to dwell'. This is something language 'tells' (or at least suggests to) us: *bin* and *bist*, the distinctively human first and second person singular, forms of *sein*, the verb 'to be', are descended from the Old High German and Old English *buan*, which means 'to dwell' (PLT 144–5). Have we then lost our humanity? Not exactly. While human beings are essentially dwellers, modern homelessness consists in the failure to 'experience and take over this dwelling' (P 257). Mostly, Heidegger and Hölderlin think, modern human beings are 'blind' to their dwelling. But blindness, Heidegger points out, 'is only possible in a being that, in its essence, is endowed with sight' (PLT 225). What this implies is that while our modern being-in-the-world is not that of dwelling, if we can overcome our 'blindness' we will recover our essence. The age of the 'death of man' has not yet arrived.

Heidegger identifies three central aspects of the homelessness of modernity which I shall first simply list, and then discuss in detail. The first is the care-less violence of modern technology. Human beings who *dwell* in their world as in a homeland take care of it. If they are places of dwelling, we care for our home and garden in a way that we do not care for the highway on which we drive, or the gas station in which we refuel our car. But in modernity, Heidegger observes in one of his popular works, the world shows up as nothing but 'a giant gas station' (DT 50).

The second aspect of homelessness is, in Hölderlin's phrase, the 'default of God' and 'the gods' (PLT 89). Without the gods, Heidegger argues, there can be no community, and without one's human environment providing the 'solidarity' (BT 122) of community, something essential to one's being-at-home-in-the-world is missing.

The third mark of homelessness is precisely the 'anxiety' about death that *Being and Time* takes to be inescapable: our inability to, in Rilke's phrase, 'read the word "death" *without* negation' (PLT 122). Again, it is clear that, as *Being and Time* indeed tells us, if one's being-in-the-world is blighted by (at best repressed) anxiety, then one cannot properly be at-home in that world.

These three aspects of modernity constitute, then, our homelessness: in Marx's language, our 'alienation' from nature, from each other, and from mortal, that is, human, being. But what, as Heidegger and Hölderlin think of it, is the underlying 'essence' of homelessness? What is its 'enabling ground'? Heidegger's answer, his diagnosis of the fundamental cause of the sickness (*Unheil*) of modernity, is, in a word, 'metaphysics', 'forgetfulness of being' (P 258, 318). It is not, to repeat, merely philosophers who have 'forgotten being', but rather the modern age as such.

The task, now, is to understand, with respect to each of the three aspects of homelessness, how it is that metaphysics is its underlying ground.

The violence of modern technology

Compare and contrast the old wooden bridge, which allows the river to remain a river, with the modern hydro-electric dam which turns it into a reservoir. Or the ancient farmer who sowed only those seeds which the climate and season could be expected to bring to fruition with the modern 'mechanised food industry' which uses artificial fertilizers, pesticides and genetic modification to compel the land to produce whatever the market demands. Whereas ancient technology represents, by and large, an accommodation of humanity to nature, modern technology seems to be a 'setting upon' (QCT 15), a violation, even a rape, of nature.

What explains this contrast between, as I shall say, the 'gentleness' of ancient technology and the 'violence' of modern technology? Heidegger holds, roughly, that how one acts is determined by how one sees the world (and by, at a deeper level, the language one speaks). 'He who ... know what is', he writes, 'knows what he wills in the midst of what is' (PLT 65). Hence the 'essence', the 'enabling ground', of a technological practice is a mode of world-experience, a mode of disclosure. What, then is the essence of modern technology? (I shall postpone until later the question of the essence of pre-modern technology.)

Heidegger's name for the mode of disclosure which both defines the modern age and accounts for the violence of its technology is *das Ge-stell*. *Ge-stell*, says Heidegger, is that mode of world disclosure in which 'the real reveals itself as resource (*Bestand*)' (QCT 23). Sharing the insight common to all the thinkers discussed in this book, Heidegger notes *Ge-stell*'s reflexive character: already in 1946, he observes with dismay the appearance in the language of the phrase 'human resource (*menschliches Material*)' (PLT 109). This is a source of dismay because 'language is the house of being' (P 145). Language determines ontology: if people show up in language as 'human resources' – as, in Weber's language, *Berufsmenschen* – then, as older forms of language pass out of use, they increasingly show up in life as 'human resources'.

Das Ge-stell is a term that defies successful translation. The standard translation, 'enframing', missing out, as it does, the definite article, is not very good. I shall, however, retain it since it has at least the virtue of helping us realize that *das Ge-stell* provides an account of the 'essence', the 'enabling ground' of the 'rationalization' Weber identifies as defining modernity. Understanding human beings, for example, as 'resource' – 'reifying' them, in the language of Horkheimer and Adorno – is the prerequisite for subjecting them to 'control through calculation'.

Since (barring the arrival of Marcuse's utopia) the need to work is universal, the requirement that 'the real' shows up in work-suitable, technological ways – that it show up as 'equipment' or as 'resource' – is universal too. What is unique to modernity, however, is that reality's disclosure as resource is its *only* mode of disclosure. Where enframing 'holds sway' it 'drives out every other possibility of disclosure' so that 'the regulating and securing [the "rationali-zation"] of resource shapes (*prägt*) all disclosure' (QCT 27). Earlier historical epochs had modes of disclosure other than the technological, with the result that the 'unconditional self-assertion' of the technological will was held in check by the 'embracing structure of the realm of culture and civilization' (PLT 109). With us, however, the real reveals itself as resource – *and nothing besides*, and it is this 'nothing besides' that explains the violence of modern technological practice.

It is not the case, that is, that modern human beings have become especially wicked: if one is confronted with a 'real estate site' then the entirely *appro-priate* thing to do is to 'develop' it. If one is confronted with a 'gas station' (p. 238 above) the appropriate thing to do is to fill up one's car. And when confronted by 'negative resources' such as pollution – which is what the Nazis held Jews, Gypsies, Slavs and homosexuals to be – the *appropriate* thing to do is to do away with it. (Once can see, here, the Heideggerian roots of Arendt's remark concerning the 'banality' of Eichmann's evil.)[13] Rather than 'wicked', the more revealing description of modernity is 'blind'. Enframing, Heidegger writes, not only 'drives out every other possibility of disclosure', it also 'conceals disclosure as such, and with it that in which unconcealment, that is to say, truth, happens (*ereignet*)' (QCT 27). The world of modernity is, that is, enframed in that the technological disclosure of reality presents itself, not *as* a disclosure, one among many, but simply as the – one and only – *way things are*. In doing so it blocks our access to the insight that truth presupposes disclosure and that disclosure is concealment. It blocks our access to 'the mystery'. Above all – as the use of *ereignet* in the above quotation tells us – it blocks our access to the *Ereignis*. Enframing, in short, is the way in which metaphysics reigns in the modern world. We live in the age of the triumph of metaphysics.

Loss of the gods

The second aspect of the homelessness of modernity consists in our loss – Hölderlin's 'default' – of God and the gods. Since living 'in the sight of the gods' is 'the ground of the possibility that man can become historical, that is, can be a community' (GA 39 216), the loss of the gods is the loss of community, the reduction of the *Gemeinschaft* of pre-modernity to the *Gesellschaft* of modernity. As *Being and Time* observes, the replacement of community by society is the loss of that authentic *Verbundenheit* ('solidarity' or 'connectedness') without which there can be no genuine 'solicitude', and its replacement by a 'distance and reserve' that is based on 'mistrust' (p. 128 above). If one's social environment is a mere *Gesellschaft*, then one is no more at home in that environment than one is at home in a business *Gesellschaft* (company). One is no more at home out of the office than in it.

The loss of the gods consists, says Heidegger, in the fact that 'no God any longer gathers (*versammelt*) men and things unto himself visibly and unequivocally, and out of such a gathering disposes of world history and of man's stay in it' (PLT 89). As we have seen, in the tradition of German communitarian thought, community is distinguished from society by the possession of what Hegel calls 'ethical substance', early Heidegger 'heritage', and Gadamer and Arendt 'tradition', a shared conception of the proper life of both community and individual. 'Devotion' (BT 122) to ethical tradition is taken to define one as a member of the community and to give meaning to one's life. For early Heidegger, Gadamer and Arendt, we have seen, the bearers of tradition are *Being and Time*'s ethical 'heroes', ethical models or exemplars. These 'heroes', it seems clear, are what reappear as 'the gods' – or 'angels' (EHP 39) – of Heidegger's later thought, the gods in whose 'sight' we must live if we are to be a community. The idea of their 'gathering', or 'collecting', us into communal ethos is an allusion to the Greek tragic festival and the medieval cathedral. According to the communitarian tradition, essential to the possession of a living ethos is what Wagner called the 'collective artwork' (p. 12 above), a sacred festival that gathers the community as a whole into a clarifying affirmation of the ethos that makes it the community that it is.

Heritage, then, requires 'the gods', but, as grounding the unity of community, it also requires, at least implicitly, that the ethos they collectively personify should be a consistent one, that the 'gathering' into community be 'unequivocal (*eindeutig*)' (PLT 89). Heidegger puts this by saying that gods must all be embraced by – be 'messengers of' – a unitary 'godhead' (PLT 147–8). This, too, as we have seen, is a thought that reaches back to the nineteenth century, to Nietzsche's (and Wagner's) critique of modernity's 'pandemonium of myths'. This critique, as we saw, reappears in Weber's critique of ethical 'polytheism', his requirement that – using the same concept as Heidegger – a 'genuine community' should possess a unifying 'godhead' (p. 12 above).

Why have we lost the gods? In the famous passage in *The Gay Science*[14] in which Nietzsche announces the 'death of God', he also says that 'we' have 'killed' him. Heidegger provides an account of how we have done this. The loss of the gods has happened, he says, on account of something 'even grimmer', the loss of the 'divine radiance (*Glanz der Gottheit*)' (PLT 89), the 'aether in which alone gods are gods', that is to say, 'the holy' (PLT 92).

There are gods and gods. There is, for example, as we have seen, the 'god of the philosophers', a god who has taken root in some forms of theology (QCT 26), the self-caused cause who is intended as a 'solution' to the cosmological question of why there is anything at all. Heidegger calls this the God of 'onto-theology', the God who is reduced to a being that belongs within the nexus of cause and effect. This, however, is not a god before whom one can 'pray or sacrifice', not a god before whom one can 'bow down in awe' (ID 72). For the gods to 'appropriate' us to the 'godhead' they personify, they must 'appear out of the holy sway' (PLT 148), must, in Weber's language, have 'charismatic' authority over us. Like the poetry which 'founds' it, however, the holy is essentially 'mysterious', is a 'dimension' that lies beyond 'everything that shows up in the light of the network of cause and effect' (QCT 26, P 258). For us, however, locked into the one-dimensional drabness of enframing, there are no mysteries. And so the holy, the essential 'abode' (PLT 90) of the gods, is absent. God and the gods, at least for the time being, are in default because the metaphysics of modernity has destroyed our capacity for reverence.

Anxiety and death

The third aspect of the homelessness of modernity is anxiety about death: our inability to 'read the word "death"' without a shudder, our inability to face death with the 'equanimity (*Gelassenheit*)' of 'the good death' (PLT 148). In *Being and Time*, we saw, Heidegger claims 'anxiety' about the nothingness of death (and hence the disposition to evasiveness) to be universal to all human beings. For later Heidegger, however, it is distinctive of modern, Western humanity. Meditating, together with Rainer Maria Rilke (another of his 'thinking poets'), he now sees the conception of death as entry into an '*empty nothing*' as a particular affliction of modernity (PLT 149), an affliction that underlies the frenetic character of modern technology: the 'unconditional ... self-assertion of technological objectification' in the modern age represents the 'constant negation of death' (PLT 109, 122). Because God is dead and we are his 'murderers', Nietzsche writes in the famous 'death of God' passage, we 'must ... ourselves become gods in order to be worthy of the deed'. Since the principal characteristic of all gods is their immortality, this must entail the abolition of death. That, Rilke and Heidegger suggest, is the unacknowledged[15] but ultimate aim of modern science and technology.

To see why modernity's inability to accept mortality is the product of metaphysics we need to return to Rilke's 'moon' analogy and to his and Heidegger's account of the overcoming of anxiety about death. Rilke writes that,

> like the moon, so life surely has a side that is constantly turned away from us, and that is not its opposite but its completion to perfection, to plenitude, to the real, whole, and full sphere and globe of being.
>
> (PLT 121)

As disclosure is always concealment, so the lighted side of the moon always conceals its dark side. What Rilke realizes through poetic insight, and the philosopher through intellectual rumination, what this confluence of *Dichten* and *Denken* realizes, is that the nothing on the other side of death is, not the 'empty' nothing, but is rather something to be understood 'positively' (PLT 122) as the nothing of 'plenitude', the plenitude of all the 'aspects (*Seiten*)' of beings that are concealed by our horizon of disclosure (PLT 121, DT 64). All this, however, is closed to one who is blinded by metaphysics. For metaphysics, it is as if the moon were a flat, illuminated disk: what lies the other side of death *is* an empty, 'nihilistic', nothing (OWL 19). In a nutshell, metaphysics fears death because it mistakes the epistemological nothing, 'the mystery', for a metaphysical nothing. Why overcoming the metaphysical nothing should make us capable of the good death we will come to shortly.

The turning

'Healing' (PLT 137) the 'sickness', the homelessness, of modernity, will require, says Heidegger, a 'turning', a turning of the 'world' (QCT 36, PLT 90) to a new, genuinely post-modern age (PLT 90). Clearly, Heidegger's, as I shall call it, 'personal turning', the turning that occurred in the 1930s in his 'path of thinking', is intended to be exemplary for this 'world turning': as the personal turning was turning from metaphysics into the gift-giving 'mystery' of the *Ereignis*, so, too, will be the world turning. The world turning will be a 're-enchantment' of the world, a return of the *Heil*, the 'hale' that can only come with a return of the *Heilige*, the 'holy' (P 267). But just how will this overcoming of metaphysics be an overcoming of homelessness, a return to dwelling? How, in other words, will the overcoming of metaphysics overcome the three aspects of homelessness outlined above?

The return of the gods

The absence of the gods, we saw, is the absence of the 'divine radiance', the 'aether' in which alone gods can be gods. But, in a way, the gods themselves are not absent at all:

> The default of God and the gods is absence. But absence is not nothing; rather it is precisely the presence, which must first be appropriated, of the hidden fullness and wealth of what has been. As such it gathers the essential: the divine in the world of the Greeks, in prophetic Judaism, in the preaching of Jesus. This no-longer is in itself a not-yet of the hidden advent of its inexhaustible nature.
>
> (GA 7 185)

In other words, the Graeco-Judeo-Christian ethical tradition, the 'heritage', of the West is still there, embodied in the lives of our gods, our ethical paradigms, available, as *Being and Time* insists, for creative 'repetition', an entirely sufficient guide to living well. All that we need is to re-'appropriate' the gods, that is, to allow them to re-appropriate us. And for that we need the return of 'the holy', the 'essential space (*Wesenraum*)' (P 258) of divine authority, a return that will constitute the overcoming of the blindness of metaphysics.

The absence of the gods was, we saw, the absence of community, and since the meaning-giving solidarity of community is an essential aspect of dwelling, the absence of community in the modern world is an aspect of its home-lessness. This raises the question of whether, if I, as an individual, follow Heidegger's path of thinking into the mystery, if I 'step back' (ID 41) out of metaphysics and into 'the full breadth of the space proper to ... [my] essence' (QCT 39), I recover my dwelling, or whether my dwelling must wait on the overcoming of metaphysics by 'the others'. The answer that is given in Heidegger's discussion of Hölderlin's 'Homecoming/to the Relatives' is that I do recover my dwelling. Even though the poet, returning to his Swabian homeland from a joyful encounter with 'the highest one' in the Alps, is in an ecstatic state, his joy is mingled with sadness that the Germans, who seem 'related' to him, are not yet fully so, because (locked into metaphysics) they have 'shut away what is most proper to them'. Heidegger says that Hölderlin's poem is not *about* homecoming, but is, rather, 'the homecoming itself' (EHP 44). So even though the 'relatives' do not yet live in the 'sight of the gods' the returning poet does. *He* is in the community, and is in community with the others, even if, mostly, they are not yet in community with him.

Becoming capable of 'the good death'

Modern homelessness, we saw, expresses itself in the inability to 'read the word "death" without negation' and hence 'anxiety' is always an element in the 'affectedness' (pp. 142–3) of the modern world disclosure. The reason for the anxiety is that, 'blind' to the other side of the 'globe of being', all that lies beyond the world, for us, is the absolute, 'empty' nothing. The turning away from metaphysics opens us to the realization that the other side of life is far from empty, is, rather, a 'plenitude' of all those aspects of reality that are concealed from us. Why, however, should this represent an overcoming of anxiety about death? Why should it make us capable of 'the good death' (p. 242 above)?

In what Heidegger calls Rilke's 'valid' verses – valid in spite of their use of the 'language of metaphysics' (PLT 94, 103)[16] – the poet pictures 'nature', the 'primordial ground' of our being, as 'throwing us forth (*loswerfen*)' into the 'danger' of its 'venture (*Wagnis*)'. Because we are 'no more dear' to the 'primordial ground' than plant or animal, it affords us 'no special protection'. But although we are thrown forth, we are 'not abandoned'. Rather, we are held 'in the balance', because 'the venture', while throwing us forth, at the same time holds us in the 'pure draft (*Bezug*)'[17] of the 'gravitational attraction' to itself as the unknown, 'unheard centre' (PLT 97–105).

There can be no mistaking the fact that in talking here about 'throwing', Heidegger is casting his mind back to the 'thrownness' that plays so central a role in *Being and Time*. We are indeed, later Heidegger agrees with his earlier self, 'thrown' into a difficult and dangerous world, a world that is now conceived as, not our own, but rather the mystery's 'venture'. Thrownness is *not*, however, as *Being and Time* supposed (pp. 129–30 above), 'abandonment'. We are *not* abandoned because – this is what *Being and Time* is blind to – the velocity of the 'throw' is, as it were, brought to a standstill by the 'gravitational attraction' towards the 'unheard centre'. In Heidegger's own language, we are, while thrown, simultaneously 'appropriated' by the mystery. Whether or not we respond to the 'attraction', being, that is, 'the mystery', 'gathers [us] ... to itself' (P 253). What in short Heidegger finds captured in Rilke's portrait of us as 'held in the balance' is an expression of the *Ereignis*.

But just how does responding to the attraction enable the good death? Rilke says that if we are open to the 'pure draft' 'we go *with* the venture, will it'. Our technological being-in-the-world will, that is, be a matter of preserving and completing the order of things that is gifted to us by the venture rather than opposing it by attempting to stamp our human order onto the world. This 'going with', as it were, the flow,

> ...[t]here, outside all [technological] protection,
> ... creates for us a safety—just there,
> Where the pure forces' gravity rules.
> (PLT 97)

It does so because, in responding to the venture's appropriation, we experience the transcendence of our mortal selves, the 'transport and enchantment', that is the *Ereignis* (p. 234 above). The 'event of appropriation' makes us its 'own' – 'owns', captivates us – in such a way that there is no longer any distinction between the 'will' of the venture and our own will. In this realization of the 'ek-static' essence of human being (P 253) – the realization that we 'stand out beyond' our mortal selves – we can no longer even repeat Jesus's words, 'not my will but thine be done', for there no longer remains any distinction between the two. Schopenhauer discusses this same phenomenon of self-transcending appropriation. 'Consciousness of the identity of one's own inner being with that of all things or with the kernel of the world' is, he says, 'the essence of all mysticism'. And he quotes Meister Eckhart's disciple as crying out, in her epiphany, 'sir, rejoice with me, I have become God'.[18]

The result of this 'appropriation', this 'transport' out of mortality, is that we enter a state in which, in Wittgenstein's words, we 'feel safe whatever happens'. We enter a 'free' region (PLT 147) in which we are 'care-less (*sorg-los*), *sine cura, securum* – secure, safe' (PLT 101, 117), a state in which we overcome anxiety and appropriate our dwelling. Notice, here, the direct rejection of *Being and Time*'s assertion that care (*Sorge*) is the human essence (p. 137 above).

Gentle technology

The hydro-electric dam, we saw, violates the river by turning it into a reservoir. This is because the river is disclosed as nothing but 'a water power supplier' (QCT 16).[19] The 'essence', the 'enabling ground', of modern technology lies in the fact that to 'enframed' modernity, everything shows up as *mere* resource. The Old Bridge celebrated in Hölderlin's ode to 'Heidelberg', by contrast, the bridge that swings 'with ease and power' over the Neckar (PLT 150), allows the river to remain a river. What, then, is the 'essence' of such 'gentle' technology?

Heidegger's paradigm of gentle technology is that of the archaic Greeks. His portrait of them is an elaboration of Hölderlin's representation of them as still 'touched by the exciting nearness of the fire from heaven' (GA 39 292), as still living in Weber's 'enchanted' world.

The world in the midst of which the ancients found themselves was not simply, prosaically, there. It was, rather, the *poiesis*, the 'bringing forth' – as it were the poem – of an unknown, but overwhelmingly powerful, agent whom they called *physis*. The meaning of this word is only dimly captured by our word 'nature' (though it 'echoes still' in Rilke's 'nature' [PLT 98]) since, for the Greeks, 'Earth', Gaya, is, as Sophocles records, 'the most sublime of the gods' (I 58). In a lifeworld that is thus a 'holy' place, technological activity, *techne*, must itself be a 'bringing forth'. What is unthinkable is the idea of a challenge to, or a remaking of, the order of things one finds oneself 'already in'. Rather, *techne* must itself be a bringing forth in which the human hand becomes the medium through which nature (Rilke's 'venture') completes herself, a 'letting what is not yet present arrive into presencing' (QCT 10). So, for example, the ancient wood turner, far from stamping his will on inert or resistant material, required himself to 'answer and respond to all the different kinds of wood and the shapes slumbering within the wood as it enters into man's dwelling with the hidden riches of nature' (WCT 14). As noted, this conception of *techne* as bringing forth survives in Michelangelo's observation that 'To sculpt means to ... liberate the figure imprisoned in the marble'. And it is echoed, too, by Emerson, who writes in *The Young American*, that

> If only the men are employed in conspiring with the designs of the Spirit who led us hither and is leading us still, we shall quickly enough advance out of all hearing of other's censures, out of all regrets of our own, into a new and more excellent social state than history has recorded.[20]

Translated into Heidegger's 'philosophy of being', the claim is that the archaic world dwelt intuitively in the 'truth of being', that in grasping its world as the self-disclosing gift of the self-concealing mystery, it was appropriated by the mystery. Ancient technology had the 'gentle' character it did because metaphysics had not yet established itself. The tragedy of modernity consists, above all, in the loss of this sense of the real: 'Above all, enframing conceals that revealing which, in the sense of *poiesis*, lets what is present come forth into appearance' (PLT 27).

In many respects, Heidegger's portrait of the ancients is clearly idealized, almost a trope. Against Heidegger, it is frequently pointed out that the Greek economy rested on slavery and it is sometimes suggested that the deforestation of the Greek countryside began in archaic times. Yet the fact that Heidegger's Greeks belong, as it were, to a dream seems to me to matter hardly at all, for what he is presenting is not history, but rather an image of the turning, the turning to the future in which we come to be, like Emerson, dwellers in our world. We can, he is telling us, overcome the violence of modern technology if – but only if – we overcome the metaphysics of enframing.

The fourfold

Heidegger's word for a technological practice that, through openness to the 'holiness' of the world, has become gentle, is 'guardianship', 'guardianship of being' (PLT 182, P 252). To dwell in the world is to be a 'guardian', and to be a guardian is to 'care-for (*schonen*)' one's world (PLT 147–9). This, he holds, is the 'appropriate' – because 'appropriated' – mode of human being-in-the-world. Heidegger's objection to 'humanism' – by which he means human chauvinism – is that it does not set the 'dignity of the human being', the task which constitutes our humanity, 'high enough' (P 251). But just what, in concrete terms, is it to be a guardian, to care-for one's world? Heidegger provides a surprisingly specific answer to this question by providing an account, first, of the to-be-cared-for, and second, of the nature of the caring-for.

From a certain point of view, the world in which we live is four-dimensional: our lives are bounded by the earth, by climate and seasons, by the norms we are subject to in our being-with-others, and by time, the finitude of our span within the other three dimensions. It is with these four dimensions in mind that Heidegger refers to the lifeworld of one who dwells as 'the fourfold (*das Geviert*)'. His description of the four elements of the fourfold is, however, very different from the neutral, quasi-scientific description that I have provided. In Heidegger's description – or evocation – of the fourfold, the geologist's 'earth' is transformed into 'the building bearer, nourishing with its fruits, tending water and rock, plant and animal ...'; the geographer's 'climate' into 'sky (*Himmel*), ... the sun's path, the course of the moon, the glitter of the stars, the year's seasons, the light and dusk of day ...'; the sociologist's 'norms' into 'the divinities, ... the beckoning messengers of the godhead'; and our temporal finitude into our accepting death as 'the shrine of the nothing', 'the shelter of being' (PLT 147–9, 175–6). Before turning to the question of what it is to care-for one's fourfold world I should like to dwell for a moment on the language Heidegger uses to describe it.

Poetry and enlightenment

Unlike mine, Heidegger's description of the fourfold is *poetic*, largely, in fact, an extrapolation from Hölderlin's poetry. The reason for this poetic evocation is to be found in two lines from the poet's 'In Lovely Blueness' to which Heidegger devotes an entire essay (PLT 211–27):

> Full of merit [for his many technological achievements, interpolates Heidegger] yet poetically, dwells / man upon this earth.

'Enlightenment', observes Heidegger, is a mode of thinking that began with Socrates and Plato and found world-historical expression in the Enlightenment. It consists in the belief that 'the thoroughgoing explanation of everything in terms of those grounds perspicuous to reason' can and should be achieved. As such, enlightenment thinking is essentially 'metaphysical': it consists in the belief (the belief in terms of which Nietzsche defines 'Socratism' [p. 17 above]) that human reason can plumb the 'deepest abysses' of being, so that what lies beyond the bounds of reason is nothing at all. Enlightenment thinking, in other words, denies 'the mystery'. When it comes to poetry that is considered to contain significant content – to be more than 'music' – enlightenment views its task as that of 'draining a marshland', of 'liberating' the 'thought' from its irrelevant 'poetic' embellishment, of 'de-mythologizing' the mythic (I 111–12). What, however, enlightenment thinking ('positivism', in other language) fails to see is that 'poetic thinking' is actually 'more rigorous' than conceptual thought (P 271) since it enables us to 'grasp ... what is ungraspable' (I 136), namely the gift-giving 'mystery'. Heidegger's own 'philosophy of being' takes us on a conceptual journey into acknowledging that *there is* a mystery, but only poetry, above all, Hölderlin's poetry, can actually bring the mystery – in its mystery – to presence. In doing so, says Heidegger, it 'measures out' the 'dimension' of the real that is hidden from modern humanity, the dimension of the 'holy'. And in doing that, it 'measures out' a place for dwelling (PLT 218–19).

This, then, is what is said in Heidegger's poetic description of the fourfold. For the four-dimensional world to show up as a dwelling place, for it to show up as a place where there is a home for the gods, where one is 'safe' in the face of death, and where one cares-for one's fellow beings, both human and non-human, it must show up in its fifth 'dimension', that of the 'the holy'. Only if it shows up 'poetically' can it show up in this dimension because it is the task and prerogative of poetry to 'found (*stiftet*) the holy' (GA 52 193, I 138, GA 4 148).

The ethics of dwelling

I return now to the question of what it is to be a 'guardian' of one's fourfold world, to care-for it. Since the fourfold has four elements, caring-for it has four aspects: caring-for earth, for sky, for gods, and for mortals. The situation is rendered more complex, however, because Heidegger distinguishes caring-for that consists in 'letting be' in the sense of 'leaving alone' – I shall refer to this as 'protection' – and 'letting be' in the sense of 'allowing to come into being', which I shall refer to as 'bringing forth' or 'completion'. Both of these senses emerge in the following, somewhat jumbled, passage:

> Mortals dwell in that they save (*retten*) the earth – taking the word in the old sense still known to Lessing. Saving does not only snatch something from a danger. To save really means to set something free into its own presencing. To save the earth is more than [not][21] to exploit it or even wear it out. Saving the earth does not master the earth and does not subjugate it, which is merely one step from spoliation.
>
> (PLT 148)

Heidegger uses the Old Bridge in Heidelberg celebrated by Hölderlin (p. 246 above) as an example of caring-for earth in both senses. In spanning rather than damming the river, in allowing it to remain a river, the bridge keeps it 'safe', protects it. But in 'gather[ing] the earth as landscape around the river', it allows the two 'edges' of the river to come forth, for the first time, as 'banks' (PLT 150), and so brings forth a hidden unity that 'completes' the landscape.

Dwellers care-for 'sky', Heidegger says, when they

> receive the sky as sky. They leave to the sun and the moon their journey, to the stars their courses, to the seasons their blessing and their inclemency; they do not turn night into day nor day into a harassed unrest.
>
> (PLT 148)

It might seem impossible for human beings to affect the seasonal and diurnal rhythms of nature, but Heidegger's point, I think, is that, if allowed, these 'natural rhythms' run, not just through nature, but also through human life. So, for instance, 'twenty-four seven' shopping, which interrupts the diurnal rhythms, and the demand for 'twenty-four twelve' fruit and vegetables, which interrupts the seasonal rhythms, are examples of the lack of care-for 'sky' that disclose modernity's homelessness. Conversely, living in the flow of such rhythms will be both a protection and a completion of 'sky'.

Caring-for 'mortals' in the sense of protecting them from environmental threats is obviously the origin of technology. Heidegger's focus, however, is on the caring for mortals (including oneself) *in their mortality*, allowing them to fully embrace their mortality. To care-for mortals is to escort (*geleiten*) their own nature – their being capable of death as death – into the use and practice of this capacity, so that there may be a good death. To initiate mortals into the essence of death in no way means to make death, as an empty nothing, the destination (*Ziel*). Nor does it mean darkening dwelling by blindly staring at the end.

(PLT 148–9)

In what might the 'protection' of the mortality of mortals consist? In, I think, a refusal to engage in all the manifestations of what *Being and Time* calls 'inauthentic being-towards-death' (pp. 143–4 above). So, for example, one will refrain from all the linguistic evasions of 'idle talk', from the embalming of corpses and from face-lifts. The 'completion', the bringing forth of death, conversely, consists in, for example, making a proper festival of death as still happens in, for example, the Polynesian *tangi*. And, of course, the bringing forth of death in its un-frightening nature, is a primary aim of Heidegger's own poetic thinking.

Heidegger turns to caring-for 'gods' in the following passage:

Mortals dwell in that they await (*erwarten*) the divinities as divinities. ... [22] They wait (*warten*) for intimations of their coming and do not mistake the signs of their absence. They do not make gods for themselves and do not live in the service of idols.

(PLT 148)

As we saw, the absence of the gods is 'not nothing'. Our ethical exemplars are preserved in our tradition. The problem is not that they are 'dead', but rather that in the absence of the 'divine radiance', they exist in, as it were, a twilight condition. How, then, can we protect and bring forth the absent gods? We protect them, Heidegger tells us (as Moses told the Israelites) by waiting for their return and not manufacturing gods, gods who, as manufactured, are false 'idols'. Evidently, if we worship idols then the space that could be occupied by the true gods is occupied. (Almost certainly there is a reference, here, to Goebbels' pioneering of modern marketing techniques to elevate Hitler to the status of a god.)

As for bringing forth the gods of heritage, since we cannot make them return to the community at large, all we, as dwellers, can do is to bring them forth in our own lives, and the lives of those who are truly our 'relatives', by living ourselves in the 'sight' of those gods.

Heidegger and Weber

In the course of this chapter I have identified a number of affinities between Heidegger and Weber: Heidegger's conception of 'enframing' is a deepening of Weber's notion of 'rationalization', his notion of 'forgetfulness of being' is a deepening of Weber's notion of 'disenchantment', and his conception of the turning as a recovered sense of the holy is an elaboration of Weber's hope for a new (or recovered) 'prophecy' possessing 'charismatic' authority. Heidegger was not given to acknowledging debts to contemporary thinkers, but he was well acquainted with Weber's work.[23] With respect to critical theory, Weber's foundational role is evident and acknowledged. But though it is less obvious, he is also a foundational influence on the later Heidegger, as he is on all the other members of the phenomenological tradition. As the title of his seminal 'The Question Concerning Technology' makes clear, Heidegger knew he was not initiating a new discussion but rather joining one that was already well established. The person who initiated that discussion for twentieth-century German philosophers was Max Weber.

Notes

1 Richardson (1974) xxii. See, further, notes 3 and 4 below.
2 As we shall see, in addition to the turning in his own 'path of thinking' Heidegger also speaks of a 'world' turning, the turning of the West to a new, *really* post-modern age. There are thus really three 'turnings' that figure in Heidegger's thought: the turning that was a biographical event in Heidegger's life; the turning we, his readers, will make if we are persuaded to follow his path of thinking; and finally the 'world turning' that is the topic of the essay 'The Turning' (QCT 36–52). A revisionist school of recent scholarship has dedicated itself to showing the continuities between *Being and Time* and later Heidegger to be so strong that, in fact, 'the *Kehre* is ... not something that happened in the 1930s' but something, rather, that 'never happened at all' (Sheehan [2001] 195). But since not only Heidegger but also the students who were closest to him, Arendt (LM II 173) and Gadamer (Palmer [2007] 360–1), assure us that it did, this, in my judgment, is a misconceived enterprise.
3 Not that they are *inconsistent* with section 44's account of truth, for they are, indeed, implicit in it. In many ways it is illuminating to view the whole of Heidegger's later philosophy as a slow grasping of all of the implications of *Being and Time*'s conception of truth. Such a description, however, while revealing an important continuity between Heidegger's later and earlier philosophy, does not undercut the idea of a radical 'turning', since, as we shall see, the grasping of those implications compelled Heidegger to reject foundational aspects of *Being and Time*.
4 Heidegger is inclined to regard this second step as even more important than the first, the reason being, I shall suggest, that it is only with the second step that his later thinking fully becomes the *religious* thinking that it essentially is. In 1966, indeed, he makes the extravagant claim that all of his thinking from 1927 to 1936 is a 'dead end (*Holzweg*)', albeit 'a necessary one', since 'one will not succeed in thinking the *Ereignis* [pp. 234–5 below] with the concept of being and the history of being' (GA 15 366). Note that *Holzweg*, here, must be used in the ordinary German sense of 'dead end', rather than in the special sense of 'path into the clearing' that it has in the title of Heidegger's essay collection *Holzwege* (GA 5), given that the path being discussed is said to precisely *not* lead into the clearing. (Apart from Heideggerians, the special sense is known only to those who speak Heidegger's Black Forest dialect in which a *Holzweg* is a path into a forest clearing in which the villagers have cutting rights.) Note, also, that 'necessary' can really only mean 'an essential part of the narrative of *my* development', essential in that by exploring a 'false' path and finding it to be a dead end, Heidegger was pointed in the direction of the 'true' path. He cannot legitimately mean 'necessary' *simpliciter*, necessary for *anyone* to arrive in the illumination to which his later thought is a testimony, because, as we shall see, he regards his later thought as an exposition of the poetry of Friedrich Hölderlin, and he knows perfectly well that Hölderlin's *Dichten* (poetry) did not need to engage in 'thinking about being and the history of being' in order to arrive in the illumination. *Heidegger* may have had to take a tortuous path through the forest to

find his way into the clearing but, as he knows, the great poet *always* stood in the 'brightening light [of] the holy' (EHP 45). This same remark applies to the 'necessary' implicit in the claim (p. 232 above) that '*only* by way of Heidegger I does one arrive at Heidegger II'.

5 Sartre (1956) 554.
6 Sartre (1956) 36.
7 Sartre (1956) 139.
8 Chesterton (2001) 463.
9 Not every project that presents itself as 'metaphysics' is metaphysical in the pejorative sense. Kant's 'metaphysics of nature', for instance, is not, since he specifically excludes the 'thing in itself' from its domain.
10 Nietzsche (2002) section 36; emphasis added.
11 Nietzsche never actually proposes the 'claim' as anything more than an hypothesis, an hypothesis that, at the end of his career, he actually rejects (see Young [2010] chapter 26). In fact, therefore, he never did more than *aspire* to be the 'last metaphysician of the West', an aspiration he finally abandoned.
12 Note that whereas *Being and Time* is concerned with 'Dasein', a concept early Heidegger insists is not to be identified with that of a 'human being' (p. 152 fn. 6 above), his later thought is unambiguously about human beings, about *us* – another sign of the 'turn' from philosophy as a 'transcendental' endeavour to philosophy as, inter alia, cultural criticism.
13 A passage in the lecture that did not appear in the printed version of 'The Question Concerning Technology' (the principal locus of Heidegger's discussion of modern technology) reads: 'Agriculture is now a motorised food-industry – in essence the same as the manufacturing of corpses in gas chambers and extermination camps, the same as the starving of nations, the same as the manufacture of hydrogen bombs' (quoted in Young [1997] 172). Note the phrase 'in essence'. Heidegger is not – as his outraged critics have claimed – suggesting a *moral equivalence* between modern agriculture and the extermination camps, but rather using 'essence' in his technical sense to claim that the 'enabling ground', enframing, is, with respect to each of these morally non-equivalent phenomena, the same.
14 Nietzsche (2001) section 125.
15 It is acknowledged, of course, by Marcuse – and apparently also by Pricilla Chan and Mark Zuckerberg who plan to use a seed fund of 3 billion dollars to 'cure, prevent and manage' all disease by the end of the twenty-first century.
16 Heidegger says that his own 'Letter on Humanism' uses 'the language of metaphysics, and does so knowingly', the 'other language remain[ing] in the background' (P 239 fn.). The other language is, I suggest, the language of poetry, which, for reasons I shall come to, Heidegger regards as, in a certain sense, 'more rigorous' than the language of metaphysics (p. 248 below). Later Heidegger eventually comes to the conclusion that on account of its substantival nature, all talk of 'being' belongs to the language of metaphysics, unavoidably makes us think of being as a substance and hence destroys the ungraspable mystery of the mystery. This is the 'dead end' mentioned in note 4 above. Later Heidegger sometimes uses the word 'being', but typically, he prefers the antique *Seyn* (the spelling that, for Hölderlin, was the normal spelling), and sometimes writes *Sein* with a crossing out through it (P 241 fn. et passim). What these devices tells us is, I think, that when we read 'being' in his later works, we should read it as nothing more than shorthand for 'the mystery', for 'the mystery that appropriates'.
17 'Draft' as in 'draft horse', a 'pull' rather than a 'push'.
18 Schopenhauer (1969) II 612–13.
19 Recall *Being and Time*'s assertion that, in Dasein's world, 'the river is water power' (BT 70).
20 Emerson (1897) 75.
21 The 'not' is missing in the German original, but the passage makes no sense without it.
22 I have excluded from the quotation 'In hope they hold up to them the unhoped-for', a sentence as to whose meaning I can make several guesses without, however, having any firm idea of which is the right one.
23 Safranski (2008) 89–92, 117–18.

Afterword

Weber, we have seen, identifies two pathologies of post-Enlightenment modernity: loss of freedom and loss of meaning. Loss of freedom consists in our reduction to robotic *Berufsmenschen*. Loss of meaning consists in ethical 'polytheism', our loss, not of meaning as such, but of *shared* meaning, the loss of a shared conception of the good life, the loss of community.

While the Frankfurt thinkers recognize loss of meaning as indeed a pathology, in practice, their attention is directed almost exclusively towards loss of freedom. Their aim is to make us clearly aware of our 'oppressed' condition in rationalized modernity, and to promote liberation: for Horkheimer and Adorno, liberation through unspecified and unspecifiable events in the future, for Habermas, liberation through a liberal democracy reinvigorated by 'communicative rationality', and for Marcuse, liberation through the dissolution of the 'performance principle' into a kind of lyrical anarchism. But concerning meaning, meaning in Weber's sense, the Frankfurt thinkers have almost nothing to say. Habermas, it is true, tries to offer 'constitutional patriotism' (p. 57 above) as a substitute for the shared meaning of the past, but, as we have seen, he is confused: constitutional patriotism is a framework designed, not for the overcoming, but for the thriving of multicultural polytheism.

The Freiburg thinkers, by contrast, while recognizing loss of freedom as an issue, attend far more closely to loss of meaning. Loss of meaning, all of them are clear, is loss of a shared ethical 'tradition': loss of what Heidegger calls 'heritage' and, later on, loss of the virtue-personifying 'gods'. If we are to recover our lost heritage, he adds, we must recover our sense of the holy; the gods must recover, in Weber's language, their 'charismatic' authority. (In the sequel to this study we shall see Walter Benjamin referring to such authority as 'aura'.) Arendt makes the point that the restoration of tradition is a task especially for educators, and Gadamer adds that the restoration of tradition is the restoration of *Bildung*, of formation through culture.

The notions of 'tradition', 'homeland', 'people', and 'community' were hijacked by the Nazis. It is unsurprising, therefore, that in mainstream post-war political thought, in Germany and elsewhere, such notions have been anathematized. Liberal, cosmopolitan, Habermasian, anti-traditional, modernity-embracing thought has been in the ascendant. What this means is that of the three values of the French Revolution, liberty, equality, and fraternity, while it has been legitimate to lament the inadequate realisation of the first and the second, the decay of the third has been, essentially, a non-issue.[1] Until, that is, very recently. What, since 2016, had become unmistakeable is the existence of a widespread revolt against the liberal hegemony, the appearance throughout the West of political movements that in every case represent, at least in part, the demand for fraternity: for the community that comes from sharing with one's neighbours what, borrowing the term from the Roman Stoics, Gadamer calls a *sensus communis* (p. 182 above), an intuitive understanding of the good life. Often, the manifestations of this demand are cynically manipulated, distorted and ugly – white nationalism, Islamophobia, homophobia, misogyny, illiberal democracy – but sometimes they evoke a greater or lesser degree of sympathy – the independence movements of Catalonia, the Basque region, Flanders, Corsica and Quebec, for example.

What these new political forces make clear is that through its sanctioning of unconstrained economic and cultural globalization, of mass immigration with little or no attempt to turn it into assimilation, the liberal orthodoxy has neglected a basic human need, the need for community. The challenge that now faces the liberal thinker is that of understanding the character of this need and of assimilating it into liberal thought. Resorting to journalistic abuse – 'nativist', 'racist', 'nationalist', and so on – is unhelpful (one calls to mind Heidegger's observation that the retreat to 'ism's is a sign that 'one no longer thinks' [P 242]). With respect to the task of understanding the communitarian need, liberal thinkers have, it seems to me, a great deal to learn from the German phenomenological tradition.

Note

1 A non-issue, that is, for most mainstream political theory and philosophy. A number of sociologists, on the other hand, have been well aware of our loss of community as a cause for extreme concern: see, in particular, Reisman (1950) and Putnam (2000).

Bibliography

Adorno, T. (1981). *In Search of Wagner*, trans. R. Livingstone (London: London Review of Books).

Arendt, H. (1958). *The Human Condition* (Chicago: University of Chicago Press).

Arendt, H. (1961). 'Freedom and Politics' in *Freedom and Serfdom: An Anthology of Western Thought*, ed. A. Hunold (Berlin: Springer), 191–217.

Arendt, H. (1969). 'Introduction' to W. Benjamin, *Illuminations* (New York: Schocken Books), 1–58.

Arendt, H. (1971). 'Thinking and Moral Considerations', *Social Research* 38. 3, 417–446 .

Arendt, H. (1974/5). 'Remembering Wystan H. Auden' in *W. H. Auden: A Tribute*, ed. S. Spender (London: Weidenfeld and Nicolson).

Arendt, H. (1977). *The Life of the Mind* (San Diego, CA: Harcourt Brace).

Arendt, H. (1978). 'Heidegger at Eighty', *New York Review of Books* XVII, Oct. 21, 50–54.

Arendt, H. (1983). *Men in Dark Times* (San Diego, CA: Harcourt Brace).

Arendt, H. (1994). *Essays in Understanding 1930–1954* (New York: Schocken Books).

Arendt, H. (2001). *The Life of the Mind*, 2 vols (New York: Harcourt).

Arendt, H. (2006). *Between Past and Future* (London: Penguin).

Benhabib, S. (2000). *The Reluctant Modernism of Hannah Arendt* (Lanham, MD: Rowman and Littlefield).

Benjamin, W. (1969). 'The Work of Art in the Age of Mechanical Reproduction' in *Illuminations*, trans. H. Zohn (New York: Schocken Books), 217–252.

Bowring, F. (2011). *Hannah Arendt: A Critical Introduction* (London: Pluto Press).

Bradley, F. H. (1962). *Ethical Studies* (Oxford: Clarendon Press).

Braver, L. (2014). *Heidegger: Thinking of Being* (Cambridge: Polity).

Canovan, M. (1992). *Hannah Arendt: A Reinterpretation of Her Political Thought* (Cambridge: Cambridge University Press).

Chesterton, G. K. (2001). *Collected Works*, vol. XX (San Francisco: Ignatius Press).

Dreyfus, H. (1991). *Being-in-the-World: A Commentary on Heidegger's Being and Time Division I* (Cambridge, MA: MIT Press).

Emerson, R. W. (1897). *Poems and Essays of Ralph Waldo Emerson* (New York: Houghton Mifflin).

Feenberg, A. (2005). *Heidegger and Marcuse: The Catastrophe and Redemption of History* (New York: Routledge).

Forster, M. N. (2007). 'Hermeneutics' in *The Oxford Handbook of Continental Philosophy*, eds. B. Leiter and M. Rosen (Oxford: Oxford University Press), 30–74.

Foucault, M. (1991). *The Foucault Reader*, ed. P. Rabinow (London: Penguin).

Frege, G. (1980). *Translations from the Philosophical Writings of Gottlob Frege*, eds. and trans. P. Geach and M. Black (Oxford: Blackwell).

Freud, S. (1939). *Moses and Monotheism* (New York: Vintage).

Freud, S. (1989). *Civilization and Its Discontents*, trans. J. Strachey (New York: Norton).

Freud, S. (2009). *Beyond the Pleasure Principle* (Mansfield Center, CT: Martino).

Gadamer, H.-G. (2004). *Truth and Method*, trans. J. Weinsheimer and D. Marshall (London: Continuum).

Galbraith, J. K. (1969). *The Affluent Society* (Boston: Houghton Mifflin).

Geuss, R. (2014). *A World without Why?* (Princeton, NJ: Princeton University Press).

Gorner, P. (2000). *Twentieth-Century German Philosophy* (Oxford: Oxford University Press).

Gottsegen, M. (1994). *The Political Thought of Hannah Arendt* (Albany, NY: SUNY Press).

Graeber, D. (2015). *The Utopia of Rules* (New York: Melville House).

Grondin, J. (2003). *The Philosophy of Gadamer* (Montreal: McGill-Queens University Press).

Habermas, J. (1977). 'Hannah Arendt's Communications Concept of Power', *Social Research* 44. 1, 3–24.

Habermas, J. (1984). *The Theory of Communicative Action*, vol. I, trans. T. McCarthy (Boston: Beacon Press).

Habermas, J. (1989). *The Theory of Communicative Action*, vol. II, trans. T. McCarthy (Boston: Beacon Press).

Habermas, J. (1990). *Die Nachholende Revolution* (Frankfurt: Suhrkamp).

Habermas, J. (1992). *Autonomy and Solidarity* (London: Verso).

Habermas, J. (1996). *Between Facts and Norms* (Cambridge: Polity Press).

Habermas, J. (1997). 'Modernity: An Unfinished Project' in *Habermas and the Unfinished Project of Modernity*, eds. M. P. d'Entrèves and S. Benhabib (Cambridge, MA: MIT Press), 38–57.

Habermas, J. (1998). *The Inclusion of the Other: Studies in Political Theory* (Cambridge, MA.: MIT Press).

Habermas, J. (2001). 'Constitutional Democracy: A Paradoxical Union of Contradictory Principles?' *Political Theory* 29, 766–81.

Habermas, J. (2015). *The Lure of Technocracy*, trans. C. Cronin (Cambridge: Polity).

Hahn, L., ed. (1997). *The Philosophy of Hans-George Gadamer* (Peru, IL: Open Court).

Heidegger, M. (1959). *An Introduction to Metaphysics*, trans. R. Manheim (New Haven, CT: Yale University Press).

Heidegger, M. (1962). *Being and Time*, trans. J. Macquarrie and T. Robinson (Oxford: Blackwell).

Heidegger, M. (1966). *Discourse on Thinking: A Translation of Gelassenheit*, trans. J. Anderson and E. Freund (New York: Harper and Row).

Heidegger, M. (1968). *What Is Called Thinking?*, trans. J. Gray (New York: Harper and Row).

Heidegger, M. (1969). *Identity and Difference*, trans. J. Stanbough (New York: Harper and Row).

Heidegger, M. (1972). *On Time and Being* (New York: Harper and Row).

Heidegger, M. (1977). *Martin Heidegger: Gesamtausgabe*, ed. F.-W. von Hermann (Frankfurt: Klostermann), publication dates 1977 onwards.

Heidegger, M. (1979). *Nietzsche*, 4 vols, trans. D. Krell (San Francisco: HarperCollins), publication dates 1979–1982.

Heidegger, M. (1982). *On the Way to Language*, trans. P. D. Herz (San Francisco: Harper and Row).

Heidegger, M. (1988). *The Basic Problems of Phenomenology*, trans. A. Hofstadter (Bloomington: Indiana University Press).

Heidegger, M. (1996). *Hölderlin's Hymn 'The Ister'*, trans. W. McNeill and J. Davis (Bloomington: Indiana University Press).

Heidegger, M. (1997). *The Question Concerning Technology and Other Essays*, trans. W. Lovitt (New York: Harper and Row).

Heidegger, M. (1998). *Pathmarks*, ed. W. McNeill, trans. various (Cambridge: Cambridge University Press).

Heidegger, M. (2000). *Elucidations of Hölderlin's Poetry*, trans. K. Hoeller (New York: Prometheus Books).

Heidegger, M. (2001). *Poetry, Language, Thought*, trans. A. Hofstadter (New York: Harper).

Heidegger, M. (2002). *Off the Beaten Track*, trans. J. Young and K. Haynes (Cambridge: Cambridge University Press).

Hirsch, E. D. (1957). *Validity in Interpretation* (New Haven, CT: Yale University Press).

Horkheimer, M. (1947). *Eclipse of Reason* (New York: Oxford University Press).

Horkheimer, M. (1980a). 'Zum Problem der Wahrheit', *Zeitschrift für Sozialforschung* 4.3, 32–42 .

Horkheimer, M. (1980b). 'Schopenhauer Today' in *Schopenhauer: His Philosophical Achievement*, ed. M. Fox (Brighton: Harvester Press), 20–36.

Horkheimer, M. (1982). *Critical Theory: Selected Essays*, trans. various (New York: Continuum).

Horkheimer, M. and Adorno, T. (2002). *Dialectic of Enlightenment: Philosophical Fragments*, ed. G. Schmid Noerr, trans. E. Jephcott (Stanford, CA: Stanford University Press).

Hume, D. (1964). *A Treatise of Human Nature*, ed. L. Selby-Bigge (Oxford: Clarendon Press).

Husserl, E. (1960). *Cartesian Meditations: An Introduction to Phenomenology*, trans. D. Cairns (The Hague: Nijhoff).

Husserl, E. (1970a). *The Crisis of European Sciences and Transcendental Phenomenology*, trans. D. Carr (Evanston, IL: Northwestern University Press,).

Husserl, E. (1970b). *Logical Investigations*, 2 vols, trans. J. N. Findlay (London: Routledge and Kegan Paul).

Husserl, E. (1982). *Ideas Pertaining to a Pure Phenomenology and a Phenomenological Philosophy: General Introduction to a Pure Phenomenology*, trans. F. Kersten (Dordrecht: Kluwer).

Husserl, E. (1989). *Ideas Pertaining to a Pure Phenomenology and a Phenomenological Philosophy: Studies in the Phenomenology of Constitution*, trans. R. Rojcewicz and A. Schuwer (Dordrecht: Kluwer).

Husserl, E. (2002). 'Philosophy as Rigorous Science' in *The New Yearbook for Phenomenology and Phenomenological Philosophy II*, 249–95.

Jünger, E. (1930). 'Die Totale Mobilmachtung' in *Krieg und Krieger* (Berlin: Junker und Dünnhaupt), 9–30.

Kant, I. (1931). *Kant's Critique of Judgment*, trans. J. Bernard (London: Macmillan).

Karlauf, T. (2007). *Stephan George: Die Endeckung der Charisma* (Munich: Blessing).

Kellner, D. (1984). *Herbert Marcuse and the Crisis of Marxism* (Berkeley: University of California Press).

Larmore, C. (1996). *The Morals of Modernity* (Cambridge: Cambridge University Press).

Lear, J. (2005). *Freud* (New York: Routledge).

Levinas, E. (1969). *Totality and Infinity* (Dordrecht: Kluwer).

Lukács, G. (1962). *Die Zerstöring der Vernunft* (Neuwied, Germany: Luchterhand).

Lukács, G. (1971). *The Theory of the Novel*, trans. A. Bostock (London: Merlin Press).

MacIntyre, A. (1984). *After Virtue* (Notre Dame, IN: Notre Dame University Press).

Marcuse, H. (1964). *One-Dimensional Man* (London: Routledge).

Marcuse, H. (1966). *Eros and Civilization* (Boston: Beacon Press).

Marcuse, H. (2005). *The New Left and the 1960s: Collected Papers of Herbert Marcuse*, vol. 3, ed. D. Kellner (London: Routledge).

Margalit, A. (2017). *Betrayal* (Cambridge, MA: Harvard University Press).

Marx, K. (1893). *Wage Labour and Capital*, trans. J. Joynes (London: Twentieth-Century Press).

Mead, M. (1952). *Sex and Temperament in Three Primitive Societies* (New York: New American Library).

Mendelson, E. (2016). 'In the Depths of the Digital Age', *New York Review of Books* LXIII.11, 34–8.

Midgley, M. (1984). *Wickedness* (Abingdon: Routledge).

Moran, D. (2012). *Husserl's Crisis of the European Sciences and Transcendental Phenomenology: An Introduction* (Cambridge: Cambridge University Press).

Müller, J.-W. (2007). *Constitutional Patriotism* (Princeton, NJ: Princeton University Press).

Nietzsche, F. (1967). *The Will to Power*, trans. W. Kaufmann and R. Hollingdale (New York: Vintage).

Nietzsche, F. (1986). *Human, All Too Human*, ed. E. Heller, trans. R. Hollingdale (Cambridge: Cambridge University Press).

Nietzsche, F. (1994). *On the Genealogy of Morals*, ed. K. Ansell-Pearson, trans. C. Diethe (Cambridge: Cambridge University Press).

Nietzsche, F. (1997). *Untimely Meditations*, ed. D. Breazeale, trans. R. Hollingdale (Cambridge: Cambridge University Press).

Nietzsche, F. (1999a). *The Birth of Tragedy*, in *The Birth of Tragedy and Other Writings*, eds. R. Geuss and R. Speirs, trans. R. Speirs (Cambridge: Cambridge University Press).

Nietzsche, F. (1999b). *Kritische Studienausgabe*, vol. 12, eds. G. Colli and M. Montinari (Berlin: de Gruyter).

Nietzsche, F. (2001). *The Gay Science*, ed. B. Williams, trans. J. Naukhoff (Cambridge: Cambridge University Press).

Nietzsche, F. (2002). *Beyond Good and Evil*, trans. J. Norman (Cambridge: Cambridge University Press).

Nietzsche, F. (2003). *Daybreak*, eds. M. Clark and B. Leiter, trans. R. Hollingdale (Cambridge: Cambridge University Press).

Nietzsche, F. (2005). *Twilight of the Idols*, in *The Anti-Christ, Ecce Homo, Twilight of the Idols and Other Writings*, ed. A. Ridley, trans J. Norman (Cambridge: Cambridge University Press).

Nietzsche, F. (2006). *Thus Spoke Zarathustra*, trans. A. del Caro (Cambridge: Cambridge University Press).

Nozick, R. (1974). *Anarchy, State, Utopia* (New York: Basic Books).

Ormison, G. and Schrift, J., eds. (1990). *The Hermeneutic Tradition* (Albany, NY: SUNY Press).

Palmer, R., ed. (2007). *The Gadamer Reader: A Bouquet of the Later Writings* (Evanston, IL: Northwestern University Press).

Putnam, R. (2000). *Bowling Alone: The Collapse and Revival of American Community* (New York: Simon and Schuster).

Quine, W. (1960). *Word and Object* (Cambridge, MA: MIT Press).

Rawls, J. (1978). *A Theory of Justice* (Cambridge, MA: Belknap Press).

Reisman, D. (1950). *The Lonely Crowd: A Study of the Changing American Character* (New Haven, CT: Yale University Press).

Richardson, W. (1974). *Heidegger: Through Phenomenology to Thought* (The Hague: Martinus Nijhoff).

Rohkrämer, T. (2007). *A Single Communal Faith?* (New York: Berghahn).

Russell, M. (2006). *Husserl: A Guide for the Perplexed* (London: Continuum).

Safranski, R. (2008). *Martin Heidegger: Between Good and Evil*, trans. E. Osers (Cambridge MA: Harvard University Press).

Sandel, M. (1984). 'The Procedural Republic and the Unencumbered Self', *Political Theory* 12. 1, 81–96.

Sartre, J.-P. (1956). *Being and Nothingness*, trans. H. Barnes (New York: Philosophical Library).

Schiller, F. (1845). *The Aesthetic Letters, Essays, and the Philosophical Letters*, trans. J. Weiss (Boston: Little, Brown).

Schopenhauer, A. (1969). *The World as Will and Representation*, 2 vols, trans. E. F. J. Payne (New York: Dover).

Schopenhauer, A. (1995). *On the Basis of Morality*, trans. E. F. J. Payne (Providence, RI: Berghahn).

Sellars, W. (1963). *Science, Perception and Reality* (London: Routledge & Kegan Paul).

Sheehan, T. (2001). 'A Paradigm Shift in Heidegger Research', *Continental Philosophy Review* 34, 183–202.

Smith, A. (2007). *An Inquiry into the Nature and Causes of the Wealth of Nations* (Amsterdam: Metalibri).

Smith, D. W. (2013). *Husserl*, 2nd edn. (London: Routledge).

Tönnies, F. (1988). *Community and Society: Gemeinschaft und Gesellschaft*, trans. C. P. Loomis (East Lansing: Michigan State University Press).

Turkle, S. (2015). *Reclaiming Conversation: The Power of Talk in a Digital Age* (New York: Penguin).

Wagner, R. (1966). *Richard Wagner's Prose Works*, 8 vols, trans. W. A. Ellis (New York: Broude Bros).

Wagner, R. (1988). *Selected Letters of Richard Wagner*, eds. and trans. S. Spencer and B. Millington (New York: Norton).

Waldron, J. (2015). 'The Lure of Technocracy', *New York Review of Books* LXII, Nov. 16, 70–2.

Warnke, G. (1987). *Hermeneutics, Tradition and Reason* (Stanford, CA: Stanford University Press).

Weber, M. (1958). *From Max Weber: Essays in Sociology*, eds. and trans. H. Gerth and C. Wright Mills (New York: Oxford University Press).

Weber, M. (1978). *Economy and Society: An Outline of Interpretative Sociology*, 2 vols, eds. G. Roth and C. Wittich, trans. various (Berkeley: University of California Press).

Weber, M. (2001). *The Protestant Ethic and the Spirit of Capitalism*, trans. T. Parsons (London: Routledge).

Weberman, D. (2000). 'A New Defence of Gadamer's Hermeneutics', *Philosophy and Phenomenological Research* LX.1, 45–65.

Wittgenstein, L. (1969). *Notebooks 1914–16*, trans. G. E. M. Anscombe (Oxford: Blackwell).

Wolin, R., ed. (1993). *The Heidegger Controversy: A Critical Reader* (Cambridge, MA: MIT Press).

Woolf, V. (2003). *Mrs Dalloway* (London: CRW Publishing).

Yaqoob, W. (2014). 'The Archimedean Point: Science and Technology in the Thought of Hannah Arendt', *Journal of European Studies* 44.3, 199–224.

Young, J. (1997). *Heidegger, Philosophy, Nazism* (Cambridge: Cambridge University Press).

Young, J. (2005). *Schopenhauer* (London: Routledge).

Young, J. (2010). *Friedrich Nietzsche: A Philosophical Biography* (New York: Cambridge University Press).

Young, J. (2013). *The Philosophy of Tragedy from Plato to Žižek* (New York: Cambridge University Press).

Young, J. (2014). *The Philosophies of Richard Wagner* (Lanham, MD: Rowman and Littlefield/Lexington Books).

Young-Bruehl, E. (1982). *Hannah Arendt: For Love of the World* (New Haven, CT: Yale University Press).

Index

operationalism 65
Orpheus 75–6

performance principle 60, 66, 71
phenomenology: ethics of 111–13; of Heidegger 121–2; of Husserl 96–100, 111–13
play 162–3
popular culture *see* culture industry
prejudice 172–3
propaganda 26

rationalization: Gadamer on 157–8; Habermas on 52; Horkheimer and Adorno on 31–3, 40, 42; Marcuse on 60; Weber on 7–9
reason: loss of objective 27–30, 40; Marcuse on 84–5; as self-undermining 28, 40
Reith, J. 38
Rilke, R. M. 242–3, 244–5
Romantic tradition: aesthetics of 160–1; critique of Enlightenment 17; hermeneutics of 167–70
Russell, M. 98, 110n17

Sartre, J.-P. 233–4
Schleiermacher, F. 168–9
Schopenhauer, A. 101n8, 245
science: Arendt on 210–12; and disenchantment 14–15; Husserl on crisis of 103–10; vs. lifeworld 107–8; and rationalization 8, 31–2; as traditional vs. critical theory 22–4
Sellars, W. 101
Smith, D. W. 95–6, 111

society: vs. community 13; as debasement 214–18
Socratism 17

Taylor, F. 9
Tönnies, F. 13, 55, 218
tradition: Arendt on 220–3, 225–8; Gadamer on 173–4, 176–7, 181–3; Heidegger on 149–51, 241; *see also* communitarianism
truth: art as disclosing 164–5; Heidegger on 134–6, 232–3; Horkheimer on 26

Universal Declaration of Human Rights 50

Wagner, R. 11
Weber, M. 7–18; and Arendt 215–17; on bureaucracy 8–9; on charismatic prophets 15–16; on collective artwork 12; as critical theorist 43; on de-Christianization 12–16; on disenchantment 14–16; Habermas's criticism of 15–16; and Heidegger 250–1; on iron cage 10–11; and Life Reform Movement 15n18; on loss of freedom 10–11; on loss of meaning 11–16; on rationalization 7–9; relativism of 11–12; and Romantic critique of Enlightenment 17; on science 22–3; on society v. community 13
Woolf, V. 96

Young-Bruehl, E. 209